CLOSED ENTRANCES

Canadian Culture and Imperialism

CLOSED ENTRANCES

Canadian Culture and Imperialism

Arnold Harrichand Itwaru
Natasha Ksonzek

TSAR
Toronto
Cardiff
1994

TSAR Publications
P. O. Box 6996, Station A
Toronto, Ontario
M5W 1X7 Canada

The publishers acknowledge generous assistance
from the Ontario Arts Council and the Canada Council.

Cover design: Natasha Ksonzek

Canadian Cataloguing in Publication Data

Itwaru, Arnold, 1942-
  Closed entrances : Canadian culture and imperialism

Includes bibliographical references.
ISBN 0-920661-25-4

1. Race discrimination - Canada. 2. Canada - Race
relations. 3. Canada - Civilization. 4. Imperialism -
Social aspects - Canada. I. Ksonzek, Natasha.
II. Title.

FC104 . I89 1994   305 . 8' 0971   C94-932241-5
F1035 . A1I89 1994

Printed and bound in Canada

Acknowledged with appreciation the assistance of the Secretary of State (Multiculturalism), in the writing of this work.

CONTENTS

Entrance

Entrances. Our world is full of so many entrances—the movement from the outside to the inside, the entering of doorways, dwelling places, homes, private spaces, intimate spaces, intimate selves. Entrances.

Being invited, being allowed in, going into, we enter and are entered and need to enter so many places, each entrance a mystery as well as the revelation of many things.

Entrances require certain expectations. These can be said to be certain points of view, that which we are expected to go along with, even if we do not totally comply. In our movement from the outside to the inside, there is a colouring of our seeing, a playing on our perceptions, sometimes subtly and sometimes conspicuously. We do not behave as we please when we enter, for example, a courtroom, a church, a shrine, a museum or a classroom. Even in our homes we make requirements of each other, and these may not always be pleasing.

The more familiar the entrance, the more unnoticeable the change. Entering, we follow the guiding steps, we go through the waiting hallways as we move along certain pathways. These pathways lead us, even as we think ourselves the wanderer, the traveller, the inquirer. Pathways lead us, and we tend to follow. Sometimes the turns in the pathways weave a rhythm into us we don't want. Sometimes these pathways are narrow and we are forced into uncomfortable positions just to remain in them. Sometimes high walls let us see no alternative, and we think that this pathway is the only way, and no other way seems in sight. This is when these patterns begin to lure, to seduce us with a certain familiarity.

These familiarities make up much of our entrances to a culture. They encourage particular ways of thinking. These ways are taught in our schools and universities, the established places of educational authority, and are widely shared by the population. They are, more often than not, taken for granted.

But this is also where closure takes place. For while at one level familiarity is reassuring, this assurance rests on the exclusion of many peoples and cultures who are often seen as a threat to the familiar and the reassuring. Sometimes these peoples so perceived are reduced into demeaning caricatures, and sometimes they are dismissed, not considered at all. In this way the familiar intensifies itself, maintaining in effect a closure.

The Canadian discourse, understandably, does not speak of this. It talks of respect for all cultures resident in Canada—Multiculturalism, Unity in Diversity. This reads so well, but many Canadian literary and museum curating practices deeply and sharply contradict this. These entrances are where the closure of vision is dangerously, unsuspectingly, even beautifully, and certainly very educationally maintained.

It is as if a certain trance, bearing unawareness, a form of awareness bearing unawareness, is at work. But what do we readily, well-behaved, fall into, fall in line with?

N A Ksonzek

A H Itwaru

Literature as Cultural Imperialism

in Canada, Glorious and Free, you say?

Arnold Harrichand Itwaru

The Imperialization of Vision

The Imperial Eye. The gaze of Empire. The gazing continuation of domination. The imperialization of vision.

The Imperial Eye is a possessive eye. It claims as its own whatever it beholds. It burns with the desire to own, to possess, to order, to control, to dominate, to destroy. This is what gives it life. It cannot exist without this. This Imperial Eye is a tyrannical eye. In its delusions of grandeur it demands obedience to its glance, homage to its presence which it thinks is Supreme, Sovereign, Majestic, Wise, born to rule, the world its stage where it struts and plays out in lofty airs its bloodthirsty avarice and insatiable greed where it is always the grand and heroic violator, pompously virtuous over the brutalized, the enslaved, the raped, the demeaned, those murdered in their sleep, those worked to death whose lament the wind of the world mourns.

The Imperial Eye is the gaze of Empire, monarch of all it surveys over land and sea and the humble lives of those who dreamed no evil. It is the watch in the pinnacle and tower of a voracious predator which waits to strike at the innocent and the unsuspecting to rob them of what they have, to force out of them their strength seen as Labour Power and used to violate the ground of their birth to furnish the palate of the minions of Civilization and Conquest. In the gaze of Empire this is the Stuff of History. This is what its citizens are taught to be proud of, this is what makes them a great people, a wealthy people. This is the backdrop, the props of the world its stage where delusions of virtue and goodness conceal the agony and the horror upon which it continually feeds to continue the atrocity of its vainglorious existence.

5

What is it that is written within the embrasures, the walls, the entrances and the exits of this imperiously contrived world-stage? The art and craft of writing, the telling of a persuasive story, the publication, reading and teaching of this, are acts of participation in certain forms of thought which make up the history of the people and place in which the literary imaginary emerges. Despite the problems in the identification of national and regional literatures, these works say a great deal of the thinking which informs the actions of the peoples in these places. More often than not they affirm and thus celebrate these features. Hence their importance in the perpetuation of highly valued ideas and attitudes among such peoples. These literatures are some of the means through which the culture in the making contemplates itself, mythologizes its history, justifies its centralizing preoccupations, constructs a vision of itself through which it gathers momentum and guards against obstacles as it seeks to ensure the conditions favourable to its notion of its own well-being. This is also true of nation-states active in the ecstasies of imperialist grandiosities.

In these the imperialization of vision teaches (among other grievous concerns) approval of the atrocity of conquest, pride in the expansion of European and British colonial military occupation "overseas" as it has been fondly styled, and is vital in furbishing the psychopathic egoism required to justify the violation and robbery of hundreds of millions of people in their own lands, including the slaughter of more than a hundred million of them—just within the last six hundred years of Empire glory.

The imperialization of vision is an imperializing dream. It is complex, this dream. It loves the sword, that sanctified weapon and emblem of imperial might and right, yet unctuously claims a monopoly on "peace" and "human relations." It is a dream in which the imperial subject orgasmically responds to the call of the bugle and drum and the warlord cries in the orders of the Commanding Officer, and proudly marches, killing strangers in their own land, and feeling just and honourable in these ghastly deeds. The suffocated agony of the maimed and the killed in the bludgeoning burst of the cannon, the sharp murderous crack of the rifle, the feel of the dagger on the Enemy's throat, the despoliation of unknown peoples and cultures inspire such individuals to greater heights of destruction to better serve their Emperors, their Kings, their Queens, their Civilization who honour them as heroes for having dishonoured and robbed others whom they call inferior.

This is an Empire Dream, this imperialization of vision. In this dream I am a caricature: I am Caliban, an inferior sordid enslaved savage evil thing. In this dream I am Friday, Crusoe's subordinate, I am Gunga-subaltern-din for the British Raj's Jewel and Crown, I am a coolie, an embarrassing primitivity who should only be too ready to serve the Light Bearers of Europe and Britain and America and Canada, their panoply of saints and sages whose domination of me is necessary so that my Heart of Darkness can be illuminated to better aid my exploitation. In this dream I am not human. I do not, cannot exist in this dream. Humans in this imperializing dream are the White caucasoid races of Europe and Britain and their progeny convinced it is their Civilized and manifest destiny to exploit the rest of humanity. In the imperialization of vision I am raw material, there to be used, to be abused with impunity, and to feel good about it.

There is a tradition in the reading of English and European literatures which refuses to consider the importance of the imperializing vision in many of these works. This refusal is in itself an example of the presence of a studied attitude of presumed aloofness from the "political"—as if writers and the things and people they write about are outside of the history of thought in which they have grown. This attitude, this disciplinary silence which stops critical inquiry into an imperialist nation-state and the literature which is produced within it which affirms its principal political action, is a form of collusion couched on the concealment of the atrocity of imperialism. The questionable claim here is that "Literature Is Above This." This is one of the ways the culture of imperialism is kept intact.

It is not surprising that in Canada, a nation-state created and upheld in the ethos of imperialism, there is virtually no interest in inquiring into this practice in its Canadian contexts. The romantic double-think trend has been to see Canada as a "young" country, "founded" by the English and the French, today both threatened and saved by the USA, with whom we are told in the tones of a peculiar pride, Canada shares the world's largest undefended border. This sharing is symbolic of shared American imperialist values, the easy flow of ideas which inform and reinforce many values and practices in Canada to such a point that there is culturally more in common than the differences between these two countries.

But what of this "founding" attributed to the English and the French, the two "founding peoples" of the nation Canada sees itself as? In typical imperialist zeal these peoples of Britain and France, two of Europe's most aggressive empire-states, came here and claimed as their own the land and birthplace of the First Peoples who lived here for millennia. In characteristic imperialist mania both the English and the French deemed these First Peoples, primitive, savage, inferior, subhuman. They mis-named them Indians, and with continuing contempt refused to recognize their own names, sought to destroy them when they refused to be servile, to be what they expected "a good Indian" to be. And this has continued in many ways. In high imperialist order the English and the French battled with each other for supremacy, meaning the sole right to exploit the land and its peoples as they saw fit. This fighting is not yet over, despite the defeat of Montcalm by Wolfe in the Plains of Abraham. These founding peoples, convinced in the delusion of their own superiority, this super-egoism so zealously assumed by imperialist cultures, sought nothing less than complete rule in the name of their imperial majesties and an arrogant and domineering Christianity—an action identical to the practices wherever euro-colonial invasion and occupation took place.

Here within the dualities of control in the institutions of the State and the Church, furbished by a self-serving educational apparatus, the Dominion of Canada emerged. Dominion, this fond Canadian term and moment celebrated each year until recently as

Dominion Day. Dominion. Sovereign authority. Lordship. Control. Rule. Government. Uncontrolled right of possession and use. The domain of a feudal lord. A district, region or country under one government. A self-governing country of the British Commonwealth. Canada. Dominion. Dominion Day. Canada Day. Independent Canada with the queen of the British monarchy as its Head of State and its closest friend and ally that Empire State which has named itself America, whose Emperor-King-President is the Commander-in-Chief of the largest and most terrifying armed imperialist military force in the world. Distressing implications, especially when the politicoes of Canada and the corporate media propagandize Canada as peacemaker to the world, and when peoples the world over called "immigrants" make up its present day population. I am one such person, but when you see me reading a book or walking in your midst remember that like you in my doing this I also bear with me other than this action in the place and moment of your seeing of me.

There are histories between us, histories in us: important differences in the particularities of our experience which are too often neglected in the emphases on what we are supposed to have in common. These emphases contain certain assumptions whose continuing presence make up dimensions of the cultural unconscious where the will of the dominant order of perception, participated in as values and conventions of thinking, is carried out without conspicuous notice. At the personal level this is experienced as forms of the familiar: the way things are done, the way one sees things, the way one has been taught to see—the habits of perception where this unconscious demonstrates its obedience to the institutions of control.

Literature (and by this I am referring to English Literature and literature written in English) is not exempt from such institutionalizing assumptions and political function, despite claims to the contrary. The approach to literature is rife with mythologies governing its production and reception. There is an order which is enshrined in much of what constitutes literary knowledge. And in

9

the problematic multicultural imaginary in which Canada has mythologized itself this raises important questions. On the one hand we have state policy upholding notions pertaining to unity in diversity, the contradictory retainance of ethnic identity as well as full participation in national life, and on the other there is the teaching and production of literature.

Is there a relationship? What perspectives are emphasized in each? What does this mean for peoples from various parts of the world whose histories have, like mine, converged in our being in Canada?

Histories are more than voices, but voices contain many histories. My speaking here is the speaking of the voices and experiences whose resonation I am. It is thus that I must talk of aspects of that history in which I have been located within the action of imperialism as one of its many subject-victims. The relationships of such actions, particularly the perspectives instilled in the ways people were groomed to think, accommodated the empire-ecstasy practices of dominion. In many ways these are upheld in Canada, despite the difference in scenarios and location.

Out of the Fields of Sugarcane Blades

There seemed to be no malice. The project of consciousness control, of trying to make us despise and forget ourselves, came to us far away from Canada in the name of Education. Canada was not even a word then on our tongue. Education was going to save us, we were told. Our parents believed it was going to get us out of the sentence of hard labour their life was. And there was some truth to this. A few were spared the agony of the fields where the British Empire extracted its toll of wealth from the peoples whom it violated with nonchalance.

And most of those so spared worked, often for the rest of their lives, serving the very forces who would have destroyed them, had they been unlucky enough to be labouring in those wealth-garnering fields of the Empire. But it all seemed so natural, hardly anyone blinked an eye. This was what doing a decent job was. Life in the fields was no life at all. Everyone knew this, and you needed this Education to get you the decent jobs. And many people did these jobs and felt decent about what they were doing.

It is not these people, but rather the obscenity of what was happening, that I want to note. For what was taking place was a particular training in seeing where decency was itself given a new meaning. Decency meant the indecency of the loyalty of the oppressed to their oppressor. It meant following with pride the order of labouring set out for them by their exploiters. It meant humility and fear before the officials of the Empire. It meant doing your duty: meaning, serve with gratitude that which perpetuates your servitude. This was what being decent was made out to be.

This indecency is the invidious infliction of unreason as part of the fundamental unreasonableness of colonial rule. But I am referring particularly to the British Occupiers of my experience and some of their practices. This Occupation affirmed its presence in the deep wounding of thought, in a psychic cruelty requiring the reformulation of thinking to accept the unreasonable as reasonable, to accommodate the atrocity of British imperial control without this being seen for what it was: British Occupation.

But this Education never mentioned Occupation, never identified the Occupiers as Occupiers. Its educators did not talk of the rule of the British Empire—this foreign imperial force laying claim to the places of our living and our lives, even our thinking— as an Occupation. This Education taught a peculiar form of awareness, one which was actually the teaching of unawareness, where awareness was construed to mean thankful servility under the Order of the Empire. Making oppression appear normal, even decent, so the civilizing imperial horde can cannibalize with imputiny and style the human beings seen as being there to nourish its all-consuming hunger.

Decency meant being grateful and faithful in thought and deed to the Empire, feeling dignity and pride in the very order of brutal rule which had made of Africans slaves in these anguished lands, which duped Indians into leaving India as indentured labour, most of whose indenture expired only in their death. It meant being loyal to the very rulers and ruling force even while it disparaged them as niggers and coolies, detritus, subhuman, uncivilized.

This Education taught us we could earn a good salary and live a decent life, doing this. After all, we were the Children of the Empire, and so were our parents. We were all children. Children of the Empire, one and all. Under the Empire we were all equals, we were all equally infantilized. We were all children.

In this infantile manner we were supposed to believe we were special, we were important, for we were heeding our call, and our call was the doing of our duty, and our duty was loyalty to this great strange proud paternal Overseas force, The British Empire, upon whose vastness, it was often boasted, the sun could never set, an empire we were to believe would never let us down.

The schooling this Education was, taught us to accept this infantile posture, to admire the Occupier, to enjoy the Occupation without seeing what was happening, without understanding what the project was all about. Our task was to learn to Read and Write, to help us find a Good Job. That was what was to be done, and to do it was to have pride in our achievement, to have dignity in knowing we were doing the sensible thing.

This was a particular instrumentalization of learning. Learning as the instrument through which the Occupation legitimated its stranglehold. Nothing new, this. Europe's philosophers of war have made a heinous art in their approval of this infamy. The Occupied should be taught to love the Occupier. In this way the rule of the Occupation will be less resisted, hence more effective, more lasting. The colonizing British and their colonizing European counterparts have demonstrated the destructive success of this strategy where they went in their delusions of grandeur to conquer and occupy in the name of their greedy majesties and their bloodthirsty self-proclaimed superior civilization.

And within the Occupation of my experience, the teaching of learning as the instrument through which you got a "good" job. Here the Occupier becomes the rewarder, the provider of these good jobs. And these were some of the jobs. A Book-Keeping Job. An Office Job. A Secretary Job. A Civil Service Job. A Police Job. A Bank Teller Job in Barclays, the English Bank or in the Royal Bank of Canada, these financial institutions which kept our earnings and used it as they saw fit in Britain and Canada, and elsewhere, but not where we lived. A Customs Job in one of the big better-paying corporations. A School Teaching Job.

In and of themselves these jobs would appear to be fine. But they were never in or of themselves. They were not simply jobs. These were the occupations which strengthened and maintained the Occupation, the Order of the Empire. They were among the vital components in the machinery of control. They served to foster the illusion that what was happening was normal, reasonable, correct. Which meant the hardship suffered by most of the peoples, the degradation, the destruction, were also correct. Education for the furtherance of the Occupation made this way of seeing possible.

It encouraged the thinking which blamed the victims for the wretchedness of their condition. They were not Educated, this thinking claimed, and because of this they did not know any better, they could not do anything better, and they thus deserved what was happening to them. And few, distressingly few, saw otherwise.

That Occupation has ended, as it has for most of those places reduced into colonies by Britain and its colonizing European counterparts, but the colonization of consciousness and the usurpation of the means for people's survival have continued, proliferating in many guises. The continuation of colonization resides within the continuing colonization of consciousness, a seeing ecstatically imbued with notions of Progress, serviced by today's technologies and industries of speedy dislocation, its ships of flight repeating what the ships of Empire have always done—taking cargo, human cargo, particularly peoples whose communities and places of birth have been ravaged by Empire Occupation—into yet another servitude. Into the largest and most terrifying of all empires, into EuroAmerica, the alliance of the discourses and strategies of imperialism, of imperialist Europe and their aggressive imperialist progeny, America.

It is where psychic torture, the brutalization of the psyche slavery inflicted in the very act of enslavement, takes on another insidious action in another elsewhere, as Glissant* has observed, Abroad, in the countries and home of the colonizer's values, whose dominant ways of seeing are necessarily hostile to these migrant peoples of hope. Where existence becomes a constant de-defining of yourself against the malignance of hateful configurations. A de-defining which also necessitates a continuing re-definition of yourself as the mode of survival in these alien cities, these centres and agencies of negation. Resistance, continuing resistance or disappear with the scrambling multitude into the obscenity of a quiet and seemingly nonintrusive exploitation. Exhausting resistance. And in this what is it that is affirmed? When does the reactivity in your having to continue to define yourself in resistance to constant disfigurations, itself begin to disfigure you?

This is the saddening unspoken despair in the continuing excoriation of the self against which you have to struggle—or disappear—after the romance of Immigration and Travel is over, as migrating labour settles in, willing to be exploited, thankful to get employed. Grateful servants, able now to afford food and shelter. We overlook our bondage in labour and debt, our unwitting indenture—the contracting of our labour to Corporation X, requiring we also cast a blind eye to what these agencies of employment are doing beyond the immediate expectations of our labour, even in our own countries.

Grateful to exist within this, and be persuaded it is good, this life. Be persuaded it is good to lose your soul in consumer happiness, to be happy you are a unit of labour whose purpose in life is to also feel happy in the mindlessness of a frenetic and obsessive mania of commodity consumption. Where who you are and what you are and what you are doing and what you are becoming, are too often not concerns of importance.

This is an attitude of hostility to yourself, a negation which works to negate you, whose success you don't want, you should never want. The negation of you is the destruction of you. It is where you disappear. The assimilated immigrant.

In the history of my experience this action of negation, the making of the subordinate subject, was my being torn between love of self and hatred of self, in which disliking me, disrespecting who I thought I was, tended to be stronger. This Education taught us in admiring our Occupiers to love what we did not know and to despise what we did, what we knew intimately, and this included ourselves. We were the inferior, the embarrassing inferior, and it was our lot to both endure and despise this. This was our psychic affliction.

This Education taught us to love a place we did not know, but knew enough of to admire, to feel good to be associated with, even proud. To do this was to somehow go beyond our inferiority, to

15

dream of Greatness without knowing what Greatness was, what this dream of Greatness meant to us, or how was it we were dreaming this dream, and whose dream was it we were dreaming. We were dreaming the dream of oppression. A dream which dreams itself in unctuous and heady scenarios of success concealing the cruel deception at work. A dreaming desire dreaming of becoming like the Occupier, whose world we were to accept was in and of itself Great, where this quality of Greatness was without question to be found. Every book this Education taught us came from this particular Occupier's world, variously and grandiosely called England, Britain, Great Britain, the United Kingdom—and with an embarrassing imaginary fondness and intimacy—the UK, the Motherland, the Centre, the Seat of the Empire whose obedient children one and all we were, who must always heed Her call.

Sadistic empire ecstasy. Harmonious infantilism.

This Education told us the men and women of Britain were brave, heroic, civilized, great. We inferiors were to admire the brave and daring exploits of the sailors and officials of that Great state, Great Britain. It told us the difficulties the Great men and women of this Great Britain had dealing with the peoples of my ancestry were because we were treacherous, barbaric, unchristian, unclean, disrespectful of Law and Order, illiterate, incapable of governing ourselves, uncivilized, and therefore were in need of the strong arm of authority from Great Britain's monarchs and officials and their loyal killers—their Great generals and admirals, their Great army and navy victorious on land and sea and in the air, their lords and ladies, their Great thinkers whose ideas of superiority furnished the barbarism of the British violation of peoples and cultures wherever it went to Occupy.

Of course, it was never said in this manner. This barbarism flattered itself in the narcissism of gentility. Its crudity required politeness. These bearers of Greatness and Decency felt they deserved respect, and especially from us. We were supposed to be respectful of them. And sadly many of us were.

This Education taught me to sing in respectful strains, God

Save Our Gracious King, and later, God save Our Gracious Queen when Elizabeth II of England was coronated. Three cheers for the Red White and Blue! and other Empire Ecstasy songs. Three cheers to Her Gracious Majesty. I was to hold my cup with the imprint of the face of this Queen of the British Empire on it and to feel she had personally sent it for me, to hold this cup and sing, Rule Britannia Rule, Britannia rule the waves, Britons will never be slaves. And we all did.

Like the others I did not know what a Briton was. Could it be that as Children of the Empire we too were among those Britons since we were not slaves and, as far as we were concerned, never would be? It did not occur to us that the Britons so celebrated were actually at one time proud enslavers and upholders of human bondage across oceans and continents. We were taught that the British abolished slavery, and for this we should wish for the continuing reign of British prosperity, and whenever we uttered this Occupier's refrain, "Long Live Great Britain, Long live Her Royal Majesty," we were to feel proud and honourable.

For many of us there was no pleasure in this kind of singing which we were forced to learn at school. We were physically assaulted by our teachers to sing praises to the continuation of the British Occupation. These teachers' ready whips and canes repeated, with our parents' problematic approval, that form of torture inflicted on resistant enslaved human beings long before our time. It was also the manifestation of the cruelty in that infamous English pedagogic adage of tyranny: Spare the rod and spoil the child. Flogging children to do what they did not understand, what they were not persuaded of. Forcing compliance through physical abuse. Torture in the euphemism Corporal Punishment. In the name of Education. A nice school-teaching job.

Empire Ecstasy. Brutal satisfaction in the infliction of pain on the weak and defenceless to facilitate the brutal order intrinsic to the Occupation. Committed by school teachers, supposedly decent people, beating children with whips and belts to sing praises to the Occupier. A singing alien to the Hindi bhajans, mantras and popular Indian songs we adored and sang, always out of school,

17

away from the world of that schooling which strictly disapproved of such uncivilized and uncivilizing utterances.

That special cup I had to hold up and sing to, that Coronation Cup, was a magical item, a very talisman of Beauty. My mother kept it for years with her select three pieces of glassware we never used. The cup with the face of the Queen had this special place in our home and all those homes fortunate enough to have it. Our colonization was our pathetic source of pride.

This education was Education, I was told. It was special, even sacred. It was not Politics. It was above Politics. It was objective. It was Education. It was not to be questioned, it was to be learned. And there was so much to learn. Only fools and troublemakers questioned Education, resisted Learning. Only the no-goods did not want to improve their Intelligence, those with no Future, no Ambition, those who had no interest in being Someone, those who would work and die in the sugarcane fields, children of misery labouring in misery until they could labour no more. It was about Teaching and Learning. The principles and practices of this Education written by select British Educators mattered. And it was my responsibility to adapt to these. That was what was going to save us, that was what was going to save me, if I wanted to matter.

And in 1953 when Great Britain sent its army and navy into my country to stop the legal electoral action for independence, for the ending of the British Occupation of our space and place— when Britain suspended my country's fledgling constitution and jailed a number of our principal proponents of independence, when battle-armed British soldiers roamed the countryside like predators, ready to attack us—the Department out of which this Education was being instilled and invigilated, saw it fit to arrange to have primary and high-school children go on tours of the Occupier's vessels of doom anchored in our harbours, as if these ominous ships were harmless curiosities whose huge guns could not be turned against us.

A remarkable accomplishment. This "educational outing" made it difficult to think that those smiling half-legible uniformed Britons whose specific reason for being there was to destroy our pursuit of independence, would want to harm us. And that perhaps certain of our own people, our politicians were really the culprits who had caused Her Majesty's honourable troops, these well-meaning Whitepeople, to come from faroff England all the way across the Atlantic to protect us and establish Law and Order for the safety of our country, and supposedly for our own good.

At one side, the side I would call home, the places I lived in before and outside of my schooling, there was the embarrassment of what I was taught to regard as backwardness. The poverty, the pain, the anguish were attributed to the peoples of my birth. It was their fault. This was what not being fully civilized, still being uncivilized, resulted in. My home-self me was a thing of shame. I felt I was somehow to blame for this, and that what I should do was there on the other side, the side of Education, there where this despicable me became my school-self "I"—a creature of hope and intelligence, dreaming heady dreams of Accomplishment, of becoming Someone, vague though this Someone was—away from there, elsewhere, always elsewhere, Abroad.

I had been quietly divided. Without knowing it I had become two forces fighting against each other in me, I was at war with myself. And in this war who was going to be the victor, who the vanquished? What would happen to me in such a war? Would I be able to survive a war against myself? Could I? Could anyone?

This is a gruesome ecstasy, this hating yourself to love yourself, this fighting with yourself to gain yourself. It is where Divide and Rule, the well-tried and repeating practice of colonial occupation, now works to divide you inside, intrapsychically, to distort your perception, to confuse, to split you apart, to make you antagonistic to yourself, and thus weakened to dominate you, to have you as servant as long as this continues, this fundamental unreasonableness which says we should hate ourselves in order to actualize ourselves. The more I hated my little pathetic home-self, the more driven the desire to become this illusion, elsewhere, this Abroad awaiting my fulfilment, my heady phantasm of ecstatic actualization.

19

And in all of this there was Literature.

* For a discussion on psychic torture, see Edouard Glissant, *Caribbean Discourse* (Charlottesville: University Press of Virginia, 1989), 14-25.

Imitating the Gateposts of Speech

Literature was insidious and enchanting.

It was there in every childhood Reader we were required to read: the Royal Reader, the Macmillan Reader, the Kate and Lay Reader. These selected stories prepared us for the formal study of Literature—where to read was to be taken in an imaginary world away from the eloquence of lotus-grown silences to the teachings the civilizing English used to instruct its empire-children in admiration and obedience—where purity was said to be as white as the snow we did not know, where important things happened in castles and palaces and royal courts in imperial intrigues and cunning we were to think were true of "the human condition."

There was no one in our midst to whom this "condition" applied. Did it mean we were not the human *the human condition* was all about? The innocence of this question touched nevertheless upon a vital truth, hidden in the very EuroEgoism informing this literature—which excluded us. Hegel's eurocentrism is but one of the examples in whose thinking History means the history of Europe, a rationalist dream of European supremacy which excludes those places in the world ravaged by Europe. It must always be remembered that in the imperious declaration of the right to rule the rest of the world, in this supremacist fantasy those whom this Europe studiedly violated in its colonial conquests have no place other than as a disparaging primitivity, but useful enough nevertheless to furnish the passion of the protagonists of the culture of imperialism among whom nothing less than aspiration towards Universal Being is contemplated.

This literature, understandably, dealt with what was relevant and important to the culture of its making, not ours. When it

21

warbled of fields of daffodils and lily of the valley and sweet eglantine we did not know, it did not have us in mind. It sang of what it knew and thought it knew, the singing of nightingales and larks we never heard, the supremacist ecstasy of "the best school of all" somewhere there in important England, not the zinc-roofed two-floor building we had our schooling in. But when this litera-ture is used as required reading upon whose knowledge you passed or failed in your Education—then this reading itself be-comes another kidnapping.

I say another kidnapping in memory of those Africans and Indians who were kidnapped, bound and gagged and taken to the labour camps of Europe's and Britain's empires, their plantations of slavery and plantocracy, peoples whose deaths are forever the blood on the hands of their torturers and killers, for whom (not only for the solitary tragic woman of nobility, Lady Macbeth) no washing, ceremonial or otherwise, will ever remove.

This kidnapping is the ensnarement of the intellect. In it kid-napping becomes the mandatory reading, for example, of the ad-venturous story of an English boy among murderous Englishmen out to rob gold and other precious items from the peoples and places in our part of the world. It is reading this and admiring the empire-son, the English boy. But perhaps more important, it is reading this and not recognizing who the dreadful natives are, not seeing how we are placed in this. This is not just that grand euphemism which claims that literature is merely a work of the imagination. What is imagined, the imaginary itself, the empha-ses in it, the use to which this has been put in terms of my history, the perception of my very existence is what this trap, this trope of thought which requires my admiration of the heroic English men and boys, works to undermine. Against these protagonists of Civi-lization I do not exist, I am the anguished absence, a confusion of silence.

These required readings took us away from the play of life in us and amidst us in the struggle for survival which our living had been made into by the Imperial Occupier. It ignored the voices in us. It taught us to disregard the lament of the speaking dead, the sweat the blood the body of memory in the ground and footpaths of our daily existences. It took us away from the ripening of rice in us, it took us outside of ourselves, away from ourselves, away from our mothers' and fathers' gaze, it deafened us against their speaking. It turned our thinking towards a deceptive inwardness, a thinking which looked towards England for meaning. This delusional gaze is just the opposite of the imperial delusion of grandeur. This delusional gaze is the gaze of dependence. It compliments the imperial gaze, validates it, and thus furthers the designation of our inferiority. The Literary induction of domination.

This mandatory formal study of select texts written by English Whitepeople telling of their and other Whitepeople's doings and thoughts which we the progeny of displaced Africans, Chinese and Indians (the designated uncivilized) had to learn, if we wanted an Education. This literature, regardless of whatever might have occasioned its writing, when used in the context of the imperialist project to which it has been put, became the teaching of a particular sensibility, an attitude of obeisance to and admiration of the literary aesthetic of the culture of the occupying force, a literary politicization of domination, one of the actions of the "triumphal art of Empire." *

The triumphal in this art works in the enchantment of the imagination, the titillation and entrapment of the intellect to derive meaning within the imaginary articulated in the scenarios of each select text, and subsequently the world inscribed in them as well as the world inscribing them. It is assumed in this premise that our thinking must necessarily be realized within the Occupier's frames of references, that these perspectives should govern the ways we reflect on our condition. And in so doing to not pay heed to the fundamental differences in the circumstances in which we are deemed subordinate, our realities subservient to the principals as well as the principles of the super-ordinating imperial order.

This Literature was not taught with a view to the development of the critical imagination of those of us who were coerced into

23

reading it. It would be too much to expect this of the Occupation, of any Occupation. Rather this literature was used to intensify the authority of the Occupier's culture, and as such its exaltation was also the arrogant manifestation of English authoritarian practice in the guise of literary advocacy, literary knowledge. Literary criticism as it was propounded provided the conceptual tools through which certain English academic literary authorities established the methods and procedures governing the modes of reading, and the analysis of these.

They were telling us how we should read these chosen works of theirs, how we should think when we imbued ourselves in such presumed higher thought. Our perspectives based on our experience, our vision, was always outside of the allowable, not even tolerated. To dare to say anything seriously critical of these works being lorded on us as Great Literature was to suffer the punishment and ignominy of failure. We mattered only in relation to our being able to demonstrate how well we could imitate these English authorities. To have success was to show how clever we were in remaining within the limits of such benevolent scholarly allowance, how well we could practise an *imitative intellectuality* in which there prevailed the odious paternalism pertaining to the English notion of the proper ways of doing this.

This paternalism required the infantilization of the conquered subject-mass to which I have earlier referred—the Children of the Empire, who one and all must also be obedient, always ready and eager to please by identifying memorizing and quoting their English Authority as demonstration of their learning, by reciting texts from English poems plays and novels and ensuring the appropriate inflections and intonations, and by being accordingly ashamed of the speech and the peoples in whose speaking they live.

Be literate: imitate.

This was not how it was said, but this was what was happening. To think of what was considered higher things was to imitate as much as possible the thinking of our designated Betters, and these writers we were dubiously fortunate enough to read were, in the order of the Occupation's ranking, our Betters. In this way imitation served to perpetuate subordination, with the more absorbing the imitation the greater the importance of the source being imitated.

This is a form of enchantment.

Enchantment does not allow for self-reflection. The enchanted is under the power of the enchanter. The relationship is a hypnogogic one for the enchanted. And enchantment with the Occupier's world, however half-dreamed, however imagined, is where the seduction in imitation holds its fatal ploy. The mask of this enchantment is imprinted with notions of dignity and pride, but we should be careful of these. What do they mean? What is it that is happening?

The disturbing truth is that the more you keep doing it, the more imitative you are, the more dependent you are. In the face of the person or source being imitated the imitator is always of lesser importance, always subservient, always unoriginal. Here imitation constructs the self as false, as inauthentic, as always inferior to that which is being imitated. Imitation is the embellishment of power relations in which the illusion of authenticity drives the imitator to enjoy being controlled. This is necromancy: the hypnogogic cortege ecstatically bearing the death of the independent self. The oblivion march.

Imitation reinforces dependency, encourages an infantile posturing where the select Children of the Empire, the Educated, are now to flatter themselves of their presumed superior knowledge and self-importance even as they absorb themselves in and are absorbed by an imitative intellectuality.

Shakespeare, wallah

This literature spoke of the winter of English Christian-toting people's civilized discontent, their hatred of the un-Christian whom they castigated as barbaric and uncivilized, and thus deserving of studied English disparagement. It told of these civilized Whitepeople's pleasures and loves, especially their murderous love of war and killing in their greed for wealth and power. This

Literature sang eulogies to the English Spring, which presumably was also a civilized and Christian occurrence, unlike the uncivilized regions of treacherous monotonous heat, the Heart of Darkness my world in the sun was deemed to be. It spoke of the midsummernights' frolics of English kings and queens, of handsome charming and brave and wise princes and beautiful lovelorn dutiful princesses dreaming of them. It spoke of noble dukes and duchesses, noble lords and ladies, and the happiness of their obsequious and sycophantic servants.

And I was expected to admire these, to find in their words and action the wisdom through which the governance of my life was to be informed. I was supposed to admire the insights of these exemplars of Empire, to draw instructive lessons from the offerings of their Literature. It did not matter that my world, my life, my experiences would never, could never correspond to any of these alien English literary obsessions. I was supposed to dream of them nevertheless, to see, to be persuaded to see in them the virtues of truth and beauty and wisdom as the properties and qualities of Whitepeople, particularly British Whitepeople. My normalcy of life worlds away was an embarrassment of sameness where nothing of significance came from or ever could, important only as sharp contrast to the climes in which the self-declared finer and elegant and noble were nurtured.

In this literature we were told that in Great Britain some men are born Great, some achieve Greatness, some have Greatness thrust upon them. It did not say what this wonderful quality of Greatness was that we should so like it, but to be born great it was clear one necessarily had to be of noble English or European blood. This certainly completely excluded us, and demeaned as inferiors, we were continually being educated to think in our midst there was no one to whom Greatness could ever be attributed. Among us no one was "born great." It was madness to think anyone from our lowly realm could ever achieve Greatness, much less have "Greatness thrust upon them." Besides, what was this Greatness that some had it "thrust upon them"? Who was this benevolent bestower of Greatness?

Greatness was not to be found among the uncivilized and the underdeveloped. Greatness was over there, in civilized Great Britain and civilized Europe, and we, the uncivilized, the underdeveloped, were required to have a proper respect for civilized and civilizing Great Britain's heroes and their marauding deeds, their acts of piracy they called "adventure," the slaughter and robbery across seas and continents and the peoples of our ancestry. We were to see in the actions and resolutions of these White invaders matters of universal importance, and to write as eloquently as we could of these proclaimed universal truths.

Like England's Shakespeare, "noble" thoughts and "noble" deeds were to be admired, sought after without our recognition that this was in effect also our upholding of that class of privileged Britons who were of titular pre-eminence above all others in Great Britain—the British nobility—who in conjunction with their status and rank in the order of exploitation were also being imbued, as Shakespeare habitually accords them, with profoundness, wisdom, goodness to the point in which, as in Shakespeare's *Hamlet, Prince of Denmark*, even a face (the Prince's, of course) is deemed noble. And when many of these Lords and Ladies of the British way went out to maintain the Empire's Occupation in its various outposts and colonies, when they lorded their will in pillage and plunder and rape and murder as they thought fit, we were expected to think their victims were culprits who deserved the cruelty inflicted on them, and that those noble and Great Britons were courageous, indeed heroes and champions, worthy of our admiration.

Consider this:

O, what a noble mind is here o'erthrown!
The courtier's, soldier's, scholar's eye, tongue, sword,
The expectancy and rose of the fair-state,
The glass of fashion and the mould of form,
The observed of all observers quite quite down,
And I of all ladies most deject and wretched
That sucked the honey of its music vows,

Now see that noble and most sovereign reason,
Like sweet bells jangled, out of tune and harsh;
That unmatched form and feature of blown youth
Blasted with ecstacy. O woe is me
To have seen what I have seen, see what I see.

Hamlet, Act 3, Scene 1

This is much more than the heartbroken Ophelia's lament upon having seen what she considers her beloved Hamlet's deterioration, the madness he is feigning but which she believes is true. This is also an ebullient poem to nobility. This daughter-of-nobility's grief sees in her princely lover a mind which she deems "noble" having been overthrown. The metaphor which informs her analogy here comes from the order of thought in which the imperial practices of battle and conquest are seen as being normal. Thus Hamlet as Prince, cannot just go mad. He has to be struck down in battle, a noble mind conquered by madness, nobility defeated, overthrown, hence tragic, and for Ophelia a double-edged grief since it involves her so intimately, the noble prince her lover now "like sweet bells jangled, out of tune and harsh," the reason for her plight. This is the imaginary in which Ophelia's woe is depicted.

In this Hamlet's noble qualities are that he is an exemplary courtier, scholar and killer, all in one, "The courtier's, soldier's, scholar's eye, tongue, sword," but more, these make him well-suited to be the future imperial lord and master of Denmark. Hamlet is "the expectancy and rose of the fair-state." The reference to the future king as the "rose of the fair-state" is the glorification of domination as well as the violation of the rose. "Fair-state" romanticizes imperial order as honest and correct. "Expectancy and rose of the fair-state." Such ooze of goodness in the man who would be king, and conspicuously stylish and good-looking too, "the glass of fashion and the mould of form" whom everyone admires, even those "quite quite down." Hamlet is "that noble and most sovereign reason." Always the superlatives for the monarchy and its imperial lineage. This is delusional thinking in

28

one of its more pronounced forms, the regal delusion of grandeur, consistent with the super-egoism in EuroEgo, convinced of its own superiority, its presumption of the right to rule. And in this play these rights/rites are authenticated.

The claims of imperious privilege are affirmed, taken as a given, and adulated. How am I supposed to feel about this? What is being said to me when I am being instructed to take pleasure in the claims of this nobility, this play about greed and the incestuousness of imperial power among European kings and queens, the treachery in their palaces and castles? The site of this drama is the possession of the rulers. In it what happens to the "noble" few is that which matters. It is where the imperial eye is monarch of all it surveys. It does not matter how corrupt or ambitious or avaricious these monarchs may be, as Shakespeare suggests at times, this assumption is always the background to their actions. It is here where the tragic is happening. This is a tragedy in which imperial domination spoken in the euphemism, "fair-state" prevails. This "fair-state" is the Kingdom of Denmark, and Hamlet is the Prince of Denmark. It is the royal domain, a pastoral fantasy where nature and monarchic control are harmonized.

The illusion pertaining to the correctness of the *imperium*, is one of the driving passions among the peoples of imperialist nation-states. Many become upset when they are asked why is it they love to be ruled in this manner. It is because these also see themselves fit to rule others, and do whenever they can. They believe in the cult of rulership in which they ascribe to the illusion that as rulers they are necessarily a superior people, a superior race. EuroEgo. Many become furious when Shakespeare, obviously their totemic of superiority, is "treated" like this. It is considered a disservice to the great genius, who it seems in this way of thinking, requires only service. And those who refuse to comply with this servile expectation are often abused by lofty condemnations like, "Oh, they do not understand Shakespeare." Understanding. Yes, problematic understanding. But what of the force of ideas whose subtle intention is the disempowerment of the persons who have been persuaded to approve of them? The order of perception which so significantly influences, is intensified in certain acts of celebration. It is where the shaping of ways of seeing in support of the hidden order prevails, where the real order beyond the facade of freedom and justice and equality, is existence as the sanctification of domination. These are the sites of "free" participation, the festivals and festivities of induction where the inculcation of particular attitudes towards power is taking place.

Shakespeare's plays are the festive sites in which the play of Good and Evil takes place within the embrasures of the *imperium*. It is here where Prince Hamlet utters the lines which have been recited and praised wherever the adulation of Shakespeare is practised.

To be or not to be, that is the question:
Whether tis nobler in the mind, to suffer
The slings and arrows of outrageous fortune;
Or to take arms against a sea of troubles,
And by opposing end them!—To die, to sleep,
No more:- And by a sleep to say we end
The heart-ache, and a thousand natural shocks
That flesh is heir to, tis a consummation
To be devoutly wish'd. To die—to sleep:
To sleep! perchance to dream: ay, there's the rub,
For in that sleep of death what dreams may come
When we have shuffled off this mortal coil,
Must give us pause. There's the respect
That makes calamity of so long life:
For who would brave the whips and scorns of time,
The oppressor's wrong, the poor man's contumely,
The pangs of despis'd love, the law's delay,
The insolence of office, and the spurns
That patient merit of the unworthy takes,
When he himself his quietus make
With a bare bodkin? who would these fardels bear
To grunt and sweat under a weary life,
But that the dread of something after death,

The undiscover'd country, from whose bourne
No traveller returns—puzzles the will
And makes us rather bear these ills we have,
Than fly to others we know not of?
Thus conscience does make cowards of us all;
And thus the native hue of resolution
Is sicklied o'er with the pale cast of thought;
And enterprises of great pith and moment
With this regard their currents turn awry,
And lose the name of action—

Hamlet, Act 3, Scene 1

There are many who are moved by such eloquence, but all is not well here. There are disturbing assumptions in this poetic meditation on life and death, and this is compounded when the speaker happens to be the Prince of Denmark. The text commences with the luxury of reflection contingent on the privileged within the cult of rulership. In it nobility's "expectancy and rose of the fair-state," Hamlet, understandably, is interested in what is "nobler" in the mind. He is assuming, as perhaps he should, that that which is "noble" is necessarily desirable, necessarily good. It is thus elevated to the realm of exemplary thought, the problematic condition of being noble "in the mind." This is the assumption nobility makes of itself. It is an idealization of the pursuits of the noble, and is one of the ways the authority of rule is made to appear both benign and profound. Let us look at what the reflection "to be or not to be," is situated in. What are the ways in which this princely mind ponders life and death?

His concern is posed within alternatives that only the privileged are positioned to contemplate, but it is uttered as if these are the fundamental dichotomies in which the question of existence hangs. It is whether "to suffer the slings and arrows of outrageous fortune/Or to take arms against a sea of troubles." But what deception is afoot here? It appears I am being told "outrageous fortune" is a form of suffering, a burdensome sufferance in which the possessor of this great wealth has to endure "slings and arrows." The pangs of wealth? Or is it that the text is buoyed upon the knowledge of the atrocities of a particular history, and thus speaks to the practices of slings and arrows in the procedures of greed whereby outrageous fortune is amassed and zealously guarded? "Outrageous fortune" is usually what the wealth of the imperium is, and is fundamental to the monarchy of which Hamlet is no less than Prince. For him this cannot be hypothetical. It is not the fantasy of someone whose condition of poverty encourages the wish for a miracle, for outrageous fortune. Hamlet's other dilemma is framed in terms of a naval military assault as the means for the resolution of difficulty. The sea is where there is trouble against which he has to take arms. The Elizabethan maritime expansionist warring among British and European empire-states becomes the motif of value here, of reference to the resolution even of personal vicissitudes. But the thought of this action, of so "opposing" to end these troubles, brings him to a suicidal contemplation, "To die, to sleep," from which he moves to a homily on death, most inappropriate for someone like him, empathy-evoking though it may be.

He tells us, "And by a sleep to say we end / The heart-ache, and a thousand natural shocks that flesh is heir to." The "we" here is the prerogative in the royal unctuousness of power which refers to itself in the plural, and it is as well a generalization pertaining to everyone else. But surely the question which has to be asked is how do the heartache and the "shocks" come about? Is it as "natural" as the Prince would have us think, so much so that "flesh is heir to" it? I understand that those who live amidst outrageous fortune, particularly members of royalty, are obsessed with inheritance, about who succeeds whom in the possession of property and rank, but if "flesh is heir" to misery who is it who so bestows this despairing burden? Who is the flesh who so suffers? And where does the Prince, as well as the sordid history of Princes, stand in this?

The odiousness in this royal utterance worsens as the speech proceeds—

For who would brave the whips and scorns of time,
The oppressor's wrong, the poor man's contumely,
The pangs of despis'd love, the law's delay,
The insolence of office, and the spurns
That patient merit of the unworthy takes,
When he himself his quietus make
With a bare bodkin? who would these fardels bear
To grunt and sweat under a weary life,
But that the dread of something after death,
The undiscover'd country from whose bourne
No traveller returns—puzzles the will
And makes us rather bear these ills we have,
Than fly to others we know not of?

"Time" here, not the actions of particular human beings, is depicted as the inflictor of whips and scorns, and existence is seen as an act of bravery against this supposedly punishing "time." But to refer to "time" in this manner is to present the idea that "whips and scorns" are natural, essential to existence. In this way attention is conveniently deflected away from the real sources through which such punishment is enacted, in which princes and rulers and the principalities of power hold gruesome significance. It is thus that Hamlet can blithely talk of oppression as wrong without heeding the fact that the order of the monarchy is based on oppression, on the actions of imperial rule which breed the misery of the poor and those who are reduced to grunt and sweat under a weary life. The agencies of this rule maintain control over those it subjugates through the repressive implementation of law which always has the force of order and command and punishment to it, and always requires obedience. It is in the service of this that "the law's delay" has its power. The gesture of a critique of this which Hamlet feigns, given his position in it, is hence fundamentally false, and gratuitous at best.

The Prince of Denmark is further saying that people endure these hardships, rather than kill themselves because of the dread of not knowing what happens after death since no one returns to tell of what it is like there. This fear, he says, "makes us rather bear these ills we have," than do something whose outcome we do not know of. Perhaps this is the reasoning of the Prince who is trying to dissuade himself from killing himself, and perhaps this is the thinking of some people persuaded by this simplistic logic. But this is also an eloquent justification of oppression. There is something after death, the Prince would have me accept, whose dread makes people endure various forms of oppression. The thought of resisting oppression, of changing the conditions in which it flourishes, leads to thoughts of death. Meaning, among other things, the order which is, is, and will always be.

The ethos of the oppressive is there also in Hamlet's references to travel and discovery. Death is the "undiscover'd country" from which no "traveller" returns. But contrary to the populism culled out of the historical glorification of imperialism, travellers cannot and do not "discover" countries. The places the traveller embarks upon have always existed before and outside of the traveller, but in EuroEgo travel is always discovery and conquest. Columbus, we are told, "discovered" the "New World" and claimed it as the property of the empire of Spain. Britain and the rest of Western Europe occupied the places which they also felt they "discovered." And this text of Shakespeare's is by no means innocent of this obsessive-compulsive euro-civilizational frenzy. Very much as in the case of taking arms against a sea of troubles, the metaphor here is affirmingly located in the values of the imperial eye, the practices of discovery and conquest which characterized colonial occupation. Here, however, it is purged of its odiousness, turned into a psychoexistential personalism, and the entire order of domination is deftly written out of recognition.

"Thus conscience does make cowards of us all," concludes the Prince. Well said, but again, all is not well here. Bravery, the combative quality of choice in the cultural delusion of supremacy, is what is required for "enterprises of great pith and moment," but for whom? These grand projects of great moment are not the actions of just anyone. They are principal in the drive and force of empire-dreamers. But the Prince says the cowards the conscious supposedly makes of us, often prevents the occurrence of many of these grand enterprises. To what end is such reasoning? Is the decision not to kill oneself an act of cowardice? Is it bravery to kill oneself? Isn't Hamlet himself in this play deemed with "great pith and moment"?

Many more questions can be asked here, but the situation is not likely to become any clearer. This is primarily due to the position the writer himself has with regard to these issues, not merely the confusion the distraught Hamlet is in. Shakespeare pays lip service to the recognition of certain conditions of human suffering while he lavishes praise and "moment" on the rulers and their conceits. It is such a conceit which leads Hamlet to so cruelly deceive the naive Ophelia. In his decision to avenge his murdered father's death obviously the noble thing to do is to demean Ophelia as part of his strategy of feigning madness. This premeditated cruelty, however, is not just the aggrieved endeavour of a son who has learned his father, contrary to what he had been led to think, was killed by his stepfather-uncle, with his mother's consent, to inherit the throne. It is also the casual cruelty and distrust which is also part of that "sovereign reason" which this Hamlet nobly bears. Everything else is inconsequential to the removal of the pretender from the seat of imperial power which belonged to Hamlet's royal father, and should now in the progeny of rule be Hamlet's. It is about the royal right, the phallocratic lineage of rule, the placing of the correct person in that sanctum where power over people is highly esteemed. That events are crossed and the tragic occurs, does not remove this concern.

The imperial phallus acts, even from the grave. It is royal wisdom returned from death to establish truth and justice. The ghost of the former king is wise and truthful. Its story is not questioned, and in the order of regal authority, of course, turns out to be the truth. This wise anguished ghost who indicts his wife and brother, will not rest until it has had revenge, whose murder his royal son, The Prince of Denmark, the phallic progeny, must necessarily now avenge. The imperium is the phallocracy of power where those who reign are the wisemen of nobility. Even in death the real king rules. It is where that imperial proclamation of statement and affirmation of continuing royal rule, "The King is dead, long live the King," holds sway. The protagonists may be all dead, but the fair-state is there to be ruled. Individuals may be villainous, and those presented as virtuous may have died, but there is no questioning of the order and values of the imperium itself. People are to be ruled. They are not to be allowed to live freely. And this right to rule is the privilege of the noble.

This, of course, is not the way this play of Shakespeare's was taught to me in my homeland or in University here in Canada. This and every one of this Englishman's plays was presented as "great" literature. Shakespeare, I was told in several ways, is a writer of "universal" importance whose appeal transcends geo-cultural boundaries. I wondered about this when I was being instructed in this Literature in that British colony, the land of my birth. If, in my father's words this *Shakespeare, wallah*, had such universal appeal why was it that hardly anyone among the people in whose midst I grew up knew of or cared to know of this writer? These were peoples of the *Ramayana,* the *Mahabharata,* the *Gita,* the *Vedas,* the *Upanishads*, people who spoke of Tulsidas and Manu, of Karma and Atma. But the pat answer has always been that they are not "educated" enough to know of or appreciate Shakespeare. And perhaps this is so. But if this is the case, if people have to be "educated," taught to think in certain ways in order to appreciate this Shakespeare, then there is something false in the grand claim pertaining to his "universal" appeal.

It is the *universalizing* of Shakespeare rather than the spurious claim that he is "universal" that needs to be looked into. In the history of my Education Shakespeare's works were required study in the syllabus for English Literature for the College of Preceptors Examination, my education in Teacher's College, the Ordinary Level and the Advanced Level of the General Certificate of Education examinations, selected by the wise men and women, the White Light Bearers of Oxford and Cambridge and London for our study. These examinations were written by us in the colonies of the British Empire and sent to them thousands of miles away to be marked in their world where Literature and the Literary happened. This is the trajectory of authority and power through which Shakespeare was inserted in my life. This is also one of the ways in which this writer has been universalized—imposed on the unsuspecting victims of colonizing British education.

Shakespeare was presented to us as Britain's greatest literary treasure, the pride of every Englishman and the Empire, the greatest writer in the world. And our appropriate appreciation of this Great writer was required, not our criticism. This was simultaneously the induction of respect for Britain which, prototypic of the EuroEgo in which it is formed, imperiously calls itself Great. At University in Toronto I studied Shakespeare's plays, but contrary to the ebullience of my professors and the acclaimed profundity of some of Shakespeare's insights, what remains disturbingly important to me is the context in which these dazzling feats of language are set. By context I do not merely mean the location in the text where a quotation has been taken from, or the surface-text description of the actions surrounding the excerpt. I am referring to the structure in which the action is contained, the nature of the thought which informs the actions of the speaker, the speaker's position and rank in the order of authority in which the drama is enacted, and the reader who is among others, a historical being, influenced and always subject to influence, but also a critical presence. Shakespeare's context is consistent in its "surfeit" of wisdom among EuroEgo's imperial hosts—its kings, its queens, its princes, its princesses, its dukes, its duchesses, its lords, its ladies, these protagonists of imperial ecstasies, and the servile cast, the commoners who serve them in pride, glad to be so ruled.

Thus to "properly appreciate" Shakespeare is to accept the views of EuroEgo's power-elite whom he depicts. This is to also accept being ruled by their descendants in the usurpations of Empire and Conquest. It is to look at these protagonists as the heroic articulators of goodness, the few whose deeds matter, whose glory transcends the rest of humanity. And all good colonial subjects were to learn this, to imitate this bard's words as universal truths, and in this imitation remain entranced in the order of the Empire, but to not recognize this demeaning truth. To instead feel wise in repeating refrains like, Portia's, "the quality of mercy is not strained," for there in that Place of Greatness there is Law and Order and Justice-for-all, not the barbarism of imperial avarice, not the officious Law and Order of the Empire, that legal mechanism of subordination and exploitative control which, in addition to ruling us, constructs us as potential lawbreakers, sees us as criminals—criminality itself being a condition of our imputed inferiority.

In *The Merchant of Venice* we are to agree with the Christians and their court's cruelty to Shylock, "the Jew," the hated Other, and not see ourselves as also the despised Other, not see ourselves as what EuroEgo abhors, as what it demeans to feel good about the abhorrence of its own exploitative pleasure. Not see how much we remind EuroEgo of its abhorrent mania, and thus how EuroEgo necessarily continues to abhor us.

The fault, dear Brutus, is not in our stars / But in ourselves that we are underlings.

In the order of the hideous imperial dream of power that this play, *Julius Caesar,* in many respects is, Cassius and Brutus are indeed underlings to Caesar who

> . . . doth stride the narrow world,
> Like a colossus; and we petty men
> Walk under his huge legs, and peep about
> To find ourselves dishonourable graves.
> > *Julius Caesar,* Act 1 Scene 2

But this is not a reference to the underlings every one of the hundreds of millions of occupied subjects of the British Empire was deemed to be. Nor does it seem to me to address, as some have touted, the condition of an individual inadequacy. Cassius is miserable because he does not have the importance and power

38

bestowed upon the warrior Caesar whom he calls ambitious. But it is also Cassius's as well as Brutus's ambitiousness for power in Rome that this discourse of empire dramatizes. Like Julius Caesar these are warrior-men whose greatness is demonstrated in their capacity to violate, to kill, to do battle with whoever the enemy is made out to be, and like Hamlet, they are noble lords, courtiers, soldiers and articulate orators and manipulators. Their military prowess, their genius in causing death and enforcing compliance by violence and the threat of violence, inflames them to further exercise their power over people from the palatial chambers of the *imperium*, to rule by heading the confederacy of warlords in the name of what is good for Rome, for their friends who are Romans and countrymen and lovers, honourable men. They cannot bear the thought of being merely "villagers," since in the *agon* in which they are active combatants, it is proper for victors to run the State.

In the *agon* combat is virtuous, victory a sacrosanct necessity. In the *agon* those who live by killing are the rulers, admired, and are often deemed Great, as in Alexander-the-Great. In the *agon* the State is an empire-state. It emerges in the violations of conquest, the construction of the Other as the dreaded enemy upon whose death it draws its momentum, its definition of itself. The *agon* feeds off death. It requires human sacrifice. This is the sanguine nature of its power. It worships war, sees in war the play of Greatness. It is nostalgic about its Great Wars, its Just Wars. It is always ready for war. It is rule as threat. Its glory is always its joy over human slaughter, its pleasure in victory, in requiring the defeat of others. It is blind to its delusions of grandeur. It has no hesitation in calling itself Brave, Great, Heroic, Wise, Good. In the *agon* existence is the sanctification of domination, and is central in the establishment and maintenance of the rule of oppressive authority. It is where EuroEgo has its recurrent moment.

It is the EuroEgoism in Cassius and Brutus and Anthony and Caesar that is at the core of this play. The imaginary is imperial-universal. Caesar struts across the world, not the blood-soaked streets of Roman gory and Colosseum killings or the bloodied waters of the river Tiber. It is this desire for such monumental significance that is the inflamed centre of EuroEgo. This play is universalized as a Great play, it is one of Shakespeare's Great Tragedies. But what does this Greatness refer to? The clever oration and the connivances of dishonourable men, men with blood on their hands, men ready to kill with daggers and swords, men adept at rationalizing their murderous acts, men who assume it is their right to rule? The *imperium* as the grand edifice of treachery and murderous deceit is not for a moment questioned. The tragedy which takes place is seen as the fault of individuals, not with the agonistic institution of values. Shakespeare as an exemplar of EuroEgo at work, has no interest in this. Greatness, it seems, is the characteristic of the dominators within this structure of domination.

Cassius and Brutus decide to change their underling status by doing what is logical in the *agon*. They kill their designated enemy and feel good about what they have done in the name of loving Rome. In typical rulership rhetoric, what they have committed is not seen as murder, but rather as a necessary and unpleasant task to rid Rome of a tyrannical ruler. An empire story, told with dramatic eloquence and insight into the progenitors of violation. Greatness? Whose greatness? Greatness for whom? And where am I in this? The placing of me in this has to be considered, for this text reaches me as I am, and in my reading of it or hearing it acted out, I am involved, but I am not a blankness, I am not consumed, I am always my history, my moment, myself. Amidst the pages of "literary appreciation" I am who I am, I am not anonymous, I cannot be. What is said is being said to me. To read this text and be anonymous is to be consumed by its levelling power.

This is not the place for me to do the thorough re-reading I would like to do of Shakespeare's plays, but it is of importance to note that the high regard there is for Shakespeare in anglophone Canada has also the affirmation of the perspectives in relation to power over people celebrated in this writer's work. For the large number of peoples resident in Canada whose former places of dwelling have been violated by the agonistic forages of EuroEgo, these issues cannot, and should not be separated from the action of the play. They are essential to the existence of the work, and it would be consequential to ignore this. A consideration of some of the implications of what is being taught to us and our children in this and similar circumstances may give proper cause for concern.

Take *The Tempest*. If I am to accept, as the surface text of this play suggests, that everything ends well, what am I really accepting? What is it that so ends? What enchantment resides in the seeming harmony here? What deceptions, what imperial discourse? Here the conspiracies of greed among a select section of European nobility within the *imperium* are rectified, wrongs are pardoned through the intervention of the "noble" Duke, the "wise" Prospero's supra-natural powers, his "charms," and the order of the rule of the nobility is re-established where Prospero is the happy and benevolent Patriarch in his "Dukedom," and his daughter is happily united with the noble personage he approves of. He even frees Caliban whom he had enslaved, and also sets Ariel free. Prospero is that dangerous contradiction, "the good ruler." In him EuroEgo is projected as benign enchanter, but his "charms" are certainly the means through which he conducts his occupation of Caliban's island. In him the insolence of rule is made to appear wholesome and wise, gracious, good, the occasion for joyous celebration. But Prospero is a slaver and a marauder. From his cell on the island which he calls "bare" Prospero rules with the powers of a sorcerer. This Duke can command obedience from the elements and the spirit-world to suit his purpose, even to torture, as he has his spirit-servant and henchman, Ariel, do to Caliban after he has occupied Caliban's homeland and imprisoned Caliban's mother.

In his *Dramatis Personae* Shakespeare refers to Caliban as a "savage and deformed slave," and in the text of his play there are numerous dehumanizing and beastly references to Caliban. He is a monster, a monster-man, a howling monster. He is a beast of burden. He is there to be violated at Prospero's whim. He is tortured and made a slave by Prospero. We are told his ancestry is evil and cursed. He is only too willing to have White Europeans as

41

his Master, especially after he has been made drunk on their intoxicant brew. He is also quite stupid. He thinks he can have Prospero's people support him against the slave-torturer-commander which the noble and wise Duke of Milan, Prospero is. He is also completely untrustworthy, as far as Prospero is concerned, since he refuses to accept being enslaved. To think of the person enslaved as having these demeaning attributes is to collude with the racist disfigurement of the original peoples to whom the euro-vampirism of Empire and Conquest did whatever harm it pleased. It is Prospero who in Crusoe-like fashion arrives on Caliban's island and decides to enslave Caliban, who besides being deemed a savage is also conceived of as being grotesque, "deformed," angry, abusive and dangerous, a rapist, a danger to the "fair" Miranda, and I suspect to all the "fair" women of noble Europe. This is the defamation of the person and humanity of those peoples Euro-empire claims it "discovered." It is the studied procedure through which EuroEgo repeatedly enacts the violation of the indigene to feed the abhorrence of EuroEgo's insatiable hunger. This is the imaginary, this atrocity of the Imperial Eye, in which Shakespeare depicts Caliban.

When the "wise" and "noble" Prospero decides to free Caliban, it is Prospero's dignity which is enhanced, not Caliban's. Indeed Prospero is the grand pardoner of even he who wanted his death, the foul Caliban. He *gives* Caliban freedom. Freedom is seen as the gift of the slave-master-torturer whose erring ways are mended, and to whom wisdom and decency are imputed. But it must be remembered, this wise giver of freedom still controls the island. Years later in euro-empire's rule, this has remarkably been the way in which the ending of slavery was depicted, as well as the "granting" of Independence to the Empire's occupied territories. Freedom and Independence as the benevolence of the royal ruler, a regal gift to the enslaved, and to the "dependent" colonies. Gifts of royal pleasure. The Empire takes and the Empire gives. The imperial bestower of freedom in which EuroEgo continues to be Master, but the names and certain circumstances are changed. In the case of Britain, the Independence it "granted" its colonies gives rise to the formation of the British Commonwealth of Nations. The extension of colonialism in the name of Independence.

In the Epilogue Prospero tells us he meant to please. He asks his audience to help him, now that his "charms are o'erthrown" and he is merely human again, leave the "bare island" to return to his Dukedom. His concluding words are, "Let your indulgence set me free." Well said, but what is it that is happening? This dramatic device works to bond the audience with the performance, and in so doing encourages a greater empathy for Prospero. I find no merit in the speculatory adulation which holds that this is Shakespeare himself bidding farewell to his audiences. This may or may not be the case. But it is remarkably ironic, isn't it, that it is Prospero who now asks his audience's aid in setting him "free"? There is nowhere in this play of domination as enchantment where Prospero is in bondage. It cannot be that he has been imprisoned on the island. He occupied the place and violated its dwellers. He is responsible for the destruction of a people which he committed, but this has no importance to this imperial figure who tells his audience his intention has been to please, and who now leaves, apparently not just unscathed by his actions, but rather transformed, transported in virtue, has become almost saintly.

In Canada, Britain and Europe, audiences are generally pleased with this performance. The pleasure here also comes from a tacit agreement with what the play celebrates, not merely the brilliance in certain lines. This is reputed to be one of Shakespeare's final plays, if not the last one, and in this the imperial correctness of EuroEgo's supremacist ecstasy is intact. The harm done to the Calibans and Sycoraxes, the ancestral inhabitants of the colonized lands, does not matter. The psychic and physical torture they are made to suffer are not important. Prospero's dukedom awaits. Ecstatic imperialism triumphs yet again. And in this scenario of thought when this happens all is said to be well. This is an exquisite imperialist discourse.

Some claim Shakespeare is reflective of the perceptions of "his time," but that he is also "timeless." I find these claims contentious. The first seeks to legitimate the values and ideas of a small number of people who dominated the era. It assumes that everyone then thought as affirmingly as this writer did of the protagonists of Empire and the rule of privilege. The second claim is the more serious one, and it is kept alive in high school and university, and supported by a veritable industry of Shakespearean theatre, with the Stratford Festival in Ontario being the most outstanding example in Canada. Shakespeare *is* Great Britain's great pride. When he is annually resurrected in Canada through huge sums of money from the Canada Council, it is more than "theatre" that is taking place. An insidious imperialism is reproduced as Great Theatre.

* Homi K Bhabha, "The Other Question: Difference, Discrimination and the Discourse of Colonialism," in *Out There: Marginilization and Contemporary Cultures*, Russel Ferguson et al. (Cambridge, Massachusetts:The MIT Press, 1992), 72.

Pathways that Lead

There are certain pathways which can lead you into the abyss of your own disappearance even while you think you're doing the correct thing. They are many, these pathways, and they are seductive. They claim to orient you, to take you to places of meaning, and they do, but where is it that you arrive? They are filled with purpose, these pathways. They are the constructs of particular perceptions, the designs of a project of power which should never be taken for granted, despite the weight and industry placed on them. The authority they hold is at the same time the pall of control, the methods and procedures through which instruction for conformity of vision takes place, the subversion of the independence of those so instructed. These pathways multiply, converge, cross each other, go out into the world and return in the serpentine of classrooms, podiums, books, essays, journals, magazines, newspapers, radio and television programmes, the boardrooms and bedrooms of editorial and publishing decisions, and the making of the reading public in these and other contexts.

Ways in which the reading of literature is taught are the pathways towards a particular moment of perception which bears always certain traditions of seeing. These traditions maintain the practices of the dominant order in the guise of cultural codes which shape one's understanding of what is being read. When you are of another cultural space these ways of reading can often read you out of existence. They amount to the institutionalizing of reading.

Is It Tragedy or Comedy or Tragicomedy?

These familiar and respected terms of classification, widely taught

45

and upheld also in Canada in extension of the anglo-european traditions of perception—the EuroEgoism to which much of Canada subscribes—are a formalism in which the approach to literature is structured by a fabrication of perspective within the fabrications of perspective that literature itself can in one way be said to be. It is where literature referred to either as tragedy or comedy or tragicomedy is also the reproduction of an attitude towards that which is defined as tragedy, comedy or tragicomedy, as far as the allowances of the genre prevail. But what are the structures that inform these allowances which are reproduced with every act of such pedagogy? And what does this form of reading and writing mean in the circumstances of those whose experience has been branded by imperialism?

To see in these terms, these constructs of tragedy and comedy, is to assume that human action is explainable within the boundaries of these contrived and simple extremes. Not only is this misleading since it does not take into consideration the complexities of human action outside of these contrivances of perspective, it disregards them, and in this it projects a disinterest in difference. This disinterest supports the conformity of vision to the dominant mode of seeing which the genre upholds and reproduces. In its exclusion of difference it politicizes its own premises as privileged. When the situation is neither tragedy or comedy it is still conceptualized as comprising elements of both: it is "tragicomedy." The pattern is the same. Everything happens within the boundaries of disciplinary governance. As I have indicated earlier, in Shakespeare in this fabrication of genre, tragedy, similar to comedy, celebrates the heroic individualism intrinsic to the aesthetic of power in the monumental imperialist ecstasies in which the nation-states of EuroEgo have their existence. In it the action of the caste of Euro-privilege in the imposition of order is not questioned. It is taken as a given, as natural, as the natural right of the rulers to rule. The gaze is centred on the actions of select British and European personages against a backdrop of faceless humanity. In this mode of fantasy there is the simultaneous elaboration of commonly held values in both Europe and Britain, a distinctive EuroEgoism of perception in which these ways of reading do not touch upon the order of domination upheld in these practices. The privileging of these perspectives is a conceit which transcends individuality. It is not just self-conceit, but rather a conceit formed in the culture of the *agon* where superiority is always a paramount obsession. This is the working of EuroEgo where the super-egoism of a universality of perspective is promoted.

In tragedy it is the "flaw" of the protagonist that leads to downfall and eventual death. Disaster comes from a personal psychic defect, not from the values of the political and social order as in themselves productive of disaster. The latter, as I have noted, is never questioned. The order is taken for granted, seen as the way things are, a sublime and unmoveable protocol, often reinforced with notions of the Divine, as in "Divine Order." In this interest in a privileged individualism, hidden always is the destruction committed by the groups these protagonists are representative of. There is also an inference here that tragedy is the personal fault of its victim. How is this to be received by those abused by the machinations of imperialism? There is something odious when such thinking leads to and is used to indict the suffering for the violations imperialism has inflicted and continues to inflict on them. This thinking would have us believe an insidious and fatal flaw in these peoples has led them to an inevitable and deserving plight, that it's their own fault.

Perhaps these tragedies do not qualify as "tragedy" in this literary form, but then what does this say of tragedy in the world outside of the niceties of such literary formalism? And what of this literary form? It seems to me that among others it valorizes the thinking in which this vision of the tragic augments an imperialist aesthetic in the construction of meaning. We should remember that while these works were being penned and dramatized Euroempire was also inflicting its cruelties on the peoples of my world.

The exportation and imposition of these views located within the curricula of literary studies, is where the project of teaching obedience to the perspectives of the ruling force of ideas realizes additional authority. In this setting there is a veiled but ominous warning also that resistance to this authority is a foolhardiness which necessarily leads to tragedy, and that there must be something wrong, some flaw in someone who so goes against the order to court what is seen as inevitable disaster. This is the order of things, the imperial order, the terrain of heroic imperialism. It is that which always prevails, whether the protagonist lives or dies, whether the ending is tragic or comical or comprises elements of both. In comedy and tragicomedy the order provides pleasure. Things end well for the principal actors who are usually the members of the nobility. The fissure of exploitation between the privileged and the common people is harmonized into an illusion of goodness, and all is said to be well that ends well, when ruler and ruled know their place in the ranking of privilege, and all are happy about it.

Does the Plot Thicken or Thin?

Plot is the traditional pathway through which much of literature is written and read. So entrenched has the plot become that when fiction or drama (the exceptional few) dispenses with it readers feel lost. In Canada, and wherever else this approach to literature is obsessively emphasized, most publishers and reviewers of books and the readers they address are uncomfortable when they do not find a plot, and many are downright hostile to works which they disparage as being "plotless." But what of this love of plot, besides the flattery the reader feels by being able to identify and follow the narrative structure of the work? What are some of the assumptions on which plot is based?

Perhaps, as some feel, plot is symptomatic of the search for coherence, the need to make sense of things within the confusion of existence. It is the structure in which "the story" is told, that through which "the theme" of the work is narrated. But this desire to know is bound to a fabrication of perspective in which meaning is problematically structured. If being coherent of the structure is what the search for coherence is presented as being, then we are in actuality more properly dealing with the closure of meaning, rather than what is thought to be the case. It is where the search is confined to the strictures of the edifice of structural identification.

The fascination with plot comes from and informs a rationality in which a plotting sensibility is esteemed. While it is true that much is learned from plots and subplots, it is *what is so learned* that has to be looked into. There is an assumption in this manner of thought that that which is meaningful is *necessarily plotted*, that life is lived according to the predetermined strictures of a plot, that experience is necessarily plotted. Plotting presumes a sense of coherence emergent out of a predetermining conspiratorial approach to meaning. The scheming plotting deliberations for conquest is an essential *strategy* in the connivances of imperialism. It furnishes the mania of power intrinsic to the perpetuation of the *agon*, and is there in the institutions of domination, the state-corporate Janus of control where strategy is as vital and highly valued as the military repressive measures of the army and the police through which force is deployed to ensure the rule of dire inequality, the siege of existence. This diabolic preoccupation of the politico-economic agencies of exploitation seeks to plot the moment and circumstances of the lives of those it dominates, to imprison the present, to possess it, to control it, and thus to control the future. Plotting is the essential strategy of domination, the deliberation through which the stratagems of control reproduce the conditions which ensure their continued existence. And in the vicissitudes bred within the unreasonableness of dire inequality, the recognition of plot, the interest in the intricacies of plot, is often experienced as comforting.

But this is a type of comfort in which the walls of containment are erroneously thought of as cradling arms, the nurturants towards the liberation of the intellect in which the real story is the imprisonment of the intellect. It is where love of plot provides an inverse pleasure. This comfort is the assurance control provides for those who have been taught to depend on it so much that it is seen as a need, and is desired. This is the making of the subject in the culture of imperialism. The comfort in the recognition of plot is also one of the principal requirements of the strategy of rule. It is where plot is seen as the exercise of intelligence, not the salutation of premeditated calculativeness.

The importance placed on plot by so many writers, publishers, teachers, reviewers and readers in Canada, demonstrates the extent to which plot is entrenched in the cultural unconscious of the society. When readers are uncomfortable in the absence of plot there is both a desire for the imposition of the control intrinsic in structure, and a fear of existing outside of such limits, a fear of being on one's own, a fear of the independence of thought. This is a form of regressive thinking. Progressive thinking moves towards freeing the self. Regressive thinking is uncomfortable without structural control. It takes pleasure in the dictums of authority, and thinks itself free.

The history of Canada, like its empire-ecstasy counterparts, has among other factors been one of plot and subplot and counterplot to facilitate the exploitative order in which it has its origin, and which it daily reproduces. It is a society in which Empire, Imperial and Royal are fond terms, used in pride in loyalty to the imperialist ethos of rule characteristic of EuroEgo.

Whose Character?

It is an institutional practice to talk of "character" and "character development" as forms of judgement in the evaluation of literature. Students are taught to see "character," and "character development," and reviewers also look for this, and proceed to praise or condemn a work, dependent on their findings. There is a presumption here that they can get to "know" these "characters." This raises many questions.

Similar to plot, the concern for "character" is part of the prescribed format of reading, and forms the basis for the dissection of the work. The desire to "know" a "character" assumes the possibility of intimacy with a fictive construct, and proposes that by paying attention to an *individuality*, the entire work can be understood. This is the perpetuation of the individualism bestowed on the protagonists of Empire. It is there in the reading which continues to look for "character" rather than the essence of the work. But what is "character"? What makes "character" what it is said to be? What are the characteristics that amount to "character"? By whose definition? Whose standards? Whose culture conceives of this notion of "character"? Does this "character" have a history, or does it have a standardized presence, occurring anywhere, a universal transarticulation?

These questions need to be asked since the practice of character-identification seems to disregard historical and cultural differences in the actions of people. How is, say, a reader from Canada, who knows virtually nothing of the peoples and customs of another society, to recognize "character" in the work of a writer from such a place? And what are the stipulates pertaining to whether this "character" has "developed" or not? Developed into what? Being credible to the person whose judgement is informed by values alien to the writer and the world being written about? Or must the writer be constrained to write to accommodate the judgemental expectations of this imputed reader?

The insistence on "character" is based on the imperialist precept that alienated individualism is the universal situation through which life happens. In this, it seems "characters" have a relation to the metaphor of size. They are talked of as being "solid" or "thin" or "flat" or "rounded." Through these vacuous stereotypes what the writer is trying to say is usually destroyed, and this is worse with works of writers outside of the empire of *EuroAmerica*. The interest in knowing the "character" here fosters the gaze of superiority where the Canadian-English-Lit expectation of what "character" should be, is the prism through which judgement is made. It is the habit of the vast majority of reviewers in Canada to cannibalize works in which their notion of "character" and "character development" does not prevail.

And what of the "flawed character"? One view holds this is the very stuff of tragedy, the tragic flaw which leads to doom. I have already remarked on this with regard to Shakespearean tragedy and heroic imperialism, but the notion of "flaw" goes much further, and is there in the other view in regard to "flawed characterization" which is that the characterization itself is incomplete, an error in the writer's depiction. This is usually related to the proprieties of "character development." The thinking which sees flaw in characterization assumes a prior and superior knowledge about what an unflawed character development ought to be. Not only is this prescriptive, it is also the action of the autocracy of a conceptual ideal of perfection, the measure against which the technicities of "character" are judged.

The belief in perfection is a discursive strategy of desire where the pursuit of the impossible is the obsessive-compulsive mania through which domination holds continuing vigil. It is where those convinced of their being disparagingly imperfect endlessly seek the abstraction of an acutely desired perfection. It is the ploy through which, for example, the imperialism of Christianity, EuroEgo's religion of choice for the last two thousand years, ensures compliance to its Order. Against the ideal of the perfect all are imperfect and in need of the mercy of the Perfect One whom they must worship with devoutness and humility their whole life through. In this trope of ecstatic control—in ritual worship, in prayer, in sin and guilt, in confession, in absolution and forgiveness, in unquestioning—people pay homage to the agents of the Omnipotent Omniscient and Omnipresent One, the Supreme Knower. A passionate supremacist totalitarian fantasy, thoroughly used in EuroEmpire's ravaging of the world.

The assumption of knowing perfection is the authoritative-authoritarian claim where the subtle presence of a castigating power ensconces itself. It constantly vilifies that which it considers imperfect. It constructs the inferior and preys on it, lords itself upon it to feed its mania of superiority. It is a predator. It destroys in numerous ways to uphold its oppressive strength.

"Character" is the conceit of the First World arbiters of taste against whom all else is inferior in character, particularly those places and peoples demeaned as third-rate, those third places, those worlds of thirdnesses, that incomplete still developing Third World, that world of flawed habitants, perpetually inferior to the self-declared First World, to glorious and knowledgeable and great EuroEgo.

Glorious and Free . . . We Stand on Guard for Thee

I who have known no glory and little freedom enter this land of the glorious and free, and without knowing it enter also the making of me into other than I am which I have to resist as long as I reside here if I am to have any dignity of self. Resistance, exhausting resistance.

I am "immigrant," the label which brands me a particular prisoner, an undesirable, a suspect, an alien, a brand which goes with me everywhere I go in this country, which I cannot remove even with having the full official status of Canadian Citizenship. It is where the human being I am has been made into a negating stereotype, smeared invisible. Yet I am visible as a "minority," I am a "visible minority." In this peculiarity of visibility I am an unimportance, an inauthenticity, a minority thing, a "visible minority," conspicuous, disliked.

The towering White policeman imperiously pulls me over.

Why? I want to know. I've not broken any traffic law.

He seems annoyed by my question. I see his hand resting as if by habit on the holster of his gun. He looks into the car at the persons with me, his face a tight reddening mask of disapproval.

You the owner of this car, sir?

Yes. Why? Is something wrong?

Your Driver's Licence and Ownership, please.

Why? What have I done?

Mouthy one, aren't you? Licence and Ownership, please, sir.

Don't argue with him, one of my companions whispers. These people are something else.

I am new here, I don't understand this. It annoys me, but I hand the policeman my papers and watch him stride in confident authority to his Cruiser.

This is not fair, I say. I've done nothing against the law, nothing wrong! It's not fair!

Fair? Boy, you think he cares about fairness? One look at us, that's all it takes. One look!

What d'you mean? I ask, feeling even more outraged. What about *us*?

A carful of Blacks and Indians, and you asking this stupid question, maan? You in Canada, you know. Not home!

The policeman is back. He returns my papers.

So you really own this car, Curly? he says.

That is *not* my name! I snap, all restraint gone.

Have a good day, sir, the policeman says and struts back in triumphant aggression to his Cruiser to maintain The Peace.

Lucky he didn't charge you with something, one of the fellows says. This en nothing, you know . . .

It is perhaps not much, there have been worse encounters, but it's enough. The policeman is not alone, he is not the only one who is like this, and the others are not confined to this military unit, the Police Force. They are also in the *Intelligentsia Academicus* where the privileging of the culture of EuroEgo is daily reproduced in the fortresses of Higher Learning, funded by the State and governed by Boards whose members are senior executives of national and multinational corporations.

In the policeman's thinking in this instance there is something wrong about a "visible minority" doing something which he and the Majority should have as their prerogative. His boldness lies in the support he has from the Majority of which he is an armed and dangerous representative. This is an example of the reproduction of the hostility to "the natives" which infuses the imperialist zeal of supremacy in the empire-forages of EuroEgo. This time we are in a place which, prototypic of the action of EuroEgo, the White-man and the Whitewoman claim as their own, and "stand on

55

guard" in the military stance of the National Anthem, in protection of. It is their "home and native land" as the Anthem proclaims and affirms. It is where the Native Peoples from whom much of this land has been stolen have been banished in the apartheid of Reservations under The Indian Act—under the Whiteman's domination. There is disapproval of our presence here. We are the "natives" of another place and as such are suspect to begin with. This is acted out in the policeman's attitude towards me. A popular Majority view today in Canada is that "Third World Peoples" are troublemakers.

When I ask the policeman what any reasonable person would, his disapproval of my being in "his" country is further expressed when he accuses me of being "a mouthy one." I am one of *them*, the despised others, and I am unpleasantly garrulous. I am not expected to speak, to question, to say anything about this harassment. I am to silently comply with the enforcer of Authority, regardless of what may be happening to me. My "visible-minority" categorization abusively equates me with criminality. And my carful of menacing Otherness is where trouble necessarily must be.

It is not easy to be this thing, this "visible minority" thing. Those who have thought it up—obviously from or in consort with the Majority—know what they had in mind. And it's not just the numbers game, not just the identification of larger numbers and smaller numbers, not just the vulgarity of quantification, although there is something vulgar in the thinking which so demeans another person. What do you do when you become a "visible minority," besides feeling despair and uncertainty?

I am doing Twentieth Century Literature at a university in Toronto. I feel like a conspicuous and offensive stain in this class of White unfriendly students. The White professor is warbling about the brilliance of certain English, Irish and American writers. White writers. But he does not refer to them this way. The best writers in the world, he claims, are writers whose meditations on the human experience are profound demonstrations of

the acute sense of self-reflection which distinguishes the civilization of which they are exemplary members.

I have read these writers with interest, and will do so repeatedly, but I cannot be as enthused about them. Today the lecture is
on D H Lawrence, and the professor is aroused by the language in
which Constance's sexual awakening is written in *Lady Chatterley's Lover.* I am unable to empathize with the ecstasies of Lady
Chatterley who I keep thinking would in my homeland be someone like the wife of one of the British Governors or Plantation
Managers, personages who would have never deigned to even
acknowledge I exist. Mellors strikes me as being the crudity
nearly everyone of the Plantation Overseers in the sugar estates
at home was. I don't have any interest in the English working
class and ruling class conflicts which Mellors resolves through the
taming of this shrew of English nobility by his own phallic domination. There is nothing about them I particularly like. And there
is something offensive in my having to study the sexual inadequa-
cies and pleasures of the English landed gentry and the romance
with the caretaker-gardener of their manorial lands.

Besides, in my readings I have come across the startling revelation that D H Lawrence held extremely disparaging views about
the peoples of my world, views which I interpret as being disturbing, as being racist. I mention this latter concern, by way of
challenging the professor's claim that Lawrence is one of the
greatest writers in the world, and I want to also know if he doesn't
consider Wilson Harris or Vidia Naipaul important writers in
Twentieth Century Literature. The professor's response remains
with me. Here's something of the flavour of it.

Race, race, the professor exclaims, and I mistake the tone of
lamentation in his voice as some kind of agreement. Then it
changes into what I recognize as a castigating parody of the
manner in which this professor obviously thinks I speak . . . Dere
are doze, the professor says, who would see race everywhere,
mohn.

Giggles in class. But they are not laughing at the ridiculous
way the professor sounds. They are laughing at me.

See, I been to Jamaica too, mohn! the professor adds, and the class bursts into a roar of laughter.

I'm *not* from Jamaica, I say, but either no one has heard or no one is paying attention to what I'm saying.

The professor continues: Ah don't know where you got your information, mohn, but it clearly is of no relevance to the appreciation of Great Writing. This, I should remind you, is a course in English Literature, not in Sociology or Political Science. And who are those—Wilson *Who*, and *what*?

Loud laughter.

Wilson Harris of Guyana! Vidia Naipaul of Trinidad!

I am shouting, and the sudden hostile silence is deafening. I realize, too late, that emotion is considered a "display " in this place, a form of threat or embarrassment, something which you do your best to repress. The professor looks uncomfortably serious, as if a wasp has just stung him in front of his class and he does not know whether to cry or not.

His voice drops to a formal solemnity, and I hear him say, This is not a course on Black Writers, you know. Shall we proceed?

But Naipaul is not a Black writer, I say.

Perhaps you're right—

I am!

—you know, I mean Third World and Commonwealth Writers. Those. And, you know, I should let you know it's your democratic right to not continue with this course if you don't care for what it addresses. As we say here, this is a free country, and I won't be offended if you or anyone else should find this course inappropriate to your interests. And now let's look at Lawrence's penetrating insight—predating Freud I might add—into the importance of sexuality in the realm of human happiness . . .

My instruction in the democratics of the acceptance of the Majority view will continue in this and many other guises in these seats of Higher Learning. It will be long after my time at this university before any course on Black or Third World or Commonwealth writers, problematic though these terms themselves are, is taught here or anywhere else in Canada. And they remain "specialty" courses, exotic fringes to the main purpose of the programmes of Departments of English in the few universities where they are currently offered. But even here one of the current newspeak buzz-word names for it is "postcolonial literature." The slave branding of EuroEmpire is burnt into this conception of the works of writers outside of EuroAmerica—while it is certainly not the practice to name the literature of EuroEgo in relation to its eras of EuroImperialism. Imperialism does not feature in the treatment of the literature of EuroAmerica, but colonialism does in the "appreciation" of the literature of EuroImperialism's Other.

Imperialism does not presence itself as a concern where its values are ingrained in the psyche as the normal and the correct. It exists within the dominant construction of perception which informs the political unconscious. It is thus that the very nature of the perception of literature is here steeped in the approach to Otherness traditional to the culture of EuroImperialism. The name and the naming derive their significance in relation to EuroImperial occupation as being so totalizing that all literature written is seen in relation to it—to colonialism—either as "colonial literature," or the continuation of the colonizational perspectives in the conceptual label, "postcolonial literature." The gaze here perceives within the preferentiality of the order of domination. It is through this that the complexity of existence within which these writers emerge is reduced to two moments within EuroImperial control, to "colonial" or "postcolonial." Thus this literature of the Other stands undermined of its originality, its authenticity, its independence. *Ergo* EuroEgo.

Salman Rushdie's phrase, "the Empire writes back to the Centre" has inspired numerous studies in "postcolonial literature" bearing this perspective, with, among others, *The Empire Writes Back,* coming out of this. But there are serious problems with this view. It presumes the continuing existence of the former "Empire" whose subject-writers are, in extension of the dependency instituted during colonialism, now writing back, talking back to the imperial centre, and in so doing are redefining themselves. Empire is conceived here both as a positivity and a reactivity, an extant consciousness outside of the former imperial centre which continues to depend on this Centre for a definition of itself. The stance is reactionary. It is post-coloniality.

Where is this Empire located which so writes back to "the Centre"? Is it in India, Pakistan, Africa, the Caribbean or elsewhere? Does the former British Empire, for example, still exist as "Empire" in the lands it once occupied so much so that its "Centre" is still Britain? It seems to me not. And if it does not exist as such how is it possible to have a situation in which "the Empire writes back to the Centre?" The vision which sees in relation to the notion that "the Empire writes back to the Centre" demonstrates the insidious play of the dialogic of imperialism. It is the circular trope of a negating self-referencing, mired in a delusion of identification—where the order of imperial domination is the trajectory in which a stylized aesthetic of resistance is conceived. In this the *imperium* prevails. Those constructed subaltern in the rule of Empire are now named the "Empire." This naming repeats the dominator's positive view of occupation and ownership where imperialist rule ceases to be oppressive, is seen as a benign order in which the oppressed are "members" who are said to be the "Empire." Who are now a literate consciousness critical of its Centre. The symbiosis of supremacy and inferiority within the order of domination is intact here.

Self-authority requires more than the reactivity of writing back to the Centre. It has to go beyond this, dispense with it, free itself from it. Critical engagement with the texts and procedurals of the Empire is not "writing back" to the imperial centre, although these works may be published in the Houses and cities of EuroAmerica. They are the instructional moments in the realization of self outside of the incarceration of Empire and Conquest. The critical moment is the act of severance.

Colonization has not ended, it has changed, become stronger, less apparently direct in most of its actions. It is now the preserve of the largest and most terrifying empire in human history,

EuroAmerica, the unification of European imperialism with its aggressive predominating progeny, American imperialism. Together these have the largest and most techno-scientifically terrifying armies of the world. They work in cooperation with each other, often side by side. Together they seek to own and control the wealth of the rest of the world. Their voracious hunger feeds upon three quarters of the earth's raw material. The work of their *Intelligentsia Academicus* has come to troubling fruition. Their universities continue to dominate the world, to presume a monopoly on knowledge. They continue their task of making virtuous the cultural assumptions of EuroEgo. Their graduates are dispersed the world over, and they are working in consort with their imperial masters, colluding in the exploitation of their own peoples and countries to furnish EuroAmerica.

I listen to the professor pontificate on Lawrence's insight into human sexuality, and I wonder who the "human" is here, knowing it certainly does not include me. I am not the "human" being talked about. I am not preoccupied with sexual repression and release as this English writer and his admirers obviously are. And I wonder as I will over the years in this place where officially there is Unity in Diversity and Multicultural harmony, I wonder what is it that is really happening here in the name of Higher Learning and Literature?

I soon learn I am supposed to be embarrassed by the accent I have. It later becomes clear it is not my accent as such, but rather that those offended by it do not want to hear what I'm saying, do not expect or want me to speak, and that this is part of the larger silence of the "visible minority" required by the Majority, who apparently must think themselves not visible. One of the assumptions here is that the "visible minority" should not have anything of importance to say, should be ashamed of the way they speak, be ashamed of themselves since to be ashamed of the way you speak is to be also ashamed of yourself. This is one of the procedures through which inferiority is reproduced and maintained in the domination discourse upheld in the primacy of the Majority, reproduced as a cultural norm, as the "status quo" in Canada where those demeaned inferior, if they speak at all must sing praises to the system which multiply exploits them in the name of Employment, seen as in and of itself fortuitous.

Before Canada, I was known by different names to different people. Seven of them. Perhaps more. These were all names in which my personness was affirmed in the experiences of people who knew me in particular circumstances of intimacy. But it is different here. There are other names, and they are far from being familiar or affirming. Here among others I am told I am "Black." A Guyanese East Indian, I am immediately jolted by the term "Black" since it is the wrong reference to me. It refuses the recognition of the distinctiveness I am, glosses over it, and stereotypes it as Black. It is where the mystification of Blackness works against the concerns of being Black in a White-dominated society.

But it's a "political term" I'm told, which refers to peoples other than Whitepeople, a term of resistance, of struggle, of solidarity. I am uneasy with these slogans, these generalizing assumptions which propose a false unity where Blackness is romanticized, reduced to terms deprived of their meaning where "resistance" and "struggle" and "solidarity" are the euphemisms of typecasting, little more than empty slogans—under the supremacy of White rule. In addition this thinking assumes there are only two peoples in the world and they are either White or Black.

My English professor did not have to know that Naipaul is an Indo-Trinidadian writer. To him "Black" and "Third World" were synonymous. From his White perspective the hundreds of millions of peoples in India and China are all Black, everyone resident in these zones of EuroEgo's Other, the third-rate world it so glibly constructs, is necessarily Black. The racism in this is the disrecognition of difference in peoples and the particularities of their concern, the continuation of the gaze of the imperial eye which sees only an undistinguished mass of Blackness against the snow-white supremacy of EuroEgo.

A current fashionable Political-correctism in multicultural Canada is the term "non-white." Non-white. The label disturbs me the first time I hear it. I cannot readily say what it is, but I feel offended by the term, despite the fact it is said by well-meaning students and professors, some of the peoples of my world and many of those educated Whites who call themselves "progressive." Yes, I tell myself, I am not White, non-white is correct, isn't it, a proper identification? Visible minorities are non-white, aren't they? Why then does the term trouble me so? I look closer. I see little difference in the racially supremacist perspective which sees the world in the Great Divide of White and Black, and what is at work here. For if I am to accept this view I am also accepting that against "White" I am a "non," a non-ness, I do not exist. If I insist I am "non-white" I am losing myself even while I am trying to do the opposite, to claim myself as distinctive from White. It is the "white" which is superior in "non-white." It is after "white" that the "non-white" exists. The "non-white" is thus inferior to the "white" from which it reactively derives its existence. This is that action of thought in the *agon* where EuroEgo conceives of itself in relation to the negation of the Other. It is the basis for the racism which is institutionalized in the cultures of imperialism. To the racist the despised races are "non."

Another current vogue of popular problematic identification—misidentification, really—is that which tells me I am "a person of colour" and that people like me are "people of colour." Colour. Doesn't every human being have colour? Why is "colour" used to label the vast numbers of the peoples of the world outside of the progeny of White Europe? One of the reasons is related to the erroneous claim so many make—that the victims of racism are violated because of the colour of their skin. There is an assumption here that beneath the colour of our skin we are the same, meaning, I suppose, biologically the same. But we are more than biology would have us think of ourselves. We are historically and culturally particular, each different, and this difference includes and goes beyond the psychology of individual differences. The abuse of the humanity of entire peoples is horribly more than the question of colour. Many of our "race relations experts" could do well by looking at the importance of the recognition and appreciation of difference rather than their habitual emphases on commonality, which at best might achieve tolerance, not acceptance.

It is years later, my twentieth year in Canada, and I'm riding a bicycle towards the Metro Reference Library in Toronto where I've been invited to read from my most recent book. A taxicab stops at the light with me and the White driver juts his head out, and in an accent similar to a Hungarian acquaintance of mine, says, Zoo?

I think he's new in the country and he does not know his way around, and I say, The zoo is far from here.

No, the driver says, I take you there. Your home, no?

The light changes and he drives off, smiling.

I ride with the sting of this stranger's abuse, wondering whether I should mention this to the audience I am going to read to, most of whom I know will be White. I decide against it. I don't want that taxi driver's ugliness to indict the people who are at the reading. A known broadcaster who tells us he is from Quebec but now lives in the Junction area in west Toronto, is hosting the proceedings. He's polite, this MC, he says complimentary things about the other writers who are also reading tonight, but I suspect he does not know any of them and has not read any of their works. He's not the only MC who is like this. His intention is to please.

Soon it is my turn and I wonder what he'll say about me. I do not know him, he does not know me, and like most of the broadcasters in Toronto, I am almost sure he has read none of my works.

He begins by talking about how rich a place multicultural Toronto is, how some of his friends are "people of colour," how instructive and helpful to him they have been, and infers that I am one of those peoples of resistance and solidarity which he now presents to the audience. The audience applauds. Audiences like to applaud, I suppose. There is something to be said about an applauding audience. But what are they applauding now? I am hurt by the MC's patronizing. Is it just due to his ignorance? Is it racist?

It feels like 90 degrees out, and I who am of the heat and

warmth of an equatorial world, begin to sweat profusely. Slowly I begin to read from the first poem in my work:

> where do you go bleeding not seen
> wailing not heard
> where do you go shadow of my shadow
> watching blinded
> what perversity lurks in the edges of the hour . . .

The audience is silent. They seem to be listening. I continue:

> Who goes there dreaming my dream?

Yes, I did not want to bring the taxi driver's vulgarity here, but it seems that that which prompted its abuse of me is here all the same. To be cast within the strictures of the MC's patronizing stereotype after having been demeaned an animal in the zoo. The taxi driver's active molestation, the MC's passive-aggressive suave articulation, are examples of the hostile desire for the absence of that Otherness I and other "visible minorities" have been constructed as being. This hostility is also there, not surprisingly, in the attitudes of the vast majority of readers who just do not read "visible minority" writers. This disregard is supported by the near absence of such writers in Canadian book publications—with the usual economistic truism which says there's no real market for such works. And the economy always prevails. In the dialectic of closure no one is to be blamed. There's just "no interest out there."

The interest shown in the few who are published is often laden with hostile attitudes towards difference. When the *Montreal Gazette* in its April 13, 1991 review uses the caption, "New Land was good to author" and follows up with, "Grants, promotion pave way for immigrant's tale"—there is hostility both to the writer, M G Vassanji, and to his work. The imputation here is that he should not have received what many other Canadian authors receive, and that there is something suspect about his using his writing grants to write his work, which is reduced to the stereotype of just another "immigrant's tale." The review mentions the grants this "minority writer" received, the CBC's coverage of the book on *The Journal,* and notes that its publisher, McClelland & Stewart is a "mainstream Canadian House." I am not aware of this practice in the review of the works of writers from the Majority, many of whom have been the recipients of much larger grants than Vassanji.

As I suspected, in its logic of exclusion it further condemns the work for lacking "focus," and sees its "characters" as not having enough "depth." The review further indicts the writer of having been apparently "schooled on the 19th-century British novel" and of using some of these techniques, with "jarring incursions by an omniscient narrator." The example given of this authorial "bursting" on to the page reads as follows: "We are but creatures of our origins, and however stalwartly we march forward, paving new roads, seeking new worlds, the ghosts from our past stand not far behind and are not easily shaken off." A profound simplicity in the common knowledge of its occurrence, marred somewhat by the military and Euro-road-paving analogies, but far from being anything like "bursting" intrusively onto the page.

This view of history is there in Henry Kreisel's esteemed work, *Betrayal.* When Stappler appears in Edmonton where students think history is only about dead bones, the ghosts of the past return. The betrayals and the self-betrayals are not easily shaken off. But it does not seem to be the substance of the excerpt which offends the reviewer. It is the style, indicted as being intrusively nineteenth-century. As I have noted elsewhere,* Vassanji's style is polysemic, told by a storyteller whose telling is nurtured in the convergences of the Islamic Asian experience in East Africa, in Indian, Arabian and English narratorial nuances where the community as sense of place is integral to the experience, and to the very writing itself.

The reviewer's inability to recognize this, and the intolerant tone of the review, are symptomatic of the iterations of excision where closure to difference is maintained in the narrow levelling eurocentric standards of judgement—like "depth" of "character" and "focus." The assumption being made is that this Tanzanian writer, and all those writers whom this review refers to as "minority writers" in Canada, have to write according to the expectations of the English-Lit Can-Lit acolytes of the Majority way. Or be condemned.

Not very dissimilar to the levelling force which augments the order of endeavour for peoples who have come from various cultures in the world to live in Canada. So well does this work that many change the way they speak the more Canadianized they think they're becoming. They lose themselves in imitation, even as their utterances imitate the sounds which negate who they are. This is how their displacement makes strangers of themselves. This is what silencing is about. The mainstreaming of the Majority discourse where compliance is disappearance.

The CBC's *Journal* coverage of the same book is, yes, a form of promotion, but the manner in which the *Journal* depicted the work is an important commentary in itself. Three White Canadian writers, none of whom had any knowledge of the cultural dislocation of the peoples the author is talking of, were selected as evaluators. The shockingly unacceptable reason given for this is that there was no suitable person from the visible minority world in Canada to make such televisual literary judgement. I know of several highly qualified persons who would have been appropriate, but none of these was contacted by the *Journal*. The *Journal* has been criticized for not having done enough homework, and there is merit to this, but this is also the demonstration of a deep institutional bias where in ethnographic parochialism, like the CBC itself and Canada at large, White Canadians continue to be depicted as the chosen images and figures of knowledge and power. One of these commentators seemed fascinated by the idea that such exotic things were going on in the Don Mills apartment building where the book is fictionally set.

This notion of the exotic continued in the *Journal's* dramatization of excerpts from the book where the principal narrator-actor had the wrong accent, sounding more like Peter Sellers vulgarizing the way some Indians speak, rather than someone from Dar.

The incident of racism in the novel is ignored. Instead there is a clip on the Muslim protagonist eating pork sausage for the first time. Honest Ed's, the Bloor Street store, is presented as a haven of inexpensive items, and the reasons for people flocking to such a store are cast aside. Turned into a show about exotic Islamic East African Asians in Toronto, the *Journal* treated the book as an exotic ethnographic object rather than a literary work.

Although the writer is careful his work is not seen as being just about race, the absence of the incident in the *Journal*'s coverage, and the accusation of rape in the work, should not be ignored. Nurdin is seen as a rapist by the White woman whom he tries to help. The woman's acute stress is the paranoic function of racism where the men of Otherness, the "visible minority," are perceived of in shades of threat, as the violators and wouldbe violators of the White woman. This denigration of the sexuality of the men of the peoples whom EuroImperialism occupied and sought to destroy, has a long history. It is based on the knowledge of EuroEgo's phallic ravishing of the women of these places, and in its hetero-sexist fear of retaliation. It presumes its acts of rape will be reacted to in kind. But this White woman in Toronto does not know this. She is not expected to. She does not have to know any of this. She is carrying out one of the principal perspectives up-held in the Majority culture of which she is a member. She is behaving the way she and others like her have been taught to think. Difference is dangerous, the man of difference is a lurking violator.

The frequency of such molestations is something the *Journal* should not look away from, but this presumes it would find this of interest. The horror of being so accused, the damage this does to one's psychic well being, the doubts and suspicions it causes even among one's family—these are touched upon in *No New Land*. Their absence in the *Journal* broadcast is significant.

Variations in Exotica Minor

This time I am being interviewed on my book, *Shanti,* at the CBC.

The host is warm. We have never met before, but there's something about her I like. She is comfortable with people, I think. She's in my most unscientific evaluation, a good person. Not too many of these around, regardless of race. Like the vast majority of the broadcasters in this publicly funded national Canadian network, she's White. She helps me feel a little less uncomfortable in the microphoned austerity of the encased room in which I am supposed to be talking about my work. She seems to have read my book and thinks well of it. She's interested in the use of "dialect" in the work. I explain it's not dialect, but the living language of daily life which I have tried to depict. She wants me to read a section of this. I wonder why since most people listening to the broadcast are likely to find this "exotic," but I read, not well as far as I'm concerned, and she likes it. She comments on my being "so alive" when I read like this, unlike the confines of English in which I have been speaking with her. I read from another place in the book where I am not so "alive" but think the narration speaks to an important moment in the work, and might interest people to want to read more of it for themselves.

After the interview, which I liked, the broadcaster and I talk of our earlier discussion about editing to fit into the air-time format of the programme. Will I have any objections if they select one of the two pieces I read for the broadcast? I have, but I don't want to offend, thinking the interest shown in my work during the interview will also be borne in the selection. It turns out I am wrong. On the evening of the actual broadcast it is the "dialect" piece which is being aired. An exotic sound on the CBC. A multicultural performance.

The setting shifts. It is a panel on TVO's *Imprint*, and I am one of the persons invited to talk on literary criticism, but the host of the show keeps referring issues pertaining to multiculturalism to me. I am not the only person on the panel who can speak to this. Multiculturalism does not simply involve me, but I am being singled out as that peculiarity, a multicultural entity. In the stereotype deployed here, my visible minority status means I would necessarily want to talk multiculturalism.

I am suddenly aware of how White this panel is, how odd I am here, how out of place.

Examples abound. Subtle, direct, institutional, individual, textual and the circumstances these texts are informed by, in the places of work and entertainment, in the street, in the very political economy of vision which sees immigrants as both threats to jobs (of the Majority) and a drain on the economy. There is an interrelationship between the seemingly "isolated" racist actions and the values of racial/cultural superiority in the foundational approaches to literature in Canada. I am not proposing that every racist has been tainted by the exposure to literature, but rather that there are similar forms of racial/cultural derogation in the attitude towards racial/cultural difference. The virtual absence of writers of difference in Canadian high school curriculums demonstrates the racial/cultural preferences being taught to these opening minds. It is also where the permutations of imperiality in racial/cultural closure are being schooled as the norm.

This, to say the least, sharply contradicts the ecstasies of multiculturality.

* *World Literature Written in English* (Spring 1991): 115.

Echoes of Empire

Natasha Ksonzek

Echoes of Empire

Forts, Churches, Castles

At Bloor and Avenue, in Toronto, even before I get to the museum, I am surrounded by cases of cold corporate steel and glass. Window cases of lit-up valuables luring us to buy. Some of these items are worn by human shapes uneasily suggesting inanimate life. I look away. Into other glass windows where people are eating. Who look like the mannequins of the adjacent displays eerily come to life.

The Royal Ontario Museum does not appear as grand as many of its European ancestors, but from across the street it seems a little fortress-like. Its high stone walls, the gargantuan Royal Canadian Flag staking its claim on top, crackling proclamations of ownership in the wind—these echo a particular tradition of fort-making claims. A tradition where the fort is seen as a place of protection and high value, even as a metaphor of the self, concealing that these values are based on conquest, that the fort as Important Place is a military place, a place of battle, of defence and attack, where one people kill another for power over territory stolen, taken as the spoils of war from the victims of a history of military victories.

Forts are taught as marvellous sites/sights of adventure and glory in Canadian classrooms. They are fondly presented as necessary stepping-stone monuments to the birth and growth of the nation. And part of this teaching has encouraged people to want to visit these official markings of our History. To see and to marvel, and to feel good about what happened there, at those preserved forts that are also now museums. Exhibited shelters of national history, sheltering the Empire view. Preserving it. Museumizing it. Like so many others, I too visited some forts with my class as part of the curriculum, and others while on vacation. We were not expected to question, and we generally did not question that these forts were the heroic testaments to the making of Canadian society.

But the Empire's past actions testify differently. *Bang bang you're dead. Bang bang we win*, echoes in the fort walls and in the culture's presentation of them. *Bang bang you're dead, bang bang we win.* It is the music and chant of Empire. The chant of the children of my childhood.

In the tower face of The Royal Ontario Museum there are echoes of a church's regality and demeanour. Tall stained-glass windows replicate the controlled arching of the *dominus* and *hallelujahs* that echo also in the contoured stone of cathedrals and basilicas of other orders and other states. There are trinities of flags over the entrance, trinities of windows, and triune dark masks for doorways that open in cold formal rigid sharp-cornered indifference. The museum's cultural mythological qualities, the imperial flags, its regality and claim of stored riches easily invokes the castles of my play.

Forts, churches, castles. From nursery rhyme and fairy tale to innocent play. Children here build castles and forts in sand. I was one of these children, not knowing then what these fortresses of my play were. Each building had to have its own important stick for a flagpole. We learned the act of staking a claim, of driving a pointed stake into the ground. We'd sometimes compete to have the biggest or tallest tower (the biggest gestural thrust? of self assertion?), the more complicated design, the highest flag, and so have the most control. We also built forts out of cushions, and bigger ones later out of wood. Shelters in trees were treeforts and caves dug in snow were snowforts. So many forts in our play.

This was in many ways the rehearsal of Empire shaped by the intimacy of my own hands, my own play. Our private spaces caught (or invaded) by the cultural preoccupations with war. Playing the game of empire building I didn't like the battles, but I think I still wanted the biggest castle and fort, and I would try to impose peace (domination nevertheless), so we could do other things besides fighting . . . in this play of battles and conquests. But the unwritten script (which was written in the very shaping of our consciousness; what better way to learn a part?) was followed, repeated, and played according to the rules we learned from those around us. War Games alright. Early education. On the side of the winners, the conquerors, the discoverers, the exploiters of the world. There were always these stories of castles and forts and churches and kings and queens and princes and princesses, stories of how good battles and conquests were. In this unconscious instilling and embracing of Empire and its values the forts and castles never seemed very related to death or destruction. And certainly not genocidal practices. No, it was Victory that was in the fortress and its populations. Bloodshed, but Victory for the self-named *civilizing* state, and that was what counted, we were taught in class, on television, and in books by the storytellers of Empire.

Its "heroes" who killed and died in service to the Empire, are praised in monuments and inscriptions throughout Canadian cities, in parks where children play on them, at schools and public sites. Statues, tanks, guns (which are still used to mark the significance of many events), warplanes, and in front of Ontario Place, a warship, the *HMCS Haida* permanently docked as a military sightseeing attraction.

On the way to my grandmother's house I would pass a big gun permanently placed on the lawn of the Salvation Army building. Many times we would play at being important on this large war monument, behind the wheel, behind the controls, discovering different (strategic) places to sit, after we had climbed up. Also there were cannons in parks, and we climbed on them too. At times we played we were soldiers. We had many kinds of guns: bee-bee guns, toy machine guns that made noises, water pistols in various designs, air rifles, dart-shooting guns, guns that would shoot plastic balls or bullets, and many less fanciful varieties. I remember liking a certain cap gun that was mine. Cap guns were a favourite. This toy gun was so widespread that the Webster dictionary uses it as the example defining "cap," not using the example of the original cap in a real gun that the toy is imitating. To use one of these while playing gave emphasis to the shooting. It sounded more real. After all, the caps were real explosive charges on a paper roll that fitted in the gun. A little bit of gunpowder for a little child to load into her little gun and pull the trigger. Just like on TV and the movies.

Sometimes the play fights of soldiers and armies, or *Cops and Robbers* or *Cowboys and Indians* or whatever combative versions were thought up, turned to real fights, testifying to the success of combat thinking in so many of us. So infested was our imagination, especially the boys' around me, that we each made our own wooden "shield" with rope handgrips and a sword. We knew about making special emblems for them, the importance of the insignia of might. There was a lion, a snake, an alligator. We were making our own Coats of Arms. These were the Empire shields which would also serve to protect us from play arrows from the bows of the "Indians" or "Redskins," who didn't have guns and so couldn't win. The shield was already here a symbol of a kind of invincibility of Empire.

The museum declares itself a particular mythological icon even as you approach it. Written in stone on one side of the entrance way, it proclaims: THE ARTS OF MAN THROUGH ALL THE AGES, and on the other, THE RECORD OF NATURE THROUGH COUNTLESS AGES. These authoritative announcements do not hesitate to greedily claim even Time itself, in a zealous empire thrust, encompassing all life in a phallocentric universalizing imaginary of "the record of nature" and "the arts of man through all the ages." The endurance of the inscribed stone attests to the endurance of the celebrated sentiments retained in the stone. An awesome territorial claim as introduction to the museum. All circumscribed within the gestural imprint of a giant arch etched triumphally in the face of the stone.

Passing beneath and through this sign you go further into the museum's austere sense of permanence where a world of masks and disquietude lurks. For what appears, hides much more than it reveals, what I identify are but masks parading as truths. It is where reality shifts. For this place of masks is a place of intimidating power, a place I have been taught to expect to find invaluable and documented Knowledge. But whose statements are these, whose knowledge? What silences lie in the seams of these constructions, the ransacked tombs, the violated dead on permanent display?

I'm always very self-conscious moving through these interiors, these giant silent watching buildings, hallways, rooms. I always feel among such hushed gloom that I'm somehow not supposed to be here. There is unease in the museum, unease beneath its grand towering ceilings and archways. Here, in the dim light and the smell of tamed stone, I am very aware of being in an Important Place. The change of light lets me know with certainty I have entered another world, and that I am a stranger here.

This is the Museum of the State where things preserved from so long ago present the past as real but reduce it into artifacts. Preserved sterility where representations are captured and held immobile for examination by our gaze as proof of the museum's version of life and history. Imagined through death. There is then a horror here in these dead things preserved as facts of the living. These Treasures of the Museum.

The presentation and tradition of knowledge-making here in Canadian/Western culture carries within it the trajectory of thought which founded this society and is rooted in the history and traditions of its interaction with other places and peoples. These echoes accompany me as I move through the Royal Ontario Museum.

Souveniring

And I enter another doorway, another of the museum's depictions of peoples and places across time. This time it is the *Into the Heart of Africa* (1989-90) exhibit whose title sounds like both an ad for a safari hunt, and Conrad's *Heart of Darkness,* this English "classic," still studied here as part of the core of literature, and usually without his dehumanizing portrayal of Africans being questioned or pointed out, his racism either unnoticed, which indicates a siding with his vision, or accepted despite the recognition, as if it were not important. As if these uglinesses are to be accepted already by the reader/student as common and appropriate ways of thinking . . . And here? What assumptions conceal which stories, revealing what kind of teller, what kind of telling?

"Africa in the nineteenth century," the first plaque begins, "was still 'the unknown continent' to most Canadians. Ignorance promoted powerful images of a mysterious land full of 'barbarous' people." It goes on to say that "Canadian soldiers and missionaries became full participants in Queen Victoria's later reign," and that "those who returned brought home souvenirs of their journey into the heart of Africa, objects that today remind us of a little remembered era in Canada's past."

But what kind of reminding? What kind of re-memberment of an era?

The portrayal of the soldiers and missionaries bringing home souvenirs sounds so innocuous. So pleasant. As if they were returning home with mementos of their holidays and travels. Like I've done so many times. But souvenir-collecting is the practice of accumulating things taken from other places. And within such a practice, a better collection usually means larger accumulations from more places. Accumulating in taking becomes the act of symbolizing a memory, a proof of having been somewhere outside of Canada. It places emphasis on taking as the act of substantiating experience. This is a learned inclination, this taking. Done as casually as remembering: possession by assumption. Empire assumptions practised again and again in apparent ordinary everyday actions of going, seeing, taking, leaving, keeping, showing and telling . . .

In the "Show and Tell" practice in many of the grade school classes I attended, the students were encouraged to bring something from home to show to the class. But the practice began to be about having things, and often those with more money had nicer things, and were envied. We were learning the cultural importance of having Things and being able to show that we have. The emphasis on having was one of the early lessons, a prerequisite to Empire-accumulation thinking whose logical extension is enacted and justified as the right to take. The nature of this celebration at the museum, of having things to show, "souvenirs" of the missionaries and soldiers, holds within it that the having and the displaying are more important than the manner of its acquisition, even if that went hand in hand with the destruction and violations of other peoples and cultures as it often did. But not much is mentioned about this. The souvenir displayed thus is not only de-contextualized, but used to convey a false notion of events and meanings even as it presumes to be representative of certain realities. The souvenirs here talk about the particular experiences, and the memories of the men and women of Empire. It is this that is being invoked here to be passed on, kept alive. Memoirs of the missionaries and soldiers, of Empire actions. Actions valorized in this case, against Africans in Africa.

This "souvenir" collection is made up of the objects claimed from the place these "collectors" went to violate. Many of these "souvenirs" came from Africans who had been or were being persuaded to live by and believe in Western dominating order and its symbologies. Whole systems of thought were made irrelevant under missionary conversion and some of the highly symbolic and sacred tools the African peoples used became "souvenirs." Like what was presented as the Diviner's basket of objects now lying in this collection as a violated site of some of the special knowledge the missionaries went specifically to destroy. So that more peoples could be reorganized into Western conformity. The missionaries went to convert, to colonize. And brought home souvenirs.

And these items turned souvenirs are also symbolic of the bounty the Europeans took from Africa, because despite the fact that many of these pieces are so-called gifts from Africans, they nevertheless represent the history of the actions of those who brought them here. The very moving of them from there to here was only possible through a chain of exploitative measures levelled at the heart of a continent they rearranged into Africa. A legacy of pillage whose totems are here used for anthropological study. A science of knowing within a history of doom-making.

I sometimes read of anthropologists scrambling to save and document information of "vanishing ways of life" where the people themselves are merely objects for study in Western science, whose way of life is being destroyed by the same West that comes to study it. It brings to mind the safari again. A kind of trophy-hunting while the game lasts in an enthusiastic gathering of data for science's later reconstruction, and representation. Kept to be used for further incursions. An arc of Empire piracy where the pirated became the "Souvenirs" of a grand greed that seems to be justified in the way it is presented here. Like the grand claims of ownership over Africa itself, by various European states.

But this exhibit is not only of "souvenirs" from Africa. There is a military helmet nestled carefully in a glass case which stands in the middle of one of the rooms. It is the first of many of what appear to be symbolic odes to soldiers and missionaries. There is a photograph of Canadian military troops departing for Ottawa. The accompanying text calls them "Defenders of the Empire," clearly demarcating the interests at work here. There is no explanation as to why there was a war, who they were going to fight, what right they had in fighting people in another country that Britain was trying to take for itself. This is not addressed. The soldiers appear as heroes, "Defenders of the Empire," not killers or invaders defending Empire greed. What is said about the Canadian soldiers as British subjects, is that "campaigning against African peoples who resisted the imperial advance and sometimes against rival European powers, they sought to extend the Pax Britannica throughout the African colonies claimed by the UK."

The queen's soldiers' "campaigning" was no less than the practice of colonization, of which two of the main facilitators were the missionaries and the enforcers, the military invaders, the "campaigners" who were trying to exercise control over another people and their land. But the eulogies written within these containers do not dwell on these aspects. They talk a treacherous talk, about the greatness of war. The view is sympathetic. In one of the display cases, a quotation from a newspaper castigates the African climate as "poison for the European" and laments how it "wrecked" one soldier's "once robust condition." Under this eulogy to the soldier are gathered the objects he brought back from Africa.

These plaques and the encased soldiers' artifacts, their helmets and personal items, their African collections, their clothing, talk about the importance of war and its symbologies. The curator has placed the military artifacts at the beginning of the exhibit, and throughout most of it, so that the military motif becomes the introduction to this presentation of Africa, and our symbolic guide to the exhibit. Almost as if it were guarding the story. (The official version of course.) Africa is thus presented at the outset as a viable place for British/Canadian military conquest. The military motif is thus the lens, the grid through which a large part of the exhibit is referenced.

There is a picture of an enlarged Canadian postage stamp dated 1898 on the wall. On it is illustrated a map of the world, and mapped on that, British controlled lands. The text underneath it says "We hold a vaster empire than has been." A blatant celebration of the occupation of territories, another celebration of taking, and also a Canadian State celebration in the sympathetic memorabilia of the stamp on the wall. Maps like these remind me of the maps in my schooling, the maps we copied. Our place was in the British Commonwealth. We were taught to identify with the British and the lands they took for their Empire.

Greeting the Stranger

"Darkest Africa" is written on the wall and on a map, with quotation marks, as are many of the stereotypes used in this show, as if implying somehow the museum's distance from the concept(s), because they are pointed out in this way. As if we are being asked to not see that they are using the same terms nevertheless, and to excuse them for using them at the same time. To not be disturbed by their use, as if the quotation marks remove the curator from the derogative stereotypes of Africa and Africans. "Darkest Africa" maintains the racist traditions of such naming, and justifies them by so using them, regardless of the stated intentions of the curator. Reusing them with the emphasis of quotation marks has the look of an apology during the act.

Ascribing "Darkness" to Africa is not an unusual stereotype among Empire writers. It evokes whole sets of assumptions and ideas described by Conrad in *Heart of Darkness*. Here the narrator, Marlow, demonstrates the ability to be somewhat critical of the brutality of the Empire when he describes the Eldorado Exploring Expedition in Africa: "To tear treasure out of the land was their desire, with no more moral purpose at the back of it than there is in burglars breaking into a safe." But we should note that at the same time he was transporting guns and other treasure for the Empire. His supposed criticism does nothing to dispel his own involvement in Empire-plundering. He seems to be merely against what he sees as the obviousness of its crudities. What might first appear as a contradiction between his vilifying racism and criticism of Empire is resolved as a consolidation of the Empire's view. In a poetic persuasiveness Conrad's reflection of the logic of Empire sees the Africans as "primitive": "dusty niggers with splay feet" (inferring, I presume, feet that had not been deformed by the wearing of constricting shoes). They "had faces like grotesque masks," with "the white of their eyeballs glistening." The African man was "the prehistoric man," "the savage," "the primate" who "was useful because he had been instructed" to serve Marlow and other Empire pirates, to look at whom "was as edifying as seeing a dog in a parody of breeches and a feather hat, walking on his hind legs." The ruined village grass walls are "pathetically childish." The land holds "an aspect of monotonous grimness." It is "savage" "always mute" yet "whispering invitations," inferring he was being invited by Africa, being secretly seduced to do what he was doing. His journeying was "a weary pilgrimage amongst hints for nightmares" being pressed upon by "the great demoralization of the land" as if it was the land which pressed upon him, not Marlow himself or other Empire people whose presence and actions and history brought on this feeling of "demoralization." This is somehow presumed to be Africa's fault. But what makes him "tingle with enthusiasm" is "the notion of an exotic Immensity ruled by an august Benevolence." The dream of Empire. There are so many of the clichés of white European racist deformation of Africans throughout Conrad's elegant and mesmerizing flow of words and evocations. It is where a disturbing commonality resides between creative higher thinking and the crudities of Empire imaginary.

These domineering civilizing echoes reside in the "Darkest" in Conrad's title, and are supported in various ways throughout the exhibit. The "Darkest Africa" written on the wall, recalling Marlow's thinking, is the darkness imagined by the explorers/colonizers who projected their own fears, this "darkness" to Africa. It reveals their responses to the unfamiliarities of other cultures, of strangers, as if these other cultures were somehow a threat to their "civilizedness." As if these peoples would, given the chance, respond with as much hostility as the Europeans had towards them. This is where these "civilized" peoples reveal their own ghosts, a legacy of thinking that does not recognize peoples who are different as being fully human. A form of barbarism belonging to those who thought this way.

In a pen-and-ink drawing called "Livingstone's last march," Livingstone is not marching, or even on his feet. He is being carried in a sling by two human beings, Africans he has doing the job of beasts of burden, while yet another two carry guns and bundles on their heads.

And rising up in front of me on a far wall, there is a larger-than-life, perhaps six-by-eight feet, illustration of a British soldier on a horse, leaning over, driving his sword through the shield and into the chest of an African, who is on foot. The caption reads "Lord Beresford's encounter with a Zulu" (*Illustrated London News*, 1879). So encountering here is killing. One meets the other to kill the other. To meet a Zulu is to kill a Zulu.

And as I go through this exhibit these images of white supremacy remain. Further along I come to an open corner arrangement looking like a Canadian/European dining room, the trophies of war hanging on the wall, telling us the familiar "context" of such collectables. There is a Zulu shield and above that is the mounted head of a deer. Together they talk about the killer's victory over them. The shield looks like Lord Beresford's victim's in the earlier illustration. Symbol of the life he took? More acceptable than the stuffed head of an African. There is a quiet horror here in this exhibit, "The Front Hallway of Beverly House." There are two European paintings on the wall here as well. There is a globe underneath, beside a chair, looking, along with the rest of the items in this "hallway," like props substantiating ownership and appropriation. The globe, the world mapped and recorded for the search for wealth, the world as conquerable world, as ownable. A pervasive universalizing agenda. The universe as trophy.

Africa is reduced here to the decor of a wealthy European, a carefully replicated monied presence celebrating the cultural violation of the African. These are displayed in the name of the owner or collector who becomes significant among objects presented as mostly authorless. As if the collector is intrinsic to the object's identity. Whose very authenticity now resides in its Taker's authority. Presented to us this way, what is African becomes a conveniently generalized metaphor and backdrop for the more clearly and sharply articulated drama of imperialistic prominence: biographical histories for the owner/appropriator, a celebration of specifics in quotations, in the soldier's or missionary's possessions, laid out as talismans of identification. What is said to be African is the possession of the Empire's soldiers. Used, as property is used in Canadian culture, to give status and power to the owner. What is African, presented here as important souvenirs and documented possessions, is lost in this possessing. They have become possessed, in the name of the soldier, the missionary, the holy reverend. Named and described by the colonizing West, made to play the mute part assigned them.

But what echoes even more loudly here is the impression that there was in Africa a sort of general inarticulateness that needed Western translation and identification. What is African is now spoken for by these various frame-ups enacted in display strategies. It seems impossible for me to be able to get a sense of anything African, for these end up being dreams of power over Africa.

I am looking at the heading "Insights and Illusions." There is a photograph of a young African woman, displayed as one more recorded object in this arranged journey called Into the Heart of Africa. Underneath, the text reads: "I had a hard time taking the photograph as the woman had to be held while I set up my camera. Just as soon as she was released and I had pressed the bulb, she ran away again. Poor creature, she thought I was going to kill her with that horrid looking thing, the camera." The words belong to Reverend A W Banfield, a Canadian missionary. The African woman in the photograph, framed by the Reverend Banfield's words, appears as the illustration for Reverend Banfield's anecdote. And for our amusement, I suppose. Reverend Banfield does not hesitate to use force against this woman in order to take this photograph of her, to have her catalogued to use as he likes. He then complains to us about the "hard time" he had in so doing. She is further incapacitated by his language which dismisses her as being unaware. She is the "poor creature" (afraid of the camera), a source of amusement. She is uncooperative, but he is an Empire man. He has his way.

The woman so photographed is nameless, she is the African woman silenced, a frightened animal, who doesn't know better. But looking upon the face of this woman I am uneasy, as if I am somehow participating in her violation. After all the view is Banfield's. I look through his imaging of her.

This Reverend, who obviously thinks he is presenting himself well in his version of the story, which the ROM also uses like this, is an example of an Empire-ordering of perception, the thinking which assumes it has rights to claim everywhere it goes, even here where a person's own image is taken and later used against her in its various re-contextualizations. In this order of perception, she is made to play the disparaging "primitive" and is dismissed.

Under the plaque heading "Civilization, Commerce and Christianity," the following: "My desire is to open a path to central Africa that civilization, commerce and Christianity might find their way there." These are the missionaries in West Africa in the early twentieth century. There is a photograph of a man and a woman on two horses, while four Africans seem like beasts of burden overladen with the missionaries' belongings. Another photograph shows several African women kneeling on the ground scrubbing while a White woman stands above them, watching. The text reads: "Taken in Nigeria about 1910, this photograph shows missionary Mrs Thomas Titcombe giving African Women 'A lesson in how to wash clothes.'" As if the women didn't know how to clean, as if it was a good thing the White lesson-giver was there, to have these women wash her clothes. Civilization, commerce and Christianity, the three major facilitators of Empire, required the servitude of the Africans.

Outside this exhibit there is a simulated market booth where objects crafted in Africa are on sale for your collection too. Where you can indulge in buying yourself some item of exotica from the world of the exhibit. You are provided with the opportunity now to have your souvenir, your trophy. Behaviours repeat themselves everywhere.

Of Histories and Absences

The *Caravans and Clipper Ships* exhibit of Fall 92 seems to be a casual homogenization of very different worlds. The "Clipper ship" reverberates with a maritime romanticism associated with the sleeker and faster ships of Western trade. The history of the European economic invasion and expansionism, presented here as "2000 Years of Trade," seems to infer some kind of mutual and equal exchange between the East and the West. But large photographs, like plaques of exotica in between the written text of the exhibit show smiling dark-skinned people selling products at markets full of colour. And this seems to say something else.

"Trade," the text tells us, "also facilitated the transmission of religious beliefs, first through activities of trading, and later by missionaries and travellers," and that, "although commercial considerations frequently overwhelmed missionary goals, initially the principles of the Christian Faith guided European expansionism. Various Christian orders endeavoured to spread their religion throughout the world." Indeed this "transmission of religious beliefs" was the facilitation of the African's slavery for Western capital, slavery to a system of values that continues to construct them as *other* and lowest in the empire hierarchy, outside of and opposite to what the West has claimed for itself: civilizedness, prosperity, superiority.

"Technical ideas and inventions as well," the text goes on, "moved freely along the trade routes." The technical is presented as that which allowed the shaping of the world, through the improvement of "vessels, maps and navigational instruments."

Shaped by trade . . . I think of countries' borders, shaped by trade, that have been redrawn by Western powers for their economic advantage, of labour markets of the world secured to produce for these colonizing countries, of much of the world shaped into poverty after Western contact. Shaped by trade.

This is the false presentation of a history of trade as a thing in itself, as something that can be seen without the horrors that accompanied it. As if wars were not fought over control of labour markets and lands. As if the history of this trade had nothing to do with bloodshed, slavery and indentured labour. This trade in the West began with the ships and men of state who came to new lands with the specific intention of exploitation, couched in various nicer-sounding versions. Trade began in Canada with the First Peoples trading valuable animal skins for which they were given in return, trinkets, disease, and the destruction of their ways of living. The trade talked about here in such grandiose niceties didn't begin with the clipper ships of modern swiftness and romance, but with every invasive act of colonization. Relations that continue in other guises today. The exhibit doesn't mention this. It looks outside of this: it looks at clipper ships and caravans.

The text accompanying the show maintains the justification of conquest by misrepresenting events in a perverted clinicalism which presents the growth of the West as falsely, gloriously unimplicated in horrors of destruction it has perpetrated. Presented this way, the "information" becomes a reaffirmation of a history of destroying. A continuing pardon allowing for continuing atrocities. This being just one of them.

Here the museum's emphasis reenacts the momentum for this travel, where there is an emphasis on an ever widening market for trade and availability of merchandises. A promotion of consumerism as items of "trade" in the cases in front of me.

Preserving Order

The pathways I follow here do not acknowledge me. Although knowledge is said to be kept here I do not feel empowered by it. In fact I feel my own life-flesh a trespass against the silence of death here, my frailty against the all-encompassing stone around me, as if I'm trading something of myself for their information. The glassed-in objects displayed are out of reach, like china in a cabinet in this culture, more valuable than my touch, reminding me of the Beverly House hallway with its formal and ostentatious display of possessions and trophies. "Don't touch" the displays say, "Look." And I see a sign reading "Mankind Discovering," and I'm excluded again. Another sign continues this talk of "mankind's efforts to discover himself and his universe." This display of glass cases rises up in a cluster of ascending levels above me like a pyramid, and there seems to be a familiar hierarchy presented here. A grandfather clock takes precedence at the top of the cases, emphasizing the rule of Western time. Just below that, an Egyptian sarcophagus stands on end, giving us Western culture's dreamed-of beginnings. But this sarcophagus is the violated coffin, a violated shelter of the dead that was dug up, whose bones were handled, examined, whose violation is somehow clinicalized as it becomes an object for study, a captured specimen. Museums haunt the living too, when they tell us their versions of other people, because these are usually very different from how these other people would tell us about themselves.

In one of the bottom cases there are smaller totems of European history, and as I am looking, a little boy, about four years old, comes over pulling earnestly at his father's hand to come to the case in front of where I am standing, his interest fired. "Daddy, I see a nice helmet!" he says over and over again. Of all the items there, this is the treasure of the museum he recognizes. He has been taught already to admire the armour of state killers.

Echoes of Empire.

Necroptic Masks in the Mausoleum of Empire

Arnold Harrichand Itwaru

At the Royal Ontario Museum

I watch with the child the objects in the glass case. The frog, the snake, the leaves, the water, seem so real, so alive. The child taps the glass once, gently, tentatively, her gaze fixed on the things inside. She taps again, harder, and looks more keenly.

Mommy, she says to the woman standing near her. Mommy it doesn't move, it won't move.

No, Honey, her mother says and ambles to the next case.

The child holds on to her mother, this life she knows but whose loving answer does not clear away the confusion.

The child looks back at the odd stillness, the puzzling lifelikeness in the glass case. Will she dream of this? What will she dream in her dreaming of this?

I'm tempted to tell her that except for the people around, nothing moves here, child. Nothing moves here. The stillness you see here, child, is the stillness of Death preserved in the illusion of Life.

This is where we are, child, in this illusion. This museum is a palace of fixity we are wandering in. Here information, preserved for our instruction, awaits us, and perhaps there is something to this, child. But what is it that we will learn in this place where we, the living, walking along these aisles, stare through these glass-case-coffins at the dead captured and displayed for us to wonder about, child?

No enchanted sleep here, child. No Sleeping Beauty awaits the phallic kiss of her prince to charm her awake and claim her as his property forever. There is another claim here, child, another claiming. Nothing moves in these display cases. You are correct. These living-looking things in these coffins don't move, they won't

93

move, they can't move. They are dead. This is how this Science works. These things are dead. They are dead. Learn this, child, learn this before you too are claimed in the claiming of this Science.

A monumental authority holds vigil in the formality of these austere columns and archways. It is here in the towering solidity of these grand walls, these vaulting stained-glass windows watching over the preserved stillness of the unliving, watching over the engulfment of corridors and stairs that take me to the undisputing silence in each vaulted chamber's display of captured evidence there for me to marvel about, to look at, to learn but not touch.

A ponderous and official anonymity requires here my anonymity too. I am faceless before the authority of these displays. In these crepuscular rooms of visiting I am the faceless visitor. In here all visitors are faceless. This facelessness is the mask of invisibility through which an insidious control works. It is where the individual is disrecognized, reduced into an anonymity, a facelessness upon which a seemingly invisible order of perception exercises its control.

Facelessness is the reductive ruse of curatorial instruction which masks me before the masks it creates. In this masking the curator's physical absence is the faceless distance where the facelessness of the authority's order of perception is reinforced. The anonymous and faceless curator instructs the anonymous and faceless visitor.

In this way the thinking in which this practice is historically situated (the construction and maintenance of such museums of grand displays) is also reproduced. The disempowerment of the visitor (facelessness) is emblematic of the daily life disempowerment of the individual, intrinsic to the dominant order. In this particular setting the mere volume of information culled out of years of hallowed scientific work and presented here as facts, is where the ponderously monumental has its intimidating presence.

94

In a way all visitors are powerless within the presence of their host unless they break the proprieties between visitor and host, destroying the thread of reciprocity in such relations. But this visit to the museum, other than using the term "visit" seems to have little in common with such notions of visiting. This is more a *visitation*. It is where the visitor comes into the embrace of the approved view, the scientific explanation of the world as *the* correct way of seeing. These visitors are that anonymity called "the public," most of whom have been schooled to think this way in the first place, and hence the authority ascribed in such articulations is thus intensified in the seemingly innocent activity which visiting the museum is generally said to be.

The child's mother is reading a text whose caption says, "Mankind Discovering." I read with her, "The Royal Ontario Museum plays a creative role in mankind's efforts to discover himself and his universe." I wonder what she thinks of this.

Where is she in this talk which talks of mankind discovering himself and his universe? Will she, like all defenders of this particular position, dismiss "mankind" and "himself" as merely the generic use of terms presumably meant to represent all of humanity? What assumptions are reinforced in this resort to generic absolution, this return to the authority of the patriarchal naming of the world? Where is she as woman and mother, among everything else she is, in the thought which thinks of *all* human beings in the patriarchal imaginary "mankind" upholds?

What of her is discovered when mankind discovers himself?

And what of "discovery" here? How does "mankind" accomplish this feat? I am reminded of the acts of "discovery" in the history of EuroEgo where discovery has been repeatedly followed by Occupation and Conquest. Discovery as domination. And in this Science the obsession to dominate nature, including the domination of human nature. The consistent text of Science, and the prevailing one here.

But self-knowledge is not discovery. One cannot "discover" oneself. To do so is to reduce oneself to an object, a thing. That which one is not. That which is so discovered is a dimension of that thing, that object of discovery which one never is, extracted from the life and consciousness of the knower whose eternal need to know makes any sort of "discovery" impossible.

What then is this claim, "mankind discovering himself"?

This is one of the palatial storehouses of an authoritarian order whose Science collects and displays in empirical confidence its findings and interpretations as Grand Fact. There is an imperialism in this claiming, this insistence on one order of seeing as *the* way through which we should understand the world as well *as the way the world is expected to function under EuroScientific domination.* The order furbishing the supremacy of conquest. Demonstrated in the realization of the project of empirical science, formulated as the *primacy of Western Science* through which imperial Britain and Europe engineered their conquests and occupations upon which their notions of supremacy are upheld. A veritable politics of Science.

In this *politics* the State Museum is the treasure house where empires and empire states declare their relationship (usually of ownership) to the things inside, and of the elaborate and gilded vaults, these monuments to pride of possession. This relationship also bears upon certain attitudes about the places and peoples from whom these objects of value have been appropriated, preserved, categorized, labelled, and displayed here, made into another story. Curated.

These curated formulations—the objects and the brief instructional note accompanying them—make up texts whose approach towards what they presume to say, and what it is that they are said to tell, are premised on particular assumptions out of which problematic meanings emerge. The claim to objectivity suggested in the unemotive tone of these curations, and esteemed by curators, is the sombre illusion in which a decided scientific bias assumes its denotative authority and presumption of correctness.

The Muse is imprisoned here in artifactual death. A taxonomic identification holds sepulchral watch in the predomination of labels, specimens, classifications. They locate and re-name that which is dislocated by placing it in another location, in this museum, and thus making of it necessarily something else. The encased object, dislocated from its unique place and meaning, and relocated, in this instance in Toronto, is relocated in permanent dislocation, stripped of its authority. It is that upon which the authority of this Science preys.

I look at the preserved remains of the violated dead in the sarcophagus upon which the disrespecting gaze of visitors falls. Egyptian mummies, one boy, no more than ten, exclaims and asks his father to take a photograph of him in front of the case. The father complies. There is a click and a flash and this peculiar ritual is over. The family moves to another exhibit, their interest in this one apparently exhausted. But there are others, not taking pictures, but fascinated, some almost gleeful. The Egyptian exhibit is a popular attraction.

The State Museums of Europe and Britain all have their Egyptian sections. In Vienna there is even an Egyptian tomb which museum-goers actually walk into. There seems to be no limit to the curiosity of the tourist or the necromancy of the archaeological imaginary in the service of commerce. But what of this morbid fascination with the Egyptian royal dead, their tombs, their burial rites?

Curiosity about an ancestral origin in which EuroEgo locates itself? This is a popular view. Egypt is romanticized as "the cradle" of European civilization, and in typical EuroEgoism there are many who hold it is *the* cradle of civilization. This interest is perhaps at one level realized in the imperialist vision which informs the archaeological preoccupation with a dynastic Egyptology—with the bodies, death shrouds and burial vessels and the buried wealth of the imperial despots, the Pharaohs, Kings and Queens of domination. And for those dominated, except for their willing servile positions, there is an absence. They are not interesting in the imperialist imaginary. What is important here is that imperialist Europe looks into its ancestral past and sees in it the virtues of an age-old, ancient, perhaps even eternal, imperialism. The continuing reign of imperial rule thus draws upon "history" to affirm its existence. But there is more to this.

This fascination with the Egyptian imperial dead, in this museum in Toronto, and elsewhere, is maintained by a Science whose curatorial ploy makes decent the sacrilege which takes place in the accumulation of these burial objects—the defiling of graves and the violation of the dead to furnish the wealth of their purchaser-owners who now so studiedly display them. The bodies removed from Egypt, like the one in this display case, are forever out of place, forever severed from their places of sacred meaning. They have been removed from death and preserved to cater to a perverse curiosity which daily abuses them.

This is the exploitation of the dead, the exploitation of death. The loss of respect of a people in the accumulative fascination that breaks into their mausoleums and tombs and makes of their embalmed bodies and burial vestments exotic objects, exhumed and removed to various select sites in EuroAmerica.

The child who so innocently has his photograph taken, is doing what is being taught to him as a cultural norm. The objects of other places and peoples of the world are there to furnish his ego. They are the backdrops, the props against which it is he who is important, he whose image is the dominating one. The world is his stage and his to stage in the primacy of his own image. He already knows, without even thinking about it, the formulation of his identity through the exploitation of the Other. And his father takes part in this. It is a family thing. . . Here's a picture of our boy in front of that Egyptian thing, that mummy . . . A day at the museum. A family outing. Yes.

*

The Royal Ontario Museum is at Queen's Park. In Ontario we treat you Royally. The Royal Ontario Museum is a good place. There are mummies there. Bug your parents to take you to the museum. Journey into The Heart of Africa at the museum. Visit the Caribbean at the Royal Ontario Museum. Pretend it's not so obviously a colonial name. Call it The ROM. Now that's a nice soft sound. Has a good *ring* to it. Befits a friendly Cultural Monument. After all, it's a Canadian Cultural Institute. And that's what's important. We should all be proud of it. Only in Canada, you say? Ignore those who malign the British Royalty as the principal British institution of imperialism. This is our *History* we're talkin' about. It's what makes us different from the Americans. The Royal Family is our Head of State. We are Canadians, Glorious and Free.

*

The signs etched at the entranceway of the Royal Ontario Museum are grandiose declarations of monumental authority, stone impositions on an unasked and unquestioning public.

The vision is imperial. This Royal house and monument, the Royal Ontario Museum, the inscriptions in stone declare, is dedicated to keeping the record of Nature through countless ages. Such a grand discourse. It talks about a "royal" interest through "countless ages" in which Nature is to be recorded. It does not say this recording is for dominion over that which is so recorded. The domination of Nature is sanctified in the realm of knowledge, accumulated through countless years.

It must never be forgotten or taken lightly that the domination of nature is also the domination of human nature, the domination of human beings. The declaration of such a magnitude of record-keeping—no less than of Nature through countless ages—strikes me as being possessive, and shares the universalist fantasy of global totalitarianism.

This theme of dominion affirming domination is there in the centre frieze above the entranceway. Here a patriarchal regal figure rises in the prototypical eurocentric mania of grandeur—the imaginary where Man as Ruler is the White man, similar to the grand narcissism and bigotry in anglo-european royal rule—holds dominance over the natural world. What am I to make of this work of sculptural art? What does it say to someone like me whose world has been repeatedly violated in so many ways by the

99

actions of this force of authority so celebrated here?

Am I to resort to that stereotypic excuse which says the sculptor as well as those responsible for the current location of this piece were simply reflecting the perceptions of their time? What of these perceptions themselves? What do they say of such times? What of the sensibility so preserved through the years, particularly the racist unconscious sculpted in the deep psyche of officialized stone here? And by implication what does this also say of the assumptions in the founders and supporters of this institutionalizing foundation which so presents itself?

This is the harmonizing of the exaltation of a racialistic supremacy, and stands today, a testament in stone affirming White supremacy in this public cultural object in Canada. It is an anglo-eurocentric imperialist sign. It is racist. And the accompanying inscription below which speaks of "the arts of Man through the years" thus talks of a "man" which excludes me and those like me, despite our legal membership in the social community of Canada. The sexism subsumes itself within the racialistically supremacist salutation. This is the *idola* through which I pass to the simulations of Nature in which I come upon necroptic masks and crepuscular discourses in this underworld of life-science facticities and empirical validities.

I read:

Life sciences expeditions involve the selective capture of specimens for collections and the recording of information through notetaking, filming and taping.

A science which names itself after life goes on ventures which, in military fashion, it names "expeditions," and similar to military action, captures selectively, kills premeditatedly and scientifically its victims. This science additionally makes of them "specimens for collections" through which the keeping of the record of Nature is done. In the name of knowledge the domination of Nature becomes invisible. Death appears so lifelike a child believes the encased specimens are alive.

"Researchers everywhere are contributing to mankind's pool of knowledge."

This is euro-scientific universalism. "Researchers everywhere" according to this text are united in the exalted task of contributing to the phallocracy (mankind) of knowledge. In this the work of these "researchers" is assumed to have an independent existence, outside of the political economies of control in which they are conducted, and whose interests they predominantly serve.

Research provides information, not knowledge. The techno-scientific stricturing of the approaches governing research provides what the procedures it uses can only do, the extraction of particular kinds of information. Knowledge is interested in trying to understand the assumptions of the action of research itself, of the compilation of data, of the very acts of selective capturing, the hoarding in the keeping of collections, of Nature turned into specimens, objects for the testing of hypotheses.

Mankind's pool of knowledge. Who is this Mankind whose pool of knowledge is being contributed to by researchers everywhere? The metaphor of possession in relation to knowledge as "Mankind's pool" constructs this research-contributing "knowledge" as property, as what is owned by "Mankind." It derives from the romance of power in private ownership, but it is presented also as the endowment of everyone everywhere. But where does this stock-piling of so universal a benefit reside?

I move to a plaque celebrating Leonardo da Vinci, Copernicus, Galileo Galilei, Newton, Karl Marx, Darwin, Freud, Einstein, as contributors to mankind's pool, and I realize this pool is a European pool, it is one which excludes most of humanity.

I pause upon the marble stairway and look again at the magnificence of speaking wood trapped amidst columns of stone, silenced. A dream of totem poles now turned into "ethnographic objects." An exotic spectacle for the wandering glance of sightseers. A thrill, and no more.

. . . Who did this? a child asks his mother as they slow down the excited pace of their steps.

The *Indians*, his mother says.

Oh, the child says, as if this means something to him, and mother and child move on to the next titillating curiosity . . .

Monumental in their dislocated location, these totem poles are now at best merely ornamental, reduced to decorative configurations, a curated display. They are the sentinels of an irretrievable loss, of a Time Past which is not contained in Time Present or Time Future. Their presence in this Royal house is also a reminder of the domination the very imperial order enshrined in this museum holds over the First Peoples of this land which the progeny of EuroEgo have named Canada.

Signs guide, signs proclaim, there are signs everywhere, but what is it that they are saying beneath the authoritative correctness of their stance?

"Writing marks the beginning of history," claims this wall/collage, tracing a map of cultures of literacy in which map-making Europe charts an acknowledgement of its self-interest.

A narrow view of history as a written record of events. Only in this limited sense can writing be seen as marking the beginning of "history." It is a view which considers the absence of what EuroEgo recognizes as "writing," as also an absence of "history," and thus not as important to the eurocentrism which reads into the written texts of other cultures its own misunderstanding and misrepresentation. Among others, it is through the violation of the texts of occupied peoples that the force of *orientalism*, as Edward Said has argued, works.

*

"The docks of London, Lisbon and Amsterdam piled high with peppers and cloves." From the exhibit: *Caravans and Clipper Ships 2000 years of Trade.*

It is not so much that those docks were piled high with peppers and cloves, but rather the romantic attitude in which "Trade" is presented here. Those caravans and clipper ships were the means through which the wealth of those pepper and clove-producing lands and peoples were exploited to provide the comforts of Europe and Britain, and later Canada and America. They were the essential links of imperialist greed. But they are celebrated in this curatorial text as wonderful sights.

Trade is not seen in relation to the violations and atrocities committed to gain these heady items of mercantile commercialism. In this manner, the sordid history of trade is not only downplayed, it is just not mentioned at all. This is a crass distortion of what happened, a historical deceit through which the imperialism-affirming vision of this Royal house is revealed.

It gets worse. Trade in luxury goods, I read, was accompanied by a reciprocal flow of ideas. It sounds so good, but the "reciprocal flow of ideas"? This is a blatant misrepresentation of the circumstances. Where did this mutual flow of ideas take place? Among the Africans, the Arabs, the Indians, and all the peoples destroyed by the machinations of this Trade? From the barrels of the guns and cannons and the artillery of imperialist glory? By the impositions of EuroImperialist education which sought the destruction of the ancestry of meanings in the places which Europe and Britain occupied? By deeming the dominated peoples savages, primitives, uncivilized, ignorant, superstitious, subhuman? By making slaves of people? By kidnapping and uprooting people and taking them to labour till death in the colonies and plantations?

Reciprocal flow. A water image conjuring up peace and harmony that never was. A reciprocal flow of ideas. But the ideas of EuroEgo clashed then with the ideas of the peoples being exploited, and continue, so much so that here *resistance* as a way of life has become vital to survival.

I am in a chamber commemorating imperial China. The valuable objects on display attest to the wealth of the imperial owners of such artistry, design and decor. Below I come upon a massive Ming tomb, and sections of the sculpture from that imperial courtyard of the privileged dead, dislocated and brought here and rearranged to demonstrate . . . what? The prestige of the museum's collection? The satisfaction of a vultural curiosity?

I am reminded of the imperialist vision in the Egyptian imaginary. The preoccupation with the perspectives and property of the imperial order of rule is repeated here. A taxonomy of artifacts from the *imperium*'s vaults and chambers of wealth is the trajectory of perception through which an elitist China is being depicted. And there is absence for the millions ruled by these protagonists of dynasty.

A sign, not curatorial this time, stops me. I look at it with an Indian couple. We are strangers, but this sight unites us in common perplexity.

Shiva, the man says in quiet intense disapproval.

It is a sign for repairs being done to this section of the museum, a caricature of a figure which borrows from the pictorial representation of Lord Shiva, one of the major Hindu deities. The figure is under the caption "Maintenance in Progress," and it is holding in its multiple arms a saw, a hammer, a nail, a drill, a paint brush and a trowel.

Although this sign cannot be attributed to any of the curatorial displays, the sensibility which it draws upon seems disturbingly similar to the ways in which the culture in which this museum is situated abuses cultures outside of EuroAmerica. That someone in the Maintenance sector has so chosen to vulgarize a principal Indian deity in this manner does not in the least strike me as being "cute" or humorous, as some Canadians are likely to see in this. Nor is this an indication of the "flow of ideas." This is a demonstration of utter contempt for a people, many of whom are resident in Canada. The image of the Creator and the Destroyer in a culture the British occupied for five hundred years, is now a crass "maintenance" sign in The Royal Ontario Museum.

I quote from one of this museum's curatorial texts entitled, The Life History of Objects in the exhibit *Into the Heart of Africa* (1989-90):

The context in which an object is used, found or viewed can significantly alter its meaning and function. What was once an African spear or shield became a trophy when collected by a Canadian soldier in Africa. It then appeared as a piece of decorative art when displayed in that soldier's home. Later in a museum collection, it was categorized as an ethnographic object. Now when viewed by you, it takes on another meaning as a museum exhibit. This transformational process is not always obvious, but it is always present. When artifacts become art, animals become natural history specimens, and objects become exhibits.

This lesson on the transformation of meaning suffers from the technicism of perspective characteristic of the attitude of the institution of empirical Science. Its assumptions are devoid of the significance of the action itself through which these objects have come into this "collection." There is no comprehension of the disturbing relationship there is between the very act of yet another White cultural institution, the Royal Ontario Museum, so exploiting the British-Canadian imperialist ecstasies in the disfiguration of the African. The critical distance the curator intended, failed, because the curatorial recourse to objectivity reinforces the very Scientific Attitude through which Africa and the African were authoritatively maligned.

The context in which "Africa" has been used in this exhibit makes of the entire continent of Africa an ethnographic object. Seen this way the historical issues of continuing importance are necessarily not taken into adequate consideration. There is already a representational abuse at work, an attribution of meaning which comes from the White dominator's world and Science. The gaze constructed in this imaginary perversely presumes the right to look "Into the heart of Africa"—the same presumption made by the imperializing actions of the British military and their colonizer-missionaries and the Canadians who heroically aided in these spurious ventures. To call it "a piece of decorative art" when it is displayed in that soldier's home, is to remove the historical significance of the imperialism through which it has been appropriated. Exploitation is sanitized, and "decorative art" becomes the new name. When an African spear or shield becomes a trophy collected by a White Canadian soldier in Africa, something violent has happened to Africa itself. This Canadian soldier is the killer-aggressor of British imperialism who, in addition to being there to take away the freedom of the African, now takes also a spear or a shield. This trophy is the totem of the oppressor's coercive superiority, a memento from one of the many "savage little wars" from "Darkest Africa."

When the museum categorizes this item in its "collection" as an "ethnographic object" it simultaneously de-politicizes the object and re-politicizes it. This African object is now under the discursive strategies of a curating science in which it will be one among numerous exotic objects to the glory of the "accumulation of knowledge." It furnishes another discourse about imperial treasures, about knowledge as possession, art as domination. In the Toronto case the ROM becomes an agency of the Ontario Ministry of Culture and Communications where the Ovimbundu proverb, "We have roots in the fields of our ancestors," has been broken with impunity.

To retrace, *without serious critical commentary,* the footsteps of Livingstone and the Canadians who violated Africa, is by implication—regardless of how unwitting this may be—to replicate the opprobrious views of those Crown-and-Empire invaders, especially those ideas which are still held by many Canadians. Like the Reverend Walter T Currie's supremacist view: "It is scarcely necessary to say that they are superstitious, for all ignorant people are more or less so." Reverend Currie's own superstition, his belief in a superior Christianity, is, of course, not mentioned. It is the beliefs of the African whose significance lies outside of the Reverend Currie's rationalism, which in effect he is ignorant of, and can never know, that are deemed superstitions.

It is thus that there's something gratuitous in the cautionary comment explaining that the experience of Africa as seen in this exhibition, was very different from the way Africans perceived themselves, their cultures, and their events. Meant perhaps as a recognition of differences in perception, and as the curator not wanting to malign, the note still does not escape the patronization in which it is instilled. It is saying the obvious for obvious reasons.

There are serious problems with the thinking which claims that when "artifacts become art, animals become natural history specimens." This is curatorial reasoning. There are millions of artifacts which have become art without the destruction of animals to make of them "natural history specimens."

Things That Speak for Themselves

This exhibit has been sponsored by the Ministry of Citizenship, Multiculturalism Strategy and two corporations, Nabisco and Imperial Oil, the latter a multinational corporate exploiter.

This museum, in addition to being funded by taxpayers' money, is supported by the new *imperium* of most of the major Canadian national and transnational corporations.

In response to angry outbursts from many Canadian citizens about *Into the Heart of Africa,* the ROM sponsored an exhibit the following year called, "Caribbean Festivals" which its advertising campaign decided to treat as another form of tourist exotica. It asked Canadians to "visit the Caribbean" at the ROM. Except for the tokenistic Hosay display, oddly foisted in this extravaganza, the rest featured the artwork of Black Caribbean artists of Caribana and Carnival and similar parade-festivities. The imaginary constructed is one of song-and-dance, and the Caribbean is Black.

What is shocking is that this appeared to have satisfied many of the same Caribbean-Canadians who were correctly angry with *Into the Heart of Africa.*

The ROM has apologized but maintained it did nothing amiss in its *Into the Heart of Africa* exhibit.

Apologies. Yes.

Indeed.

Selected Readings

Ames, Michael. *Cannibal Tours and Glass Cases*. Vancouver: University of British Columbia Press, 1992.

Ashcroft, et. al. *The Empire Writes Back*. London: Routledge, 1989.

Bhabha, Homi, K. *Nation and Narration*. London: Routledge, 1990.

Baudrillard, Jean. *Simulations*. New York: Semiotext(e), 1983.

Brydon, D. (ed). *World Literature Written in English*. Spring, 1991.

Cannizzo, Jeanne. *Into the Heart of Africa*. Toronto: Royal Ontario Museum, 1990.

Conrad, Joseph. *Heart of Darkness*. Middlesex: Penguin Books, 1902.

Glissant, Edouard. *Caribbean Discourse*. Charlottesville: University of Virginia Press, 1989.

Greenblatt, S. *Marvellous Possessions*. Chicago: University of Chicago Press, 1991.

Itwaru, A H. *Body Rites*. Toronto: TSAR Publications, 1991.

Itwaru. A H. *The Invention of Canada*. Toronto: TSAR, 1990.

Itwaru, A H. "Open Closures." *Toronto South Asian Review*, Vol 10, No 3, 1992.

Karp and Levine. *Exhibiting Cultures*. Washington, DC: Smithsonian Institute Press, 1991.

Lawrence, D H. *Lady Chatterley's Lover*. London: Octopus Books, 1960.

Said, Edward. *Orientalism*. New York: Vintage, 1979.

Said, Edward. *Culture and Imperialism*. New York: Knopf, 1993.

Schiller, Herbert. *Culture Inc*. New York: Oxford University Press, 1989.

Thomas, Nicholas. *Entangled Objects*. Cambridge, Massachusetts: Harvard University Press, 1991

Shakespeare, W. *The Illustrated Stratford Shakespeare*. Chancellor Press, 1983.

Torgovnick, M. *Gone Primitive*. Chicago: University of Chicago Press, 1990.

Vassanji, M G. *No New Land*. Toronto: McClelland & Stewart, 1991.

Viswanathan, G. *Masks of Conquest*. New York: Columbia University, 1969.

THE AUTHORS

Natasha Ksonzek is an artist, writer and book cover illustrator.

Arnold Harrichand Itwaru is a writer of fiction and poetry and is also a social and cultural theorist.

Doris Lessing was born of British paren[...] (now Iran) in 1919 and was taken to Southern Rhodesia (now Zimbabwe) when she was five. She spent her childhood on a large farm there and first came to England in 1949. She brought with her the manuscript of her first novel, *The Grass is Singing*, which was published in 1950 with outstanding success in Britain, in America, and in ten European countries. Since then her international reputation not only as a novelist but as a non-fiction and short-story writer has flourished. For her collection of short novels, *Five*, she was honoured with the Somerset Maugham Award. She was awarded the Austrian State Prize for European Literature in 1981, and the German Federal Republic Shakespeare Prize of 1982. Among her other celebrated novels are the five-volume *Children of Violence* series, *The Golden Notebook*, *The Summer Before the Dark*, and *Memoirs of a Survivor*. Many of her short stories have been collected in two volumes entitled *To Room Nineteen* and *The Temptation of Jack Orkney*, while her African stories appear in *This Was the Old Chief's Country* and *The Sun Between Their Feet*. *Shikasta*, the first in the series of five novels with the overall title of *Canopus in Argos: Archives*, was published in 1979. Her novel *The Good Terrorist* won the W. H. Smith Literary Award for 1985, and the Mondello Prize in Italy that year. *The Fifth Child* won the Grinzane Cavour Prize in Italy, an award voted on by the students in their final year in school. *The Making of the Representative for Planet 8* was made into an opera with Philip Glass, libretto by the author, and premiered in Houston.

By the same author

DORIS LESSING

Martha Quest

Book One of
'Children of Violence'

Paladin

An Imprint of HarperCollins*Publishers*

Paladin
An Imprint of HarperCollins*Publishers*
77–85 Fulham Palace Road,
Hammersmith, London W6 8JB

Published by Paladin 1990
9 8 7 6 5 4 3

Previously published by Grafton Books 1966
Reprinted sixteen times

First published in Great Britain by
Michael Joseph 1952

Copyright © Doris Lessing 1952

The Author asserts the moral right to
be identified as the author of this work

ISBN 0 586 08998 5

Set in Melior

Printed in Great Britain by
HarperCollinsManufacturing Glasgow

Martha Quest

Part One

I am so tired of it, and also tired of the future before it comes
— OLIVE SCHREINER

Chapter One

Two elderly women sat knitting on that part of the veranda which was screened from the sun by a golden shower creeper; the tough stems were so thick with flower it was as if the glaring afternoon was dammed against them in a surf of its own light made visible in the dripping, orange-coloured clusters. Inside this coloured barrier was a darkened recess, rough mud walls (the outer walls of the house itself) forming two sides, the third consisting of a bench loaded with painted petrol tins which held pink and white geraniums. The sun splashed liberal gold through the foliage, over the red cement floor, and over the ladies. They had been here since lunchtime, and would remain until sunset, talking, talking incessantly, their tongues mercifully let off the leash. They were Mrs Quest and Mrs Van Rensberg; and Martha Quest, a girl of fifteen, sat on the steps in full sunshine, clumsily twisting herself to keep the glare from her book with her own shadow.

She frowned, and from time to time glanced up irritably at the women, indicating that their gossip made it difficult to concentrate. But then, there was nothing to prevent her moving somewhere else; and her spasms of resentment when she was asked a question, or her name was used in the family chronicling, were therefore unreasonable. As for the ladies, they sometimes allowed their eyes to rest on the girl with that glazed look which excludes a third person, or even dropped their voices; and at these moments, she lifted her head to give them a glare of positive contempt; for they were seasoning the dull staple of their lives – servants, children, cooking – with a confinement or scandal of some kind; and since she was reading Havelock Ellis on sex, and had taken good care they should know it, the dropped voices had the quality of an anomaly. Or rather, she was not actually reading it: she read a book that had been lent to her by the Cohen boys at the station, while Ellis lay, like an irritant, on the top step, with its title well in view. However, there are certain rites in the talk of matrons and Martha, having listened to such talk for a large part of her life, should have learned that there was nothing insulting, or even personal, intended. She was merely expected to play the part 'young girl' against their own familiar roles.

At the other end of the veranda, on two deck-chairs planted side by side and looking away over the bush and the mealie fields, were Mr Quest and Mr Van Rensberg; and they were talking about crops and the weather and the native problem. But their backs were turned on the women with a firmness which said how welcome was this impersonal talk to men who lived shut into the heated atmosphere of the family for weeks at a time, with no refuge but the farmwork. Their talk was as familiar to Martha as the women's talk; the two currents ran sleepily on inside her, like the movements of her own blood, of which she was not conscious except as an ache of irritation when her cramped position made her shift her long, bare and sunburnt legs. Then, when she heard the nagging phrases 'the Government expects the farmers to . . .' and 'The kaffirs are losing all respect because . . .' she sat up sharply; and the irritation overflowed into a flood of dislike for both her parents. Everything was the same; intolerable that they should have been saying the same things ever since she could remember; and she looked away from them, over the veld.

In the literature that was her tradition, the word *farm* evokes an image of something orderly, compact, cultivated; a neat farm-house in a pattern of fields. Martha looked over a mile or so of bush to a strip of pink ploughed land; and then the bush, dark green and sombre, climbed a ridge to another patch of exposed earth, this time a clayish yellow; and then, ridge after ridge, fold after fold, the bush stretched to a line of blue kopjes. The fields were a timid intrusion on a landscape hardly marked by man; and the hawk which circled in mile-wide sweeps over her head saw the house, crouched on its long hill, the cluster of grass huts which was the native compound huddled on a lower rise half a mile away; perhaps a dozen patches of naked soil – and then nothing to disturb that ancient, down-peering eye, nothing that a thousand generations of his hawk ancestors had not seen.

The house, raised high on its eminence into the blue and sweeping currents of air, was in the centre of a vast basin, which was bounded by mountains. In front, there were seven miles to the Dumfries Hills; west, seven miles of rising ground to the Oxford Range; seven miles east, a long swelling mountain which was named Jacob's Burg. Behind, there was no defining chain of kopjes, but the land travelled endlessly, without limit, and faded into a bluish haze, like that hinterland to the imagination we cannot do without – the great declivity was open to the north.

Over it all curved the cloudless African sky, but Martha could not look at it, for it pulsed with light; she must lower her eyes to the bush; and that was so familiar the vast landscape caused her only the prickling feeling of claustrophobia.

She looked down at her book. She did not want to read it; it was a book on popular science, and even the title stiffened her into a faint but unmistakable resentment. Perhaps, if she could have expressed what she felt, she would have said that the calm factual air of the writing was too distant from the uncomfortable emotions that filled her; perhaps she was so resentful of her surroundings and her parents that the resentment overflowed into everything near her. She put that book down and picked up Ellis. Now, it is hardly possible to be bored by a book on sex when one is fifteen, but she was restless because this collection of interesting facts seemed to have so little to do with her own problems. She lifted her eyes and gazed speculatively at Mrs Van Rensberg who had had eleven children.

She was a fat, good-natured, altogether pleasant woman in a neat flowered cotton dress, which was rather full and long, and, with the white kerchief folded at the neck, gave her the appearance of a picture of one of her own grandmothers. It was fashionable to wear long skirts and tie a scarf loosely at the neck, but in Mrs Van Rensberg the fashion arranged itself obstinately into that other pattern. Martha saw this, and was charmed by it; but she was looking at the older woman's legs. They were large and shapeless, veined purple under the mask of sunburn, and ended in green sandals, through which her calloused feet unashamedly splayed for comfort. Martha was thinking with repugnance, Her legs are like that because she has had so many children.

Mrs Van Rensberg was what is described as uneducated; and for this she might apologize, without seeming or feeling in the slightest apologetic, when a social occasion demanded it – for instance, when Mrs Quest aggressively stated that Martha was clever and would have a career. That the Dutchwoman could remain calm and good-natured on such occasions was proof of considerable inner strength, for Mrs Quest used the word 'career' not in terms of something that Martha might actually do, such as doctoring, or the law, but as a kind of stick to beat the world with, as if she were saying, 'My daughter will be somebody, whereas yours will only be married.' Mrs Quest had been a pretty and athletic-looking English girl with light-brown hair and blue eyes as candid as spring sunshine; and she was now exactly as she would have been had she remained in England: a rather tired and disappointed but decided matron, with ambitious plans for her children.

Both ladies had been living in this farming district for many years, seventy miles from the nearest town, which was itself a backwater; but no part of the world can be considered remote these days; their homes had the radio, and newspapers coming regularly from what they respectively considered as Home – Tory newspapers from England for the Quests, nationalist journals from the Union of South Africa for the Van Rensbergs. They had absorbed sufficient of the spirit of the times to know that their children might behave in a way which they instinctively thought shocking, and as for the book Martha now held, its title had a clinical sound quite outside their own experience. In fact, Martha would have earned nothing but a good-natured and traditional sigh of protest, had not her remaining on the steps been in itself something of a challenge. Just as Mrs Quest found it necessary to protest, at half-hourly intervals, that Martha would get sunstroke if she did not come into the shade, so she eventually remarked that she supposed it did no harm for girls to read that sort of book; and once again Martha directed towards them a profoundly scornful glare, which was also unhappy and exasperated; for she felt that in some contradictory way she had been driven to use this book as a means of asserting herself, and now found the weapon had gone limp and useless in her hands.

Three months before, her mother had said angrily that Epstein and Havelock Ellis were disgusting. 'If people dug up the remains of this civilization a thousand years hence, and found Epstein's statues and that man Ellis, they would think we were just savages.' This was at the time when the inhabitants of the colony, introduced unwillingly through the chances of diplomacy and finance to what they referred to as 'modern art', were behaving as if they had been severally and collectively insulted. Epstein's statues were not fit, they averred, to represent them even indirectly. Mrs Quest took that remark from a leader in the *Zambesia News*; it was probably the first time she had made any comment on art or literature for twenty years. Martha then had borrowed a book on Epstein from the Cohen boys at the station. Now, one of the advantages of not having one's taste formed in a particular school is that one may look at work of an Epstein with the same excited interest as at a Michelangelo. And this is what Martha did. She felt puzzled, and took the book of reproductions to her mother. Mrs Quest was busy at the time, and had never found an opportunity since to tell Martha what was so shocking and disgusting in these works of art. And so with Havelock Ellis.

13

Now Martha was feeling foolish, even let down. She knew, too, that she was bad-tempered and boorish. She made resolutions day after day that from now on she would be quite different. And yet a fatal demon always took possession of her, so that at the slightest remark from her mother she was impelled to take it up, examine it, and hand it back, like a challenge – and by then the antagonist was no longer there; Mrs Quest was simply not interested.

'Ach,' said Mrs Van Rensberg, after a pause, 'it's not what you read that matters, but how you behave.' And she looked with good-natured affection towards Martha, who was flushed with anger and with sunshine. 'You'll have a headache, my girl,' she added automatically; and Martha bent stubbornly to her book, without moving, and her eyes filled with tears.

The two women began discussing, as was natural, how they had behaved when young, but with reservations, for Mrs Van Rensberg sensed that her own experience included a good deal that might shock the English lady; so what they exchanged were not the memories of their behaviour, but the phrases of their respective traditions, which sounded very similar – Mrs Van Rensberg was a member of the Dutch Reformed Church; the Quests, Church of England. Just as they never discussed politics, so they never discussed – but what did they discuss? Martha often reflected that their years-old friendship had survived just because of what had been left out, everything of importance, that is; and the thought caused the girl the swelling dislike of her surroundings which was her driving emotion. On the other hand, since one lady was conservative British and the other conservative Afrikaans, this friendship could be considered a triumph of tact and good feeling over almost insuperable obstacles, since they were bound, by those same traditions, to dislike each other. This view naturally did not recommend itself to Martha, whose standards of friendship were so high she was still waiting for that real, that ideal friend to present himself.

'*The Friend*,' she had copied in her diary, '*is some fair floating isle of palms eluding the mariner in Pacific seas. . .*'

And so down the page to the next underlined sentence: '*There goes a rumour that the earth is inhabited, but the shipwrecked mariner has not seen a footprint on the shore.*' And the next: '*Our actual friends are but distant relations of those to whom we pledged.*'

And could Mrs Van Rensberg be considered even as a distant relation? Clearly not. It would be a betrayal of the sacred name of friendship.

Martha listened (not for the first time) to Mrs Van Rensberg's long account of how she had been courted by Mr Van Rensberg, given with a humorous deprecation of everything that might be described (though not by Martha, instinctively obedient to the taboos of the time) as Romance. Mrs Quest then offered an equally humorous though rather drier account of her own engagement. These two heavily, though unconsciously, censored tales at an end, they looked towards Martha, and sighed, resignedly, at the same moment. Tradition demanded from them a cautionary moral helpful to the young, the fruit of their sensible and respectable lives; and the look on Martha's face inhibited them both.

Mrs Van Rensberg hesitated, and then said firmly (the firmness was directed against her own hesitation), 'A girl must make men respect her.' She was startled at the hatred and contempt in Martha's suddenly raised eyes, and looked for support towards Mrs Quest.

'That's right,' said Mrs Quest, rather uncertainly. 'A man will never marry a girl he does not respect.'

Martha slowly sat up, closing her book as if it were of no more use to her, and stared composedly at them. She was now quite white with the effort of controlling that hatred. She got up, and said in a low tight voice, 'You are loathsome, bargaining and calculating and . . .' She was unable to continue. 'You are *disgusting*,' she ended lamely, with trembling lips. Then she marched off down the garden, and ran into the bush.

The two ladies watched her in silence. Mrs Quest was upset, for she did not know why her daughter thought her

15

disgusting, while Mrs Van Rensberg was trying to find a sympathetic remark likely to be acceptable to her friend.

'She's so difficult,' murmured Mrs Quest apologetically; and Mrs Van Rensberg said, 'It's the age, my Marnie's just as bad.' She did not know she had failed to find the right remark: Mrs Quest did not consider her daughter to be on a level with Marnie, whom she found in altogether bad taste, wearing grown-up clothes and lipstick at fifteen, and talking about 'boys'. Mrs Van Rensberg was quite unconscious of the force of her friend's feeling. She dismissed her strictness with Martha as one of those English foibles; and besides, she knew Marnie to be potentially a sensible woman, a good wife and mother. She continued to talk about Marnie, while Mrs Quest listened with the embarrassment due to a social *gaffe*, saying 'Quite' or 'Exactly', thinking that her daughter's difficulty was caused by having to associate with the wrong type of child, meaning Marnie herself. But the Dutchwoman was unsnubbable, since her national pride was as deep as the Englishwoman's snobbishness, and soon their conversation drifted back to servants and cooking. That evening, each would complain to her husband – one, with the English articulateness over matters of class, that Mrs Van Rensberg was 'really so trying', while the other, quite frankly, said that these rooineks got her down, they were all the same, they thought they owned the earth they walked on. Then, from unacknowledged guilt, they would ring each other up on the district telephone, and talk for half an hour or so about cooking and servants. Everything would continue as usual, in fact.

In the meantime, Martha, in an agony of adolescent misery, was lying among the long grass under a tree, repeating to herself that her mother was hateful, all these old women hateful, every one of these relationships, with their lies, evasions, compromises, wholly disgusting. For she was suffering that misery peculiar to the young, that they are going to be cheated by circumstances out of the full life every nerve and instinct is clamouring for.

After a short time, she grew more composed. A self-preserving nerve had tightened in her brain, and with it her limbs and even the muscles of her face became set and hardened. It was with a bleak and puzzled look that she stared at a sunlit and glittering bush which stood at her feet; for she did not see it, she was seeing herself, and in the only way she was equipped to do this – through literature. For if one reads novels from earlier times, and if novels accurately reflect, as we hope and trust they do, the life of their era, then one is forced to conclude that being young was much easier then than it is now. Did X and Y and Z, those blithe heroes and heroines, loathe school, despise their parents and teachers who never understood them, spend years of their lives fighting to free themselves from an environment they considered altogether beneath them? No, they did not; while in a hundred years' time people will read the novels of this century and conclude that everyone (no less) suffered adolescence like a disease, for they will hardly be able to lay hands on a novel which does not describe the condition. What then? For Martha was tormented, and there was no escaping it.

Perhaps, she thought (retreating into the sour humour that was her refuge at such moments), one should simply take the years from, let us say, fourteen to twenty as read, until those happier times arrive when adolescents may, and with a perfectly clear conscience, again enjoy themselves? How lucky, she thought, those coming novelists, who would be able to write cheerfully, and without the feeling that they were evading a problem: 'Martha went to school in the usual way, liked the teachers, was amiable with her parents, and looked forward with confidence to a happy and well-spent life!' But then (and here she suffered a twisting spasm of spite against those cold-minded mentors who so persistently analysed her state, and in so many volumes), what would they have to write about?

That defensive spite released her, and it was almost with confidence that she again lay back, and began to consider herself. For if she was often resentfully conscious that she was expected to carry a burden that young people of earlier times knew nothing about, then she was no less conscious that she was developing a weapon which would enable her to carry it. She was not only miserable, she could focus a dispassionate eye on that misery. This detached observer, felt perhaps as a clear-lit space situated just behind the forehead, was the gift of the Cohen boys at the station, who had been lending her books for the last two years. Joss Cohen tended towards economics and sociology, which she read without feeling personally implicated. Solly Cohen was in love (there is no other word for it) with psychology; he passionately defended everything to do with it, even when his heroes contradicted each other. And from these books Martha had gained a clear picture of herself, from the outside. She was adolescent, and therefore bound to be unhappy; British, and therefore uneasy and defensive; in the fourth decade of the twentieth century, and therefore inescapably beset with problems of race and class; female, and obliged to repudiate the shackled women of the past. She was tormented with guilt and responsibility and self-consciousness; and she did not regret the torment, though there were moments when she saw quite clearly that in making her see herself thus the Cohen boys took a malicious delight which was only too natural. There were moments, in fact, when she hated them.

But what they perhaps had not foreseen was that this sternly objective picture of herself merely made her think, no doubt unreasonably, Well, if all this has been said, why do I have to go through with it? If we *know* it, why do we have to go through the painful business of living it? She felt, though dimly, that now it was time to move on to something new, the act of giving names to things should be enough.

Besides, the experts themselves seemed to be in doubt as to how she should see herself. There was the group which stated that her life was already determined when she still crouched sightless in the womb of Mrs Quest. She grew through phases of fish and lizard and monkey, rocked in the waters of ancient seas, her ears lulled by the rhythm of the

18

tides. But these tides, the pulsing blood of Mrs Quest, sang no uncertain messages to Martha, but songs of anger, or love, or fear or resentment, which sank into the passive brain of the infant, like a doom.

Then there were those who said it was the birth itself which set Martha on a fated road. It was during the long night of terror, the night of the difficult birth, when the womb of Mrs Quest convulsed and fought to expel its burden through the unwilling gates of bone (for Mrs Quest was rather old to bear a first child), it was during that birth, from which Martha emerged shocked and weary, her face temporarily scarred purple from the forceps, that her character and therefore her life were determined for her.

And what of the numerous sects who agreed on only one thing, that it was the first five years of life which laid an unalterable basis for everything that followed? During those years (though she could not remember them), events had occurred which had marked her fatally forever. For the feeling of fate, of doom, was the one message they all had in common. Martha, in violent opposition to her parents, was continually being informed that their influence on her was unalterable, and that it was much too late to change herself. She had reached the point where she could not read one of these books without feeling as exhausted as if she had just concluded one of her arguments with her mother. When a native bearer came hastening over the veld with yet another parcel of books from the Cohen boys, she felt angry at the mere sight of them, and had to fight against a tired reluctance before she could bring herself to read them. There were, at this very moment, half a dozen books lying neglected in her bedroom, for she knew quite well that if she read them she would only be in possession of yet more information about herself, and with even less idea of how to use it.

But if to read their books made her unhappy, those occasions when she could visit them at the store were the happiest of her life. Talking to them exhilarated her, everything seemed easy. She walked over to the kaffir store when her parents made the trip into the station; sometimes she got a lift from a passing car. Sometimes, though secretly, since this was forbidden, she rode in on her bicycle. But there was always an uneasiness about this friendship, because of Mrs Quest; only last week, she had challenged Martha. Being what she was, she could not say outright, 'I don't want you to know Jewish shopkeepers.' She launched into a tirade about how Jews and Greeks exploited the natives worse than anyone, and ended by saying that she did not know what to do with Martha, who seemed bent on behaving so as to make her mother as unhappy as possible. And for the first time that Martha could remember, she wept; and though her words were dishonest, her emotion was not. Martha had been deeply disturbed by those tears.

Yesterday, Martha had been on the point of getting out her bicycle in order to ride in to the station, so badly did she need to see the Cohen boys; when the thought of another scene with her mother checked her. Guiltily, she left the bicycle where it was. And now, although she wanted more than anything else to tell them about her silly and exaggerated behaviour in front of Mrs Van Rensberg, so that they might laugh good-naturedly at it, and restore it to proportion, she could not make the effort to rise from under the big tree, let alone get out the bicycle and go secretly into the station, hoping she would not be missed. And so she remained under the tree, whose roots were hard under her back, like a second spine, and looked up through the leaves to the sky, which shone in a bronze clamour of light. She ripped the fleshy leaves between her fingers, and thought again of her mother and Mrs Van Rensberg. She would *not* be like Mrs Van Rensberg, a fat and earthy housekeeping woman; she would *not* be bitter and nagging and dissatisfied like her mother. But then, who was she to be like? Her mind turned towards the heroines she had been offered, and discarded them. There seemed to be a gap between herself and the past, and so her thoughts swam in a mazed and unfed way through her mind, and she sat up, rubbing her stiffened back, and looked down the aisles of stunted trees, over a wash of pink feathery grass, to the red clods of a field which was invisible from the house.

There moved a team of oxen, a plough, a native driver with his long whip, and at the head of the team a small black child, naked except for a loincloth, tugging at the strings which passed through the nostrils of the leaders of the team. The driver she did not like – he was a harsh and violent man who used that whip with too much zest; but the pity she refused herself flooded out and surrounded the black child like a protective blanket. And again her mind swam and shook, like clearing water, and now, instead of one black child, she saw a multitude, and so lapsed easily into her familiar daydream. She looked away over the ploughed land, across the veld to the Dumfries Hills, and refashioned that unused country to the scale of her imagination. There arose, glimmering whitely over the harsh scrub and the stunted trees, a noble city, set foursquare and colonnaded along its falling flower-bordered terraces. There were splashing fountains, and the sound of flutes; and its citizens moved, grave and beautiful, black and white and brown together; and these groups of elders paused, and smiled with pleasure at the sight of the children – the blue-eyed, fair-skinned children of the North playing hand in hand with the bronze-skinned, dark-eyed children of the South. Yes, they smiled and approved these many-fathered children, running and playing among the flowers and the terraces, through the white pillars and tall trees of this fabulous and ancient city . . .

It was about a year later. Martha was seated beneath the same tree, and in rather the same position, her hands full of leaves which she was unconsciously rubbing to a green and sticky mess. Her head was filled with the same vision, only more detailed. She could have drawn a plan of that city, from the central market place to the four gates. Outside one of the gates stood her parents, the Van Rensbergs, in fact most of the people of the district, forever excluded from the golden city because of their pettiness of vision and small understanding; they stood grieving, longing to enter, but barred by a stern and remorseless Martha – for unfortunately one gets nothing, not even a dream, without paying heavily for it, and in Martha's version of the golden age there must always be at least one person standing at the gate to exclude the unworthy. She heard footsteps, and turned her head to find Marnie picking her way down the native path, her high heels rocking over the stones.

'Hey,' said Marnie excitedly, 'heard the news?'

Martha blinked her eyes clear of the dream, and said, rather stiffly, 'Oh, hullo.' She was immediately conscious of the difference between herself and Marnie, whose hair was waved, who wore lipstick and nail varnish, and whose face was forced into an effect of simpering maturity, which continually vanished under pressure from her innate good sense. Now she was excited she was like a healthy schoolgirl who had been dressing up for fun; but at the sight of the sprawling and undignified Martha, who looked rather like an overgrown child of eleven, with a ribbon tying her lanky blonde hair, and a yoked dress in flowered print, she remembered her own fashionable dress, and sat primly on the grass, placed her black heels together, and looked down at her silk-stockinged legs with satisfaction.

'My sister's getting married,' she announced.

There were five sisters, two already married, and Martha asked, 'Who, Marie?' For Marie was next, according to age.

'No, not Marie,' said Marnie with impatient disparagement. 'Marie'll never get herself a man, she hasn't got what it takes.'

At the phrase 'get herself a man,' Martha flushed, and looked away, frowning. Marnie glanced doubtfully at her, and met a glance of such scorn that she blushed in her turn, though she did not know what for.

'You haven't even asked who,' she said accusingly, though with a timid note; and then burst out, 'Man, believe it or not, but it's Stephanie.'

Stephanie was seventeen, but Martha merely nodded.

Damped, Marnie said, 'She's doing very well for herself,

too, say what you like. He's got a V-8, and he's got a bigger farm than Pop.'

'Doing well for herself' caused Martha yet another internal shudder. Then the thought flashed across her mind: I criticize my mother for being a snob, but despise the Van Rensbergs with a clear conscience, because my snobbishness is intellectual. She could not afford to keep this thought clear in her mind; the difficult, painful process of educating herself was all she had to sustain her. But she managed to say after a pause, though with genuine difficulty, 'I'm glad, it will be nice to have another wedding.' It sounded flat.

Marnie sighed, and she glanced down at her pretty fingernails for comfort. She would have so much liked an intimate talk with a girl of her own age. Or rather, though there were girls of her own age among the Afrikaans community growing up around her father's farm, she would have liked to be friends with Martha, who she admired. She would have liked to say, with a giggle, that she was sixteen herself and could get a man, with luck, next year, like Stephanie. Finding herself confronted by Martha's frowning eyes, she wished she might return to the veranda, where the two mothers would be discussing the fascinating details of the courtship and wedding. But it was a tradition that the men should talk to the men, women with women, and the children should play together. Marnie did not consider herself a child, though Martha, it seemed, did. She thought that if she could return by herself to the veranda, she might join the women's talk, whereas if Martha came with her they would be excluded. She said, 'My mom's telling your mom.'

Martha said, with that unaccountable resentment, 'Oh, she'll have a wonderful time gossiping about it.' Then she added quickly, trying to make amends for her ungraciousness, 'She'll be awfully pleased.'

'Oh, I know your mom doesn't want you to marry young, she wants you to make a career,' said Marnie generously.

But again Martha winced, saying angrily, 'Oh she'd love it if I married young.'

'Would you like it, hey?' suggested Marnie, trying to create an atmosphere where they might 'have a good talk'.

Martha laughed satirically and said, 'Marry young? Me? I'd die first. Tie myself down to babies and housekeeping . . .'

Marnie looked startled, and then abashed. She remarked defiantly, 'Mom says you're sweet on Joss Cohen.' At the sight of Martha's face she giggled with fright. 'Well, he's sweet on you, isn't he?'

Martha gritted her teeth, and ground out, '*Sweet* on!'

'Hell, he likes you, then.'

'Joss Cohen,' said Martha angrily.

'He's a nice boy. Jews can be nice, and he's clever, like you.'

'You make me sick,' said Martha, reacting, or so she thought, to this racial prejudice.

Again Marnie's good-natured face drooped with puzzled hurt, and she gave Martha an appealing look. She stood up, wanting to escape.

But Martha slid down a flattened swathe of long grass, and scrambled to her feet. She rubbed the back of her thighs under the cotton dress, saying, 'Ooh, taken all the skin off.'

Her way of laughing at herself, almost clowning, at these graceless movements, made Marnie uncomfortable in a new way. She thought it extraordinary that Martha should wear such clothes, behave like a clumsy schoolboy, at sixteen, and apparently not mind. But she accepted what was in intention an apology, and looked at the title of the book Martha held – it was a life of Cecil Rhodes – and asked, was it interesting? Then the two girls went together up the native path, which wound under the low scrubby trees, through yellow grass that reached to their shoulders, to the clearing where the house stood.

It was built native style, with mud walls and thatched roof, and had been meant to last for two seasons, for the Quests had come to the colony after seeing an exhibition in London which promised new settlers that they might become rich on maize-growing almost from one year to the next. This had not happened, and the temporary house was still in use. It was a long oval, divided across to make rooms, and around it had been flung out projecting verandas of grass. A square, tin-roofed kitchen stood beside it. This kitchen was now rather tumble down, and the roof was stained and rusted. The roof of the house too had sagged, and the walls had been patched so often with fresh mud that they were all colours, from dark rich red through dulling yellow to elephant grey. There were many different kinds of houses in the district, but the Quests' was original because a plan which was really suitable for bricks and proper roofing had been carried out in grass and mud and stamped dung.

The girls could see their mothers sitting behind the screen of golden shower; and at the point where they should turn to climb the veranda steps, Martha said hastily, 'You go,' and went off into the house, while Marnie thankfully joined the women.

Martha slipped into the front room like a guilty person, for the people on the veranda could see her by turning their heads. When the house was first built, there had been no verandas. Mrs Quest had planned the front of the house to open over the veld 'like the prow of a ship,' as she herself gaily explained. There were windows all around it, so that there had been a continuous view of mountains and veld lightly intersected by strips of wall, like a series of framed 'views'. Now the veranda dipped over them, and the room was rather dark. There were chairs and settees, and a piano on one side, and a dining table on the other. Years ago, when the rugs and chintzes were fresh, this had been a pretty room, with cream-washed walls and smooth black linoleum under the rugs. Now it was not merely faded, but dingy and overcrowded. No one played the piano. The silver teatray that had been presented to Mrs Quest's grandfather on retirement from his bank stood on the sideboard among bits of rock, nuts and bolts from the ploughs, and bottles of medicine.

When Mrs Quest first arrived, she was laughed at, because of the piano and the expensive rugs, because of her clothes, because she had left visiting cards on her neighbours. She laughed herself now, ruefully, remembering her mistakes.

In the middle of the floor was a pole of tough thornwood, to hold the end of the ridgepole. It had lain for weeks in a bath of strong chemical, to protect it from ants and insects; but now it was riddled with tiny holes, and if one put one's ear to it there could be heard a myriad tiny jaws at work, and from the holes slid a perpetual trickle of faint white dust. Martha stood beside it, waiting for the moment when everyone on the veranda would be safely looking the other way, and felt it move rockingly on its base under the floor. She thought it typical of her parents that for years they had been reminding each other how essential it was to replace the pole in good time, and, now that the secretly working insects had hollowed it so that it sounded like a drum when tapped, remarked comfortingly, 'Well, it doesn't matter, the ridgepole never really rested in the fork, anyway.' And indeed, looking up at the thatch, one could see a clear two inches between the main spine of the roof and its intended support. The roof seemed to be held well enough on the web of light poles which lay under the thatch. The whole house was like this – precarious and shambling, but faithful, for it continued to remain upright against all probability. 'One day it'll fall on our heads,' Mrs Quest would grumble when her husband said, as usual, that they could not afford to rebuild. But it did not fall.

At a suitable moment, Martha slipped into the second room. It was her parents' bedroom. It was a large square, and rather dark, for there were only two windows. The furniture was of petrol and paraffin boxes nailed together and painted and screened by cretonne. The curtains, originally bought in London, had faded to a yellowish grey. On the thin web of the stuff, which hung limp against the glare, showed a tenacious dark outline of strutting peacocks. There were two large iron beds standing side by side on one wall, a dressing table facing them on the other. Habit had not dulled Martha into blindness of these things, of the shabby neglect of the place. But the family lived here without *really* living here.

The house had been built as temporary, and was still temporary. Next year they would go back to England, or go into town. The crops might be good; they would have a stroke of luck and win the sweepstake; they would find a gold mine. For years Mr and Mrs Quest had been discussing these things; and to such conversations Martha no longer listened, for they made her so irritable she could not stand them. She had seen clearly, when she was about eleven or twelve, that her parents were deluding themselves; she had even reached the stage where she could say, if they really wanted to move, they would. But this cold, exasperated thought had never been worked out, and she still shared her parents' unconscious attitude, although she repudiated their daydreaming and foolishness, that this was not really her home. She knew that to Marnie, to others of their neighbours, this house seemed disgracefully shabby, even sordid; but why be ashamed of something that one has never, not for a moment, considered as home?

When Martha was alone in this room, and had made sure the doors were closed, she moved carefully to the small square mirror that was nailed to the centre of the window, over the dressing table. She did not look at the things on the dressing table, because she disliked them. For many years, Mrs Quest had been describing women who used cosmetics as fast; then she saw that everyone else did, and bought herself lipstick and nail varnish. She had no instinct for them and they were the wrong colour. Her powder had a musty, floury smell, like a sweet, rather stale cake. Martha hastily put the lid on the box and slipped it into a drawer, so as to remove the smell. Then she examined herself in the mirror, leaning up on her toes, for it was too high; Mrs Quest was a tall woman. She was by no means resigned to the appearance her mother thought suitable. She spent much time at night, examining herself with a hand mirror; she sometimes propped the mirror by her pillow, and, lying beside it, would murmur like a lover, 'Beautiful, you are so beautiful.' This happened when Mrs Quest had made one of her joking remarks about Martha's clumsiness, or Mr Quest complained that girls in this country matured so early.

She had a broad but shapely face, with a pointed chin, severe hazel eyes, a full mouth, clear straight dark brows. Sometimes she would take the mirror to her parents' bedroom, and hold it at an angle to the one at the window, and examine herself, at this double remove, in profile; for this view of herself had a delicacy her full face lacked. With her chin tilted up, her loose blonde hair falling back, her lips carefully parted in an eager expectant look, she possessed a certain beauty. But it seemed to her that her face, her head, were something quite apart from her body; she could see herself only in sections, because of the smallness of the mirror. The dresses her mother made looked ugly, even obscene, for her breasts were well grown, and the yokes emphasized them, showing flattened bulges under the tight band of material; and the straight falling line of the skirt was spoiled by her full hips. Her mother said that girls in England did not come out until at the earliest sixteen, but better still eighteen, and girls of a nice family wore dresses of this type until coming out. That she herself had not 'come out', and that her family had not by many degrees reached that stage of *niceness* necessary to coming out, was not enough to deflect her. For on such considerations is the social life of England based, and she was after all quite right in thinking that if only she had married better, or *if only* their farming had been successful, it would have been possible to arrange with the prosperous branch of the family that Martha should come out. So Martha's sullen criticisms of her snobbishness had no effect at all; and she would smooth the childish dresses down over Martha's body, so that the girl stood hunched with resentment, and say with an embarrassed coyness, 'Dear me, you are getting a pouter pigeon, aren't you?'

Once, Mrs Van Rensberg, watching this scene, remarked soothingly, 'But, Mrs Quest, Martha has a nice little figure, why shouldn't she show it?' But outwardly the issue was social convention, and not Martha's figure; and if Mrs Van

Rensberg said to her husband that Mrs Quest was going the right way to make Martha 'difficult' she could not say so to Mrs Quest herself.

This afternoon was a sudden climax after a long brooding underground rebellion. Standing before the mirror, she took a pair of scissors and severed the bodice from the skirt of her dress. She was trying to make the folds lie like Marnie's, when the door suddenly opened, and her father came in. He stopped, with an embarrassed look at his daughter, who was naked, save for a tiny pair of pink drawers; but that embarrassment was having it both ways, for if Martha was still a child, then one could look at her naked.

He said gruffly, 'What are you doing?' and went to a long cupboard beside his bed, formed of seven petrol boxes, one above another, painted dark green, and covered by a faded print curtain. It was packed with medicine bottles, crammed on top of each other so that a touch might dislodge them into an avalanche. He said moodily, 'I think I'll try that new stuff, I've a touch of indigestion,' and tried to find the appropriate bottle. As he held them up to the light of the window, one after another, his eyes fell on Martha, and he remarked, 'Your mother won't like you cutting her dresses to pieces.'

She said defiantly, 'Daddy, why should I wear dresses like a kid of ten?'

He said resentfully, 'Well, you are a kid. Must you quarrel all the time with your mother?'

Again the door swung in, banging against the wall, and Mrs Quest entered, saying, 'Why did you run off, Martha, they wanted to tell you about Stephanie, it really is rude of you – ' She stopped, stared, and demanded, 'Whatever are you doing?'

'I'm not wearing this kind of dress any more,' said Martha, trying to sound calm, but succeeding only in her usual sullen defiance.

'But, my dear, you've ruined it, and you know how badly off we are,' said Mrs Quest, in alarm at the mature appearance of her daughter's breasts and hips. She glanced at her husband, then came quickly across the room, and laid her hands on either side of the girl's waist, as if trying to press her back into girlhood. Suddenly Martha moved backwards, and involuntarily raised her hand; she was shuddering with disgust at the touch of her own mother, and had been going to slap her across the face. She dropped her hand, amazed at her own violence; and Mrs Quest coloured and said ineffectually, 'My dear . . .'

'I'm sixteen,' said Martha, between set teeth, in a stifled voice; and she looked towards her father, for help. But he quickly turned away, and measured medicine into a glass.

'My dear, nice girls don't wear clothes like this until – '

'I'm not a nice girl,' broke in Martha, and suddenly burst into laughter.

Mrs Quest joined her in a relieved peal, and said, 'Really my dear, you are ridiculous.' And then, on a more familiar note, 'You've spoiled that dress, and it's not fair to Daddy, you know how difficult it is to find money . . .' She stopped again, and followed the direction of Martha's eyes. Martha was looking at the medicine cupboard. Mrs Quest was afraid that Martha might say, as she had said to her, that there must be hundreds of pounds worth of medicines in that cupboard, and they had spent more on Mr Quest's imaginary diseases than they had spent on educating her.

This was, of course, an exaggeration. But it was strange that when Martha made these comments Mrs Quest began arguing about the worth of the medicines: 'Nonsense, dear, you know quite well it can't be hundreds of pounds.' She did not say, 'Your father is very ill.' For Mr Quest was really ill, he had contracted diabetes three or four years before. And there was an episode connected with this that neither Martha nor Mrs Quest liked to remember. One day, Martha was summoned from her classroom at school in the city to find Mrs Quest waiting for her in the passage. 'Your father's ill,' she exclaimed, and then, seeing that Martha's face expressed only: Well, there's nothing new in that, is there?, added hastily, 'Yes, really, he's got diabetes, he must go to the hospital and have tests.' There was a long silence from

Martha, who at length muttered, like a sleep-walker, '*I knew it.*' Almost the moment these words were out, she flushed with guilt; and at once she hastened to the car, where her father sat, and both women fussed over him, while Mr Quest, who was very frightened, listened to their assurances.

When Martha remembered that phrase, which had emerged from her depths, as if it had been waiting for the occasion, she felt uneasy and guilty. Secretly, she could not help thinking, He wanted to be ill, he likes being ill, now he's got an excuse for being a failure. Worse than this, she accused her mother, in her private thoughts, of being responsible.

The whole business of Mr Quest's illness aroused such unpleasant depths of emotion between mother and daughter that the subject was left alone, for the most part; and now Mrs Quest said hastily, moving away to the window, 'You're upsetting your father, he worries about you.' Her voice was low and nagging.

'You mean *you* worry about me,' said Martha coldly, unconsciously dropping her voice, with a glance at her father. In a half-whisper she said, 'He doesn't even notice we're here. He hasn't *seen* us for years . . .' She was astounded to find that her voice shook, she was going to cry.

Mr Quest hastily left the room, persuading himself that his wife and daughter were not quarrelling, and at once Mrs Quest said in a normal voice, 'You're a worry to us. You don't realize. The way you waste money and – '

Martha cut it short, by walking out of the room and into her own. The door did not lock, or even fasten properly, for it hung crooked. It had been formed of planks, by a native carpenter, and had warped in the rainy seasons, so that to shut it meant a grinding push across a lumpy and swelling lintel. But though it did not lock, there were moments when it invisibly locked, and this was one of them. Martha knew her mother would not come in. She sat on the edge of her bed and cried with anger.

This was the pleasantest room of the house, a big square room, freshly whitewashed, and uncrowded. The walls rose clear to the roof, which slanted down on either side of the ridgepole in a gentle sweep of softly glistening thatch, which had turned a greyish gold with the years. There was a wide, low window that looked directly over a descent of trees to an enormous red field, and a rise on the other side, a fresh parklike bush – for it had never been cut to feed mine furnaces, as had most of the trees on the farm – and beyond this slope rose the big mountain, Jacob's Burg. It was all flooded with evening sunlight. Sunset: the birds were singing to the day's end, and the crickets were chirping the approach of night. Martha felt tired, and lay on her low iron bedstead, whose lumpy mattress and pillows had conformed comfortably to the shape of her body. She looked out past the orange-tinted curtains to the sky, which was flooded with wild colours. She was facing, with dubious confidence, what she knew would be a long fight. She was saying to herself, I won't give in. I won't; though it would have been hard for her to define what it was she fought.

And in fact the battle of the clothes had begun. It raged for months, until poor Mr Quest groaned and went out of the room whenever the subject was raised, which was continuously, since it had become a focus for the silent struggle between the women, which had nothing to do with clothes, or even with 'niceness'.

Mr Quest thought of himself as a peace-loving man. He was tall and lean and dark, of slow speech and movement; he was handsome too, and even now women warmed to him, and to the unconscious look of understanding and complicity in his fine, dark eyes. For in that look was a touch of the rake; and at these moments when he flirted a little with Mrs Van Rensberg, he came alive; and Mrs Quest was uneasy, and Martha unaccountably rather sad, seeing her father as he must have been when he was young. His good looks were conventional, even dull, save for his moments of animation. And they were rare, for if Mr Quest was a rake, he did not know it.

When Mrs Quest said teasingly, but with an uneasy undertone, 'Mrs Van Rensberg, poor soul, got quite flustered this afternoon, the way you flirted with her,' Mr Quest said, rather irritated, 'What do you mean, I flirted? I was only talking for politeness' sake.' And he really believed it.

What he liked best was to sit for hours on end in his deck-chair on the veranda, and watch the lights and shadows move over the hills, watch the clouds deploying overhead, watch the lightning at night, listen to the thunder. He would emerge after hours of silence, remarking, 'Well, I don't know, I suppose it all means something'; or 'Life is a strange business, say what you like.' He was calm, even cheerful, in his absent-minded way, as long as he was not disturbed, which meant these days, as long as he was not spoken to. At these moments he became suffused with angry irritation; and now both women were continually appealing for his support, and he would reply helplessly, 'For heaven's sake, what is there to quarrel *for*? There isn't anything to quarrel *about*.' When his wife came to him secretly, talking insistently until he had to hear her, he shouted in exasperation, 'Well, if the child wants to make herself ridiculous, then let her, don't waste your time arguing.' And when Martha said helplessly, 'Do talk to her, do tell her I'm not ten years old any longer,' he said, 'Oh, Lord, do leave me alone, and anyway, she's quite right, you're much too young, look at Marnie, she makes me blush wriggling around the farm in shorts and high heels.' But this naturally infuriated Martha, who did not envisage herself in the style of a Marnie. But the women could not leave him alone, several times a day they came to him, flushed, angry, their voices querulous, demanding his attention. They would not leave him in peace to think about the war, in which he had lost his health, and perhaps something more important than health; they would not leave him to dream tranquilly about the future, when some miracle would transport them all into town, or to England; they nagged at him, as he said himself, like a couple of darned fishwives! Both felt that he let them down, and became irritable against him, so that at such times it was as if this very irritation cemented them together, and against him. But such is the lot of the peacemakers.

Chapter Two

Early in her sixteenth year, Martha was expected to pass the matric – it goes without saying, quite brilliantly. She did not even sit the examination; and it was not the first time she had withdrawn from a situation through circumstances which it occurred to no one, particularly Martha herself, to call anything but bad luck. At eleven, for instance, there had been just such a vital examination, and she had become ill the week before. She was supposed to be exceptionally musical, but by some fatality was always prevented from proving it by gaining the right number of marks. She was prepared for confirmation three times, and in the end the whole thing was allowed to drop, for it appeared that in the meantime she had become an agnostic. And now here was this important examination. For months Mrs Quest was talking about university and scholarships, while Martha listened, sometimes eagerly, but more often writhing with embarrassment. A week before the vital date, Martha got pink eye, which happened to be raging through the school. Not a very serious affliction, but in this case it appeared Martha's eyes were weakened.

It was October, the month of heat and flowers, and dust and tension. October: the little town where Martha was at school was hung with flowers, as for a festival. Every street was banked with purple-blooming trees, the jacarandas held their airy clouds of blossom over every sidewalk and garden; and beneath them blew, like a descant, the pale pink-and-white bauhinias; and behind, like a deep note from the trumpet, the occasional splash of screaming magenta where a bougainvillaea unloaded its weight of colour down a wall.

Colour and light: the town was bombarded by light, the heat beat down from a whitish sky, beat up from the grey and glittering streets, hung over the roofs in shimmering waves. The greens of the foliage were deep and solid and shining, but filmed with dust; like neglected water where debris gathers. As one walked past a tree, the light shifted glittering from facet to facet of a branch or leaf. How terrible October is! Terrible because so beautiful, and the beauty springs from the loaded heat, the dust, the tension; for everyone watches the sky, and the heavy trees along the avenues, and the sullen clouds, while for weeks nothing happens; the wind lifts an eddy of dust at a street corner, and subsides, exhausted. One cannot remember the smell of flowers without the smell of dust and petrol; one cannot remember that triumphant orchestra of colour without the angry, white-hot sky. One cannot remember ... Afterwards Martha remembered that her eyes had ached badly, then they closed and festered, and she lay in half-darkness making jokes about her condition because she was so afraid of going blind. She was even more afraid of her fear, because nothing could have been more absurd, since half the girls in the school were similarly afflicted. It was merely a question of waiting till her eyes grew better. She could not bear to lie in bed and wait, so she pestered the nurse until she could sit on a veranda, screened by a thick curtain of golden shower from the street, because she could assure herself she was not blind by looking through her glowing eyelids at the light from the sky. She sat there all day, and felt the waves of heat and perfume break across her in shock after shock of shuddering nostalgia. But nostalgia for what? She sat and sniffed painfully at the weighted air, as if it were dealing her blows like an invisible enemy. Also, there was the examination to be taken; she always relied on intensive study during the last fortnight before an examination, for she was the kind of person with a memory that holds anything, almost photographically, for about a month; afterwards what she had learned disappeared as if she had never known it.

35

Therefore, if she took the examination, she would probably pass, but in a mediocre way.

Mrs Quest was told that her daughter had pink eye. Then she got a letter from Martha, a very hysterical letter; then another, this time flat and laconic. Mrs Quest went into town, and took her daughter to an oculist, who tested her and said there was nothing wrong with the eyes. Mrs Quest was very angry and took her to another oculist; the anger was the same as that she directed towards those doctors who did not immediately accept her diagnoses of her husband's condition. The second oculist was patient and ironical and agreed to everything Mrs Quest said.

Curious that Mrs Quest, whose will for years had been directed towards Martha distinguishing herself – curious that she should accept those damaged eyes so easily, even insist that they were permanently injured when Martha began to vacillate. For as soon as Mrs Quest arrived in town and took the situation in hand, Martha found herself swept along in a way she had not foreseen. If one can use the word 'see' in connection with anything so confused and contradictory. The end of it was that Martha went back to the farm – 'to rest her eyes,' as Mrs Quest explained to the neighbours, with a queer pride in the thing that made Martha uneasy.

So here was Martha at home, 'resting her eyes' but reading as much as ever. And how curious were the arguments between the two women over this illogical behaviour. For Mrs Quest did not say, 'You are supposed to have strained your eyes, why are you reading?' She made such remarks as 'You do it on purpose to upset me!' Or 'Why do you have to read that kind of book?' Or 'You are ruining your whole life, and you won't take my advice.' Martha maintained a stubborn but ironical silence, and continued to read.

So here was Martha, at sixteen, idle and bored, and sometimes secretly wondering (though only for a moment, the thought always vanished at once) why she had not sat that examination, which she could have passed with such ease. For she had gone up the school head of her class, without even having to work. But these thoughts could not be clearly faced, so she shut them out. But why was she condemning herself to live on this farm, which more than anything in the world she wanted to leave? The matric was a simple passport to the outside world, while without it escape seemed so difficult she was having terrible nightmares of being tied hand and foot under the wheels of a locomotive, or struggling waist-deep in quicksands, or eternally climbing a staircase that moved backwards under her. She felt as if some kind of spell had been put on her.

Then Mrs Quest began saying that Marnie had just passed the matric, and she said it unpleasantly: Look, if she can pass it, why not you?

Martha did not want to see Marnie, and it was easy to avoid doing so, for the Van Rensbergs and the Quests were drifting apart. It was more than one of those inexplicable changes of feeling between neighbours; there was a good reason for it. Mr Van Rensberg was becoming violently nationalist, and Mrs Van Rensberg had an apologetic look on her face when she saw Mrs Quest at the station. And so, by a natural reaction, the Quests began saying, 'These damned Afrikaners,' although the two families had been friends, shelving the question of nationality for so many years.

Martha did not want to think of these things, she was turned in on herself, in a heavy trancelike state. Afterwards she was to think of this time as the worst in her life. What was so frightening was this feeling of being dragged, being weighted. She did not understand why she was acting against her will, her intellect, everything she believed. It was as if her body and brain were numbed.

There was nothing to do. The farm lay about her like a loved country which refused her citizenship. She repeated the incantatory names of childhood like a spell which had lost its force. The Twenty Acres, the Big Tobacco Land, the Field on the Ridge, the Hundred Acres, the Kaffir Patch, the Bush by the Fence, the Pumpkin Patch – these words became words; and, walking by herself across the Twenty Acres, which was bounded on three sides by a straggle of gum trees (a memory of her father's afforestation phase), a patch of sloping land tinted pink and yellow, full of quartz reefs and loose white pebbles, she said to herself scornfully, Why Twenty Acres? It's about twelve acres. Why the Hundred Acres, when it is only seventy-six? Why has the family always given large-sounding names to things ordinary and even shabby? For everything had shrunk for her. The house showed as if an unkind light had been shone on it. It was not only shabby, it was sordid. Everything decayed and declined, and leaned inwards.

And, worse, far worse, she was watching her father with horror, for he was coming to have, for her, a fatal lethargy of a dream-locked figure. He had the look of a person half claimed by sleep. He was middle-aged, she told herself, neither young nor old; he was in the long middle period of life when people do not change, but his changelessness was imposed, not by a resisting vigour but by – what? He was rising late in the morning, he dreamed over his breakfast, wandered off into the bedroom to test himself for his real disease and for various imaginary ones; returned early from the farmwork to lunch, slept after it, and for a longer time every day, and then sat immobile in his deck-chair, waiting for the sunset. After it, supper – a calculatedly healthy meal – and an early bed. Sleep, sleep, the house was saturated by it; and Mrs Quest's voice murmured like the spells of a witch, 'You must be tired, darling; don't overtire yourself, dear.' And when these remarks were directed at Martha, she felt herself claimed by the nightmare, as if she were standing beside her father; and, in fact, at the word 'tired' she felt herself tired and had to shake herself.

'I will *not* be tired,' she snapped to her mother, 'it's no good trying to make me tired': extraordinary words; and even more extraordinary that Mrs Quest did not question them. Her face fell in patient and sorrowful lines, the eternal mother, holding sleep and death in her twin hands like a sweet and poisonous cloud of forgetfulness – that was how

Martha saw her, like a baneful figure in the nightmare in which she herself was caught.

But sometimes their arguments were more sensible. 'You are terribly unfair to your father,' Mrs Quest complained. 'He's ill, he's really ill.'

'I know he's ill,' said Martha, miserably, feeling guilty. Then she roused herself to say, 'Look at Mr Blank, he's got it, too, he's quite different.' Mr Blank, over the other side of the district, had the same disease, and much more seriously than Mr Quest, and led an active life, as if this business of injecting oneself with substitute gland juices once a day was on the same level as cleaning one's teeth or making a point of eating fruit for breakfast. But Mr Quest was completely absorbed in the ritual of being ill, he talked of nothing else – his illness and the war, the war and illness; it was as if a twin channel drove across his brain, and if his thoughts switched from one subject, they must enter the other, like a double track leading to the same destination.

It even seemed to Martha that her father was pleased that the Van Rensbergs no longer visited them, because with Mr Van Rensberg he talked about the farm, while with Mr McDougall, who took his place, he shared memories of the trenches.

Martha, coming down the veranda, a silent and critical figure, would see her father at one end, leaning back in his deck-chair like a contemplative philosopher, and hear his voice: 'We were out in no man's land, six of us, when the star shells went up, and we saw we weren't three paces from the Boche trenches and . . .'

At the other end of the veranda, Mrs Quest was talking to Mrs McDougall. 'That's when we got the wounded in from Gallipoli and . . .'

Martha listened, absorbed in these twin litanies of suffering in spite of herself, for they been murmuring down her childhood as far back as she could remember, and were twined with her deepest self. She was watching, fearfully, the effect on herself of the poetry of suffering; the words 'no man's land', 'star shells', 'Boche', touched off in her images like those of poetry; no man's land was the black and wasted desert between the living forces; star shells exploded in coloured light, like fireworks, across her brain, drenched in reminiscence; Boche was fearful and gigantic, nothing human, a night figure; the tripping word 'Gallipoli' was like a heroic dance. She was afraid because of the power of these words, which affected her so strongly, who had nothing to do with what they stood for.

On one such afternoon, when she was standing on the steps, listening, her father called out to her, 'Matty, did I ever tell you about – ' and she said ungraciously, but with discomfort, 'Quite a thousand times, I should think.'

He jerked up his head and stared at her, and on to his face came that look of baffled anger. 'It's all very well for you,' he said. 'We came out of the trenches, and then suddenly the war was bad form. The Great Unmentionable, that's what you called it.'

'*I* didn't call it anything,' she remarked at last, sullenly humorous.

She moved away, but he called after her, 'All you pacifists, there were pacifists before the last war, but when it started, you all fought. You'll fight, too, you'll see.'

Martha had never thought of herself as a pacifist, but it seemed she was one: she played this part against her father's need, just as, for him, she was that group of people in the Twenties who refused to honour the war, although the Twenties were the first decade of her life, and she could hardly remember them. She was creating them, however, for herself, through reading, and because of this, the mere sound of the word *young*, which had apparently been some sort of symbol or talisman during that decade, sprung in her a feeling of defiance and recklessness.

Similarly, when Mr Quest complained about the international ring of Jews who controlled the world (which he had taken to doing lately, after reading some pamphlet sent to him through the post), Martha argued against him, in the most reasonable and logical manner; for one does not learn so young that against some things reason is powerless. And when Mrs Quest said that all the kaffirs were dirty and lazy and inherently stupid, she defended them. And when both parents said that Hitler was no gentleman, an upstart without principles, Martha found herself defending Hitler too; it was this which made her think a little and question her feeling of being used, her conviction that when her parents raised their voices and argued at her, on a complaining and irritable note, insisting that there was going to be another war with Germany and Russia soon (this was at a time when everyone was saying another war was impossible, because whom would it benefit?), this new war was in some way necessary to punish her, Martha, who talked of the last one so critically.

Jonathan Quest, the younger brother, came home for the holidays from his expensive school, like a visitor from a more prosperous world. For the first time, Martha found herself consciously resenting him. Why, she asked herself, was it that he, with half her brains, should be sent to a 'good school', why was it he should inevitably be given the advantages? There was something uneasy in this criticism, for she had been telling her mother fiercely that nothing would induce her to go to a snob school, even if her eyes did get better. She was becoming aware of several disconnected strands of her thinking. And this was brought to a climax by Jonathan himself. He was a simple, good-natured boy, very like his father to look at, who spent his holidays visiting the neighbouring farmers, riding in to the station to visit Socrates the Greek, and the Cohen family at the little kaffir store. He was on the best of terms with everyone. But it struck Martha as unjust that this brother of hers who despised the Afrikaners (or rather, who took up the orthodox British attitude towards them, which was the same thing) should spend the day at the Van Rensbergs' house like a second son, and drop in for a chat with the Cohen brothers as if it was the most natural thing in the world.

Martha asked him sarcastically. 'How do you reconcile the Jews ruining the world with going to see Solly and Joss?'

Jonathan looked uncomfortable and said, 'But we've known them all our lives.'

When she looked pointedly quizzical, he said, 'But you never go and see them at all.'

'That's not because I feel the way you do.'

Jonathan was embarrassed, because he would not have said he felt any way rather than another; he merely repeated what his parents said, and what he had heard at school. 'Well, if you think Hitler all right, how do you reconcile that?'

'But I never said he was all right, all I said was – ' She stopped and blushed; and it was his turn to look quizzical. It was true that all she had said was that Hitler's being an upstart was no criticism of his capabilities, but in this household it was as good as a defence.

She began a long rational argument; he refused to argue, merely teasing her, 'Matty's lost her temper, Matty's lost her temper,' singing it like a child.

'You're nothing but a baby,' she concluded scornfully, which was how their arguments always ended, and she turned away. Now, that act of turning away implies something one turns towards – and she picked up a book, at random, from the bookcase. This was also a familiar act. How many times had she not simply reached for the nearest book, as if to remark, 'I have authority for what I say'?

It occurred to her that the phrase 'Martha is a great reader' was being used by herself exactly as her mother used it, and with as little reason. For what was she reading? She read the same books over and over again, in between intervals of distracted daydreaming, in a trance of recognition, and in always the same place, under the big tree that was her refuge, through which the heat pumped like a narcotic. She read poetry, not for the sense of the words, but for the melodies which confirmed the rhythm of the moving grasses and the swaying of the leaves over her head, or that ideal landscape of white cities and noble people which lay over the actual vistas of harsh grass and stunted trees like a golden mirage.

She went through the house searching for something

different. It was full of books. Her own room had shelves packed with fairy stories from her childhood, and with poetry. In the living room, her parents' bookcases were filled with the classics, Dickens and Scott and Thackeray and the rest, inherited from prosperous Victorian households. These she had read years before, and she now read them again, and with a feeling of being starved. One might equate the small black child with Oliver Twist – but what then? There were also, lying everywhere, books on 'politics' in her parents' sense of the word, such as the memoirs of Lloyd George, or histories of the Great War. None of these seemed to have any reference to the farm, to the gangs of native labour, to what was described in the newspapers, or even to *Mein Kampf*, which had started this restless condition of mind.

But one day, slipped behind the rows of dusty books, she found a volume of H G Wells, and, as she held it in her hand, was very conscious of a dull feeling of resistance, a disinclination. It was so strong that she nearly put it down and reached as usual for Shelley or for Whitman; then she became conscious of what she was doing and stood wondering at herself. For she had felt this before. She looked at the book again. It was the *Concise History of the World*, and the name on the flyleaf was 'Joshua Cohen'. Now, she had dropped her childish friendship with the Cohen boys from the moment Marnie had said, 'Joss Cohen is sweet on you.' She missed them. And yet she could not face them. At first it was because the relief of escaping the barrage of criticism was so great: there was no longer any necessity to read their books, examine her own ideas. Recently it had been because of some obscure and unadmitted shame about her strained eyes. She took the book to her refuge, the tree, and read it through; and wondered why it was that she could read the most obscure and complicated poetry with ease, while she could not read the simplest sort of book on what she called 'facts' without the greatest effort to concentration. She brought herself to decide she would make an effort to renew that friendship with the Cohens, for there was no one else who could help her. She wanted them to tell her what she must read. For there are two ways of reading: one of them deepens and intensifies what one already knows; from the other, one takes new facts, new views to weave into one's life. She was saturated with the first, and needed the second. All those books she had borrowed, two years before – she had read them, oh yes; but she had not been ready to receive them.

And now what was she to do? For she had behaved very badly to the Cohen boys. She saw them at the station sometimes. Now, to avoid *seeing* people one has known for years is something of a feat, and Martha achieved it by the simple device of saying to herself, They wouldn't think *that* of me – '*that*' being anti-Semitism – and smiling at them constrainedly, like an acquaintance. They nodded back, and left her alone, as she apparently desired.

The village held about fifty souls, and had sprung up untidily around the first store, owned by Socrates the Greek, who was known to the farmers as Sock. There was a garage, run by a Welshman; a farmers' hall; the station beside the railway, a long tin-roofed shack on wooden piles; a ganger's cottage; and a hotel, also owned by Socrates, in which there was a bar, which was the real social centre of the district. These buildings were scattered over a few acres of red dust; and along the railway line was a stretch of brownish water, where ducks swam until Mrs Socrates came out to catch one for the hotel dinner, and where the oxen from the farmers' wagons were unyoked while the wagons were loaded, and stood knee-deep in green scum, raising their eyes tranquilly as the train thundered past over their heads. There were two trains a week, and twenty miles away was the end of the line, for beyond was the long ascent to the great escarpment at the verge of the Zambesi Valley. But there was a great deal of road traffic, and all day the cars stood in the dust outside the bar.

Years before, the Quests used to make the trip in to the station twice a week, for Mrs Quest was sociable; but Mr Quest disliked being disturbed so much that now they went once a month, and Mrs Quest must begin fighting with her husband at least a week before.

'Alfred,' she would say, with a sort of offhand defiance, 'remember, we are going in to the station tomorrow.'

He did not hear. Or rather, he raised vaguely irritable eyes towards her, and dropped them again, hunching his shoulders against her voice.

'Do listen, dear. I told you, we are out of flour, and the boys need new aprons, and the sugar's practically finished.'

He kept his eyes lowered, and his face was stubborn.

'Alfred!' she shouted.

'What *is* it?' he demanded, and glared at her.

Startled by the glare, which nevertheless she had been provoking and facing with obdurate strength for years, she murmured, abashed but determined, 'We must go to the station.'

'We can send the wagon,' he said hastily, getting up to escape.

'No, Alfred, you know you always say you can't spare the wagon, and it's silly to send the wagon for two sacks of . . .' He was at the door, on his way out; but she raised her voice after him: 'Besides, I want to see if they've any nice materials: I'm really down to my last rag.'

And now he stopped, and gave her another glare, in which there was guilt and reproach, for she was using the weapon he dreaded most: she was saying, The very least you can do is to let me have a little trip once a month, when you've made me live on this awful farm, and we're so poor, and my children have been dragged down to the level of the Van Rensbergs and . . .

'Oh, all right, all right, have it your own way,' he said, and sat down, reached for the newspaper, and covered himself with it.

'Tomorrow,' she said. 'We will go in after lunch, and Martha can help me get ready.'

Her husband's defiant eyes were hidden by the newspaper, which nevertheless gave a small protesting shake; but Martha's eyes were lifted towards her, with the sullen enquiry. 'Why do we have to *get ready* for half an hour's trip?'

'Oh well – you know – with everything . . .' Mrs Quest lapsed into confusion.

'Good Lord,' said Martha irritably, 'to hear us talk, you'd think we were off to England or something.'

This was a familiar joke, and allowed Mrs Quest to give her girlish and rather charming laugh; though no one else laughed. 'Well, with this family I've got, and no one lifts a finger but me . . .' This was not a grumble, but an appeal that please, please, for pity's sake, they should laugh, this irritable, resisting couple, and make things easier. She sighed, as Martha's face remained glum and the newspaper was held firmly upright against her.

Next morning at breakfast she said, 'Don't forget we're going to the station.'

Now he was resigned, '*Must* we?'

'Yes, we must. Besides, you know you'll enjoy it once we get there.'

This was a mistake. 'I do not enjoy it. I loathe it. Besides, we haven't any petrol.'

'There's a spare tin in the storeroom,' said Mrs Quest firmly. And now there was no help for it; Mr Quest groaned, and accepted his fate; and as he went off to the garage he even looked interested; the cloud of introspection was lifting, and his eyes intently followed what his hands did. It always worried Martha, made her uneasy, to see how those brooding eyes must concentrate, force themselves outwards, watching his hands as if they were clumsy creatures that were separate from himself.

The garage was a roof of tin over two walls of plastered logs, open at each end; and he reversed the car slowly out into the bush, so that it bounced and jerked over the rough ground, and then forwards into an empty space. Then he got out, and stood frowning at the car. It was a very old Ford; the paint had gone; there were no side curtains – they had been lost somewhere; one door was tied with rope; and a part of the canvas hood, which had decayed into holes, was thatched over. He had bought it for thirty pounds, ten years before.

'The engine's as good as ever,' he murmured proudly. And he called Martha to say, 'It isn't the body of a car that matters. Only fools pay good money for paint and varnish. What matters is the engine.' He liked to have Martha there when he attended to the car; he would even send the servant to fetch her. Now, Martha did not mind about how cars looked; but she was irritated because of this one's extreme slowness; so her face was as absent and dreamy as his own while he fetched water in a watering can, and fed the radiator, and took off the rope from the useless handle and retied it. Slowly, because he got no response to his remarks, he began glaring at her. 'It's all very well,' he would begin, 'it's all very well for *you* . . .' More often than not, the sentence was never finished, for a humorous look would come over her face, and their eyes met.

'Oh, Daddy,' she protested, grumbling, 'why is it all very well, I haven't said a word!' Here she might begin edging away, with longing glances at the house. It was so hot; the heat and light glittered into her eyes from the battered old car. 'Where are you going?' he demanded, sounding offended; and she returned to sit on the running board, opening the book she had held in her hand. Now he was mollified, and he sounded cheerful, as he stroked the warm thatch on the roof, and said, 'I always did like thatching, there's something about the look of a nice piece of thatch. I remember my cousin George – he was an expert thatcher, back home. Of course, he knew his job, not like these damned niggers, they slam it on any old how. When you go back to England, Matty, the first thing you must do is go to Colchester and see if George's kids are half the man their father was – if so, you'll see a piece of thatching you'll find nowhere else in the world. *Matty!*' he shouted at her bent and absorbed head.

'*What?*' she asked, exasperated, lifting her eyes from the book.

'You're not listening.'

'I am listening.'

'It's all very well for *you*,' came the grumbling voice.

When he had fiddled with the car for an hour or so, he came back to the house, followed by Martha, and demanded tea. He would not go down the farm that day. And then, about twelve o'clock, he began worrying that the lunch was late and they would never get off that afternoon.

'But Alfred,' said poor Mrs Quest, 'first you won't go at all, and then you start fussing hours before – '

'It's all very well, you haven't got to nurse a twenty-year-old car over these roads.'

Martha gritted her teeth in anger. Standing on the hill, one could see the other farmers' cars racing through the trees, like tiny black beetles, the red dust spurting up behind them. Other people made the journey to the station in a few minutes.

After lunch, the anxious Mr Quest went to the car and again tested the radiator. It was likely to be empty; and then he would call for half a dozen eggs, and break them one after another into the cavity. The eggs would form a sticky sediment over the leaky bottom of the radiator. Once someone had suggested mealie meal, which he had tried immediately, with all the cautious enthusiasm of the scientific experimenter. 'There must be something in it,' he murmured as he poured handfuls of the white floury stuff into the car. But halfway along the track, the cap shot off with an explosion, and lumps of porridge flew all over the windscreen, so that the car came to a blind and sliding stop against a large tree. 'Well,' said Mr Quest thoughtfully, 'that's interesting. Perhaps if one used a finer grain it might . . .'

On the whole, eggs were more predictable; though it was important not to drive too fast, and to stop frequently, so that the engine might cool, as otherwise the water might boil the clotted egg off the bottom of the radiator, and then . . .

After lunch Mr Quest called peremptorily, 'May! Matty! Come on, the engine's started, we must go.' And Mrs Quest, half laughing, half grumbling, ran to the car, adjusting her hat, while Martha followed unhurriedly, with a look of exhausted resignation.

The car was poised at the edge of a flattish space, on the brow of the hill. Mr Quest sat urgently forward, clasping the brake with one hand, hugging the steering wheel with the other.

'Now!' he exclaimed, letting go the brake. Nothing happened. 'Oh, damn it all,' he groaned, as if this were the last straw. 'Come on, then.' And he and Mrs Quest began swinging back and forth in their seats, so the car was joggled inch by inch over the edge, and slid precariously down the rutted pebbly road to the foot of the hill, where there was a great ditch. Into this it slid, and stopped. 'Oh, damn it *all*,' Mr Quest said again, on a final note, and looked around at his women in an aggrieved way.

He tried the starter, without much hope. It worked at once, and the car flew up over the edge of the ditch in a screeching bounce, and down the track between the mealie fields. The maize stood now in its final colouring, a dead silvery gold, dry as paper, and its whispering against the wind was the sound of a myriad fluttering leaves. Below this Hundred Acres Field lay the track, the old railroad track, and now Mr Quest stopped the car, got out, took off the radiator cap, and peered in. There was a squelchy bubbling noise, and a faintly rotten smell. 'It's all right so far,' he said, with satisfaction, and off they went.

Halfway, they stopped again. 'At three and a half miles, the petrol ought to show . . .' murmured Mr Quest, looking at the petrol gauge. For it was seven miles to the station. Or rather, it was five and three-quarters; but just as it was seven miles to the Dumfries Hills (in fact, six) and seven to Jacob's Burg (at least nine), so the distance to the station must be seven miles, for to have a house in the dead centre of a magically determined circle offers satisfaction beyond all riches, and even power. But a poetical seven miles is one thing, and to check one's petrol gauge by it another; and Mr Quest frowned and said, 'I'd better take the thing to the garage. I cannot understand – if these people can make an engine to last a lifetime, why is everything else so shoddy?'

At the station, Mrs Quest descended at Socrates' with her shopping lists, and Mr Quest drove off to the garage. Martha lagged on the veranda until her mother had forgotten her in her eager talk with the other women at the counter, and then walked quickly to the belt of trees which hid the kaffir store. It was a large square brick erection, with a simple pillared veranda. Martha went through the usual crowd of native women with their babies on their backs, pushed aside the coloured bead curtain at the door, and was inside the store. It had a counter down the centre, and on it were jars of bright sweets, and rolls of cotton goods. There were sacks of grain and sugar around the walls, bicycles, cans of paraffin, monkey nuts. Over the counter, cheap beads, strips of biltong, mouth organs and glass bangles dangled and swung together. The smell was of sweat and cheap dyes and dust, and Martha sniffed it with pleasure.

Old Mr Cohen nodded at her, with a distance in his manner, and, having asked politely after her parents, who owed him fifty pounds, waited for an order.

'Is Solly in?' she asked rather too politely.

The old man allowed his eyebrows to lift, before replying, 'He's in, for anyone who wants to see him.'

'I would like to see him,' she said, almost stammering.

'You used to know the way,' he said laconically, and nodded at the closed flap of the counter, under which she had ducked as a child. She had expected him to lift it for her now; clumsily, she tried to move it, while he watched her. Then, taking his time, he lifted it, and moved aside so that she might go through.

She found herself saying, 'You're mistaken, I didn't mean . . .'

His eyes snapped around at her, and he said sarcastically, 'Didn't mean what?' He at once turned away to serve a native child, who was so red with dust from the road that his black skin had a rusty look, some acid-green sweets from a jar.

Martha walked into the back room, and found the Cohen

boys reading, one in each of the two big easy chairs, which she privately thought in unpleasant taste, as was the whole room, which was very small, and crowded with glossy furniture and bright china ornaments; there was an effect of expensive ostentation, like the display window of a furniture store. And in this ugly and tasteless room sat Solly and Joss, the intellectuals, reading (as she took care to see) Plato and Balzac, in expensive editions.

After a startled look at her, they looked at each other, and after a long pause Solly remarked, 'Look who's here!' while Joss returned, 'Well, well!' and they both waited, with blandly sarcastic faces, for her to speak.

She said, 'I've brought back a book of yours,' and held it out.

Solly said, 'My grateful thanks,' extended a hand, and took it.

Joss was pretending to read, and this annoyed her; for, as Mrs Van Rensberg had suggested, he had once been her particular friend. But it was also a relief, and she said, rather flirtatiously, to Solly, 'May I sit down?' and sat forthwith.

'She's got to be quite a smart girl, h'm?' said Solly to Joss, as the boys openly and rudely examined her.

As a result of her quarrels with Mrs Quest, she was now making her own clothes. Also, she had starved herself into a fashionable thinness which, since she was plump by nature, was not to everyone's taste. Apparently not to the Cohen boys', for they continued, as if she were not present:

'Yellow suits her, doesn't it, Solly?'

'Yes, Joss and that cute little slit down the front of the dress, too.'

'But too thin, too thin, Solly, it comes of giving up that rich and unhealthy Jewish food.'

'But better thin and pure, Joss, than fat and gross and contaminated by – '

'Oh, shut up,' she said, in discomfort; and they raised their eyebrows and shook their heads and sighed. 'I know you think . . .' she began, and once again found it hard to continue.

'Think *what*?' they demanded, almost together, and with precisely the keen, sarcastic intonation their father had used.

'It isn't so,' she stammered, sincerely, looking at them in appeal; and for a moment thought she was forgiven, for Joss's tone was quite gentle as he began: 'Poor Matty, did your mummy forbid you to come and see us, then?'

The shock of the words, after the deceptively gentle tone, which reached her nerves before the sense, caused her eyes to fill with tears. She said, 'No, of course she didn't.'

'Mystery,' said Joss, beginning the game again, nodding at Solly; who sighed exaggeratedly and said, 'We're not to know, dear, dear.'

Suddenly Martha said not at all as she had intended, but with a mixture of embarrassment and coyness, 'Mrs Van Rensberg was gossiping.' She glanced at Joss, whose dark face slowly coloured; and he looked at her with a dislike that cut her.

'Mrs Van Rensberg was gossiping,' said Solly to Joss; and before the exchange could continue, she cut in: 'Yes, and I suppose it was silly, but I couldn't – take it.' The defiant conclusion ended on a shortened breath; this interview was not as she had imagined.

'She couldn't take it,' sighed Joss to Solly.

'She couldn't take it,' Solly sighed back; and with the same movement, they picked up their books, and began to read.

She remained where she was, her eyes pleading with their averted faces, trying to subdue the flood of colour she could feel tingling to the roots of her hair, and when, after a long silence, Solly remarked in a detached voice, 'She couldn't take us, but she's still here,' Martha got up, saying angrily, 'I've apologized, you're making a mistake. Why do you have to be so thin-skinned?' She went to the door.

Behind her back, they began laughing, a loud and unpleasant laughter. 'She's cut us dead for two years, and she says we're thin-skinned.'

'I *didn't* cut you – why must you talk about me as if I weren't here?' she said, and stumbled out, past Mr Cohen.

She found the flap of the counter down, and had to wait, speechless, for him to lift it, for she was on the verge of crying.

He looked at her with what she thought was a tinge of kindliness; but he opened the flap, nodded quietly, and said, 'Good afternoon, Miss Quest.'

'Thank you,' she said, with the effect of pleading, and walked back up the dusty path to the village, as the bead curtain swung and rattled into stillness behind her.

She walked over the railway tracks, which gleamed brightly in the hot sunlight, to the garage, where Mr Quest was in absorbed conversation with Mr Parry. He was repeating urgently, 'Yes there's going to be a war, it's all very well for you people . . .'

Mr Parry was saying, 'Yes, Captain Quest. No, Captain Quest.' In the village, the war title was used, though Mr Quest refused it, saying it was not fair to the regular soldier. Martha used to argue with him reasonably, thus: 'Are you suggesting that it is only the peace-time soldier who deserves his title? Do you mean that if civilians get conscripted and killed it's on a different level from . . .' and so on and so on – ah, how exasperating are the rational adolescents! For Mr Quest gave his irritable shrug of aversion and repeated, 'I don't like being Captain, it's not fair when I haven't been in the Army for so long.' What Martha thought privately was, How odd that a man who thinks about nothing but war should dislike being Captain; and at this point, the real one, was of course never mentioned during those *reasonable* discussions.

Mr Parry was listening nervously to Mr Quest, while his eyes anxiously followed his native assistant, who was dragging an inner tube through the hot dust. At last he could not bear it, saying, 'Excuse me, but . . .' he darted forward and shouted at the native, 'Look you, Gideon, how many times have I told you . . .' He grabbed the tyre from the man's hand, and took it over to a tub of water. Gideon shrugged, and went off to the cool interior of the garage, where he sat on a heap of outer tyres, and began making patterns on the dust with a twig. 'Look you, Gideon . . .' shouted Mr Parry; but Gideon wrinkled his brows and pretended not to hear. Mr Parry's Welsh speech had lost nothing of its lilt and charm; but the phrases had worn slack; his 'Look you' sounded more like 'Look ye'; and when he used the Welsh 'whatever', it came haphazard in his speech, with a surprised, uncertain note.

Mr Quest, disappointed of a listener, came to the car, climbed in, and said, 'They don't listen. I was telling him the Russians are going to join with the Germans and attack us. I know they are. Just after the war – *my* war – I met a man in a train who said he had seen with his own eyes the way the Russians were kidnapping German scientists and forcing them to work in their factories so they could learn how to make tanks to smash the British Empire. I said to Parry here . . .'

Martha heard these words somewhere underneath her attention, which was given to her own problems. Mr Quest looked over his shoulder at her, and said sarcastically, 'But don't let me bore you with the Great Unmentionable. Your time'll come, and then I can say I told you so.'

Martha turned her face away; her lids stung with tears; she felt the most rejected and desolate creature in the world. It occurred to her that the Cohen boys might have felt like this when she (or so it had appeared) rejected them; but she dismissed the thought at once. The possessors of this particular form of arrogance may know its underside is timidity; but they seldom go on to reflect that the timidity is based on the danger of thinking oneself important to others, which necessitates a return of feeling. She was saying to herself that she could not imagine the clever and self-sufficient Cohen brothers caring about her one way or the other. But we were friends all our childhood, a voice said inside her; and that other voice answered coldly, Friends are whom you choose, not the people forced on you by circumstances. And yet she was nearly crying with misery and humiliation and friendlessness, in the hot back seat of the car, while grains of sunlight danced through the fractured roof, and stung her flesh like needles. For the first time, she said to herself that the Cohens were almost completely isolated in the district. The farmers nodded to them, offered remarks about the weather, but never friendship. The Greek family maintained a complicated system of friendship with the other Greeks from stores all along the railway line. The Cohens had relations in the city, no one nearer.

At last Mr Parry found a trail of bubbles sizzling up through the dirty water from the tube, and shouted to Gideon, 'Come ye, now, you lazy black loafer, and do it quick whateffer you do, and listen well, now.'

Gideon indolently lifted himself and went to mend the puncture, while Mr Parry came back to the car in order to resume his conversation with Mr Quest.

'Sorry, Captain, but if you want a good job, you do it yourself, whateffer else, it's no good trusting the blacks, they've no pride in their work.'

'As I was saying, you people have your heads buried in the sand. Anyone can see war is coming. If it's not this year, it'll be the next, as soon as they're strong enough.'

'You think the Jerries'll have another shot at us?' asked Mr Parry, polite but doubtful, and turned so that he might keep an eye on Gideon.

Another native came loping across the railway tracks and stopped by the car. 'Baas Quest?' he asked.

Mr Quest, once again interrupted, turned his darkly irritable eyes on him. But Martha recognized him: he was the Cohens' cook; and she reached for the parcel he held.

'For me,' she said, and asked the man to wait. He went off to help Gideon with the tyre.

The parcel was a book from Joss, entitled *The Social Aspect of the Jewish Question*, and inside was a note: 'Dear Matty Quest, This will be good for your soul, so do, *do* read it. Yours thin-skinnedly, Joss.'

She was filled with outrageous delight. It was forgiveness. She interrupted her father once again to borrow a pencil, and wrote: 'Thanks for the book. As it happened, I borrowed it from you and of course agreed with it, three years ago. But

55

I shall read it again and return it next time we come to the station.' She was determined that would be very soon.

Next mail day she suggested that they should make the trip, but her father refused, with an air of being exploited.

'Why do you want to go?' asked Mrs Quest curiously; and Martha said, 'I want to see the Cohen boys.'

'You're making friends with them?' demurred Mrs Quest.

'I thought we always were friends with them,' said Martha scornfully; and since this put the argument on that hypo-critical level where it was maintained that of course the Quests did not think Jews, or even shopkeepers, beneath them, and the only reason they did not continually meet was an inconvenience of some sort, Mrs Quest could not easily reply.

Martha telephoned the McDougalls to ask if they were going to the station. They were not. She asked the Van Rensbergs; Marnie said awkwardly that Pop didn't often go to the station these days. Finally she telephoned Mr McFarline, the old miner from the small working in the Dumfries Hills; and he said yes, he was going to town tomorrow. She told her mother she would get a lift back (for 'town' in this case meant the city, not the station, as it sometimes did), and added, with the apparently deliberate exaggeration which was so infuriating, 'If I don't get a lift, I'll walk.' Which of course was absurd, infringed one of the taboos – 'a young white girl walking alone', etc. – and was calculated to provoke an argument. The argument immedi-ately followed; and both women appealed to Mr Quest

'Why shouldn't she walk?' demanded Mr Quest vaguely. 'When I was a young man in England, I used to walk thirty miles an afternoon and think nothing of it.'

'This isn't England,' said Mrs Quest tremulously, filled with horrid visions of what might happen to Martha if she encountered an evil native.

Martha came back with, 'I walk miles and miles all over the farm, but that doesn't matter for some reason. How can you be so illogical?'

'Well, I don't like it, and you promised not to go more than half a mile from the house.'

Martha laughed angrily, and chose this moment to say what until now she had been careful to keep dark: 'Why, I often walk over to the Dumfries Hills, or even to Jacob's Burg, I've been doing it for years.'

'Oh, my dear,' said Mrs Quest helplessly. She had known quite well that Martha was doing this, but to be told so now was another thing. 'What would happen if a native attacked you?'

'I should scream for help,' said Martha flippantly.

'Oh, my dear . . .'

'Oh, don't be ridiculous,' said Martha angrily. 'If a native raped me, then he'd be hung and I'd be a national heroine, so he wouldn't do it, even if he wanted to, and why should he?'

'My dear, read the newspapers, white girls are always being ra – attacked.'

Now, Martha could not remember any case of this happening; it was one of the things people said. She remarked, 'Last week a white man raped a black girl, and was fined five pounds.'

Mrs Quest said hastily, 'That's not the point; the point is girls get raped.'

'Then I expect they want to be,' said Martha sullenly; and caught her breath, not because she did not believe the truth of what she said, but because of her parents' faces: she could not help being frightened. For they were united for once, in genuine emotion, and began lecturing her on the consequences of her attitude. It ended with 'and so they'll drive us into the sea, and then the country will be ruined, what would these ignorant blacks do without us.' And the usual inconsequent conclusion: 'They have no sense of gratitude at all for what we do for them.' It had all been said so often that it rang stale and false for both sides; and Martha remained silent in a way which they could take as an agreement, for comfort's sake.

Next morning she was waiting down on the track, by the

signpost in the long grass, for Mr McFarline; and they made the journey to the station in just over ten minutes.

Mr McFarline was a charming and wicked old Scotsman, who lived alone on his mine, which he worked in a way which cost him the very minimum in money, but a good deal in human life. There were always accidents on his mine. Also, his native compound was full of half-caste children, his own. He was extremely wealthy, and very popular. He gave generously to charity, and was about to stand for Parliament for one of the town constituencies. Because of the work in connection with getting himself elected, he often went into town.

As the car raced dangerously through the trees, he squeezed Martha's knee in an experimental way and tried to put his hand up her skirt. She held the skirt down, and moved coolly away to the other side of the car, as if she had not noticed the action. So he took his hand away, and concentrated on showing her how nearly it was possible to escape death, with perfect sangfroid, at every bend of the road. He took the paint off his back mud-guard at the last raking turn; and they stopped before Sock's store in a billowing cloud of dust. Martha's heart was beating wildly for several reasons. No one had ever tried to put his hand up her skirt before, and she was petrified at the wild driving. She looked confused and alarmed; and the old Scotsman decided to see her as the little girl he had known for years. He took a ten-shilling note from his stuffed wallet, and gave it to her.

'For when you go back to school,' he said bluffly.

Martha almost handed it back; but was unable to partly because ten shillings was such a large sum for her, and partly because of a feeling which she described to herself as: If I refuse it, he will think it's because of the way he tried to touch me. She thanked him politely for the lift, and he roared away over the railway track on the road to the city, singing, 'You're a bonny lassie . . .'

She had the book on the Jewish question (which she had not re-read, thinking it unnecessary to gild the already sound coinage of her opinions) under her arm. She went over to the kaffir store. Mr Cohen greeted her, and lifted the counter for her. He was a short, squat man; his hair was a close-growing, crinkling cap of black; his skin was pallid and unhealthy. He had, she thought secretly, the look of a toad, or something confined and light-shunning; and in fact he was hardly ever away from his counter; but the commercial look of the small shopkeeper was tempered in him by purpose and dignity, which was not only because of his ancient culture, but because this penniless immigrant from Central Europe had chosen such a barren place, such exile, for the sake of his brilliant sons. His eyes were black and wise and shrewd, and it was impossible not to like him. And yet Martha found him repulsive, and was guilty; it was strange that she could find the oily fatness of the Greek Socrates repulsive without any sense of guilt at all, but this question of anti-Semitism, this shrinking nerve, put her on guard against herself, so that her manner with Mr Cohen was always strained.

In the back room Martha found Solly, alone; and was pleased that the brotherly solid act could not be repeated. Besides, there was something uneasy and false in it, for there was a strong current of antagonism between the two brothers, a temperamental difficulty which expressed itself politically – Solly being a Zionist, while Joss was a Socialist. Solly was a lanky, tall youth, with a big head on a long thin neck, and big bony hands at the end of long arms; he was altogether knobbly and unintegrated, and his enormous, sombre black eyes brooded abstractedly on the world around him in a way that gave Martha a feeling of kinship to him; but this was perhaps not an altogether welcome relationship, reminding her, as it did, of her father. If she was to fight the morbid strain in herself, which was her father's gift, then how could she admire Solly wholeheartedly, as she wished to do? On the whole, she was easier with Joss, who was short and compact and robust, with humorous direct eyes and a sarcastic practicality, as if he were always saying, 'Well, and what's the fuss about, it's all quite easy!'

Solly took the book, without any sign of the hostility of the previous meeting; and no sooner had she sat down than Mrs Cohen came in with a tray. The older Cohens were strictly kosher, and the sons were lax. For years Mrs Cohen had been scrupulously sorting her crockery and cutlery, washing them herself, forbidding the native servants even to touch them; but at the table, Joss and Solly, usually deep in bitter argument, would reach for the wrong knives, and stack the plates carelessly about them, while Mrs Cohen scolded and pleaded. By now she had learned to say, 'I'm too old to learn new ways,' and with a sorrowful tolerance, she continued to wash and sort her things, but made no comment if her sons misused them. It was a compromise in which Martha could see no sense at all; if her own parents had been guilty of *unreasonable* behaviour, how irritably would she have argued with them! In Mrs Cohen, however, it merely struck her as charming. The mere sight of the plump old Jewish woman, with her fine, dark sad eyes, made her feel welcomed; and she at once accepted, enthusiastically, when she was bidden, 'You'll stay eat with us?' In a few moments they were talking as if she had never absented herself from the family for two years.

Solly was leaving shortly to study medicine in Cape Town, and Mrs Cohen was urging him to live with her cousin there. But Solly wanted independence, a life of his own; and since this vital point was never mentioned, the argument went on endlessly about buses and transport and inconvenience; and it reminded Martha of her own home, where this kind of surface bickering was equally futile.

Joss came in, gave Martha an ambiguous look, and forbore to comment, in a way which made her voice rise to a jaunty brightness. He was intending to study law, but was staying at home with his parents until they could move into town, which they planned to do. The store was to be sold. This solicitude for his father and mother only struck Martha as a kind of betrayal to the older generation; she found it extraordinary; even more strange that he sided with his parents against Solly's desire to fend for himself. He sounded more like an uncle than a brother.

They sat down to table, and Mrs Cohen asked, 'And when are you going back to your studies, Matty? Your mother must be worrying herself.'

Martha replied awkwardly, 'My eyes aren't better yet,' and lowered them towards her plate. When she raised them, she found Joss critically studying her in the way she had feared.

'What's wrong with them?' he inquired bluntly. She gave an uncomfortable movement with her shoulders, as if to say, 'Leave me alone.' But in this family everything was discussed; and Joss said to Solly, 'Her eyes are strained, well, well!'

Solly refused, this time, to make the alliance against her, and asked, 'What's it got to do with you?'

Joss raised his brows, and said, 'Me? Nothing. She used to be such a bright girl. Pity.'

'Leave her alone,' said Mr Cohen unexpectedly, 'she's all right.' Martha felt a rush of warmth towards him, which as usual she could not express, but dropped her eyes, and even looked sullen.

'Of course she's all right,' said Joss carelessly; but there was a note in his voice . . .

Martha looked quickly at him, and at once interpreted his agreement as a reference to her own appearance; and this she half resented, and half welcomed. Since her incarnation as a fairly successful imitation of a magazine beauty, the Cohen boys were the first males she had tried herself against. But she had never said to herself that her careful make-up and the new green linen had been put on to impress them, and therefore she felt it as a false note that either should mention or even react to her appearance – a confusion of feeling which left her silent, and rather sulky. After the meal, Mr Cohen went back to the shop, and Mrs Cohen to her kitchen, with the mis-handled crockery; and the three young people were left together. Conversation was difficult, and soon Martha felt she should leave. But she lingered; and it was Solly who at last went out; and at once she and Joss were at ease, as she and Solly were, by themselves: it was three of them together that set up the jarring currents.

At once Joss inquired, 'And now what's all this about not going to university?'

The direct question, which she had never put to herself, left her silent; but he persisted. 'You can't hang about this dorp doing nothing.'

She said, 'But you are at home, too.'

His look said that she must see this was no analogy; he tried not to sound bitter as he remarked, 'My parents have no friends in the village. It'll be different when they're in town.'

Again she was silent, feeling apologetic for herself and for her parents. She got up and went to the bookcase, to see what was new in it; but this represented the family: the Jewish classics, books on Palestine, Poland and Russia; this was the source of the rapidly diverging streams which were Solly and Joss; and these new books would be in their shared bedroom. Into this room it was impossible to go, since she was now Miss Quest; and the glance she directed towards Joss was troubled.

He had been watching her, and, at the glance, he lifted from a table beside him a large pile of books and handed them to her. Again she felt that flush of delight; for he must have prepared them for her. He remarked calmly, 'Take these, good for your soul.'

She looked at the titles, and was at once indignant, as a child might be if a teacher urged her to study subjects she had mastered the year before.

'What's the matter?' he asked sardonically. 'Not up your street?'

She said, 'But I know all this.' At once she wished the words unsaid, for they sounded conceited. What she meant was, 'I agree with all the things these books represent.'

He studied her, gave an incredulous grimace, and then fired the following questions at her, in the offhand indifferent manner of the initiate to a breed utterly without the law:

'You repudiate the colour bar?'

'But of course.'

'Of course,' he said sardonically. And then: 'You dislike racial prejudice in all its form, including anti-Semitism?'

'Naturally' – this with a touch of impatience.

'You are an atheist?'

'You know quite well that I am.'

'You believe in socialism?'

'That goes without saying,' she concluded fervently; and suddenly began to laugh, from that sense of the absurd which it seemed must be her downfall as a serious person. For Joss was frowning at the laugh, and apparently could see nothing ridiculous in a nineteen-year-old Jewish boy, sprung from an orthodox Jewish family, and an adolescent British girl, if possible even more conventionally bred, agreeing to these simple axioms in the back room of a veld store in a village filled with people to whom every word of this conversation would have the force of a dangerous heresy.

'You sound as if you were asking a catechism,' she explained, giggling irrepressibly.

He frowned again; and at once she felt indignant that he might be surprised because she had made the same intellectual journey he had. 'So what are you going to do about it?' he demanded practically. Also, he sounded aggressive; she was beginning to feel childish and wrong for having laughed; she felt she had hurt him.

'I don't know,' she said, and there was an appeal in it. She raised her eye to his and waited. Because of the look on his face, she at once became conscious of the picture she presented, standing there in front of him, a young girl in a green linen frock that emphasized every line in her body.

'I suppose you are all right,' he conceded slowly, looking at her with approval; and she felt the unfairness of it. This was an intellectual discussion, wasn't it? Why, then, that note in his voice?

Her look at him was now as aggressive as his had been. 'It's all very well for you, you're a man,' she said bitterly, and entirely without coquetry; but he said flippantly, even suggestively, 'It will be all quite well for you too!'

He laughed, hoping she might laugh with him. But she stared at him in dismayed outrage, then muttered, 'Oh, go to hell,' and for the second time left that room, and went out into the glaring sunlight. No sooner had she gone than she understood she had been as touchy and thin-skinned as she had said he was, and almost went back. Pride forbade it; and she went into the village.

The place had a deserted look. Four in the afternoon: the sky was huge and cloudless, the sun loomed swollen through a reddish haze, and the tin roofs reflected a dulled and sombre light. It was likely to rain soon; but now the long brown pond had shrunk within lips of cracked mud to a narrow scummy puddle. Outside the bar stood half a dozen big cars, outside the station about twenty shabbier cars. Among them was the Van Rensbergs'; and they were packed with children of all ages.

What the British referred to as 'the Afrikaans element' had come in for their mail.

Now, it is quite easy to remark the absurdities and contradictions of a country's social system from outside its borders, but very difficult if one has been brought up in it; and for Martha, who must have seen that sight dozens of times before, it was a moment of illumination, perhaps because she was feeling sore and rejected under Joss's treatment of her; and there was something in that bearing and character of those people kin to what she felt.

On mail days there were cars of every degree of wealth, from the enormous American cars of the tobacco farmers down to eccentric creations like the Quests', but the owners of these cars met together without any consciousness of degree. English and Scotch, Welsh and Irish, rich and poor, it was all backslapping and Christian names, a happy family atmosphere which had a touch of hysterical necessity in it, since the mail days, gymkhanas and dances were false tokens of community – for what is a community if not people who share their experience? The fact was, this district was divided into several separate communities, who shared nothing but Christian names, cards at Christmas, and a member of Parliament. The eastern part of the district, all along the flanks and slopes of Jacob's Burg, was where the tobacco families lived, and here the common denominator was wealth; they were regarded by the rest with tolerance, for they went in for bottle parties, divorces, and modern restlessness. North and west of the Quests' farm Scots families were settled, mostly related, hard-working, modest, sociable people who visited a great deal among themselves. Half a dozen Irish inhabited the slopes of the Oxford Range; but this was not a group; one cannot think of the Irish except as picturesque individualists. Near them were five farms where lived a collection of the English eccentrics who reach their richest bloom only in the colonies. Colonel Castairs, for instance, who lived by himself in a ranging stone mansion, sleeping all day and reading all night, preparing himself to write that history of melancholia through the ages which he would one day begin; he was now over seventy. There was Lord Jamie, who walked naked around his farm, and ate only fruit and nuts; and quarrelled bitterly with his wife because she clothed their children, for he held the view that even so much as a diaper on a baby was an insult to God who created Adam and Eve. There was a story that once he had come raking into the village on a great black horse, quite naked, with his wild red beard and his mane of red hair sparking fire in the sunlight, a great rough-cast man, whose fiercely innocent blue eyes stared out from the waving locks of his hair like the eyes of an inquiring savage. He dismounted from his horse, and went into the store to buy a pound of tobacco, a bottle of whisky, and the weekly newspaper; and it seemed that everyone in the store greeted him as casually as if he were as decently dressed as they. Then they began talking about the weather; and so it had never happened again; and the incident retreated into the fabulous past of kaffir wars, and pioneers, and violence. How exciting life must have been then, sighed the people in the district, remembering their distant origins – and yet the district had not been settled much more than thirty years. How wonderful if that wild man on the black horse appeared again in his scandalous glory! How wonderful if Commander Day walked into the store (as he had once, in the golden age) flanked by his two half-tamed leopards, with his three native concubines behind him – but alas, alas, he did not, they did not, the time for the creation of legends was past.

For many years, between this essential group of gentle maniacs and the Quests' farm there had been hundreds of acres of empty ground, considered too poor to farm. On its verge, sharing a boundary with the Quests, were the Van Rensbergs, like the solitary swallow which would one day make a summer; for five years before another Afrikaans family arrived, rocking along the track in a hooded wagon, a vehicle which had, to this district, only literary associations from the Great Trek. Soon there came another family, and then another . . . And now, inside this district whose pattern of living was a large farm and two or three children, with a governess and maybe an assistant, grew up a close-knit, isolated community of Dutch people, who worked fifty and a hundred acres where the British used thousands, and made their farming pay; who bred healthy children, eight and ten to a family; who built their own hall, and a thatched church where they worshipped their angry God. And their speech had the rich cadences of a living religion.

They came to fetch their mail on a day when the village would be empty. Their cars drew up together outside Socrates' store; moved away together to the garage across the railway track; returned together to the station building, one after another in a file, with the slow deliberation that suggested a team of covered wagons.

So it was today. There were eleven cars, standing behind each other; and from them had come enough people to populate a small village, men, women and children, talking, reading mail, playing in groups.

Martha stood on Socrates' veranda among the grain sacks and looked at them, and tried to find what it was which gave these people their look of cohesion. Physically they were strong and broadly built, with the blunt open features of their Dutch ancestry; but the word 'Dutch' surely suggests a picture of fair skin and hair, blue eyes, and easy health? These people tended to be dark, as if the sun had fed a strain of resistance into defenceless light skin and the light hair that becomes dry and limp in the south. The older women wore black – here the colour of respectability, though in other cultures, other contexts, it may be the colour of mourning or sophistication. The younger women wore print frocks that were pretty rather than smart; some of the children wore the flapping sunbonnets of the tradition; the men were in the male uniform of the country, khaki shorts and open-necked shirts. No, the clothing here expressed only a restlessness, a movement, even uncertainty; for if it was true that the pretty sunbonnets could have been seen nowhere else, the little girls' frocks were likely to have been made by a pattern from an English magazine; and if no one but a certain type of Dutchwoman would wear those black lace hats (so that, catching sight of one a hundred yards away, one might imagine the face under it, broad, practical, humorous, earthy), then the black dress she wore with it was probably mass-produced in America.

The closeness of this group expressed itself somewhere else, perhaps in the look of dogged self-sufficiency, the look of the inveterate colonizer; but in that case, they were colonizers in a country which considered itself past the colonizing stage. Not so easy to put flesh and blood on the bones of an intellectual conviction; Martha was remembering with shame the brash and easy way she had said to Joss that she repudiated race prejudice; for the fact was, she could not remember a time when she had not thought of people in terms of groups, nations, or colour of skin first, and as people afterwards. She stood on the veranda of Socrates' store, and looked over the empty dusty space to the railway line, and thought of the different people who passed there: the natives, the nameless and swarming; the Afrikaans, whose very name held the racy poetic quality of their vigorous origins; the British, with their innumerable subgroupings, held together only because they could say, 'this is a British country' – held together by the knowledge of ownership. And each group, community, clan, colour, strove and fought away from the other, in a sickness of dissolution; it was as if the principle of separateness was bred from the very soil, the sky, the driving sun; as if the inchoate vastness of the universe, always insistent in the enormous unshrouded skies, the enormous mountain-girt horizons, so that one might never, not for a moment, forget the inhuman, relentless struggle of soil and water and light, bred a fever of self-assertion in its children like a band of explorers lost in a desert, quarrelling in an ecstasy of fear over their direction, when nothing but a sober mutual trust could save them. Martha could feel the striving forces in her own substance: the effort of imagination needed to destroy the words *black, white, nation, race*, exhausted her, her head ached and her flesh was heavy on her bones. She looked at the Van Rensbergs' car, and thought that she had known them for years, and yet she was reluctant even to cross the dust and greet them. She walked off the veranda and towards the car, smiling rather queerly, for when it was too late to retreat it occurred to her that they might not wish to have their friendship with the Quests so publicly emphasized.

She came to a standstill at the car door, and said good afternoon to Mr Van Rensberg. He nodded at her, and went on reading the newspaper, having made a hunching movement with his shoulder towards the back of the car, where Marnie was sitting between two married sisters who held small babies. There was a young man beside Mr Van Rensberg, who greeted Martha, and she smiled at him hastily, thinking, This must be a cousin; for his face was the family face.

Marnie was smiling with constrained pleasure, and looked uncomfortably at her father's back; and this made Martha wish she had not come. Over his shoulder, she could see the name of the most rabid nationalist journal from the south; while she did not know the language, there was hardly any need to, for the words and phrases of nationalism are the same in any tongue, but the knowledge that the brain behind the close-cropped black head beside her was agreeing with what was bound to be a violent complaint about the very existence of the British made her drop her voice like a guilty person as she said to Marnie, 'Why don't you come over and see me soon?'

'I'd like to, man. I'd like to,' agreed Marnie, in the same low tone, and with another glance at her father. 'Your dress is the tops, Martha,' she added. 'May I have the pattern?'

'Of course,' said Martha, with an involuntary glance at Marnie's matronly body. 'Come over for the day . . .' She had lowered her voice almost to a whisper; the absurdity of it made her angry. She and Marnie quickly said goodbye, smiling at each other like conspirators; she dropped another smile in the direction of the attentive young man in the front seat, and hastily retreated back to the store.

She had no lift home. She would have liked to walk; she intended to, but . . . She imagined that eyes would follow her, queerly, as she set off, on foot, along a road where a dozens cars might be expected to pass that afternoon. *White girls do not* . . . As she was hesitating on the veranda, she saw Joss approaching, and smiled with what was, had she known it, a tenderly amused appreciation of the figure he cut. He wore a respectable dark suit, he carried books under his arm, he moved in a careful, constrained way, eyes watching the direction of his feet, his shoulders a little hunched. He seemed, in fact, already the sober professional man he intended to become; he was altogether out of place among these khaki-clad, open-air people; and knew it, and approved. For these farmers, these men of the soil: when they approached, one saw first the exposed developed limbs, the body; one marked the hard muscled forearm perhaps, or the bronze knotted pillar of the thigh, or the stride, or the swing of the arms; they moved magnificently, at ease, slowly, to match the space and emptiness of the country – no suggestion here of limbs grown cautious and self-contained, against possible undesired contact. Yes, here one stands at a distance from a man, a woman, and sees them whole. First the way of walking, the stance of the body. Then lift your eyes to the face, and the first impression is confirmed: what fine, exposed, frank faces, wholesomely weathered, unafraid, open to every glance. And then (but lastly) the eyes, look straight at the eyes – which of course meet yours with the completest frankness. Nothing to hide here, they say; everything above-board, take it or leave it. But always, behind the friendly brown eyes, the welcoming blue ones, is the uneasiness; something not easily defined. but expressed best, perhaps, in a moment of laughter. The man laughs out loud, an infectious wholehearted laugh; but there is a faint sideways flickering movement of the eyes, the eyes are not altogether there, there is an absence, something blank and empty. Take, for instance, that contingent of fine young colonials marching down the Strand with their English cousins. What fine young men, what physique; a head taller than the rest, bronzed, muscled, strong as horses. Then look at the eyes. But the eyes seem to say, 'What do you want with us? Aren't our bodies enough for you?' There is a pale and fretful look; the soft and luminous darkness that should lie behind the iris is simply not there. Something is missing.

And so it seems that one cannot have it both ways, one has to choose; and Joss chose, without any hesitation.

Martha, watching him approach, was conscious of the most perverse but definite feeling of pity. Why pity? She envied him almost to the point of bitterness, knowing exactly what he wanted, and how to get it. She saw how the compact, neat body, hidden under dark grey flannel, moved carefully across the sunlit, filthy dust, as if every nerve and muscle were connected direct to his will; she saw how his eyes were focused, steady and direct, the whole of himself behind them, so that it was only when one looked into his eyes that one saw him; she saw the great difference there was between Joss and these farmers, and she half envied, half pitied him. Pity? What for? One does not pity a person who knows what it is he chooses and why.

Martha was watching him in a way which would allow

her to pretend, to herself at least, that she was not; she was afraid he might go past her with another of his formal nods. He came straight towards her, however, extended the books, and said brusquely, 'I thought you'd like these.'

'How did you know I was still here?' – with feminine obliquity.

'I can see the store through the trees.'

For a moment Martha was irrationally angry, as if she had been spied upon; then he asked, 'How are you getting home?' and she replied defiantly, 'I'm walking.' It seemed, however, that Joss could see no reason why she should not walk; and after a hesitation he merely said, 'So long!' and walked back across the dust. Martha was disappointed – he might have asked her back to his home, she thought. Then she understood that he was waiting for her to invite herself; and this confused her. She shrugged away the thought of Joss, who always made her feel deficient in proper feeling; and with the parcel of books under her arm, which gave her confidence, she walked away off Socrates' veranda, and along the road home.

She had never made this journey on foot; always by car, or, as a child, perched on top of the hot hairy grain sacks on the wagon. During the first mile she was remembering the creaking sway of the old wagon, which seemed always as if it might spring apart between the dragging weight of the sacks and the forward-heaving oxen; there was a place towards the front of the wagon where it seemed that the tension was localized, and here she liked to sit, shuddering with excitement, because of the groaning timbers under her, which always were on the point of flying asunder, but never did, carrying their burden mile after slow and labouring mile. She was remembering the alarming way the sacks shifted under her; heavy sacks they were, but sliding and subsiding easily with the sway of the vehicle. She remembered the pleasurable warm smell of the cow droppings falling plop, plop in the red dust, and releasing, deliciously, the odours of fresh grass; so that, although the wagon wheels perpetually flung up rivers of red sand, and she travelled in a column of whirling ruddy dust, the sweet perfumes of newly cudded grass mingled with it, mile after mile, as if the four-divided stomachs of the great oxen were filled with nothing but concentrated memories of hours of grazing along the water heavy vleis.

Later, she hesitated outside the McDougall's farm; for if she went in she would be given a wonderful Scotch tea of bannocks and griddle cakes and newly churned butter. But she did not go in, for the McDougalls had not yet noticed that she was now Miss Quest; they still treated her like a child, and this she could not bear.

She walked more slowly now, not wanting the journey to end; she was savouring freedom: the station far behind, where she was convinced everyone remarked her, commented on her; the house not yet in sight, where the mere existence of her parents was like a reminder that she must be wary, ready to resist. Now there was no one to mark her, not a soul in sight; and she dawdled along the track, skipping from one run to another, and pulling from their delicate green sheaths the long sweet-tasting grass stems that are as pleasant to chew along a dusty road as sticks of sugar cane. She was happy because she was, for the moment, quite free; she was sad because before long she would reach home; these two emotions deepened together, and it flashed across her mind that this intense, joyful melancholy was a state of mind she had known in the past and – But at once she dismissed the thought; it passed as lightly as the shadow of a wing of a bird, for she knew that the experience associated with that emotion was not to be courted. One did not lie in wait for it; it was a visitor who came without warning. On the other hand, even the fact that the delicious but fearful expectation had crossed her mind at all was enough to warn it away; the visitor liked the darkness, this Martha knew, and she hastened to think of something else. At the same time, she was thinking that she had associated the experience with what she now, rather scornfully, called her 'religious phase'; and becoming an atheist, which she had done from one day to the next, as easily as dropping a glove, had been painful only because she imagined she must pay the price for intellectual honesty by bidding farewell to this other emotion, this fabulous visitor. It seemed, then, that no such price had been asked of her, it seemed that –

Martha caught herself up, already bad-tempered and irritable: she must *not* analyse, she must not be conscious; and here she was, watching the movements of her mind as if she were observing a machine. She noted, too, that she was walking very fast, quite blind to the beauties of the trees and grass. For it was evening, and very beautiful; a rich watery gold was lighting the dark greens of the foliage, the dark red of the soil, the pale blonde of the grass, to the solemn intensity of the sunset hour. She noted a single white-stemmed tree with its light cloud of glinting leaf rising abruptly from the solid-packed red earth of an anthill, all bathed in a magical sky-reflecting light, and her heart moved painfully in exquisite sadness. She consciously walked more slowly, consciously enjoyed the melancholy; and all at once found herself on a slight rise, where the trees opened across a wide reach of country; and the sight, a new one, caused her to forget everything else. She could see their house, crouched low on the green-shrouded hill, and between was an unbroken stretch of silver-gold mealies; it was perhaps five miles from where she stood to the Van Rensbergs' boundary, a dark belt of trees behind which solemn blue sky rose like a wall. The mealies swayed and whispered, and the light moved over them; a hawk lay motionless on a current of blue air; and the confused and painful delirium stirred in her again, and this time so powerfully she did not fear its passing. The bush lay quiet about her, a bare slope of sunset-tinted grass moving gently with a tiny rustling sound; an invisible violet tree shed gusts of perfume, like a benediction; and she stood quite still, waiting for the moment, which was now inevitable. There was a movement at the corner of her eye, and she turned her head, cautiously, so as not to disturb what was swelling along her nerves, and saw a small buck, which had come from the trees and stood quietly, flicking its tail, a few paces away. She hardly dared to blink. The buck gazed at her, and then turned its head to look into the bush laying its ears forward. A second buck tripped out from the trees, and they both stood watching her; then they walked daintily across the ground, their hooves clicking sharp on the stones, the sun warm on their soft brown hides. They dropped their heads to graze, while their little tails shook from side to side impatiently, with flashes of white.

Suddenly the feeling in Martha deepened, and as it did so she knew she had forgotten, as always, that what she had been waiting for like a revelation was a pain, not a happiness; what she remembered, always, was the exultation and the achievement, what she forgot was this difficult birth into a state of mind which words like *ecstasy*, *illumination*, and so on could not describe, because they suggest joy. Her mind having been formed by poetic literature (and little else), she of course knew that such experiences were common among the religious. But the fact was, so different was 'the moment' from what descriptions of other people's 'moments' led her to believe was common, that it was not until she had come to accept the experience as ordinary and 'incidental to the condition of adolescence' as she put it sourly, and with positive resentment, that it occurred to her. Why, perhaps it is the same thing, after all? But if so, they were liars, liars one and all; and that she could understand, for was it not impossible for her to remember, in between, how terrible an illumination it was?

There was certainly a definite point at which the thing began. It was not; then it was suddenly inescapable, and nothing could have frightened it away. There was a slow integration, during which she, and the little animals, and the moving grasses, and the sunwarmed trees, and the slopes of shivering silvery mealies, and the great dome of blue light overhead, and the stones of earth under her feet, became one, shuddering together in a dissolution of dancing atoms. She felt the rivers under the ground forcing themselves painfully along her veins, swelling them out in an unbearable pressure; her flesh was the earth, and suffered growth like a ferment; and her eyes stared, fixed like the eye of the sun. Not for one second longer (if the terms for time apply) could she have borne it; but then, with a sudden movement forwards and out, the whole process stopped; and *that* was 'the moment' which it was impossible to remember afterwards. For during that space of time (which was timeless) she understood quite finally her smallness, the unimportance of humanity. In her ears was an inchoate grinding, the great wheels of movement, and it was inhuman, like the blundering rocking movement of a bullock cart; and no part of that sound was Martha's voice. Yet she was part of it, reluctantly allowed to participate, though on terms – but what terms? For that moment, while space and time (but these are words, and if she understood anything it was that words, here, were like the sound of a baby crying in a whirlwind) kneaded her flesh, she knew futility; that is, what was futile was her own idea of herself and her place in the chaos of matter. What was demanded of her was that she should accept something quite different; it was as if something new was demanding conception, with her flesh as host; as if it were a necessity, which she must bring herself to accept, that she should allow herself to dissolve and be formed by that necessity. But it did not last; the force desisted, and left her standing on the road, already trying to reach out after 'the moment' so that she might retain its message from the wasting and creating chaos of darkness. Already the thing was sliding backwards, becoming a whole in her mind, instead of a process; the memory was changing, so that it was with nostalgia that she longed 'to try again'.

There had been a challenge that she had refused. But the wave of nostalgia made her angry. She knew it to be a falsity; for it was a longing for something that had never existed, an 'ecstasy', in short. There had been no ecstasy, only difficult knowledge. It was as if a beetle had sung. There should be a new word for *illumination*.

She saw that she was standing off the road in the grass, staring at the two little bucks, who indifferently flicked their tails and grazed their way off into the bush. Martha thought that she had often shot these little creatures, and that she would never do so again, since they had shared the experience with her. And even as she made the decision, she was as helplessly irritable as if she had caught herself out in a lie which was pointless. She felt, above all, irritable; not sad, merely flat and stale; the more because not five minutes after 'the moment' it had arranged itself in her mind as a blissful joy; it was necessary, apparently, to remember the thing as an extremity of happiness.

She walked slowly homewards, taking a short cut along the fence through the mealies. The ground was hard and packed, cracked across with drought under her feet, which ached, for her sandals were meant for show and not for use. She climbed the hill draggingly, and went to her room, so as to compose herself before meeting her parents, or rather, her mother, for to *meet* her father was rather like trying to attract the attention of an irritable spectre.

Alas for visions and decisions. In her bedroom she felt nothing but angry resentment: against the people in the district, against Mr McFarline, against Marnie, who would now 'drop over' and borrow patterns.

Her mother entered with the oil lamp, for it was dusk, and exclaimed, 'My dear, I was worrying, and you don't even tell me you're home.'

'Well, there's no harm done, safe and sound and still a virgin.'

'My *dear* – ' Mrs Quest checked herself, and hung the lamp on the wall. The flame vibrated bluely, then sent a pleasant yellow glow over the uneven plaster, and up to the thatch, where a strand of tarnished silver glistened among shadow. 'How did you get back?' asked Mrs Quest cautiously.

'Walked,' Martha said aggressively; and even felt disappointed because Mrs Quest did not protest.

'Well, come on, we're going to have supper now.'

Martha followed her mother obediently, and suddenly found herself saying, in a bright flippant voice, 'That dirty old man, Mr McFarline, he tried to make love to me.' She

76

looked at her father but he was slowly crumbling his bread in time with his thoughts.

Mrs Quest said hastily, 'Nonsense, you're imagining it, he couldn't have done.'

The suggestion that she was too young for such attentions made Martha say, 'And then he had an attack of conscience, and offered me ten shillings.' She giggled uncomfortably, with another glance at her abstracted father; and Mrs Quest said, 'He knows better, he's too nice.'

'Nice,' said Martha acidly, 'with a compound full of his children.'

Mrs Quest said hastily, with a glance at the servant who was handing vegetables, 'You shouldn't listen to gossip.'

'Everybody knows it, and besides, I heard you saying so to Mrs McDougall.'

'Well, but that doesn't mean – I don't think . . .'

'Damned hypocrisy,' said Martha, 'all this colour-bar non-sense, and Mr McFarline can sleep with whoever he likes and – '

'My dear,' said Mrs Quest, with a desperate look towards the impassive servant, 'do think of what you're saying.'

'Yes, that's all you think of, provided all the lies and ugliness are covered up.'

Mrs Quest raised her voice in anger, and the battle was on; mother and daughter said the things both had said so often before; not even waiting for the other to finish a sentence, until the noise caused Mr Quest to snap out, 'Shut up, both of you.'

They looked at him immediately, and with relief; one might have supposed this was the result they intended. But Mr Quest said no more; after a baffled and exasperated glare, he dropped his eyes and continued to eat.

'You hear what your father says?' demanded Mrs Quest unfairly.

Martha was filled with frightened pain, at this alliance against her; and she exclaimed loudly, 'Anything for peace, you and your Christianity, and then what you do in practice . . .' But almost at once she became ashamed, because of the childishness of what she was saying. But the things we say are usually on a far lower level than what we think; it seemed to Martha that perhaps her chief grievance against her parents was this: that in her exchanges with them she was held down at a level she had long since outgrown, even on this subject, which, to her parents, was the terrifying extreme outpost of her development.

But her remark at least had had the power to pierce her father's defences, for he raised his head and said angrily, 'Well, if we're so rotten, and you haven't time for us, you can leave. Go on,' he shouted, carried away by the emotions his words generated, 'go on, then, get out and leave us in peace.'

Martha caught her breath in horror; on the surface of her mind she was pointing out to herself that her own father was throwing her out of her home – she, a girl of seventeen. Deeper down, however, she recognized this for what it was, an emotional release, which she should ignore. 'Very well,' she said angrily, 'I will leave.' She and her father looked at each other across the breadth of the table – her mother sat in her usual place at the head; and those two pairs of dark and angry eyes stared each other out.

It was Mr Quest who dropped his head and muttered, half-guiltily, 'I simply cannot stand this damned fight, fight, fight!' And he pettishly threw down his napkin. Immediately the servant bent and picked it up, and handed it to his master. 'Thanks,' said Mr Quest automatically, arranging it again across his lap.

'My *dear*,' said Mrs Quest, in a small appealing voice to her husband.

He replied grumblingly, 'Well, fight if you like, but not when I'm around, for God's sake.'

Now they all remained silent; and immediately after the meal Martha went to her bedroom, saying to herself that she would leave home at once, imagining various delightful rescues. The parcel of books lay unopened on her bed. She cut the string and looked at the titles, and her feeling of being let down deepened. They were all on economics. She had wished for books which might explain this confusion of violent feeling she found herself in.

Next day she rose early, and went out with the gun and killed a duiker on the edge of the Big Tobacco Land (where her father had grown tobacco during his season's phase of believing in it). She called a passing native to carry the carcase home to the kitchen which, as it happened, was already full of meat.

But put this way it implies too much purpose. Martha woke early, and could not sleep; she decided to go for a walk because the sunrise was spread so exquisitely across the sky; she took the gun because it was her habit to carry it, though she hardly ever used it; she shot at the buck almost half-heartedly, because it happened to present itself; she was surprised when it fell dead; and when it was dead, it was a pity to waste the meat. The incident was quite different from actually planning the thing, or so she felt; and she thought half-guiltily, Oh, well what does it matter, anyway?

After breakfast she again looked at Joss's books, skimming through them rapidly. They were written by clearly well-meaning people who disliked poverty. Her feeling was, I know this already; which did not only mean that she agreed with any conclusion which proved hopelessly unfair a system which condemned her, Martha Quest, to live on the farm, instead of in London with people she could talk to. She made this joke against herself rather irritably, for she knew it to be half true. What she felt was, Yes, of course poverty is stupid so why say it again? How do you propose to alter all this? And 'all this' meant the farm, the hordes of deprived natives who worked it, the people in the district, who assumed they had every right to live as they did and use the natives as they pleased. The reasonable persuasiveness of the books seemed merely absurd when one thought of violent passions ranged against them. She imagined the author of books like these as a clean, plump, suave gentleman, shut in a firelit study behind drawn curtains, with no sound in his ears but the movement of his own thoughts.

She kept the books a week, and then returned them on a mail day with the postboy. She also sent a note saying: 'I wish you would let me have some books about the emancipation of women.' It was only after the man had left that the request struck her as naïve, a hopeless self-exposure; and she could hardly bear to open the parcel which was sent to her. Inside was the note she had expected: 'I'm glad you have absorbed so much knowledge of economics in three days. What a clever girl you are. I enclose a helpful handbook on sexual problems. I could ask Solly, who has a fine collection of psychology, etc., but alas, he has gone off to "live his own life", and our relations are not such that I could handle his books without asking him.' The enclosed book was Engels' *Origin of the Family*. Martha read it, and agreed with every word of it – or rather, with what she gained from it, which was a confirmation of her belief that the marriages of the district were ridiculous and even sordid, and most of all old-fashioned.

She sat under her tree, hugging her sun-warmed arms, feeling the firm soft flesh with approval, and the sight of her long and shapely legs made her remember the swollen bodies of the pregnant women she had seen, with shuddering anger, as at the sight of a cage designed for herself. Never, never, never, she swore to herself, but with a creeping premonition; and she thought of Solly's books, now out of bounds, because he and Joss so unreasonably insisted on quarrelling; and she thought of Joss, for whom she was feeling a most irrational dislike. At one moment she scorned him because he had dared to treat her like an attractive young female; and the next because he had taken her at her word, and simply offered books; and the confusion hardened into a nervous repulsion: Well, she could do without Joss!

She returned Engels with such a formal note that no further word came from Joss, though she was waiting for one; and then melancholy settled over her, and she wandered around the farm like a girl under a spell of silence.

One morning she came on her father, seated on a log of wood at the edge of a field, watching the natives dig a furrow for storm water. Mr Quest held his pipe between his teeth, and slowly rolled plugs of rich dark tobacco between his palms, while his eyes rested distantly on his labourers.

'Well, old son?' he inquired, as Martha sat beside him; for he might call either his male or his female child 'old son'.

Martha rested the rifle across her knees, pulled herself some chewing grass, and lapsed into his silence; for these two, away from Mrs Quest, were quite easy together.

But she could not maintain it; she had to worry at him for his attention; and soon she began to complain about her mother, while Mr Quest uneasily listened. 'Yes, I daresay,' he agreed, and 'Yes, I suppose you are right'; and with every agreement his face expressed only the wish that she might remove this pressure on him to consider not only her position but his own. But Martha did not desist; and at last the usual irritability crept into his voice, and he said, 'Your mother's a good woman,' and he gave her a look which meant 'Now, that's enough.'

'Good?' said Martha, inviting him to define the word.

'That's all very well,' he said, shifting himself slightly away.

'What do you mean by "good"?' she persisted. 'You know quite well she's – I mean, if goodness is just doing what you want to do, behaving in a conventional way, without thinking, then goodness is easy enough to come by!' Here she flung a stone crossly at the trunk of a tree.

'I don't see where you end, when you start like this,' said Mr Quest, complainingly. For this was by no means the first time this conversation had taken place, and he dreaded it. They were both remembering that first occasion, when he had demanded angrily, 'Well, don't you love your mother, then?' and Martha had burst into peals of angry laughter, saying 'Love? What's love got to do with it? She does exactly as she wants, and says, "Look how I sacrifice myself," she never stops trying to get her own way, and then you talk about love.'

After a long silence, during which Mr Quest slowly slid away into his private thoughts, Martha said defiantly, 'Well,

I don't see it. You just use words and – it's got nothing to do with what actually goes on . . .' She stopped, confused; though what she felt was clear enough; not only that people's motives were not what they imagined them to be, but that they should be made to see the truth.

'Oh Lord, Matty,' said Mr Quest, suddenly bursting into that helpless anger, 'What do you want me to do? The last year has been hell on earth, you never stop bickering.'

'So you want me to go away?' asked Martha pathetically and her heart sang at the idea of it.

'I never said anything of the sort,' said poor Mr Quest, 'you're always so extreme.' Then, after a pause, hopefully: 'It wouldn't be a bad idea, would it? You always say you've out-grown your mother, and I daresay you have.'

Martha waited, and it was with the same hopeful inquiry she had felt with Joss: she was wanting someone to take the responsibility for her; she needed a rescue. Mr Quest should have suggested some practical plan, and at once, very much to his surprise, he would have found an amenable and grateful daughter. Instead, the silence prolonged itself into minutes. He sighed with pleasure, as he looked over the sunlit field, the silent, heat-slowed bush; then he lowered his eyes to his feet, where there were some ants at work in an old piece of wood.

Suddenly he remarked, in a dreamy voice, 'Makes you think, doesn't it, seeing these ants? I wonder how they see us, like God, I shouldn't be surprised? When that soil specialist was out last year, he said ants have a language, and a police force – that sort of thing.'

There was no reply from Martha. At last he shot her an apprehensive glance sideways, and met eyes that were half angry, half amused, but with a persistent criticism that caused him to rise to his feet, saying, 'How about going up to the house and asking for some tea? Weather makes you thirsty.'

And in silence the father and daughter returned to the house on the hill.

Chapter Three

Mrs Quest watched her daughter and husband returning from the fields, with nervous anticipation. The night before, in the dark bedroom, she had demanded that he must speak to Martha, who wouldn't listen to her own mother, she was ruining her future. Mr Quest's cigarette glowed exasperatedly, illuminating his bent and troubled face; and at the sight of that face, Mrs Quest leaned over the edge of the bed towards him, and her voice rose into peevish insistence; for as long as the darkness allowed her to forget her husband's real nature, she spoke with confidence. And what was he expected to say? he demanded. 'Yes, yes, I daresay,' and 'I am quite sure you're right,' and 'Yes, but, May, old girl, surely that's putting it a bit strongly?'

Mrs Quest had lain awake most of the night, framing those angry complaints against him in her mind that she could not say aloud. Since it had always been understood that only bad luck and ill-health had brought the family to such irremediable if picturesque poverty, how could she say now what she thought: For heaven's sake, pull yourself together, and run the farm properly, and then we can send Martha to a good school which will undo the bad effects caused by the Van Rensbergs and the Cohen boys?

She thought of writing to her brother; she even made this decision; then the picture of Martha in a well-regulated suburban London household, attending a school for nice English girls, entered her mind with uncomfortable force. She remembered, too, that Martha was seventeen; and her anger was switched against the girl herself; it was too late, it was much too late, and she knew it. Thoughts of Martha always filled her with such violent and supplicating and angry emotions that she could not sustain them; she began to pray for Martha: please help me to save her, please let her forget her silly ideas, *please let her be like her brother*. Mrs Quest fell asleep, soothed by tender thoughts of her son.

But it seemed that half an hour's angry and urgent pleading last night had after all pricked Alfred into action. There was something in the faces of these two (they were both uncomfortable, and rather flushed) that made her hopeful. She called for tea and arranged herself by the tea table on the veranda, while Martha and Mr Quest fell into chairs, and each reached for a book.

'Well, dear?' asked Mrs Quest at last, looking at them both. Neither heard her. Martha turned a page; Mr Quest was filling his pipe, while his eyes frowningly followed the print on the pages balanced against his knee. The servant brought tea, and Mrs Quest filled the cups.

She handed one to Mr Quest, and asked again, 'Well, dear?'

'Very nice, thank you,' said Mr Quest, without looking up.

Her lips tightened, and as she gave Martha her cup she demanded jealously, 'Had a nice talk?'

'Very nice, thank you,' said Martha vaguely.

Mrs Quest regarded them both, and with a look of conscious but forgiving bitterness. Her husband was half hidden in a cloud of lazy blue smoke. He was the very picture of a hard-working farmer taking his repose. Martha, at first sight, might pass for that marriageable and accomplished daughter it seemed that Mrs Quest, after all, desired. In her bright-yellow linen dress, her face tinted carefully with cosmetics, she appeared twenty. But the dress had grass stains on it, was crumpled, she was smoking hungrily, and her fingers were already stained with nicotine, her rifle was lying carelessly across her lap, and on it was balanced a book which, as Mrs Quest could see, was called *The Decay of the British Empire*. That Martha should be reading this book struck her mother as criticism of herself; she began to think of the hard and disappointing life she had led since she came to the colony; and she lay back in her chair, and onto her broad square, rather masculine face came a look of patient regret; her small blue eyes clouded, and she sighed deeply.

The sigh, it appeared, had the power to reach where her words could not. Both Martha and Mr Quest glanced up, guiltily. Mrs Quest had forgotten them; she was looking through them at some picture of her own; she was leaning her untidy grey head against the mud wall of the house; she was twiddling a lock of that limp grey hair round and round one finger – a mannerism which always stung Mr Quest – while with the other hand she stroked her skirt, in a tired hard, nervous movement which affected Martha like a direct criticism of ingratitude.

'Well, old girl?' demanded Mr Quest, with guilty affection.

She withdrew her eyes from her private vision, and rested them on her husband. 'Well?' she returned, and with a different intonation, dry and ironic, and patient.

Martha saw her parents exchange a look which caused her to rise from her chair, in order to escape. It was a look of such sardonic understanding that she could not bear it, for it filled her with a violent and intolerable pity for them. Also, she thought, How *can* you be so resigned about it? and became fearful for her own future, which she was determined would never include a marriage whose only basis was that ironic mutual pity. Never, never, she vowed; and as she picked up her rifle and was moving towards the steps she heard a car approaching.

'Visitors,' she said warningly; and her parents sighed at the same moment, 'Oh, *Lord*!'

But it was Marnie sitting beside one of her sisters' husbands.

'Oh, Lord,' said Mr Quest again. 'If she's wearing those damned indecent shorts, then . . .' He got up, and hastily escaped.

The car did not come close to the house, but remained waiting on the edge of the small plateau in front. Marnie approached. She was not wearing shorts, but a bright floral dress, with a bunch of flowers and lace at the neck. She was now very fat, almost as large as her mother; and her heavy browned arms and legs came out of the tight dyed crepe like the limbs of an imprisoned Brünhilde. Her hair was crimped into tight ridges around the good-natured housewife's face.

'I haven't come to stay,' she called from a distance, and quickened her steps. Martha waited for her, wishing that her mother also would go away; but Mrs Quest remained watchful above the teacups. So she walked down to meet Marnie, where they might both be out of earshot.

Marnie said hastily, 'Listen, Matty, man, we're having a dance, well, just friends, sort of, and would you like to come. Next Saturday?' she looked apprehensively at Mrs Quest, past Martha's shoulder.

Martha hesitated, and found herself framing excuses; then she agreed rather stiffly, so that Marnie coloured, as if she had been snubbed. Seeing this, Martha, with a pang of self-dislike, said how much she had been longing to dance, that in this district there was nothing to do – even that she was lonely. Her voice, to her own surprise, was emotional; so that she too coloured, as at a self-betrayal.

Marnie's good heart responded at once to what must be an appeal, even a reproach, and she said, 'But Matty, I've been wanting to ask you for ages, really, but I thought that ...' She stumbled over the unsayable truth, which was half a complaint against the snobbish English and half an explanation of her father's attitude. She went on in a rush, falling back into the easy, suggestive raillery: 'If you knew what my brother Billy thinks of you, oh, man! He thinks you're the tops.' She giggled, but Martha's face stopped her.

The two girls, scarlet as poinsettias, were standing in silence, in the most confusing state of goodwill and hostility, when Mrs Quest came down the path. From a distance, they might have been on the point of either striking each other or falling into each other's arms; but as she arrived beside them Martha turned and exclaimed vivaciously, 'I'm going to dance at Marnie's place on Saturday night!'

'That's nice, dear,' she said doubtfully, after a pause.

'It's only just informal, Mrs Quest, nothing grand,' and Marnie squeezed Martha's arm. 'Well, be seeing you, we'll come and fetch you about eight.' She ran off, calling back, 'My mom says Matty can stay the night, if that's all right.' She climbed heavily into the car, sending back beaming smiles and large waves of the hand; and in a moment the car had slid down off the hill into the trees.

'So you're making friends with the Van Rensbergs,' said Mrs Quest reproachfully, as if this confirmed all her worst fears; and a familiar note was struck for both of them when Martha said coldly, 'I thought you and the Van Rensbergs had been *friends* for years?'

'What's all this about Billy?' asked Mrs Quest, trying to disinfect sex, as always, with a humorous teasing voice.

'What about him?' asked Martha, and added, 'He's a very nice boy.' She walked off towards her bedroom in such a state of exaltation that a voice within her was already inquiring, Why are you so happy? For this condition could be maintained only as long as she forgot Billy himself. She had not seen him for two or three years, but it occurred to her that he might have caught sight of her somewhere; for surely he could not have tender memories of their last encounter? Martha, on a hot, wet, steamy afternoon, had spent two hours wriggling on her stomach through the undergrowth to reach a point where she might shoot a big koodoo that was grazing in a corner of the Hundred Acres. Just as she rested the rifle to fire, a shot rang out, the koodoo fell, and Billy Van Rensberg walked out from the tree a few paces away, to stand over the carcase like a conqueror. 'That's my koodoo!' said Martha shrilly. She was covered with red mud, her hair hung lank to her shoulders, her eyes trickled dirty tears. Billy was apologetic but firm, and made things worse by offering her half; for it was not the meat she cared about. He bestrode the carcase, and began stripping off the hide: a brown, shock-headed lad, who occasionally lifted puzzled blue eyes towards this girl who walked around and around him, crying with rage, and insisting, 'It's not fair, it's not fair!' Finally she said, as the hot smell of blood reeked across the sunlight, 'You're no better than a butcher!' With this, she marched away across the red clods of the field, trying to look indifferent. Martha had long since decided that this incident belonged to her childhood, and therefore no longer concerned her; and it made her uncomfortable that Billy might still be remembering it. Altogether the mere idea of Billy aroused in her an altogether remarkable resentment; and she chose not to think of him.

This was on a Wednesday. During the next day or two she could scarcely eat or sleep; she was in a condition of restless expectation that was almost unbearable. The Saturday dance seemed like an entrance into another sort of life, for she was seeing the Van Rensbergs' house magnified, and peopled with youthful beings who had less to do with what was likely than with that vision of legendary cities which occupied so much of her imagination. The Quests were watching, with fearful amazement, a daughter who was no longer silent and critical, but bright-eyed and chattering and nervous: a proper condition for a girl going to her first dance.

Martha was agonized over what to wear, for Marnie, who had been wearing grown-up clothes since she was about thirteen, would of course have evening dresses. Mrs Quest hopefully offered a frilly pink affair which had belonged to a ten-year-old cousin, saying that it came from Harrods, which was a guarantee of good taste. Martha merely laughed, which was what Mrs Quest deserved for she was seeing her daughter as about twelve, with a ribbon in her hair, an Alice-in-Wonderland child, for this vision made the idea of Billy less dangerous. There was a quarrel: Martha began sarcastically to explain why it was that even if she had been twelve she could not have worn this pink frilled georgette to the Van Rensbergs' house, since nice little English girls were not for export. At length, Mrs Quest withdrew, saying bitterly that Martha was only trying to be difficult, that she needn't think they could afford to buy her a new one. She had the pink dress ironed and put on Martha's bed; Martha quickly hid it, for she was really terrified at what the Van

Rensbergs might say if they ever caught sight of that charming, coy, childish frock.

On the Friday morning she telephoned Mr McFarline, and was down at the turn-off waiting for him before nine in the morning.

Mr McFarline drove more slowly than usual to the station. He was nervous of Martha, who had accepted ten shillings from him, like a child, but who was now using him with the calm unscrupulousness of a good-looking woman who takes it for granted that men enjoy being used. She was looking, not at him, but out of the window at the veld; and he asked at last, 'And what's the great attraction at the station?'

'I'm going to buy material for a dress,' she announced.

He could think of no approach after that impersonal statement that might make it possible to joke with her, or even ask her for a kiss; and it occurred to him that the stern young profile, averted from him as if he were not there, was not that of a girl one might kiss. Mr McFarline was made to think, in fact, of his age, which was not usual for him. Two years before, this girl and her brother had come riding on their bicycles, over to his mine, eating chocolate biscuits, and listening to his tales of adventurous living, accepting his generous tips with an equally generous embarrassment. No more than two years ago, he had slapped Martha across the bottom, pulled her hair, and called her his lassie.

He said sentimentally, 'Your father has no luck, but he's got something better than money.'

'What's that?' asked Martha politely.

He was driving along a piece of road that was dust between ruts, on a dangerous slant, and it was not for several seconds that he could turn his eye to her face. She was looking at him direct, with a slow quizzical gleam that made him redden. An outrageous idea occurred to him but he dismissed it at once, not because he was afraid of his neighbours knowing his life, but because Martha was too young to acknowledge that she knew: there was something in her face which made him think of his children in the compound, and even more of their mothers.

With a short, amused laugh, Martha again turned to the window.

He said gruffly, 'It's a fine thing for your father, a daughter like you. When I look at you, lassie, I wish I had married.'

Once again Martha turned to look at him, her eyebrows raised, her mouth most comically twisted. 'Well,' she said, 'you couldn't marry them all, one can see that.'

They had reached the station, and he dragged at the brakes. His heavy, handsome face, with its network of tiny red veins, was now a uniform purple. Martha opened the door, got out and said, very politely, 'Thanks for the lift.' She turned away, then over her shoulder gave him a delightful amused smile, which at once infuriated Mr McFarline and absolved him of guilt. He watched her walk away, in her rather stiff awkward manner, to Socrates' store; and he was swearing, Damn little ... Then he, too, laughed and went off to town in the best of spirits, though at bottom he was very shocked; for when he was drunk he enjoyed thinking of himself as a sinner, and it was in these moods that the local charities were sent such generous cheques.

Martha went into the Greek store. It was empty. Socrates was behind the counter, as usual, reading a murder story. He greeted her as 'Miss Quest', and showed her what materials he had, apologizing for not having anything good enough for such a fine young lady. He was a short, plump man, with black eyes like raisins, and a pale, smooth skin, and a manner of suggesting that Mr Quest owed him a hundred pounds; and Martha said coldly, 'No, I'm afraid you're quite right, you have nothing very attractive, have you?' She walked out, reluctantly, for there was a piece of green figured silk she would have liked to buy.

On the veranda she stood hesitating, before plunging into the glare of that dusty space, where the sunlight lashed up from tin roofs and from the shrinking pond. A dark greasy cloud held light like a vast sponge, for the sun rayed out whitely from behind it, like incandescent swords across the sky. She was thinking apprehensively, I hope he doesn't get angry and send Daddy a bill. She was also thinking, Damned little dago; and checked herself, with guilt, for 'dago' was a word she had outlawed.

She narrowed her eyes to a slit of light, and walked out towards the Cohens' store. She parted the bead curtain with relief, though blindly, and expected her eyes to clear on the sight of Mr Cohen; but it was Joss who stood there, palms down on the counter, like a veritable salesman, waiting for a native to make up his mind over a banjo. This man, seeing a white person enter, moved aside for her, but she saw Joss's eyes on her, and said in kitchen kaffir, 'No, when you've finished.' Joss gave a small approving nod; and she watched the man finger the instrument, and then another, until at last he began counting sixpences and shillings from a piece of dirty cloth that was suspended from his neck. The banjo cost thirty shillings, which was two months' wages to this farm-worker, and when he left, clutching the instrument with a childlike pleasure, she and Joss exchanged looks which left nothing to say. She even felt guilty that she was coming to buy anything so frivolous as an evening frock; and with this feeling was another, an older one: helpless anger that her father's debt of a hundred pounds at Sock's store was more than the farm-worker might earn in the whole of his short life.

Joss said, 'And what can I do for you?' and she watched him pull out the heavy rolls of stuff and stack them along the counter.

'Why are you still here?' she asked, acknowledging to herself that she had come to get some news of him.

'Delay over the sale. Sock's working a pretty point. He knows we're keen to sell out.'

'And so you can't start university. I don't see why you should sacrifice yourself,' she said indignantly.

'My, my, listen to the rebel who never leaves home,' he remarked, raising his eyes to the fly-covered ceiling, while he competently slipped yards of pink cotton from hand to hand.

'That isn't why I don't leave home,' said Martha stiffly, as if he had been accusing her of wrong feelings.

'You don't say,' he said, sarcastically; and then, more gently, when she lifted troubled eyes to his face: 'Why don't you be a brave girl and get into town, and learn a thing or two?'

She hesitated, and her look was appealing; and he said, 'I know you're very young, but you could get into a girls' hostel, or share a flat with someone, couldn't you?'

The idea of a girls' hostel struck Martha before the kindness of his intention, and her eyebrows swiftly rose in derision.

He gave her a look which said plainly, 'What the hell do you want then?' and became impersonal. 'I don't think we have anything suitable, you'd better try Sock, he's got a consignment of new materials.'

'I've been to Sock,' she said plaintively, feeling abandoned.

'Then if he hasn't, we certainly haven't.' He laid his palms downwards again, in the salesman's gesture which annoyed her, like an affectation. But she still waited. Soon he let his hands fall from the counter, and looked at her seriously. He was relenting. 'I'll choose something for you,' he said at last, and looked along the shelves. Martha, thinking of their tasteless back room, was momentarily alarmed, and ashamed of herself for the feeling; but he reached down a roll of white cotton, and said with a rough, unwilling tenderness, which touched her deeply, 'White. Suitable for a young girl.'

She saw at once it would make an attractive dress, and said, 'I'll have six yards.' And now his look seemed to say that she had agreed too quickly; and she fingered the crisp material to please him, while her mind already held a picture of how it would look made up. 'I'm going to dance at the Van Rensbergs',' she remarked, with a confused intention; and his face stiffened, after a quick glance, and he cut the material without speaking.

'Why don't you come and dance with me?' he asked with a challenge.

'Why don't you ask me?' she replied quickly. But there

was no response. He was folding the material, smoothing it in a way which kept her looking at his hands; and at last he tied it and handed it to her with a slightly sardonic bow. 'On the account?' he inquired.

'No, I'm paying.' She handed over the money, and waited for at least a look from him; but he said, 'So long!' and went quickly into the back part of the building, leaving the store quite empty. So she began the hot, wearying walk home, but this time was overtaken by the McDougalls before she had gone more than a few hundred yards.

As soon as she had reached her room, and spread the material on her bed, Mrs Quest entered, saying virtuously, 'Oh my dear, we've been so worried . . .' Then she saw the material, and reddened with anger. 'How dare you waste your father's money when you know we haven't got it and we owe Sock so much money as it is?'

'I paid for it myself,' said Martha sullenly.

'How could you pay for it yourself?'

'There was the money from last Christmas, and the ten shillings Mr McFarline gave me.'

Mrs Quest hesitated, then chose a course and insisted, 'The money wasn't given to you to waste, and in any case . . .'

'In any case, what?' asked Martha coldly.

Again Mrs Quest hesitated; and at last her feelings expressed themselves in a voice that was uncertain with the monstrousness of what she was saying: 'Until you're twenty-one, you've no right to own money, and if we took it to court, the judge would . . . I mean, I mean to say . . .' Martha was quite white, and unable to speak; it was her silence, the bitter condemnation in her eyes, which caused her mother to walk out of the room, saying unhappily: 'Well, at least, I mean, I must speak to your father.'

Martha was exhausted with the violence of what she felt, and it was only the thought that this was midday Friday, and the dress must be ready tomorrow, that enabled her to go on sewing.

At suppertime Mrs Quest was bright and humorous, and

there was an apology in her manner which Martha might have answered; but she was repeating to herself that the incident over the money was something she would never, never forget – it was to join the other incidents chalked up in her memory. Mr Quest ate his meal in peace, gratefully persuading himself that this unusual silence between his womenfolk was one induced by harmony and goodwill.

Immediately after supper Martha went to her room, and soon they heard the whirr of the sewing machine. Mrs Quest, in an agony of curiosity, timidly entered her daughter's room, towards midnight, saying, 'You must go to bed, Matty, I order you.'

Martha did not reply. She was sitting on the bed, surrounded by billowing folds of white. She did not even lift her head. Mrs Quest tugged the curtains across invading moonlight that flung a colder greener light over the warm dull lampshine, and said, 'You'll spoil your eyes.'

'I thought my eyes were already spoiled,' said Martha coldly; and for some reason Mrs Quest was unable to answer what seemed to be an accusation. She left the room, saying ineffectually, 'You must go to bed at once, do you hear me?'

The machine whirred until nearly morning, an unusual undercurrent to the chirping crickets, the call of the owl. Mrs Quest woke her husband to complain that Martha would not obey her; but he said, 'Well, if she wants to make a fool of herself let her,' and turned over in bed with a clanging of the ancient springs. Martha heard both these voices, as she was meant to; and though she had been on the point of going to bed, since the sky was greying the square of the window and she was really very tired, she made a point of working on for another half hour.

She woke late, from a dream that she was wearing her white frock in a vast ballroom hung with glittering chandeliers, the walls draped with thick red crimson; and as she walked towards a group of people who stood rather above the floor, in long fluted gowns, like living statues, she noticed a patch of mud on her skirt and, looking down, saw that all her dress was covered with filth. She turned helplessly for flight, when Marnie and her brother came towards her, bent with laughter, their hands pressed over their mouths, gesturing to her that she must escape before the others, those beautiful and legendary beings at the end of the long hall, should catch sight of her.

She sat up in bed, and saw that the room was filled, not with sunlight, but with a baleful subdued glare reflected from clouds like still mountains. It was nearly midday, and if she was to finish her dress she must hurry. But the thought of it was no longer a pleasure; all the delight had gone from it while she slept. She decided, tiredly, that she would wear an ordinary dress; and it was only because Mrs Quest put her head around the door to say that lunch was ready, and Martha must come at once, that she replied she would not take lunch, she had to finish the dress.

Work on it restored the mood she had lost; and when it began to rain, her exultation was too great to be deepened – these were the first rains of the season; and she sat on the bed clicking her needle through the stiff material, and while overhead the old thatch rustled as the wet soaked in, as if it remembered still, after so many years, how it had swelled and lifted to the rain when it stood rooted and uncut. Soon it was soaked, and the wet poured off the edge of thatch in glittering stalactites, while the grey curtain of rain stood solid behind, so dense that the trees barely twenty paces away glimmered like faint green spectres. It was dark in the room, so Martha lit a candle, which made a small yellow space under the all-drenching blackness; but soon a fresh coloured light grew at the window, and, going to it, Martha saw the grey back of the storm already retreating. The trees were half emerged from the driving mists, and stood clear and full and green, dripping wet from every leaf; the sky immediately overhead was blue and sunlit, while only a few degrees away it was still black and impenetrable. Martha blew out the candle, and put the last stitches in her dress. It was only four in the afternoon, and the hours before she would be fetched seemed unbearable. At last, she went in to supper in her dressing gown; and Mrs Quest said nothing, for there was a dreamy, exalted look on her daughter's face which put her beyond the usual criticisms.

Five minutes before eight o'clock, Martha came from her room, a candle in each hand, with her white dress rustling about her. To say she was composed would be untrue. She was triumphant; and that triumph was directed against her mother, as if she said, You can't do anything about it now, can you? She did not look at Mrs Quest at all, but passed her steadily, her naked brown shoulders slightly tensed. Nor did her pose loosen, or she stand naturally, until she was before her father, where she waited, her eyes fixed on his face, in a look of painful inquiry. Mr Quest was reading a book printed by a certain society which held that God had personally appointed the British nation to rule the world in His Name, a theory which comforted his sense of justice; and he did not immediately raise his eyes, but contracted his brows in protest as the shadow fell over his book. When he did, he looked startled, and then gazed, in a long silence, at Martha's shoulders, after a quick evasive glance at her demanding, hopeful eyes.

'Well?' she asked breathlessly at last.

'It's very nice,' he remarked flatly, at length.

'Do I look nice, Daddy?' she asked again.

He gave a queer, irritable hunch to his shoulders, as if he disliked a pressure, or distrusted himself. 'Very nice,' he said slowly. And then, suddenly, in an exasperated shout: 'Too damned nice, go away!'

Martha still waited. There was that most familiar division in her: triumph, since this irritation was an acknowledgment that she did in fact look 'nice'; but also alarm, since she was now abandoned to her mother. And Mrs Quest at once came forward and began, 'There you are, Matty, your father knows what is best, you really cannot wear that frock and . . .'

The sound of a car grew on their ears; and Martha said, 'Well, I'm going.' With a last look at her parents, which was mingled with scorn and appeal, she went to the door, carefully holding her skirts. She wanted to weep, an impulse she indignantly denied to herself. For at that moment when

96

she had stood before them, it was in a role which went far beyond her, Martha Quest: it was timeless, and she felt that her mother, as well as her father, must hold in her mind (as she certainly cherished a vision of Martha in bridal gown and veil) another picture of an expectant maiden in dedicated white; it should have been a moment of abnegation, when she must be kissed, approved, and set free. Nothing of this could Martha have put into words, or even allowed herself to feel; but now, in order to regain that freedom where she was not so much herself as a creature buoyed on something that flooded into her as a knowledge that she was moving inescapably through an ancient role, she must leave her parents who destroyed her; so she went out of the door, feeling the mud sink around her slight shoes, and down the path towards a man who came darkly against stars which had been washed by rain into a profusely glittering background to her mood. Martha, who had known Billy Van Rensberg all her childhood, who had been thinking of him during the last half hour with suppressed resentment, as of something she must bypass, an insistent obstacle, found herself now going towards him half fainting with excitement. For she at once told herself this was not Billy; this man, whose face she could clearly see in the bright glow, might be a cousin of some kind, for he had a family likeness.

Martha found herself on the back seat of the car, on his knee, together with five other people, who were so closely packed together it was hard to know whose limbs were whose. Marnie's half-smothered voice greeted her from the front seat. 'Matty, meet – Oh, George, stop it, I've got to do the intros, oh, do stop it. Well, Matty, you'll have to find out who everybody is.' And she stopped in a smother of giggles.

While the car slid greasily down the steep road, and then skidded on its brakes through the mealie-fields, Martha lay stiffly on the strange man's knee, trying to will her heart, which was immediately beneath his hand, to stop beating. His close hold of her seemed to lift her away from the others into an exquisite intimacy that was the natural end of days of waiting; and the others began to sing, 'Horsey, keep your tail up, keep your tail up, keep your tail up'; and she was hurt that he at once joined in, as if this close contact which was so sweet to her was matter-of-fact to him. Martha also began to sing, since it appeared this was expected of her, and heard her uncertain voice slide off key; and at once Marnie said, with satisfaction, 'Matty's shocked!'

'Oh, Matty's all right,' said the strange man, slightly increasing the pressure of his hand, and he laughed. But it was a cautious laugh, and he was holding her carefully, with an exact amount of pressure; and Martha slowly understood that if the intimacy of the young people in this car would have been shocking to Marnie's mother, or at least to her own, it was governed by a set of rigid conventions, one of which was that the girls should giggle and protest. But she had been lifted away into a state of feeling where the singing and the giggles seemed banal; and could only remain silent, with the strange man's cheek against hers, watching the soft bright trees rush past in the moonlight. The others continued to sing, and to call out, 'Georgie, what are you doing to Marnie?' or 'Maggie, don't let Dirk get you down,' and when this attention was turned to Martha and her partner, she understood he was replying for her when he said again, 'Oh, Matty's all right, leave her alone.' She could not have spoken; it seemed the car was rocking her away from everything known into unimaginable experience; and as the lights of her own home sank behind the trees, she watched for the light of the Van Rensbergs' house as of the beacons on a strange coast. The singing and shouting were now a discordant din beneath the low roof of the car; and in their pocket of silence, the man was murmuring into Martha's ear, 'Why didn't you look at me then, why?' With each 'why' he modified his hold of her in a way which she understood must be a divergence from his own code; for his grip became compelling, and his breathing changed; but to Martha the question was expected and delightful, for if he had been looking for her, had she not for him? A glare of light swept across the inside of the car, the man swiftly released her, and they all sat up. The Van Rensbergs' house was in front of them, transfigured by a string of coloured lights across the front of the veranda, and by the moonlit trees that stood about it.

They tumbled out of the car, and nine pairs of eyes stroked Martha up and down. She saw she was the only person in evening dress; but at once Marnie said, in breathless approval, 'You look fine, Matty, can I have the pattern?' She took Martha's arm, and led her away from the others, ignoring the lad with whom she had been in the car. Martha could not help glancing back to see how he took what she felt as a betrayal, for she was dizzy and shocked; but George had already slipped his arm around another girl, and was leading her to the veranda. She looked round for her own partner, feeling that surely he must come forward and claim her from Marnie, but the young man, in a tight uncomfortable suit whose thick texture her fingers knew, and whose appearance had the strangest look of alienation, was bending, with his back to her, over the open engine of the car, reaching down into it with a spanner.

So she went forward with Marnie, on to the wide veranda, which was cleared for dancing. There were about a dozen people waiting. She knew them vaguely by sight, having seen them at the station, and she smiled in the manner of one who has been prevented from achieving friendship by all manner of obstacles. Marnie took her through the veranda and into the room behind, where Mr Van Rensberg was sitting in his shirt sleeves, reading a newspaper beside an oil lamp. He nodded, then raised his head again and stared rudely; and Martha began to feel ashamed, for of course her dress was too elaborate for the occasion; and it was only Marnie's exclamations of delight and admiration that kept her mood from collapsing entirely.

Martha watched her friend rub lipstick on to protruding, smiling lips before the mirror, and waited on one side, for she did not want to see herself in the glass; but as they returned to the veranda she caught sight of herself in a windowpane; she did not know this aloof, dream-logged girl who turned a brooding face under the curve of loose blonde hair; so strange did it seem that she even glanced behind her to see if some other girl stood there in just such another white dress, and noticed her escort standing outside the door to the veranda.

'You're all right,' he said impatiently, as if he had been kept waiting; and an old gramophone began to play from behind a window.

At once the space filled with couples; and Martha, lagging back to watch, to adjust herself, was dismayed by a savage discrepancy between what she had imagined and what was happening; for dancing may mean different things to different people, but surely (or so she felt) it could not mean this. Male and female, belly to belly, they jigged and bounced, in that shallow space between roof and floor of the veranda which projected out into the enormous night, in a good-natured slapdash acceptance of movement, one foot after another, across the floor, as if their minds owned no connection with what their bodies and limbs were doing, while the small tinny music came from the neat black box. It was a very mixed group – that is, it must appear so to an outsider, though Martha felt the partners were chosen according to certain invisible obligations. The one link missing was joy of any kind. The married couples walked themselves cheerfully around; partners of marked family resemblance stuck together as if their very features bound them; the only members of the party who seemed unbound by these invisible fetters were several small girls between nine or ten and fifteen, who danced together, politely adjusting their movements, while their eyes watched the older members of their society with patient envy, as if anticipating what must seem to them a delicious freedom. The women wore ordinary dresses, the young men stiff suits, in which they looked ugly, or the easy khaki of their farmwear, which made them into handsome peasants. Martha was again humiliated because of her dress, though there was no criticism, only detached curiosity, in the glances she received.

She looked instinctively towards her partner for support, feeling that his appreciation would sustain her. And this time she really looked at him, and not at the mental image created by the idea of dancing, of one's 'first dance'. He was a half-grown, lanky youth, with light hair plastered wetly across a low forehead, and the heavy muscles of shoulders and arms – too heavy for the still boyish frame – distorted the neat clerkly suit. He was regarding her with embarrassed pride, while he jerked her loosely around the dancing space, one stride after another, his arms pumping, with a check at each corner so that they might achieve a change of direction. The truth came into her mind, and at the same moment she stammered out, 'I don't know your name', and he at first stretched his mouth into a polite laugh, as at a jest, and then stopped dead, and dropped his arms, and stood staring at her, while his blunt and honest face went crimson.

'What's my name?' he asked; and then, to save them both: 'You've got a funny sense of humour.' Again he held her in a dancing position, while his limbs laboured through the movements dictated by his mind, and they continued self-consciously around the veranda.

'Well, I haven't seen you for so long,' she apologized, and again, even as she spoke, understood that it was he who had sat beside his father at the station; she could not imagine how she had failed to see Billy in this young man.

'Oh, all right, all right,' he muttered; and then suddenly burst out singing, in Afrikaans, which was as good as saying, 'We have nothing to say to each other.'

Others joined in; it was a folk tune, and the small jazzy tune stopped, and someone put on another record. Now all the people on the veranda had arranged themselves quickly into two long lines, facing each other, while they clapped their hands. Martha, who had never seen the old dances, shook her head and fell out, and, as soon as the dancing began, found the spontaneous joy of movement that had been lacking in the other. Everyone enjoyed himself, everyone smiled, and sang; for the few minutes the music lasted, every person on the veranda lost self-consciousness and became part of the larger whole, the group; their faces were relaxed, mindless, their eyes met those of the men and women they must meet and greet in the dance with an easy exchange. It was no longer their responsibility; the responsibility of being one person alone, was taken off them. And soon the music stopped, and the other, newer music, with its wailing complaint, took its place. But Martha had fled, to collect herself, into the kitchen, where Mrs Van Rensberg was arranging the supper.

Marnie ran after her, pulled her aside and said, 'It's all right. I've told him you didn't mean it, you're not stuck-up, you're just shy.'

Martha was resentful that she had been thus discussed, but found herself being pushed forward into Billy's arms, while Marnie patted them both encouragingly, saying, 'That's right, that's the idea, don't take offence, man, the night is yet young.'

Billy held her at arm's length, and gave her troubled but pleading glances; and she chattered brightly, on a note she knew was false. But she felt cold, and nervous. She wished bitterly she had not come; and then that she was better able to adjust herself, and the small tight critical knot in her could dissolve, and she become one with this friendly noisy crowd of people. She set herself to be nice to Billy, and for this he was half grateful, or at least took it as better than nothing. As the night slowly went by, and they made repeated trips to the buffet inside, where there were ranks of bottles of Cape brandy, and ginger beer, another illusory haze formed itself, within which she was able to persuade herself that Billy was the culmination of the last few days of helpless waiting: even, indeed, that the white frock had been made for him.

By midnight the house was filled with singing and laughter and the thin churning gramophone music could be heard only in snatches. The crowd had a confined look; the rooms were too full, and couples continually moved to the veranda steps, laughing and hesitating, because outside the ground was churned to a thick red mud, and the moon shone on the puddles left by the storm. Some made a tentative step down, while the others shouted encouragement; then owned themselves beaten, and went to find a private corner in one of the busy rooms, or in the kitchen, where Mrs Van Rensberg stood, hour after hour, slicing the bread, piling cream and fruit on the cakes. Martha saw Marnie seated on the knee of a strange youth while both talked to Mrs Van Rensberg; and she wished enviously that her own mother might be as tolerant and generous. For while she watched Marnie, as a guide to how she might behave herself, she knew it was impossible for her to do the same: she was not so much shocked as dismayed at the way Marnie was with one young man after another, as if they were interchangeable. She saw, too, that it was not her formal dress but the fact that she was dancing only with Billy that set her apart from the others. Yet she could not have gone with anyone else; it would have driven across the current of feeling which said that Billy – or rather, what he represented – had claimed her for the evening; for alcohol had strengthened the power of that outside force which had first claimed her four days before, at the moment she agreed to go to the dance. She was not herself, she was obedient to that force, which wore Billy's form and features; and to the others it seemed as if she was as helpless to move away from him as he was reluctant to let her go. This absorbed couple who moved in a private dream were felt to be upsetting; whichever room they entered was disturbed by them; and at length Mr Van Rensberg broke the spell by arresting Martha as she trailed past him on Billy's arm, by pointing his pipestem at her and saying, 'Hey, Matty, come here a minute.' She faced him, blinking and visibly collecting herself. The soft look on her face disappeared and she became watchful, gazing straight at him.

Mr Van Rensberg was a short, strong, thickset man of about sixty, though his round bristling black head showed not a trace of grey and his weathered face was hardly lined. He wore a dark-red scarf twisted thick around his bull neck, though it was swelteringly hot; and over it the small black, mordant eyes were as watchful as hers.

'So your father lets you come visiting us, hey?' he demanded.

Martha coloured; and half laughed, because of this picture of her father; and after a hesitation she said, consciously winsome and deferential, 'You used to come visiting us, not so long ago.' She checked herself, with a quick glance at the others – for there were several people listening; she feared he might resent this reminder of his long friendship with the Quests.

But he did not take her up on this point. With a kind of deliberate brutality, he lifted his pipestem at her again, and demanded, Did she admit that the English behaved like brutes in the Boer War?

At this, she could not help laughing, it was (to her) such an irrelevance.

'It's not a funny matter to us,' he said roughly.

'Nor to me,' said Martha, and then, diffidently: 'It was rather a long time ago, wasn't it?'

'No!' he shouted. Then he quietened, and insisted, 'Nothing has changed. The English are arrogant. They are all rude and arrogant.'

'Yes, I think that's true,' said Martha, knowing it was often true; and then could not prevent herself asking that fatally reasonable question, 'If you dislike us so much, why do you come to a British colony?'

There was a murmur from the listening people. There seemed to be many more people in the room than before, they had been crowding in, and Martha found herself thinking how different was this man's position in his household to her father's: the silence was due to him as a spokesman, he was a patriarch in a culture where the feared and dominating father is still key to the family group; and Martha felt a twinge of fear, because she understood this was not to be taken as a personal conversation, she was being questioned as a representative. And she did not feel herself to be representative.

Mr Van Rensberg dropped his pipe in dramatic comment, with a nod at the others, and remarked heavily, 'So! So!'

Martha said quickly, with the defensive humour which

she could not prevent, though she knew he found it insulting, 'I don't see why you shouldn't come, why shouldn't you? As far as I am concerned, you're welcome.'

There was a silence, he seemed to be waiting for more; then he said, 'There should be equal rights, there should be rights for both languages.'

Martha was remembering, very ruefully, that other conversation, with Joss. She smiled and said firmly, with considerable courage, considering the nature of her audience, that she believed in equal rights for all people, regardless of race and –

Billy tugged at her from behind, and said in an urgent voice, 'Hey, Matty, come and dance.'

Mr Van Rensberg, who had dismissed the improbable suspicion from his mind as soon as it appeared said, rather taken aback, 'Well, that's all right, then, that's all right.' Afterwards, he would call Martha a hypocrite, like all the English.

On the veranda, Billy called her one to her face, without knowing he was doing so. 'Why don't you learn to speak Afrikaans?' he asked, as if this followed naturally from what he had heard her say.

But to Martha this was narrowing the problem away from its principles, and she said, half flippantly, 'Well, if it's a question of doing justice to majorities, one'd have to learn at least a dozen native languages as well.'

His hand tightened across her back. To him it was as if she put the Afrikaans language on a level with those of the despised kaffirs. It was a moment of hatred; but at last he gave a short, uncomfortable laugh, and bent his head beside hers, closing his eyes to the facts of her personality, wishing to restore this illusory unity. It was late, some of the people had already left, and Martha was dancing in his arms stiffly and unwillingly, frowning over the incident that had just occurred. He felt that dancing would no longer be enough – or rather, that it was too late to wait for the spell to settle over them again. He drew her to the veranda steps. The moon was now standing level with the tops of the trees, the mud of the clearing was glimmering with light. 'Let's go down for a minute,' he said.

'But it's all muddy.'

'Never mind,' he said hastily, and pulled her down.

Once again the wet squelched around her shoe, and she picked her way from ridge to ridge of hardening mud, hanging on Billy's arm, while he steered them both to the side of the house out of sight. She tried to hold her skirts clear of the mud, while he pinned her arms down with his, and kissed her. His mouth was hard, and ground her head back. She resented this hard intrusive mouth, even while from outside – always from outside – came the other pressure, which demanded that he should simply lift her and carry her off like booty – but to where? The red mud under the bushes? She pushed aside this practical and desecrating thought, and softened to the kiss; then she felt a clumsy and unpractised hand creeping down her thigh, and she jerked away, saying in a voice that annoyed her, because of its indignant coldness: 'Stop it!'

'Sorry,' he said at once, and let her go, with a humility that made her loathe him.

She walked away in front, leaving him to follow as he wished, and walked confusedly up the steps, because the few couples that were watching them with derisive smiles, and none of the communal teasing that had been drawn by the other couples. Martha saw the eyes drop to her skirt, and looked down, and saw that the hem was dragging heavy wth red mud.

Marnie came running forward, exclaiming, 'But Matty, your lovely dress, you've spoilt it . . .' She clicked over Martha for a moment, then tugged her through the house on her hand, saying, 'Come and wash it off, before it dries.'

Martha went, without so much as a glance at the unfortunate Billy, grateful for Marnie, who thus took her back into the group.

'You'd better take that dress off,' said Marnie. 'You're staying the night, so it doesn't matter.'

'I forgot my suitcase,' said Martha awkwardly, leaving

herself completely in Marnie's hands. For she had forgotten to pack her night things; her imagination had reached no further forward than the dancing and the exaltation.

'Doesn't matter, I'll lend my pyjamas.'

Mrs Van Rensberg came fussing in, pleasant and maternal, saying she would ring Mrs Quest. It seemed that Martha ruining her dress while making love to her son was the most natural thing in the world. She kissed Martha, and said she hoped she would sleep well, and she mustn't worry, everything was all right. The warm and comfortable words made Martha want to cry, and she embraced Mrs Van Rensberg like a child, and like a child allowed herself to be led to her room, and left alone.

It was a larger room built to the back of the house, lit by two tall candles, one on either side of the vast double bed spread with white. The windows were open to the veld, which was already greying to the dawn, and the moon had a pallid, exhausted look. A sheet of silver, inclining at the end of the room, took Martha's attention, and she looked again, and saw it was a mirror. She had never been alone in a room with a full-length mirror before, and she stripped off her clothes and went to stand before it. It was as if she saw a vision of someone not herself; or rather, herself transfigured to the measure of a burningly insistent future. The white naked girl with the high small breasts that leaned forward out of the mirror was like a girl from a legend; she put forward her hands to touch, then as they encountered the cold glass, she saw the naked arms of the girl slowly rise to fold defensively across those breasts. She did not know herself. She left the mirror, and stood at the window for a moment, bitterly criticizing herself for allowing Billy, that impostor, to take possession of her at all, even for an evening, even under another's features.

Next day she took breakfast with the Van Rensbergs, a clan of fifteen, cousins and uncles and aunts, all cheerfully mingled.

She walked home through the bush, carrying the dress in a brown paper bag, and, halfway, took off her shoes for the pleasure of feeling the mud squeeze and mould around her feet. She arrived untidy and flushed and healthy, and Mrs Quest, in a flush of relief, kissed her and said she hoped she had enjoyed herself.

For a few days, Martha suffered a reaction like a dulling of all her nerves. She must be tired, murmured Mrs Quest, over and over again, you must be tired, you must sleep, sleep, sleep. And Martha slept, hypnotized.

Then she came to herself and began to read, hungrily, for some kind of balance. And more and more, what she read seemed remote; or rather, it seemed that through reading she created a self-contained world which had nothing to do with what lay around her; that what she believed was separated from her problems by an invisible wall; or that she was guided by a great marsh light – but no, *that* she could not afford, not for a moment, to accept. But not merely was she continuously being flooded by emotions that came from outside, or so it seemed; continuously other people refused to recognize the roles they themselves had first suggested. When Joss, for instance, or Mr Van Rensberg, posed their catechism, and received answers qualifying her for their respective brotherhoods, surely at that moment some door should have opened, so that she might walk in, a welcomed daughter into that realm of generous and freely exchanged emotion for which she had been born – and not only herself, but every human being; for what she believed had been built for her by the books she read, and those books had been written by citizens of that other country; for how can one feel exiled from something that does not exist?

She felt as if a phase of her life had ended, and that now a new one should begin; and it was about a fortnight after the Van Rensbergs' dance that Joss wrote: 'I heard there was a job going, at the firm of lawyers where my uncles are both partners. I spoke to them about you. Get a lift into town and interview Uncle Jasper. Do it quickly. You must get yourself out of this setup. Yours, Joss.' This was hastily scribbled, as if in a hurry; and there followed a neat and sober postscript: 'If I'm interfering, I'm sorry.'

She wrote back that she would at once apply for the job, and gratefully thanked him. She sent this letter by the cook, so urgent did it seem that he should at once know her reaction.

With Joss's letter in her hand, she walked onto the veranda, and informed her parents, in a hasty way, that she was taking a job in town; and she hardly heard their startled queries. It all seemed so easy now. 'But you can't expect me to stay here for the rest of my life!' she demanded incredulously, just as if she had not been 'here' for two years, apparently as if she considered there could be no possible end to it.

'But why Joss – I mean, if you felt like this, we could ask our friends . . .' protested poor Mrs Quest, helplessly.

She was thinking in terms of the future, something unpleasant to be faced, perhaps, next week; and when she heard that Martha intended to go into town, with Mr McFarline, the very next morning, she said she forbade it. Martha made no reply, and she suddenly announced she was coming into town with her.

'Oh, no, you're not,' said Martha, in the deadly tone of unmistakable hatred which always disarmed Mrs Quest, who had never admitted that hatred inside a family was even possible.

Martha was not in the house that last afternoon, so Mrs Quest went into her bedroom, and looked helplessly around it for some kind of clue to her daughter's state of mind. She found Joss's note, which struck her unpleasantly; she found the soiled white dress, still crushed into the paper bag and already going green with mildew; she looked at the books on the table by the bed, with a feeling that they must be responsible; but they were Shelley and Byron and Tennyson and William Morris; and though she had not read them herself since she was a girl, she thought of them as too respectable to be in any way dangerous.

Martha, in the meantime, was consciously bidding farewell to her childhood. She visited the ant heap where she had knelt in ecstatic prayer during her 'religious phase'; and she walked through the thick scrub to the quartz reef under which a spring came bubbling clear and cold, where she had lain thinking of the stream that must reach the sea hundreds of miles away; she walked through the compound, where she had secretly played with the native children against her mother's orders. She paid a last visit to the big tree. It was all useless; her childhood, it seemed, had already said goodbye to her, nothing had power to move her.

Next day she went to town with Mr McFarline, who tried to impress her with the fact that he had just been elected member of Parliament for one of the city constituencies, but received only an abstracted politeness for his pains. She interviewed Mr Cohen, the uncle, got the job, and found herself a room before nightfall. Her parents expected her home. She sent them a wire saying would they please send on her books and clothes. 'Do not worry, everything fine.'

And a door had closed, finally; and behind it was the farm, and the girl who had been created by it. It no longer concerned her. Finished. She could forget it.

She was a new person, and an extraordinary, magnificent, an altogether *new* life was beginning.

Part Two

The worst of a woman is that she expects you to make love to her, or to pretend to make love to her.

— BARON CORVO

Chapter One

The offices of Robinson, Daniel and Cohen were crushed
into the top floor of a building on Founders' Street, a
thoroughfare which marked the division between that part
of the town built in the 1890s and the centre, which was
modern. From the windows one looked away left over the
low tin roofs and shantylike structures which were now
kaffir stores, Indian stores, and the slum of the coloured
quarter. To the right rose gleaming white buildings fronted
with glass, and at the end of the street was the rambling,
pillared, balconied brown mansion known as McGrath's
Hotel, whose erection was remembered by old inhabitants
as a sign of the triumph of progress: the first modern hotel
in the colony. Founders' Street was narrow and shabby; and
although it was named to commemorate those adventurers
who had come riding over the veld to plant the Union Jack,
regardless of the consequences to themselves or to anybody
else, it was now synonymous in the minds of the present
citizens with dubious boardinghouses and third-rate shops.
This building shared the doubtful quality. On the ground
floor was a large wholesale business, so that as one mounted
the central iron staircase, which spiralled up like an out-
sized corkscrew, it was to look down on a warren of little
offices, each inhabited by a man in shirtsleeves, half buried
in papers, or by a girl with a typewriter; while at the back
was a narrow strip of counter where the 'samples' were
stacked. With what relief did the romantic eye turn to that
counter, past the hive of impersonal offices! For the half-
dozen coloured blankets, the dozen rolls of material, which
surely, from a practical point of view, were as good as

useless, seemed to suggest that the owner, a brother of Mr Cohen upstairs, a cousin of Mr Cohen from the kaffir store, also felt a need to remind himself and others of the physical existence of machinery, textiles, and a thousand other fascinating things which were sold through this office by means of those little bits of paper. Perhaps Mr Cohen, who had made his fortune in another small native store just down the street, regretted those days when he handled beads and bicycles and stuffs, and kept that counter embedded among the desks and filing cabinets as a nostalgic reminder of personal trading, trade as it should be. On the counter were big tinted pictures of shipping, locomotives, the ports of the world. No one seemed to penetrate to it save old Mr Samuel Cohen himself, who might be observed (by someone climbing the iron staircase) handling the blankets and rearranging the pictures.

The first and second floors were let as rooms, and the less said about them, the better. Clients ascending to the sober legal offices above might catch sight of a woman in a dressing-gown hurrying (but aggressively, since she had paid her rent and had the right to it) to the bathroom. At night, working late the partners had been known to telephone the police to quell a brawl or eject an improper person. In fact, this layer of the building was altogether undignified and unsuitable; but, as the partners were waiting to rebuild, everything was allowed to remain. Martha discovered a familiar atmosphere almost at once when she heard Mr Cohen say to a client, 'I must apologize for the surroundings, but we really aren't responsible.' This although the building was owned and controlled by him; because he planned a change, he could not be considered as *really* being here.

On the other hand, the very age of the place gave it dignity. People from older countries might think it strange to describe a building dated 1900 as old; but it had been the first to raise its three storeys above the bungalows and for this it was affectionately remembered, and one entered it with a comforting sense of antiquity – as in Spain one lifts one's eyes from the guidebook murmuring reverently, 'This was first built three centuries before Christ, think of that!' and afterwards poverty and squalor seem merely picturesque.

This, the oldest legal firm in the city, was known as Robinson's on account of the first Mr Robinson, now dead; for the young Mr Robinson gave precedence to both Mr Cohens, and to Mr Daniel when he was there, which was seldom, for he was a member of Parliament, and therefore very busy. But all this became clear to Martha slowly; for she was too confused, to begin with, to understand more than her own position, and even that was not so simple.

The partners each had a small room, reached by squeezing through the main room, which was packed tight with typewriters and filing cabinets and telephones; but though this main room at first sight looked like chaos, holding as it did fifteen women of varying ages, certain divisions soon became apparent. The chief one was that the four senior secretaries sat at one end, with telephones on their desks; but Martha was so ignorant of office routine she did not at first notice this. She arrived on the first morning in a state of keyed desire to show impossible heights of efficiency: arrived half an hour before anyone else, and sat waiting for the demands on her to begin. But the other girls drifted in, talked a little; and then came the partners; and still no one asked her for anything. She was left sitting until a slight, sparrowlike woman, with bright fringed hair and round blue eyes, came past and remarked warningly that she should keep her eyes open and learn the ropes. From which Martha gathered that she had already failed in her first duty, and opened them again from a vision of herself receiving quantities of illegible scrawl and transforming it, as if by magic, into sober and dignified legal documents of the kind Mrs Buss produced from her typewriter. She forced herself to watch what was going on around her.

At lunch hour she stayed at her desk, because she had ten shillings between herself and the end of the month, and told herself it would be good for her figure. She went from typewriter to typewriter to see what kind of work she would be asked to do, and felt dismayed in spite of her large intentions; for these legal documents – no, no, it was as if she, Martha, were being bound and straightened by the formal moribund language of legality.

Just before the others were due back, the door marked 'Mr Jasper Cohen' opened, and he came out, stopping in surprise when he saw her. He laid some documents on Mrs Buss's desk and went back again. Almost at once a buzzer sounded, and then, while she confusedly looked for the right instrument, the door opened again and he said, 'Never mind the telephone. You won't mind my asking – have you any money, Miss Quest?'

For some reason she protested, 'Oh, yes, quite a lot,' and then blushed because it sounded so childish.

He looked at her dubiously, and said, 'Come into my office for a moment,' and she followed him. It was very small; he had to squeeze past the corner of the big desk to the corner he sat in. He told her to sit down.

Mr Jasper Cohen already owned her heart because of a quality one might imagine would make it impossible: he was hideously ugly. No, not hideously: he was fantastically ugly, so ugly the word hardly applied. He was short, he was squat, he was pale; but these were words one might as justly use for Joss, his nephew, or his brother, Max. His body was broad beyond squareness; it had a swelling, humped look. His head enormous; a vast, pale, domed forehead reached to a peak where the hair began, covering a white, damp scalp in faint oily streaks, and breaking above the ears into a black fuzz that seemed to Martha pathetic, like the tender, defenceless fuzz of a baby's head. His face was inordinately broad, a pale, lumpy expanse, with a flat, lumpy nose, wide, mauvish lips, and ears rioting out on either side like scrolls. His hands were equally extraordinary: broad, deep palms puffed themselves into rolls of thick white flesh, ending in short, spatulate fingers almost as broad as long. They were the hands of a grotesque; and as they moved clumsily in a drawer, looking for something, Martha watched them in suspense, wishing she might offer to help him. She longed to do something for him; for this ugly man had something so tender and sweet in his face, together with the stubborn dignity of an afflicted person who intends to make no apologies or claims for something he cannot help, that she was asking herself, What is ugliness? She was asking it indignantly, the protest directed against nature itself; and perhaps for the first time in her life, she wondered with secret gratitude what it would be like to be born plain, born ugly, instead of into, if not the aristocracy, at least the middle classes of good looks.

He at last found what he wanted. It was a roll of notes, and he took five of them, sliding them free of each other with an awkward movement; and said, 'You are only getting a small salary, and so . . .' As Martha hesitated, he continued quickly, 'It was my fault for not remembering you might be short of money, coming in from the farm like that. Besides, you are an old friend of my nephew.' That clinched the thing for him; and Martha took the money, feeling guilty because she had not been a good friend to Joss. She thanked him with emotion, which seemed to upset him, and he said hurriedly, 'In a day or two we'll give you something to do. Just pick up what you can, it must be strange to you if you've never been in an office before.'

The interview was over. She went to the door and, as she opened it, heard him say, 'I shall be pleased if you do not mention this to Mrs Buss. There is no reason why she should know.' She glanced incredulously at him, for he sounded apprehensive; she was even ready to laugh. But he was looking at some papers.

She went out, and met the other Mr Cohen returning. She disliked him as much as she liked his brother. He was ordinary in appearance, smartly commonplace: a neat, pale, respectable Jewish-looking person, in a striped business suit, and his manner was snappy but formal, as if he tried to cover a natural ill-humour by the forms of good feeling. And where his brother swelled and protruded into large shapes, he seemed concerned to give the opposite impression. His hair lay in a smooth black cap; his hands were neatly moving, and weighted on either little finger with a heavy signet ring; his tie lay safely behind a narrow gold chain; a gold watch chain confined his neat little stomach.

Martha returned to her desk as the other girls came in, and spent the afternoon watching them. There was no need to be told (as Mrs Buss made a point of telling her) that this was an easy office to work in. There was no feeling of haste; and if they paused in what they were doing for a chat, or a cigarette, they did not pretend otherwise if one of the partners came through. When Mr Max Cohen entered with work for his secretary, he asked politely, 'Would you mind doing this for me, when you've finished your tea?' And his secretary finished her tea before even looking to see what he had brought her to do. All this was strange to Martha, although she had not known what she must expect. Perhaps she was remembering what her father had said of his days in an office in England, for it was to escape from that office that he had come farming: 'I simply couldn't stick it. Day in and day out, damned routine, and then, thank God, there was the war, and then, after *that*, going back to the office was nothing but purgatory, sitting at a desk like a mouse in a hole.' So it may have been that Martha was unconsciously expecting a purgatory, and had now found this pleasant working place; but of course she had not yet so much as lifted her fingers to the typewriter.

Two incidents occurred that first afternoon. At a table near the door where the clients came in sat a young woman whose task it was to take money from debtors. They came in, one after another, white, black and coloured, to pay off small sums on what they owed. The young woman was strictly impersonal; and because of this, Martha's first impulse towards pity was dulled. But almost immediately after the midday break a shabby woman entered, with a small child on either hand, and began to cry, saying she could not pay what was due and perhaps her creditor would let her off that month? The impersonal young woman argued with her in a warningly low voice, as if to persuade the shabby one to lower hers. But all the typists were watching, and Martha saw they glanced towards Mrs Buss.

Sure enough, it was not very long before the dues collector went to Mrs Buss and said, 'Can you talk to Mr Cohen? You know, she really does have a hard time, and she's having another kid, too.'

Mrs Buss said flatly, 'Well, whose fault is it she has a new kid every year?'

'But – '

'I'm not going to ask Mr Cohen, he'll give in to her again, and anyway she's a fraud – she was drunk in McGrath's last night, I saw her.'

The shabby woman began to cry. 'Let me explain to Mr Cohen, just let me explain,' she pleaded.

Mrs Buss kept her head stoically down over the typewriter and her fingers drummed angrily, until the door behind her opened and Mr Jasper Cohen came out.

'What's all this?' he demanded mildly.

'Nothing,' said Mrs Buss indignantly, 'nothing at all.'

Mr Cohen looked over the listening heads of his staff to the weeping woman.

'Mr Cohen,' she wept, 'Mr Cohen, you've got a good heart, you know I try my best, you can put in a good word for me.'

'You did promise, you know,' said Mr Cohen, and then hastily: 'Very well, don't cry, I'll write to our clients. Make a note of it, Mrs Buss.' And he escaped quickly into his room.

The woman left the office, wiping her eyes, with a triumphant look at Mrs Buss; while Mrs Buss let her hands fall dramatically from her machine, like a pianist at the end of a piece, and exclaimed, 'There, what did I tell you?'

The dues collector looked positively guilty under that blue and accusing stare, and murmured, 'Well, he's got a right to decide.'

'Yes,' said Mrs Buss tragically. 'Yes, and that's what always happens. I do my best to protect him, but ... Well, when we get into the new offices this sort of thing won't happen, believe *me*!' And she lifted her hands to the keys again.

The second incident was similar. Charlie, the office-boy, came round with a tray of tea, and then went to speak to Mrs Buss, while she let those dedicated hands rest on the keys like someone not prepared to be interrupted.

'No,' she said loudly, 'no, Charlie, it's no good.' And she began typing.

Charlie raised his voice over the noise; she typed faster; he cried, 'Madam!'

She stopped suddenly, in a dramatic silence, glared at him, shouted '*No!*' and at once rattled on.

Charlie gave an immense, good-natured shrug, and went out. Immediately, Mrs Buss rested her hands, looked around the office, and demanded breathlessly, 'What do you think of that for cheek?' The girls laughed sympathetically and, it seemed, did not need to be told why it was cheek.

Martha, who was at sea, looked closely at Charlie when he came back to collect the empty cups. He was a tall and handsome young man, with a dark bronze skin, a small toothbrush moustache, and careless eyes. He was whistling a dance tune under his breath.

Mrs Buss watched him over her jigging hands, and then protested sharply, 'Charlie!'

'Yes, madam?' he answered at once, turning to her.

'We know you're a dancing champion, you don't have to whistle like that,' she said, without expecting an answer, for she tore a sheet of paper out of her machine and inserted another without looking at him.

Charlie stopped his muted whistle; and then, with his black and gallant eyes fixed on her, sidled past her towards Mr Cohen's door.

'It's all right, I'll get his cup,' she said firmly, flushed with anger. She glared at him; he looked back with, it seemed, appreciation of the duel, for his eyes were snapping with amusement.

'Charlie,' she said furiously, 'you're not going to ask Mr Cohen for that money!'

'No, madam,' he agreed, and gave a large and fatalistic

shrug. With a humorous look at her, he went out and began a shrill whistle just outside the door.

'Did you ever see anything like it?' asked Mrs Buss, faint with indignation. 'He'd go past *me*, into Mr Cohen's office, and ask for an advance!'

Suddenly Martha asked, 'What does he earn?' and knew at once she should not have asked, or at least not in that tone of voice.

Mrs Buss said aggressively, 'He earns five pounds a month. It's more than he's worth, by about four pounds. Have you ever heard of an office-boy earning that much? Why, even the head cook at McGrath's earns only seven! Mr Cohen's so softhearted . . .' She was overcome by inarticulate indignation, and continued to type like a demon.

Martha reflected uneasily that she herself was to earn twelve pounds ten shillings, and an altogether unreasonable protest was aroused in her; for if she supported the complete equality of all races, then she must applaud this small advance towards it. On the other hand, because of her upbringing, she was shocked. She asked the blonde young woman next to her what Charlie did in the office, and was told that he delivered letters by hand, sent others to the post, made the tea and ran errands for the girls in the office.

'He's a real character, Charlie is,' the girl added good-humouredly.

'Mr Cohen makes a joke. He says, "The two best-dressed men in town are my brother" – that's Max, you know – "and my office-boy."' She looked at Martha to make sure she would laugh, and when Martha did she continued, 'I like Charlie. He's much better than most of the niggers, and that's saying something, isn't it?'

Martha agreed absent-mindedly that it was, while she argued with the voices of her upbringing. She had never heard of a native being paid more than twenty shillings a month. Her father's boss-boy earned twenty, after ten years' service. With half her emotions she commended Mr Cohen for his generosity, both to herself and to Charlie, and with the other she fought down an entirely new fear – new to her,

121

that is: she could not help feeling afraid that the gap between her and Charlie was seven pounds and ten shillings, in hard cash.

At half past four something happened which cannot be described as an incident, since she understood it occurred every day. The girls were covering their typewriters when the door swung open and in came a tall, fair woman, who simply nodded at Mrs Buss and stood waiting. Mrs Buss lifted her telephone receiver.

'Here's our beauty,' muttered the blonde girl to Martha. 'I wouldn't mind her clothes, would you? These Jews always give their wives everything they want.'

Well, of course; what could Mr Cohen's wife be called, if not 'beauty'? But Martha was troubled by something else — that she was not the only female creature prepared to overlook Mr Cohen's appearance. It had never entered her head that there could be a Mrs Cohen; but almost immediately the balance was redressed by a fresh conviction of injustice. Mrs Cohen was not, Martha decided, in the least beautiful; whereas Mr Cohen was — in any sense that mattered. Conventionally, she might be called tall, slim and elegant; Martha preferred to describe her as bony, brassy-haired and over-dressed. She wore a clinging white crepe afternoon suit, a white cap with dangling black plumes, and a great deal of jewellery. The jewellery was sound, but colourful. When Mr Cohen came out in answer to Mrs Buss's call, Martha was still able to feel sorry for him; but she was at once forced to examine this emotion when she understood that all the women around her were feeling the same thing.

'Poor man,' said Mrs Buss calmly, as she came pushing her own narrow hips this way and that around the sharp desks, and pulling on black suede gloves. 'Poor man. Oh, well, it's not my affair.' And she went out, at a discreet distance from her employer and his wife, watching them jealously.

Chapter Two

When Martha arrived in the room she was prepared to call her home, her mother and father were there, and she was angry. She had not expected them for at least a week; it seemed to be monstrously unfair that she had been tormented for years by those terrible preparations for the excursions over a seventy-mile stretch of road, and now, it seemed, there was no more necessity for preparations. Mr and Mrs Quest, like anybody else, had 'come in for the afternoon'. Mr Quest was talking about the Great War with Mrs Gunn, the landlady, when Mrs Quest gave him an opportunity, for she was concerned to get Mrs Gunn to agree that girls were headstrong and unsatisfactory. Martha could hear this talk going on in the back veranda, through the fanlight of her room, which opened on to it. She sulkily refused to join them, but sat on her bed, waiting for what she expected would be a battle.

The room was large, and plainly furnished. The iron bed was low and spread with white, and reminded her of her own. There was simple brown coconut matting on the red cement floor, and a French door opened into a small garden filled with flowers. Beyond the garden lay a main road, and the noise was difficult for a country person who had learned *not* to hear only the din of thunder, the song of the frogs, the chirping crickets. As she sat waiting on her bed, Martha was conscious of strain. She understood that her eardrums, like separate beings, were making difficult and painful movements to armour themselves against the sound of traffic. There was a quivering sensitiveness inside her ears. A big lorry roaring down the tarmac ripped across tender flesh, or so it felt; the *ching-ching* of a bicycle bell came sharply, almost as if it were in the room. She sat listening and painfully attentive, and at the same time marked the progress of the conversation next door. Her father was winning Mrs Gunn's attention; it was becoming a monologue.

'Yes, that was two weeks before Passchendaele,' she heard. 'And I had foreknowledge of it, believe it or not. I wrote to my people, saying I expected to be killed. I felt as if there was a black cloud pressing down on me, as if I was inside a kind of black velvet hood. I was out inspecting the wire – and then the next thing I knew, I was on the hospital ship.'

That these words should be following her still made Martha feel not only resentful but afraid. In spite of herself, even as she isolated each traffic sound in a difficult attempt to assimilate it, even while she looked at the rough and hairy surface of the coconut matting, she was seeing, too, the landscape of devastation, shattered trees, churned and muddy earth, a tangle of barbed wire, with a piece of cloth fluttering from it that had once been part of a man's uniform. She understood that the roar of a starting car outside had become the sound of an approaching shell, and tried to shake herself free of the compulsion. She was weighted with a terrible, tired, dragging feeling, like a doom. It was all so familiar, so horribly familiar, even to the exact words her father would use next, the exact tone of his voice, which was querulous, but nevertheless held a frightening excitement.

When the door opened and her parents came in, Martha rose to meet them with the energy of one prepared to face the extremities of moral and physical persuasion; but all she heard was a grumbling note in Mrs Quest's voice as she said, 'It wasn't polite of you not to come and have tea when you were asked.' It was exactly as she might complain of Martha's rude behaviour to visitors on the farm; and Martha was surprised into silence. 'Well, dear,' continued Mrs Quest, briskly moving around the room as if it were her own, 'I've unpacked your things and arranged them, I don't know whether you've noticed, and I moved the bed, it was in a draught, and you must be careful to sleep a lot.' Noticing the look on Martha's face, she hurried on: 'And now Daddy and I must go back to the farm, we really hadn't time to leave it, but you're such a helpless creature, you look tired, do go to bed early.'

Martha, as usual, pushed away the invading feeling of tiredness and pointed out to herself that her sudden guilt was irrational, since she had not asked them to leave the farm and come in after her. She decided to leave this room at once for another which would be free of her mother's atmosphere and influence.

Mr Quest was standing at the french door, his back to the women. 'Mr Gunn must have been an interesting chap,' he said thoughtfully. 'He was in the Somme country. Must have missed him by two weeks. Get Mrs Gunn to tell you about him some time, Matty, old chap. Died of gas from the war, she says. Pity those War Office blokes never understood that people could be ill because of the war, and it only showed afterwards. He got no compensation, she says. Damned unfair.' He turned himself around, and his face had put on its absorbed, devoted look. He reached for a bottle in the skirts of his bush shirt – he always refused to change from his farm clothes when he came into town – and stood holding it, helplessly looking around. 'A glass?' he asked. Mrs Quest took it from him, measured his dose at the washstand, and he drank it down. 'Well?' he asked irritably, 'it's quite a way back, you know, with our old car.'

'Coming,' said Mrs Quest, guiltily, 'coming.' She moved Martha's things on the dressing table to her own liking, and changed the position of a chair. Then she went across to Martha, who stood stiffly, in nervous hostility, and began patting her shoulders, her hair, her arms, in a series of fussy little pushes, as a bad sculptor might ineffectually push and pat a botched piece of work. 'You look tired,' she murmured, her voice sinking. 'You look tired, you must sleep, you must go to bed early.'

'*May!*' exclaimed Mr Quest irritatedly, and Mrs Quest flew

to join him. Martha watched them drive away, the thatched, rattling, string-bound machine jogging through the modern traffic. People turned and smiled indulgently at this reminder that it was a farming country – even, still, a pioneer country. Martha could not manage a smile. She stood tensely in the middle of the room and decided to leave at once.

Mrs Gunn knocked. The knock, a courtesy to which she was not accustomed, soothed Martha, and she said politely, 'Come in.'

Mrs Gunn was a tall, large-framed woman with abundant loose flesh. She had faded reddish hair, pale, pretty blue eyes, and an air of tired good nature. 'It was nice to speak to your mother,' she said. 'I couldn't help wondering, a young thing like you by yourself.'

Martha was trying to frame words, which would convey, politely, that she was leaving, and that it was no fault of Mrs Gunn that she must. But Mrs Gunn talked on, and she found herself without the courage to say it.

'. . . your mother says you don't eat, and I must make you. I said you were providing for yourself, but I'd do what I could.'

'There's no need, Mrs Van Rens—' Martha stopped, confused. 'I mean, Mrs Gunn. I eat like a horse.'

Mrs Gunn nodded comfortably. 'You look as if you had a head on your shoulders. I told her, girls have sense these days. My Rosie was out and about two years before she married, and I never had to raise my voice to her. The thing is you must keep men in their place, so they know from the start they're not getting something for nothing.'

Martha was ready to be sarcastic at this remark; but Mrs Gunn came over and kissed her, and she was warmed by gratitude into good humour.

'If you want anything, just come to me. I know young things don't want to be nagged at, but think of me like a mother.'

'Thank you, Mrs Van R— Mrs Gunn,' said Martha gratefully, and Mrs Gunn went out.

Martha gazed around the room with as much dislike as if

it had been contaminated. She looked into her drawers, and every crease and fold of her clothing spoke of her mother's will. But she had paid the rent till the end of the month, and she could not afford to move. She flung all the clothes out onto the floor, and then rearranged them to her own taste, though no outsider would have seen any difference; she pushed the bed back to what she imagined had been its old position, but she was unobservant and did not accurately know what that position had been. Having finished, she was very tired; and although it was early, she undressed, and stood by the door and watched the cars go racing past, while their lights spun over her in blotches and streaks of gold, and over the flowers in the garden, touching them into sudden colour. Beyond the garden and the street, there were black shapes of trees against a dim night sky. It was the park. And beyond, the city; but she imagined its delights in terms of what she had read of London and New York. She dreamed of the moment when she would be invited to join these pleasures, while her eyes remained on the trees and she unconsciously compared their shapes with those of the skyline on the farm; and soon it was as if the farm had stretched itself out, like a long and shadowy arm across the night, and at its end, as in the hollow of a large, enfolding palm, Martha stood like a pigmy and safely surveyed her new life. And when she awoke in the morning and saw the sunlight warm and yellow over the coconut matting, she wondered sleepily if the water-cart brakes had given, for it was making such a noise; and she sat up, while the new room rearranged itself about her; and now her ears had been informed by her brain that this was not the water-cart but a delivery van, they began to ache in protest.

At the office that day, she was left to 'keep her eyes open' until after the lunch hour. Then Mr Max Cohen brought her a document to copy. She was so nervous, she had to start afresh three time; and when he came to fetch it, all that had been achieved were the words 'Memorandum of an Agreement of Sale' typed raggedly across the top of the sheet. She shrank under his impatient assurance that it did not matter in the least, and she must take her time. Her fingers were heavy and trembling, and her head was thick. To type two pages of his small neat writing into something clean and pleasant to look at seemed to her, just then, an impossibly difficult task. He went home without coming to her desk again; and she flung a dozen sheets of paper into the wastepaper basket, and decided she would come early next morning and do it before anyone else arrived.

Mrs Buss, on her way out, asked, 'Have you got any certificates?' Martha said no, she had learned to type at home. Mrs Buss said nothing consoling, but merely nodded absent-mindedly, for her eyes were on the elegant Mrs Jasper Cohen.

Martha left the office so humiliated she could hardly see where she was going. She was filled with a violent revulsion against the law and everything connected with it. What she said to herself was, I won't spend the rest of my life typing this stupid jargon.

She stood at the corner of the street, with Mr Jasper Cohen's money – or rather what was left of it – in her handbag, and watched a crowd of carefree young people going into McGrath's Hotel, and felt sick with envy. Then she crossed the street and went into the offices of the *Zambesi News*. She was going to see Mr Spur, an old journalist, whom she had known 'as a child' – that is to say, she had spent a month's holiday with him and his wife about four years before. She was in the building about half an hour, and when she came out her face was hot with embarrassment. It had been so painful she could not bear to remember what had happened. What she must remember was that she had no qualifications whatsoever.

She understood, finally, the extent of the favour Mr Cohen was doing her; and next morning she was at her desk in a very chastened frame of mind. Her eyes were certainly opened, but she had no time to use them, for long before that first document was finished, several more arrived on her desk, and it was lunchtime before she knew it. She was very incompetent. She tried to persuade herself that the papers she sent in, neatly clipped and tied with green tape in the form of the exquisite, faultless documents Mrs Buss turned out with such ease, were satisfactory. Mr Max Cohen received them with a noncommittal glance and a nod; and later Martha saw Mrs Buss doing them again. She was given no more. For a whole day she sat idle at her desk, feeling sick and useless, wishing that she could run away, wondering what would happen.

The fair, plump girl, Miss Maisie Gale, who sat next to her said consolingly, 'Don't lose any sleep over it. Just do what you can get away with, that's my motto.'

Martha was offended, and replied with a stiff smile. Later, she was told to go to Mr Jasper Cohen's office, and she went, while her heart beat painfully.

The ugly man was waiting quietly in his chair. It seemed to Martha that the pale face was paler than ever, and the flat, brownish-mauve lips moved several times before any sound came out. Then he pulled himself together. He settled the ungainly body firmly back in his chair, lifted a pencil with that fat protuberant hand, and said gently, 'Miss Quest, I think we were mistaken in putting you on to skilled work so soon. I thought you said you had learned to type.'

'I thought I had,' said Martha ruefully; and she was conscious that in using that tone she was again trading on the personal relation.

'Well, well, it doesn't matter; it couldn't have been easy, learning by yourself, and I propose you take the following course. Will you go down to the Polytechnic and take lessons in shorthand and typing for a few months, and in the meantime you can work with Miss Gale. You must learn to file too, and it won't be wasted, in the long run.'

Martha eagerly assented, and at the same time registered the fact that working with Miss Gale was beneath her. She was surprised and flattered, for all the women in the office seemed so immeasurably above her, in their self-assurance and skill, that she saw them through a glowing illusion. She understood, too, that Mr Cohen was now about to give her a lesson, very kindly and tactfully, and she must listen carefully.

'You see, Miss Quest, you are very young – you won't mind me saying that, I hope? It is obvious you are intelligent, and – well, if I may put it like this, you're not considering getting married next week, are you?' He was smiling, in the hopeful but uncertain way of a person who finds it hard to make amusing remarks; and Martha quickly laughed, and he gratefully joined in. 'No. Of course not. At eighteen there's plenty of time. You shouldn't marry too quickly. In this country I think there's a tendency – however, that's not my affair. Well, most girls work in an office simply to pass the time until they get married – nothing wrong with that,' he hastened to assure her. 'But my policy – our policy – is, I think, rather unusual: that we do not believe married women make bad workers. Some firms dismiss women as soon as they marry, but you will have noticed that all our senior girls are married.'

Martha saw, with fresh humiliation, that she had been expected to notice things of this sort, and she had not.

'My policy – our policy – is, that there is no reason why girls should not have a good time and work well too, but I would suggest to you that you don't get into the way of some girls we have – oh, they're very useful, and we couldn't do without them, but they seem to think that because they will get married one day, that is all that can reasonably be expected of them.' Here Martha glanced quickly at him; there was a resentful note that could have nothing to do with herself. Again Mr Cohen eased his great body in his chair, fingered the pencil, seemed to be on the point of speaking, and then said abruptly, 'I think that's all. You will forgive me for making these remarks. I feel, we feel – in short, you have undoubted capacities, Miss Quest, and I hope you will use them, for efficient secretaries are rare. Which is remarkable, when you think of it, since most women these days seem to train to be secretaries?' On that query he paused and reflected and then said, 'I hope you don't feel that being a secretary is not a worth-while career?'

Martha assured him that she wanted to be an efficient secretary, even while she felt quite indignant; she felt herself capable of much more. She thanked him, went back to her desk, and once again sat idle. She was waiting for someone to direct her; then she understood she was now expected to direct herself, and went to Mrs Buss, asking for information about the Polytechnic.

Mrs Buss's face cleared into a gratified relief that seemed to Martha offensive; and she took a piece of paper from her desk, with clear directions as to classes and times. Then she delivered herself – with a pause between each, for assent – of the following remarks: 'I'm glad you've got some sense . . . You don't want to get like these girls here, sitting with their eyes on the clock, just waiting till their boy friends fetch them at half past four, and out all night and then so tired next day they just sit yawning . . . There's plenty of work here, believe me, for those with the intention to do it.' And finally, her china-blue eyes fixed on Martha's: 'When you've got someone to work for as good as Mr Cohen, then you work your best?' Martha said yes; but it was not enough. 'I've worked for my living since I was fifteen, and in England till two years ago, and in England girls are expected to be efficient, it's not like here, where they can get married for the asking, and I've never known anyone like Mr Cohen.' Martha said yes; and Mrs Buss insisted challengingly, 'He's got a heart as big as his body,' and this time Martha said yes with real feeling, and she was released.

And now Martha was able to understand – but only since it had been pointed out to her – the real division in this closely packed mass of women. When Miss Gale leaned over and whispered, like a schoolgirl, 'Get off easily?' she replied coldly, 'I'm going to the Polytechnic,' and Miss Gale shrugged and looked indifferently away, like one who does not intend to show she feels her cause has been deserted. But Martha looked away from this group she had been put into with envy and admiration for the four secretaries and for the two accountants who sat side by side over their big ledgers. She intended, in fact, to emulate the skilled; and her eyes, when she regarded the complacent Miss Gale, were scornful. These women had in common not that they were younger, or even more attractive, than the others, but a certain air of tolerance; they were paying fee to something whose necessity they entirely deplored.

After work, Martha walked the hundred yards or so to the Polytechnic, which was further down Founders' Street. It was a low brown building, though now it swarmed with activity; and its front was barricaded by stacked bicycles. Martha, as usual doing nothing by halves, enrolled herself for classes which would take up every evening of her week, and walked home through the park, where the paths already glimmered pale among the darkening trees, her mind filled with visions of herself in Mrs Buss's place, though they were certainly lit by the highly coloured experimental glow that had coloured earlier visions of herself as a painter, a ballet dancer or an opera singer, for like most people of her age and generation she had already tasted every profession, in mind at least.

When she reached her room, she imagined for a moment she had come to the wrong place, for through the light curtains across the french door she could see a shape she did not know. She hesitantly entered at last, and there stood a young man who asked, 'Martha Quest? My mother had a letter from your mother and – ' He stopped, and looked appreciatively at Martha; for until then he had been speaking with a politeness that said quite plainly, 'I'm doing this because I've been told to.'

He was a youth of about twenty. Martha, who had known only the physical, open-air men of the district, and the Cohen boys, who were all she had met of the student type, and her brother, who was a student because it was expected of him, found in Donovan Anderson something quite new. He was a rather tall, broad-framed handsome young man, wearing a sharply-cut light summer suit, and a heavy gold signet ring on one hand. She was not observant, but because of this impression of broad-shouldered masculinity she was instinctively looking for resemblances, and her eyes lingered on the way his shirt front caved inwards under the flowing blue tie; for if Billy or her brother had been wearing that suit it would have bulged out, and the sleeves would have been filled with muscle. Looking upwards from the hollow chest, she received from that correctly arranged healthily sun-burned face – large nose, square jaw, open brow – an altogether incongruous impression of weakness.

He said gracefully, 'We were expecting a nice girl from the wide-open spaces, we heard you were sporting and hunted big game.'

At first Martha started at the 'we'; then she laughed, and averred that she loathed sport of any kind, as if this was a claim to grace in itself.

'That's a relief, because I'm ever such an indoor type, and I was expecting to have to take you to something energetic.'

Martha said spitefully that she was surprised he did as he was ordered; to which he returned a politely appreciative laugh, and said, 'Well, then, I'll take you to the pictures instead. You must come and meet my mamma. It is what both our mammas would expect.'

Martha agreed that she would like to do this, and it was arranged that it would all take place the following evening – which, incidentally, meant that she must postpone her first lesson in shorthand. They informed each other that they insisted on being called respectively Don and Matty. His mamma, said Donovan, called him Donny, but one knew what mammas were. He most elegantly shook her hand, and told her that she must not be late tomorrow, for if there was one thing he could not endure it was being kept waiting by girls. He then took his leave.

Martha wandered around her room in a state of breathless exhilaration, already picturing Donovan as a lover, but in an extraordinarily romantic light, considering the nature of the books she read. The time between the present and tomorrow evening must be lived through; she felt she could not bear it, and just as she had decided she would go to sleep, in order to dispose of as much of it as possible in oblivion, Mrs Gunn knocked and asked anxiously if she would like some supper. Martha refused, because of the anxious note, which automatically stiffened her resistance. Yet she had hardly eaten since she came to town; she had too little money to 'waste on food' – in other words, she was by no means finished with that phase of her life when she was continuously thinking about food, not because she intended to eat any, but because she meant to refuse it. She would think of the next meal due to her according to convention, assess it in terms of flesh, and then nervously pass her hands downwards over her hips, as if stroking their outlines smaller.

Before she went to bed that night, she ironed the dress she intended to wear the following evening. An instinct she did not know she possessed chose it from the point of view of a Donovan, and the same instinct made the downward-stroking movement over hips and thighs appreciative and satisfied. She had slimmed herself during the past two years so that the bones of her pelvis were prominent, and this gave her great pleasure; and she went to bed vowing she must not put on weight.

At the office next day she helped Miss Gale with the filing, and found that she liked her after all; for some reason, there was a flow of sympathy between them, and more than once Mrs Buss looked sharply towards them and they lowered their voices guiltily.

Half past four soon came, and Martha flew home to dress, though Donovan was not expected until six. She annointed and prepared herself with the aid of mirrors large and small, a bathroom next door, and no Mrs Quest likely to interrupt. She bathed, painted her fingernails and – for the first time, and with a delicious sense of sinfulness – her toenails, powdered her body, plucked her eyebrows, which did not need it, and arranged her hair; and all this under the power of that compulsion that seemed to come from outside, as if Donovan's dark and languid eyes were dictating what she must do, even to the way her hair should lie on her shoulders. For the first time, she knew the delight of dressing for a man: her father never noticed what she wore, unless it was pointed out; her brother had not gone beyond the stage of defensive derision, or at least not with her; and a Billy Van Rensberg was likely to approve anything she wore.

But when Donovan arrived and she presented herself to him (still in the power of that outside necessity), he behaved in a way she had never imagined any man might behave. He looked at her, critically narrowed his eyes, and even walked around her thoughtfully, his head rather on one side. She could not resent it, for it was quite impersonal. 'Yes,' he murmured, 'yes, but . . .' He lifted her hair back from her face, studied her anew, then let it fall back, and nodded. To Martha it was an extraordinary sensation, as if he were not only receiving her appearance as an impact, but as if he were, for the moment, herself, and her clothing covered him, and he felt the shape and lines of her dress with the sympathy of his own flesh. It was like being possessed by another personality; it was disturbing, and left her with a faint but pronounced distaste.

Donovan emerged from this prolonged study, saying thoughtfully, 'You know what this dress needs, my dear? What you need is . . .' He went to the wardrobe as if he had been using it for years, flung it open, and searched for something that already existed in his mind. 'You must buy a black patent belt tomorrow,' he announced firmly. 'About an inch and a half wide, with a small, flat buckle.' And he was right, Martha saw that at once. 'You must ask my mamma about clothes,' he continued pleasantly. 'She's very good at them. Now come on, she doesn't like being kept waiting.' And he led the way to his car.

It was a small open car, dark green, shabby but highly polished and when he climbed into the front seat and sat languidly waiting for her to join him, the man and the car instantly became a unit. 'Like it?' he enquired indifferently. 'Got it for twelve pounds ten last month. We junior civil servants must make do on other people's leavings.' Yet he was indifferent because he knew he might be quite satisfied with both himself and the car.

They drove a short way out of town; that is to say, when they had left behind them the avenues of old houses that had been built between 1900 and 1920, there was about half a mile of tree-lined dust track to cover before they came to a signboard which said 'The Wellington Housing Estate'. Here they turned off on to another dust track which would one day be a street between houses, because the foundations of the houses were already lightly sketched, in cement, in the raw-surfaced earth; and piles of red brick lay everywhere.

'We got in early and bought the first lot while it was dirt cheap, but it's already expensive, this is going to be ever such a smart place to live,' Donovan said; and she saw that he was politely pointing out what things she should admire, as he had done over the car. And so it was when they reached the house, the only completed house, which stood like a narrow brick box, spotted with round windows like portholes, and laced with a great deal of scrolled iron-work. 'My mamma thought she would like a Spanish house,' said Donovan, apparently meaning the iron; and again Martha knew she was being instructed.

Inside while they waited for Mrs Anderson, Martha was shown the ground-floor rooms, and found them smart and expensive, as Donovan said they were; and apparently he was satisfied with her response, for her politeness might easily be taken for the same thing as that negligence he was careful to maintain. Now, Martha was adapting herself to Donovan according to that outside pressure which said that she must; and yet this pliability was possible only because something was still informing her, in a small voice but a clear one, that this had nothing to do with her; in fact, it could be said she was so easy and comfortable with him just because of this fundamental indifference.

When they had finally settled in the big drawing room, an incident occurred which was final as far as Martha was concerned. She reached for a book from the big bookcase, to see what kind of people these were, as she always did in a new house, and heard Donovan say, 'Oh, my dear, it's no use looking at the books. We have nothing new in the place.'

Martha left her hand on the book, while she turned her stern, derisive eyes on Donovan as if she could not possibly have heard aright. 'What do you mean, nothing new?' she inquired, in a voice he had not heard from her and was not likely to, or at any rate, not yet.

'My mamma forgot to send to England for the new books. All these are last year's best sellers.'

Martha stared, then a movement of laughter disturbed her face, but at once vanished; she dropped her hand from the book, and in the same movement sank into a chair, in a pose that suggested a compliant willingness to be everything he might wish. And so Mrs Anderson found them when she came sweeping into the room, her hands outstretched so that she might pull Martha to her feet and give her a quick, assessing glance that took in everything, before laying a perfumed cheek against hers, in lieu of the kiss which might disturb her make-up. Then she allowed Martha to fall back on the chair, and turned to her son so that he might kiss her.

She was a tall, large lady, firmly corseted, dressed in black-and-white silk, with waved fair hair and large, white, firm hands whose capability contradicted the rest of her appearance, which aimed at an impression of useless elegance. She placed herself on a low purple satin chair, and her son sat in another, immediately opposite, in a way which showed this was a habit with both of them. They proceeded to tease each other, good-humouredly affectionate, about his lateness that morning for breakfast, about her wasting the whole afternoon at the hairdresser's, about her dress, which, it seemed, was new and expensive. Martha listened, for she was excluded, though they did not mean to be impolite. She understood that this teasing was a way of finding out about each other's movements without direct questioning: for as soon as Mrs Anderson had learned that Donny had not been late for the office, with which girl he had taken lunch, and what cinema he intended to visit with Martha, as soon as Donovan had told her she must go to bed early – 'because old women need a good night's rest' – and had been scolded for his impertinence, she rose and kissed Martha again. Or rather, she made all the preparatory motions towards a kiss and concluded by faintly laying her cheek against Martha's; and asked to be forgiven, for she was going out to dinner, and the young people must amuse themselves. She then asked Donovan to be sure a tray was sent up to his father, who did not feel like taking a proper dinner.

She was moving towards the door, with the voluminous lightness of a sailing ship, her skirts flowing, a scarlet chiffon handkerchief trailing from her hand, when Donovan asked, in a voice that held a grumbling, offended note that Martha had not yet heard, 'Who are you going to dinner with?'

Mrs Anderson paused, her back to them, a stiffened and wary back, and began touching some dark-yellow poppies that stood on a low table beside the door. 'No one you know, dear,' she replied cautiously, but with an unmistakably warning note. The scarf caught and dragged out a poppy, so that it lay in a pool of water on the polished table. Martha, who was watching, though Donovan could not since his face was sullenly averted, saw Mrs Anderson's smooth and handsome face darken with anger. 'Oh, damn,' she muttered crossly, and glanced at her son; and then she hastily wiped away the spilt water with her handkerchief, and stood holding the crumpled ball of stuff delicately between finger and thumb, while a smile slowly spread over her face and she gave Martha a long, amused, but wickedly guilty look; and although Martha did not know what misdemeanour she was being invited to share, she could not help smiling back.

When Donovan saw Martha's smile, he turned to his mother, his eyes accusing. Mrs Anderson came smoothly forward, holding the poppy. She bent over him, and inserted it in his lapel. 'For my little boy,' she murmured, and kissed the top of his head. Then she ruffled the carefully arranged hair with the tip of a long, firm finger, so that a lock of hair stood up, giving Donovan a ridiculous look. 'He looks so beautiful,' she said. Again, her tongue caught between her teeth, she smiled wickedly at Martha, allowed her eyes to return towards the accusing ones that were fixed on her, and suddenly flushed. 'I'm late,' she said firmly, and hurried out, her skirts disturbing the flowers for the second time as she passed them.

Donovan lay stiffly in his chair, frowning, smoothing back

138

his hair with his manicured hand. Martha was astounded when he at last spoke, for this self-possessed man sounded like a deserted little boy, his voice shrill and complaining. 'She's out every night, and Father has to lump it. God knows what he does with himself all the time, reading in his room – ' He stopped himself, leaped to his feet, and said, in a normal tone, 'Well, let's go and see what my erring mamma has left us to eat.'

They sat at opposite ends of a long dining table, served by a native in the conventional uniform: red fez, white starched tunic, an impassive face. This man brought in a tray for Donovan to examine. There was nothing on it but some bread, a boiled egg and a lump of quivering green jelly.

'My father has ulcers,' announced Donovan, as if this was a personal affront to himself. 'Take it away,' he said, waving his hand at the servant; then: 'No, wait.' The tray was returned for Donovan's inspection; and with a slow, wicked smile very like his mother's, he took the yellow poppy from his lapel, tucked it into the napkin ring, and waved the tray away for a second time. 'Well,' he said, with grumbling grace, 'you have a glimpse of the home life of the Andersons.'

But he looked at Martha challengingly, and Martha could not immediately meet the challenge. She was sorry for Donovan, but elderly ladies (she must be at least fifty) with the wayward charm of Mrs Anderson had never come her way before. Also, the word 'ulcers' had struck a deeper chord than she liked. At last she sighed and said, 'Yes, it's all very difficult, isn't it?' But this was too strong a note, and he began to defend his mother and explain what a terrible life of it she led with Mr Anderson.

When the meal was finished, he said, 'And now we must hurry. I suppose I should take you to meet my papa? But no, you don't want to meet him, do you.'

Martha therefore followed him to the car; and during the weeks she was to visit this house, she saw the old gentleman no more than half a dozen times. He had been an important civil servant – something to do with finance, Donovan airly explained. If he came down to a meal, he sat silent, as Martha was accustomed to see a father behave, while Donovan and his mother kept up a lively conversation. In the drawing room he never appeared at all; there sat mother and son, on the low purple satin chairs, flirting, chattering, teasing, and always with a watchful look in their eyes. Martha was as relieved as they when he chose not to descend from his room, for a nerve in her, sensitized long before its proper time, predisposed her uncomfortably to watch Mr Anderson, that morose, silent gentleman, rather like a dapper little monkey in his careful clothes – but an old and misanthropic monkey; she looked from him to the charming young man, his son, and wondered how soon the shrill and complaining strand in his character would strengthen until he too became like his father, a bad-tempered but erudite hermit among his books – but no, that transformation was impossible to imagine. And where did Martha gain the idea that Mr Anderson was erudite? Simply from the fact that he spent his time reading. She had an altogether romantic picture of him, and the background of that picture was the wall of a library, sober with dark, leather-bound volumes.

One afternoon Martha came into the house to find it empty, and climbed the stairs to Mr Anderson's room, aided by the self-possession of an attractive girl accustomed to find herself welcomed, and opened the door and went in – but she was not to be allowed into his room under any such passport. Mr Anderson was reading in a big chair by a window which framed a view of veld crossed and recrossed by telephone wires. When he demanded gruffly what she wanted, she instinctively switched off the charming manner, sat down, and asked him about his book, confident that *that* was the key. But no, he thankfully laid the book aside. She saw it was called *Three Days to the Moon*, and on the cover was a picture of something that looked like a bomb with a window in it, through which peered a man and a girl, both half naked. Beside his chair were stacked dozens of similar books. On the table, however, were blue books, reports and newspaper clippings; and she understood at last where his heart was, when he began to talk of a recent Government commission on population, and as abruptly stopped himself with the bitter comment, 'However, at sixty it seems I'm too old to take an intelligent interest.'

Rather nervously, she mentioned Donovan; and Mr Anderson appeared to be dismissing both of them when he said gruffly, 'Of course, I suppose you find this sort of thing dull. But at his age ... However, nowadays it seems sex is enough.' She was embarrassed, but not for the reason he imagined.

There were voices and laughter downstairs, and she got up and thanked him (automatically 'charming' again, under the invisible influence of mother and son, whom she was to join) for entertaining her.

'Well, well,' Mr Anderson said forbearingly, and picked up his science fiction again. She left him, with a pang for that window and its view of the sun-soaked grasses; and another, much deeper one, of fear that at sixty a window, some tedious reports and bad novels were all that one could reasonably expect to enjoy.

But on that first evening, her idea of Mr Anderson was crystallized by an invalid's tray, with a crumpled yellow poppy stuck into a silver napkin ring.

When Martha asked what film they were going to see, Donovan replied that he always went to the Regal, in his manner of pointing out something she must copy. She was still silent, trying to approve this way of choosing one's entertainment, when they arrived. The Regal was a large, shabby building in the centre of town, decorated to surface splendour with coloured lights and posters of film stars. As they walked towards it, Donovan took Martha's arm, and she looked instinctively to see why, for this was not the sort of gesture one associated with him. She found they were progressing slowly through groups of people whom Donovan was greeting, and when she examined them she felt his obvious pleasure and excitement affect her: the pavement was a dull city pavement, the posters on the wall were garish, but the place was transformed into something very like one of her private dreams. Everyone was young, throngs of young men and girls were everywhere, and they all knew each other, or so it seemed; for as she and Donovan slowly pressed their way through, she found herself introduced to faces who smiled through a blur of excitement, she found herself shaking dozens of hands; and as they left the crowded foyer and climbed the staircase, she heard him say, 'Well, you're a great success, Matty, they were all wanting to see the new girl come to town.'

She was startled, and glanced back to see this crowd under the new light of a unifying 'they', and saw that she was being watched by what seemed to be dozens of pairs of eyes. Straightening herself and tossing her hair back, she climbed onwards, still supported by Donovan's arm, which, however, withdrew itself the moment the crowd was left behind.

He said again, with his self-satisfied note, 'There, now, you've made your début.'

Martha was resentful; or rather, a small critical nerve in Martha was struck unpleasantly. At the same time, excitement was flooding into her at the idea that she was being displayed; and this confusion of feeling persisted while they entered the cinema and once again Donovan began waving and calling to innumerable people. She was prepared to become absorbed by the film, for this was the first she had seen, apart from the few shown at school; but it soon became clear that seeing the film was the least of the reasons which brought Donovan to the cinema. While it was running, he talked to her and to the people behind him; in fact, there was a continuous murmur of talk, and when someone shouted 'Hush!' it hushed only for a moment.

At the interval, Martha ate ice cream in the foyer with a group of young people to whom, it seemed, she had already been introduced; for they called her Matty, and knew not only where she worked but where she lived; and one youth asked if he might pick her up at Mrs Gunn's the following evening, only to be informed curtly by Donovan that she was already engaged. Martha was annoyed. As they returned to their seats, he said, 'You don't want to get mixed up in that Sports Club crowd, my dear, they're not in our line.'

After the film was over, Martha found herself going into McGrath's together, it seemed, with everyone who had been at the cinema. McGrath's lounge was a vast brownish room, with a beige ceiling of heavy plaster divided into squares, like a mammoth slab of staling chocolate, which had been further moulded to form superimposed circles and scrolls and shells and flowers, and finally swabbed with pailfuls of gilt. The walls were also sculptured and panelled and made to glitter with gold. The room was divided down the centre with heavy fluted and gilded columns. But the floor of this old-fashioned room was crowded with slender black glass tables and chromium chairs, and these were crowded with young people. After some minutes, Martha realized that a band was playing, and on a platform decorated like an altar with flowers and statuary she saw half a dozen black-coated men making the movements of those who create music; and straining her ears, she heard the ground rhythm of a waltz. The musicians were talking and laughing with each other as they played, and with the people at the tables under the platform; the waiters who hurried through the crowd carrying trays laden with glass mugs of beer smiled when they were hailed by their Christian names. It all had the atmosphere of a festival, and Martha found herself transported into delight, and forgot her resentment, and sat by Donovan drinking beer and eating peanuts and talking to the people around her so animatedly that she was not at first aware of Donovan's silence. When she looked around, he appeared sulky, and as soon as their beer was finished he refused to join in another round, and said, 'Matty and I must be going.' There were humorous groans from the young men; and Martha was astounded and infuriated to hear them calling out to the dignified Donovan, as he walked with her to the door, 'Oy-oy! Spoilsport! Meany!'

On the pavement he said gruffly, 'Don't take any notice.' But he was certainly pleased; and that pleasure offended her; and she could not help glancing back to where the light spilled from the great columned door, with the music and the sound of laughter and young voices. They were singing now, inside; and unaccountably her eyes filled with tears. It seemed as if she were being snatched away from her birthright before she had even stretched out her hands to take it.

Donovan strolled beside her to the car, and said, 'Well, it's quite early, what shall we do? Of course, we'll follow the custom. You haven't been up the kopje, have you? That's where all we boys and girls go, to look at the lights and hold hands.' He was now light and careless again; and they found the shabby but correct little car and drove away downtown, through the slums and kaffir stores, until a low hill rose before them. They spiralled slowly up it; and near the top there was a flat space, filled with parked cars, lightless and apparently deserted. Donovan at once got out and led her to the edge of the flat space. For a moment Martha felt herself carried away, for it was with a violent mingling of fear and delight that she struggled with the sensation that she was back home, looking away over the darkened veld, under the stars. But now the great hollow before her was scattered with light – it seemed as if a large hand had flung down stars caught from the sweep of the Milky Way over her head, to mark the streets and houses of the little town. At her feet rustled the veld grass, and the scent of the violet tree swept across her face. But Donovan said, 'And so here we are, we must admire the lights and feel romantic.'

At once she sobered, and listened as he pointed out the compact blur of light which was McGrath's Hotel; an irregular dark space, surrounded by light, which was the park; and away over a blank darkness that seemed to suffuse with an internal glow, to the sparkle which was his own house, where the smart new suburb would soon rise from the veld grasses. What a small town it was, seen thus from above! And its smallness defined in Martha's mind what had till then mazed and confused in streets, parks, suburbs, without limit or direction. They were all here, her experiences of the last few days, shrunk to a neat pattern of light. They were dismayingly shrunk and at once her mind tugged to soar away from Donovan and from the town itself; but he kept pulling her down, pointing out this building and that, once even gaining her willing attention by directing her gaze to a building that stood by itself, so brightly lit that even from here she could make out the tiny black strokes which were the pillars of the veranda.

'The Sports Club,' he said, and she heard the reluctance in his voice. 'I'll take you there when there's a nice dance.' She did not answer, but he continued, 'And while we're about it, I'm booking the Christmas Dance, and the New Year's Dance, and the Show Ball.' He added, grumbling humorously, 'It's disgusting, booking a girl up months ahead, but what can one do, one must pay the penalty for living in the colonies, where there's a woman shortage.'

She laughed and, examining her experiences of that evening, realized that in those crowds there had been far more men than girls; and immediately her heart lifted on a wave of reckless power. She laughed again, and there was an unscrupulous note.

'You'll get spoiled,' said Donovan gloomily. 'You all do. All the same, it does go against the grain to book one's girl up a year in advance.'

It was in this manner that Martha learned she was Donovan's girl; and instinctively she turned towards him, in a moment of swelling gratitude and warmth; she was prepared to accept him in short, as her man, since he had laid that claim on her; but Donovan was standing there, hands in his pockets, staring moodily down at the lights of the town. The moment passed, and she was left feeling blank, rather foolish, and unaccountably tired.

'Well,' he remarked, 'so now we've done the expected. Come on.'

They stumbled back over the stony ground, past a big beacon, a great post stuck into a heap of whitewashed stones. She stopped to look at it, and he said, giggling, 'Just imagine the pioneers climbing all this way to stick the flag on the top of a kopje!'

As they descended, a curve of the hill shifted, slightly,

and she saw below her another expanse of sparsely lit country, though this time there was no neat pattern of streets, only an apparently limitless darkness irregularly marked by small yellow lights, 'The location,' said Donovan indifferently. 'Kaffirtown.' Involuntarily, she stopped. 'The cemetery's this side of it,' he added. 'Come on, do, Matty, it's getting late.' She followed him obediently, with a glance downwards at Kaffirtown. Her social conscience was troubling her, pointing out that she should remonstrate with Donovan; it was also saying that Donovan was an unworthy successor to Joss – she had forgotten Billy altogether by this time. However, follow him she did, for she was intoxicated.

They were now passing the silent and darkened cars, and, as if he was reminded by them of something he should do, he put his arm carelessly about her, and so they went to theirs. At the door of her room, he kissed her lightly on the cheek, which Martha accepted as the seal she was instinctively waiting for.

'And now,' he said firmly,' 'let's fix up.' He took a little book from his pocket and turned so that the light from the street lamp might fall on it. 'Tomorrow evening?' he inquired.

'I'm going to take lessons at the Polytechnic,' she replied uncertainly; and she would have thrown it all up at a word from him.

But no: he said approvingly, 'That's a good girl, we must all get efficient and earn lots of money.' He considered for a moment, and said, 'You must arrange to be finished by seven every evening, otherwise it will be ever such a dull life for both of us. I'm supposed to be studying for some kind of an exam myself. We can fit it in.' He put away his book, waved a cheerful goodbye, and went away to his car, leaving Martha to go to bed if she chose.

But she could not. She was walking, in that familiar dazed and delirious condition, for some hours around her room; it was not until the stars were dimming that she dragged herself unwillingly to bed; and she was late for the office next morning.

146

Maisie was a few minutes later; and, as always, she walked composedly through her already busy companions, pulling off her white beret and smiling in vague goodwill. She lazily settled herself, took off the cover of her typewriter, and lit a cigarette, which she smoked to the end before beginning work. The main filing cabinet was in front of Martha's desk, and as Maisie pulled out the drawers and began sorting files, she said pleasantly to Martha, 'Well, did you have a good time last night?'

'Why – were you there?' asked Martha.

'You didn't see me,' said Maisie, laughing suggestively. 'And you looked through me at McGrath's too.'

'I'm sorry.'

'It's OK.' She laughed again, and said, 'So our Donny-boy's got hold of you, has he?'

This had more than a suggestion of contempt, and Martha replied quickly, 'My mother knew his mother.'

Maisie worked for a few moments in silence, humming under her breath. She wore a tight white linen dress, and as she lifted her arms to slide the drawers the soft bulges of flesh above her petticoat, and the lace of the petticoat itself, showed clear through the thin white. Also, there were large wet patches under her arms, and the tendrils of loose hair on her neck were damp. From time to time she paused, and gazed out of the window in gentle reflection, towards the kopje that rose above the dingy, slumlike streets, while she rested her hand on the edge of a drawer. Those damp patches, and a dust mark on the white skirt, seemed inoffensive, even attractive, on this cheerful slattern whose whole appearance, way of talking and happy-go-lucky movements took their assurance from the life she led outside the office. And when Mrs Buss asked, with indignant politeness, if the filing was finished, she replied, 'It's going along fine,' and gave a calm laugh. Before she sat down she inquired, 'Good-looking young lad our Donny?' and waited for an answer.

Martha assented, though oddly enough she had not thought of Donovan as good-looking; and now she was asking herself why she had not, since of course he was –

now it had been pointed out, she could see it. Could it be that this had something to do with that notion (firmly inculcated in her by her mother, whether she liked it or not) that one loved a man not for his looks, but for what he *was*? Mrs Quest, who believed this, had married an extremely good-looking man – but this was an altogether unsettling line of thought, and Martha's mind refused to follow it; for it grew dim, and she shook her head to clear it.

Maisie said comfortably, 'Well, we've only got one life, that's what I say, so let's enjoy it.' She went back to her desk, where she lit another cigarette.

But Martha had resolved not to smoke in the office, and kept it up for half the morning; and she worked as well as she could for thinking of the evening ahead of her. At half past four she went dutifully to the Polytechnic, and stayed there until Donovan fetched her at seven.

Chapter Three

At the end of a month she found she had passed one examination, and moved to another room in the Polytechnic where she took shorthand from a Mr Skye, a small, dark, restless man who encouraged his pupils by taking it for granted that they would all, and very soon, be doing two hundred words a minute, as he could. This was friendly of him, but not the best method for someone like Martha, who already tended to think too much of an end before she had mastered a beginning. His restlessness fed itself by speeding up his girls; for after reading a long passage (which he must have read a thousand times before) he would say impatiently, 'Now, that's fine. You did that in ten minutes. You did get it, didn't you? Now let's speed it up.' There were good-natured groans, but everyone picked up her dulled pencil and flew after his reading. At the end he came round, glancing rapidly for form's sake over their shoulders, saying, 'Fine, fine, you did get it.' And by this means when Mrs Buss asked her how she was getting along, Martha was able to say that her speed was one hundred and twenty.

'You're a fast worker,' said Mrs Buss unbelievingly, and Martha laughed and said that she was. Mrs Buss spoke to Mr Cohen, and Mr Cohen invited Martha into his office for dictation, which she managed better than he had expected but much worse than she had. So she was now promoted, not to the status of the skilled, but somewhere in between; half her time she spent helping Maisie with the filing and copying, and for the rest did easy letters for Mr Cohen, and even, when Mrs Buss was pressed, some of the more simple

149

documents. She felt an altogether unreasonable astonishment that the work she had put in at the Polytechnic had, in fact, lifted her one degree up the ladder towards efficiency; as if the progress of painfully learning a thing could have nothing to do with her for herself. But it was considered to be only a beginning; she felt it to be a beginning – and yet . . .

The truth was, she was slackening off. She was really tired; and she had every reason to be. Since she had come to town, she had been carried on the same impulse which had first made her take flight from the farm. She had never paused to think where she was going, she was too busy. She woke early for the delight of finding herself alone and no pressure on her but the necessity to be at the office more or less on time. She forced herself to give as much attention to the dry legal stuff as she could, pretending that it did not bore her intolerably. She ate sandwiches at lunchtime, and read alone in the office. After work in the afternoon, she went, most days, to the Polytechnic, was picked up by Donovan and went on with him to a sundowner party, where they ate as many peanuts and snacks as they could, since as Donovan pleasantly but frankly pointed out, they got them for nothing. She was seldom in bed before one or two in the morning. She even woke hungry.

This business of food: how little one should take it for granted! For it might be considered strange that until thirteen or fourteen Martha's appetite was so hearty it was positively embarrassing; and now that hungry and affectionate child had vanished so completely that she could not eat without feeling guilty and promising restitution to herself by giving up the next meal. On the other hand, she would suddenly turn aside into a shop, without even knowing she had intended to, and buy half a dozen slabs of chocolate, which she would eat, secretly, until she was sickened and very alarmed, saying she must be careful, for she would certainly lose her figure if she went on like this. And when her mother sent in parcels of butter, fresh farm cheese, eggs, exactly as she had when Martha was at school, Martha gave them to Mrs Gunn, saying airily that it was a nuisance to have the smell in her room. But for all this, she was putting on weight; for if she did not eat she drank, as everyone did. From the first sundowner, gulped down hastily to give her vitality after the hours of work, she drank steadily through the evening until she arrived back in her room in the small hours, slightly tipsy, if not drunk. She was only doing as everyone else did; and if someone pointed out to her, 'You are living on sandwiches, sundowner snacks and alcohol, you are sleeping three hours a night,' he would probably have got for his pains a dark and uncomprehending stare; for that was not how life felt to Martha; it was a rush of delicious activity, which, however, was just beginning to flag.

It was six weeks or so after she had come to town that Joss walked into the office, in the same dark businessman's suit he had worn in the red dust of the station and behind the counter of the kaffir store; and as he passed through, asked her to come and have tea with him. He was leaving that night for Cape Town, where the university term was just starting. He dismissed Martha's rather embarrassed objections, saying that of course old Uncle Jasper wouldn't mind. He went into his uncle's office.

Maisie said, without envy, 'You've got all sorts of irons in the fire, haven't you?' She was smiling at Martha, while she filed her nails.

But Martha said indignantly, 'I've known Joss for years.'

Maisie nodded. 'I've known marriages come out of boy-and-girl romances before.' She held up her white hand and looked at it critically, flicked a bit of cuticle dust from a shining red nail, and added, 'Of course, romancing with a Jew-boy is one thing, and marrying's another, I can see that.' She glanced up, and her frank blue eyes grew startled: what had she said to earn that deadly and contemptuous stare from Martha? 'It's not my affair, of course,' she said hastily, looking hurt.

Joss returned, saying, 'It's OK.' Martha picked up her bag and followed him out. They went to McGrath's lounge, which in the morning was filled with shopping women. The band played, the palms quivered as the great doors unceasingly swung; and Martha ordered beer, from habit, when asked what she would have. Joss had been going to have tea, but ordered beer, and then looked straight at her and demanded, 'What's the matter with you? Don't tell me my uncle is working you too hard? You look like something the cat's brought in.'

She did not have to mind this, for he looked concerned and affectionate. She said, laughing, 'Your uncle's an angel. He's the sweetest thing that ever lived.'

He drank his beer and regarded her, half with admiration and half critically. Martha knew this criticism was of the new skilled vivacity which was part of her equipment, as girl about town; she had not learned it, it had offered itself to her, together with a new vocabulary and the ability to drink all night without showing it unpleasantly.

'You look to me as if you could do with some sleep,' he remarked.

'I could,' she laughed. 'I'm exhausted. You've no idea how exhausting life is.'

She chatted on and he listened, nodding from time to time; and when she paused, thinking it was his turn to be self-revealing, he replied to the real sense of what she had said: 'So now you've got all the boys queuing up, eh?'

She coloured, because now she could see she had been boasting, and he went on:

'It's all very well, Martha Quest, but – ' He stopped, looking annoyed, and added, 'It's nothing to do with me.'

She wanted it to be his affair, and said 'Go on.'

'Who's the boy friend?' he asked bluntly.

'I haven't got one,' she said quickly; and it was true, for, sitting with Joss, the sober, the responsible, the intelligent and manly Joss, how could she own to Donovan?

'Good,' he said simply, without impertinence or self-interest. 'You'd better be careful, Martha. After all, if you wanted to get married, you could have stayed on the farm.'

'But I'm not getting married,' she laughed; and he said

quietly, 'That's the ticket,' and looked at his watch. 'I've got to pack. My mother's busy settling in the new house. They've bought a plot in a new suburb called Wellington or something like that, but in the meantime they've got something temporary. Our store has got "Sock's Kaffir Emporium" written over it now,' he ended, looking at her so that she might share his regret and amusement, which she did.

'I wish you weren't going away,' she said impulsively, holding out her hand; and he took it and squeezed it before replacing it gently in her lap, as if rebuking her for being careless with it. 'When are you coming back? Are you going to work with your uncles when you've finished university? Will you be away long?' she chattered, in an effort to keep him.

'My uncles want me, but I want to go overseas,' he said.

'Ah, *yes*,' she breathed out, and with such envy that he glanced quickly at her and said gently, 'Never mind, your turn will come.' She found her eyes swimming; it seemed to her, just then, that Joss was the only person she had ever known who knew exactly how she felt, with whom she might behave as she liked – *and get away with it*, a critical voice added inside her.

He came with her to the door of the office. 'And how does my Uncle Jasper strike you?' he asked.

'He's very nice,' she said, but he pointed out impatiently, 'Surely you can see he's very ill?'

'I didn't know.'

He gave her a rather irritated look. 'My cousin's business isn't helping much – though of course Abe was right to go.'

She looked at him helplessly.

'Surely you know about my cousin?'

'No one ever mentioned him,' she excused herself.

'My Cousin Abraham went off to Spain last year, and no one's heard a word from him for months.'

'The Spanish Civil War?' she asked doubtfully.

Again that look. 'What's the matter with you? A bit out of touch, aren't you?' She nodded guiltily. 'Well, my aunt treats my Uncle Jasper as if it was all his fault. And it is, too – *her* son would never have the guts or intelligence to know one side of the Spanish business from the other . . .' Here Martha looked down, blushing. 'But Uncle Jasper may be a slow old man, but he's all right. And Abe's all right too,' he concluded, and sounded envious and sad. 'I should have gone. If it wasn't for my parents, I'd have gone, I should have gone in any case.' Here he stopped, looking guilty. 'Even that romantic fool, my brother, had that much sense.'

'You mean Solly's in Spain?'she asked incredulously.

'No, he got as far as England and then he got mixed up with some girl, and now he's on his way back. But at least he started in the right direction.'

'Give Solly my – regards,' she said reverently.

'I'll give him your love,' he said promptly; and she was delighted to hear that he sounded grudging. 'He always had a soft spot for you. God knows why,' he added, smiling; and this shy smile completely transformed what was a rather solemn and stiff face. 'Good luck,' he said, and walked away from her. He called back, 'I've given your name to some friends of mine.' And he ran quickly down the iron staircase.

Back at her desk, she repeated to herself that Joss was going away; to her, he was off overseas, Cape Town being merely a resting place in his voyaging; she thought of him as a citizen of Europe, with the freedom of the big cities, and melancholy and envy fused into a bitter, frustrated sadness. And yet, while she was seeing herself, attractive and intelligent Matty, caged behind the desk of a legal office, she heard Maisie ask, 'Pleasant dreams?' and understood – even as she indignantly asked, 'What do you mean?' – that she had been smiling. Maisie only gave her a good-natured laugh and yawned.

Under the spell of Joss, Martha completely repudiated Donovan; and this revulsion lasted through that day and the next, when there was the following letter for her:

Dear Martha,
I enclose a list of various people you should look up. There's a discussion group, Left Book Club, they only talk, but it's better

than nothing. My Cousin Jasmine might be worth your while, she's in a receptive state due to being heartbroken over my Cousin Abraham. Who else? I'm afraid stony soil, but even in the provinces (!) there is work to do, and you might perhaps lead that ass Robinson to a meeting or two, he's going into Parliament, so it would be a good idea if he had at least one or two ideas in his head. As for my Uncle Max, he's a born fascist, so don't waste your time.

Sincerely,
Joss

Martha read this letter with difficulty – as an English person reads Scots dialect, for instance. There were a number of assumptions in it that it seemed Joss took for granted were hers as well; and this was flattering, but she felt ignorant. He made no secret of the fact that he considered her lazy, but at the same time it appeared she possessed a quality which would enable her to influence others. What quality, then, was it? It was as if he were handing on a torch. Reading the letter again, she was struck by a grudging and acrimonious undertone, and when she came to the word 'fascist' it sounded exaggerated, so that she suddenly giggled, and Mrs Buss looked inquiringly over the desks.

She glanced down the list of addresses, seven of them, and felt a curious disinclination, as mental images of seven (at least) new people to be approached and known rose in her mind. Martha Quest, who thought of herself as so adventurous, so free and unbounded – the fact was, even the idea of picking up a telephone and making herself known to a new person troubled her: she made excuses, she could not do it.

But the difficulty was solved when the telephone rang and a small, precise, slow voice introduced itself as Jasmine's, with a suggestion that Martha should go to such an address on the following afternoon. It was not a meeting, but Martha might find it interesting. There was a lazy, even slighting, tone to this voice, which struck Martha: Jasmine, like Joss, seemed more struck by what this new group of people lacked than by what they possessed; and this contempt extended itself, or so it seemed, to Joss himself, for when the name was introduced the voice poised on an upward note, as if it expected Martha to join in a good-natured laugh. Martha did not laugh, feeling indignant on Joss's behalf; but she said she would be there tomorrow.

She told Donovan, when he telephoned to book her for the usual sundowner party, that she was engaged; and even was irrational enough to feel hurt when he remarked huffily that in that case he would take someone else.

On the following afternoon she spent a long time getting dressed; and then, ten minutes before she was due to be fetched, flung off the clothes that had been suggested, even created, by Donovan – white linen slacks and a checked shirt – in favour of a simple dress. In her mind, the man who was coming to fetch her was identical with Joss; they stood for the same thing. What social current, flowing through such devious channels, reached this room, so that Martha felt that the casual gamin-like appearance Donovan liked was wrong – even that the linen dress as arranged by Donovan was too sophisticated? She arranged a coloured scarf loosely around her neck, clasped an embroidered belt at her waist, and let her hair fall in untidy curls. There was a touch of the peasant in her now, and she went to meet Mr Pyecroft with confidence. At once she was disappointed, for he struck her as elderly. As they drove uptown, she chattered in her 'attractive' manner, although she felt obscurely, without being able to alter it, that there was a discrepancy between her appearance and the manner that had been brought into being by Donovan.

It was a beautiful afternoon; there had been a storm, and the sky was full and clear, with shining masses of washed clouds rolling lightly in bright sunlight. The trees in the park glistened a soft, clean green; the puddles on the pavements reflected foliage and sky; and as the car turned into the grounds of the school where Mr Pyecroft was headmaster, these puddles became ruffled brown silk, and above them, all down the drive, grew massed shrubs, glistening with wet. On a deep-green lawn were several deck-chairs. From them two men rose as Martha approached; and again she thought, disappointedly, But they are old.

They were, in fact, between thirty and forty; they wore flannels, open shirts, sandals; they were of the same type: all long, thin, bony men, with intellectual faces, spectacles, thinning hair. It would be untrue to say that Martha made any such observations or even compared them with Joss. When she met people, she felt a dazzled and confused attraction of sympathy, or dislike. Now she was in sympathy; she responded to the half-grudging deference older men offer a young girl. She answered their questions brightly, and was conscious of her appearance, because they were.

Mr Pyecroft said that his wife would not be long, she was giving the children their tea; the other two men also apologized for the absence of their wives, and Martha accepted these social remarks not at their social value, but with the statement which she imagined sounded light and flippant, but actually sounded hostile: 'Children are a nuisance, aren't they?'

Soon three women came from a veranda of the big school building, shepherding half a dozen children and two native nannies to another lawn, about a hundred yards away, which was sheltered by a big glossy cedrelatoona tree. As soon as the women appeared, the voices of the men acquired a touch of heartiness that had not been there before, grew louder; and they turned their shoulders on these domestic arrangements with an uneasy determination which at once struck Martha, for she felt it herself. She was watching the scolding and fussy women as if her eyes were glued to them in fierce horror; she said to herself, Never, never, I'd rather die; and she reclined in her deck-chair with a deliberate coolness, a deliberately untroubled look.

When Mrs Pyecroft, Mrs Perr, and Mrs Forester came to join the men, they apologized, laughing, together and separately, for being a nuisance, and explained how the children had been troublesome, and went into details (and in a way that made it seem as if it were an accusation against the men themselves) of how Jane was off her food, while Tommy was in a trying psychological phase. The men listened, politely, from their chairs; but they were not allowed to remain in them, for it appeared that the whole group must be rearranged, an operation which took a great deal of time. Martha was more and more hostile and critical – the women seemed to her unpleasant and absurd, with their fuss and demands; she was as much on the defensive as if their mere presence were a menace to herself.

She looked at their dresses, as Donovan had taught her to look, but understood at once that here was a standard that refused to acknowledge Donovan. Their appearance had something in common which was difficult to define; Martha made no attempt to define it, she merely felt derisive. They were not at all unashamedly housewifely women of the district; nor were they fashionable – clearly they disdained fashion. Their dresses tended to be discordantly colourful, and too long for the year; their hair was looped or braided or fringed, in a consciously womanly way; they wore bright beads and 'touches' of embroidery – Martha found herself fiddling with her embroidered belt and with her scarf, which was now uncomfortable. She was stifled by it.

A native servant rolled a wagon with tea things across the lawn, and there began a business of pouring, handing cups and passing cakes. Martha joked and lit a cigarette, and said she was slimming. The women looked sharply at her, and said that at her age it was ridiculous; they looked at the men for support, and did not find it. If there was an edge on their voices when they spoke to her, they could hardly be judged for it; for Martha's gaze was expressing the most frank criticism, even scorn; and she, in her turn, ranged herself with the men as if it were her due to have their support.

With the arrival of the ladies, the rights of the intellect were at once asserted; and Martha was informed of times of meetings, the origin of the Left Book Club, the courage and force and foresight of a Mr Gollancz, and that *we* were trying to raise aid for Spain. But no sooner had this conversation begun than the children began to shriek, and all three women rushed off, as one, to the rescue, in spite of the two native nannies, who might have been considered sufficient to deal with them. And so it went on: the three women came back, hurriedly apologizing, firmly took up the threads of their respective remarks, a general conversation began to develop, and then either a child would come rushing across the lawn, shouting 'Mummy, Mummy!' or one, or all, of the women found it necessary to go to the children.

And Martha heard that fierce and passionate voice repeating more and more loudly inside her, I will *not* be like this; for, comparing these intelligent ladies, who nevertheless expressed resentment against something (but what?) in every tone of their voices, every movement of their bodies, with the undemanding women of the district, who left their men to talk by themselves while they made a world of their own with cooking and domesticity – comparing them, there could be no doubt which were the more likeable. And if, like Martha, one had decided to be neither one nor the other, what could one be but fierce and unhappy and determined?

She did not know when she had spent a more uncomfortable afternoon. It was not until the women had gone off, saying brightly and irritably, 'Well, I suppose now we've got to return to our chores,' and Martha was left with the men, that she felt at all at ease, but by now the men had acquired, in her eyes, a pathetic and hangdog look, and she was impatient.

She rose, saying, 'I'm afraid I must go, I've got a sundowner party.'

There was a slight hesitation before Mr Pyecroft inquired, in the humorous light tone which was the counter of conversation among the men (though certainly not the women), 'And so I take it you agree with us?'

Martha replied, even rather offended that the question could be put at all, 'But of course.'

'And we can expect you at the meetings?'

'Oh, yes,' said Martha lightly; but more was being asked of her than that light statement.

'What newspapers do you take?' asked Mr Perr suddenly. She had gathered that he was the chairman of the Left Book Club, the leader of the group. His length of body and face, his bony look, his humorousness, were distinguished from the others by an emphasis in everything. He must be well over six feet, the flesh of his face was hollowed over big bones as if by a bold sculptor, and everything he said had a cautious space around it, while he curled his large mouth in a deprecating smile. 'Newspapers are everything,' he remarked humorously. 'One must be certain of the complete impartiality of one's sources.' And he spoke as if he were amused at himself, and at the idea of any newspaper, or in fact anything at all, being taken seriously.

'I – I read the *Observer*,' confessed Martha, understanding that he did not mean local newspapers.

They involuntarily exchanged glances. Mr Pyecroft said reproachfully, 'But, Miss Quest, surely . . .'

Martha flushed and said quickly, 'But I've never been introduced to any other.'

At the appeal, the men looked relieved, and were able to say protectively that this was easily remedied. Mr Pyecroft picked up a journal that was lying on the grass by his side, apologized that it was damp, and offered it to her. 'I think you will find you will never read another,' he suggested.

Martha thanked him and said goodbye, and suggested she should walk home. Mr Pyecroft would not hear of this, so she said goodbye again and they went to the car.

Inside, she looked at the paper and saw the name *New Statesman and Nation*. It was familiar, because the local newspaper used it whenever it wanted to frighten its readers with a suggestion of sinister lawlessness. They were bad words, like 'Fabian' or 'Communist'. Martha felt that warmth of recognition with which one greets a person one had heard about from friends.

She was leafing curiously through it when Mr Pyecroft said, 'Here's our Jasmine,' and drew the car in under a tree. Walking slowly towards them was a small, dark girl in orange slacks and a purple sweater. At first glance she might be taken for a child, she was such a miniature figure, her black hair curled all over her head and held with a ribbon. But the walk was composed and mature, even dignified; and Mr Pyecroft said with a laugh, 'Our Jasmine always takes her time.' It was a critical laugh; and Martha, in her turn, was critical that every member of this group seemed to find the others absurd, or, at the most, tolerable.

Jasmine at last came to a stop beside the car door, and said, 'Hya.' This bizarre greeting was made additionally extraordinary by the careful way she used it; it was as if she were saying, very formally, 'Good afternoon.' To Martha she said, with casual dignity, 'Oh, hullo, so there you are at last,' and added some information about the next meeting. It appeared she was secretary and intended to behave only in this capacity, for, having told Mr Pyecroft that she was having some trouble with the press – information which he understood at once, for he nodded casually – and that these reactionaries were getting her down, she said, 'Well, I'm in a terrible hurry,' and nodded and walked on, with neat, slow, precise steps.

'Our Jasmine is an interesting figure at the moment, because her great love has gallivanted off to Spain,' said Mr Pyecroft, as he started the car; and he said it with what can only be described as a sneer.

Martha was altogether at sea. If Abraham was not to be approved, who was? 'Don't you like Abraham?' she inquired like a child.

Mr Pyecroft glanced at her, and said immediately in a sentimental voice that Abe was a fine chap, an altogether unusually intelligent chap; he added at once, however, in his customary light, denigrating way, that all one had to do these days to be a hero was to go dashing off to Spain. He glanced again at Martha, inviting her to laugh with him, and saw her huddled away from him, inside her shawl-like scarf, which she was holding close around her throat as if she were cold, her eyes bent down, her face puzzled and frowning.

He was silent, waiting for the self-possessed young woman to reappear, for this stubborn child was not at all to his taste.

As for Martha, she had discovered she disliked Mr Pyecroft. She thought dimly, It's all very well for these old people . . . and sympathetically dreamed of Jasmine, who loved a modern hero.

When they reached her room she was opening the car door, prepared to thank him politely and get out, when he asked, 'Perhaps you'd like to come and have supper with me one evening?'

She was struck by an eager but uneasy look on his face. At once she went scarlet, and said quickly, 'I'll be seeing you at the meetings, I expect.' She ran away from the car, repeating to herself, 'Dirty old man'; and she did not look around until the car, after a long silence, began to grind its gears. 'Disgusting, filthy, horrible,' she muttered angrily to herself, inside her room; and poor Mr Pyecroft had assumed, in her eyes, the very figure of an old lecher. But in her hand was his *New Statesman*, and she went to the telephone and left a message with Mrs Anderson that she was ill and could not go to the sundowner party with Donovan.

Then she lay on her bed and read the journal; for she had already decided to cancel the *Observer* and order this instead. Perhaps it is not correct to say that she read it, for unfortunately the number of people who actually read magazines, papers or even books is very small indeed. As she turned the pages and the lines of print came gently up through her eyes to her brain, without assault, what she gained was a feeling of warmth, of security; for here were ideas which she had been defending guiltily for years, used as the merest commonplaces. She was at home, she was one of a brotherhood. Yet when she laid down the journal she could not have said in detail what she had read, what were the facts; but she gave, unconsciously, a great quivering sigh, and lay back on her bed, eating chocolate and dreaming of a large city (it did not matter which, for it shared features of London and New York and Paris, and even the Moscow of the great novelists) where people who were not at all false and cynical and disparaging, like the men she had met that afternoon, or fussy and aggressive, like the women – where people altogether generous and warm exchanged generous emotions.

Apart from this dream she passed to her older one, so much older than she knew, of that golden city whose locality was vague, but until now had been situated somewhere between the house on the kopje and the Dumfries Hills (which area was in fact inhabited by the Arikaans community), the white-piled, broad-thoroughfared, tree-lined, four-gated dignified city where white and black and brown lived as equals, and there was no hatred or violence.

Towards morning she awoke, rather stiff and cold, and went to the french door which stood open to the garden. She leaned her head against the doorframe, and shivered at the cold and starlit sky. There was no moon. Along the silent street came the clip-clopping of hooves. A small white donkey glimmered into sight, and behind it a milk cart, rattling its cans, and behind that ran a small and ragged piccaninny, a child of perhaps seven years, whose teeth were rattling so loudly they sounded like falling pebbles even across the width of the garden. She felt sad and depressed; the ideas with which she had fallen asleep seemed ridiculous now; she thought dimly that if the world was going to be changed it would not be changed by the people she had met the previous afternoon, and at that decision she became even sadder. She shut the door and decided that, since it was already four o'clock and she must be at the office by eight, it would be a waste of time to sleep. She looked for a book among the piles on the dressing table, the table, even on the floor. She wanted something which would include that deprived black child, her own fierce unhappiness (which was likely at any moment, as she knew, to turn into as fierce a joy); even the unattractive and faithless group of people whom Joss very properly despised. She wanted it all explained. The titles of her book seemed faded, what the print said had nothing to do with her life; and as the sun rose, Martha was lying fully dressed on the floor, copying out titles of books advertised in the *New Statesman*, which had no better recommendation than their names were included in the glow which surrounded that magic title.

She had decided she would go to the next meeting of the Left Book Club, but would treat Mr Pyecroft coldly, as he deserved, for even the thought of him filled her with the most violent disgust.

She was just about to telephone Jasmine, when the phone rang for her; but not at all as simply as that statement sounds. First, the instrument on Mrs Buss's desk gave a shrill and prolonged peal, so that Martha, who had been about to pick it up, jumped and went back to her desk, already jarred, even apprehensive. She saw Mrs Buss give her an interested and then emotional look as she switched the instrument through to Mr Jasper Cohen. Mrs Buss continued to type, her vivid, but now professionally reticent, gaze hovering around Martha. Then the instrument clicked, Mrs Buss listened again, and switched it through to Mr Max. Finally, Martha was called into Mr Jasper Cohen's office, where she was told kindly that her father was ill and she must hurry back to her room, where her mother was waiting for her. Martha's irritation that her mother's sense of drama had succeeded in disturbing two busy men, and in fact the whole office, over what should concern herself alone, was only just allayed by concern over her father. She left the office with all those interested eyes following her, while she instinctively modulated her walk to one of deprecating dignity. Mrs Buss did not fail to point out that this was the second time within a week that Martha had allowed 'personal matters' to call her out of the office, and Mr Cohen was kindness itself.

Martha walked as fast as she could along the few streets which led to her room, and found her mother there alone, waiting at the door, restless with energetic excitement.

'So there you are,' she exclaimed reproachfully, and, as she kissed her daughter's cheek, announced, 'Your father's really ill, he really is very ill, Matty.'

Martha felt guilty, as usual, and inquired, 'What's the matter?'

She expected to hear of some crisis in the diabetes; but Mrs Quest said, 'Well, we're not quite sure, they're finding out at the hospital. I've left him there for the day.' Mrs Quest was drawing on her gloves, and was looking at a list of things she must do, which she had taken from her bag.

'Why did you call me at the office, then?' inquired Martha sullenly.

'I don't like driving in town, you can drive for me,' said Mrs Quest, and Martha said angrily, 'I can't just leave the office to act as your chauffeur.'

'But your father's ill,' said Mrs Quest antagonistically; and Martha exclaimed, '*Mother!*' Mrs Quest, evading the accusing eyes, said briskly, 'I must go and see Mrs Anderson, she wrote to me, and I think it would be nice if you were there, too.'

'Mother, what is the matter with Daddy?'

'I told you, they're finding out. He's having a barium meal,' announced Mrs Quest, using the technical words with a satisfaction which reminded her daughter that she had been a nurse.

Hastily, in order to avoid the repulsive details which would certainly follow, described with the same cool satisfaction, Martha said, 'I can't possibly spend all day having tea and gossiping. You didn't tell Mr Cohen you wanted me as a chauffeur, did you?'

'He was very kind,' said Mrs Quest, smiling. 'And now let's go quickly, Matty, because it will be too late for the morning tea otherwise.'

'I'm not taking you to tea with Mrs Anderson, what do you want to see her for – ' She stopped, on the verge of saying, 'behind my back.' As usual she was feeling the impotent resentment that as soon as she made a friend, created anything of her own, her mother followed her, assuming first place. She spoke as if she had been an intimate friend of Mrs Anderson for years, whereas they had not seen each other since they met on the boat when the Quests first arrived in the colony.

'Don't be so unreasonable, Matty. It's only natural the two mothers should want to talk over their children.' And she looked suggestive and coy.

'What have you got into your head now?' asked Martha disgustedly; but Mrs Quest, not at all upset, said impatiently, 'Oh, come along, Matty, don't waste time.'

'I'm not coming,' said Martha, with calm fury.

Seeing her face, Mrs Quest said hurriedly, 'Well, you needn't stay, just run me over and leave me there. You can walk back, it isn't far.' She looked into the mirror, composing her face and adjusting her hat, which was a severe navy-blue felt and suited her regular, dominant features. Her suit was of navy linen, squarely cut, and she looked altogether an efficient woman, a committee woman. Martha thought of the perfumed, billowing Mrs Anderson, and wanted to laugh. On a wave of good spirits, inspired by the malicious thought of 'the nice talk' the two ladies would have, she became suddenly amenable, even affectionate and she drove Mrs Quest without protest to the Andersons' house, where she left her, and walked quietly to the office.

And here she leaned her head on her hands, oblivious of the interested eyes of the other women, who were longing to be sympathetic if she would only give them the chance, and thought miserably of her own lack of feeling. She only felt resentful that at any moment it might be used as an emotional argument against her. She knew she should be thinking of Jasmine, and making arrangements to know her better, and yet all she could think of was her mother, at that moment discussing her with Mrs Anderson. She knew that because of her mother's interference something unpleasant would happen, because it always did. Why had she not said that she had quarrelled with Donovan? It was as good as the truth. Why ... But soon she ceased to think, she merely waited, in a condition of locked and irritable unhappiness.

Later that afternoon Jasmine telephoned her and asked her to come to tea. She heard Martha's remote, nervous voice saying yes, she would try, but it was difficult, and perhaps it would be better if . . .

Jasmine, who had telephoned the ladies Forester, Pyecroft and Perr for what she described half humorously as a 'report' on Martha, had been told she was conceited, affected, and her level of political understanding was indicated by the fact that she read the *Observer*. The last was the contribution of Mrs Pyecroft, who added that Joss must be influenced by Martha's looks: Martha would be quite attractive if she weren't so conscious of being attractive. Jasmine therefore gave Martha up as a waste of time, on hearing these ineffectual excuses.

By now Martha was nearly hysterical, for she had been sent a letter, by office-boy, from Donovan, saying she must meet him at McGrath's immediately after office, because it was very urgent.

And when she threaded her way between the crowded tables, smiling automatically, like royalty, at the people who greeted her, shaking her head with playful regret when they asked her to join them, she could see Donovan energetically defending the empty seat beside him, and knew that he was very angry: he looked exactly like his father, morose and bad-tempered.

'Matty *dear*,' he said shrilly, as she struggled to her seat, 'what's all this about your mamma and my mamma? My mamma has telephoned me for the third time, and she is really furious.'

'I'm not responsible for my mother,' Martha said flatly, and added, 'For God's sake get me a drink.'

He ordered two enormous glass jugs of the strong local beer, and went on: 'What are we to do, Matty? I told my mamma that I hadn't seen you for as good as a week, you've practically thrown me over, but she wouldn't listen.'

This was an invitation to confess what she had been doing, but Martha said impatiently, 'Yes, but what's happened?'

'Why haven't you been seeing me? A little bird told me that you were all mixed up with the local Reds, and that won't do you any good, Matty dear. Did you know the police go to their meetings? They'll put you in prison one of these days.'

Martha laughed crossly, and said, 'Oh don't be such a baby.'

The beer was slammed down in front of them by one of the hurrying waiters, and Martha seized hers and drank half of it.

'You're getting quite a little toper, Matty dear,' said Donovan unpleasantly.

'Well, one must do something,' said Martha defensively. She unconsciously glanced at her fingers: on both hands, they were stained to the middle joints with nicotine. As she decided she would cut down smoking, she reached for her bag and lit a new one from the stub of the last, and thought, I'll stop smoking when this business with my mother is settled.

'They're a bunch of Jews, too,' said Donovan gracefully. 'After knowing me for so long, you should have learned discrimination.'

'But they aren't all Jews – ' Martha began, and stopped, furious with herself. 'I thought you had asked me here to discuss our respected parents?' she inquired at last, and with that rueful smile she knew put him at a disadvantage.

'You're a naughty girl,' said Donovan, more gently. 'My mamma says she wants to see us. It's a crisis, Matty, a crisis.'

A group of lads in black-and-white-striped jerseys and white shorts, which exposed what seemed to be several yards of long, thick, red-brown thighs, entered the lounge and emitted a series of shrieks and yodels, began slapping the seated men nearest to them across the shoulders, and bending over the girls with yearning, sentimental faces.

'Now here are the Sports Club crowd,' said Donovan sulkily. 'If you let them sit here, it's the end, really it is.

Seeing Martha, the lads let out a yell expressing agonized frustration, and came pushing towards her. 'Matty, Matty,' they moaned inarticulately, 'beautiful Matty.' They were watching a passing waiter, and, even as they paid their fee to beauty, reached out for mugs of beer and turned their backs as the waiter protested, 'Baas, baas, someone else paid for this beer.'

'Beautiful,' continued the ringleader, ignoring the waiter, 'why are you so toffee-nosed, why – '

'This table is engaged,' said Donovan, rising to the bait as he had been intended to.

'Keep your hair on,' said the sportsman, and he lifted his glass mug and tilted his head back, exposing a long, lumpy throat, and began to drink.

'Down, down, down,' chanted the people at the tables nearby. 'Here's to Donny, drink it down . . .' The Adam's apple moved steadily up and down, the golden liquid sank in its foam, and everyone began to clap. The young man set down his mug, which had held nearly a quart of beer, and looked about proudly, so that the applause grew louder. Then he shook his hands together in self-congratulation over his head, and, his eyes happening to fall on Martha, turned up his eyes and staggered away, clutching his brow in a parody of despair. Everyone laughed, while Donovan sat moodily silent.

'If you can tear yourself away from these fascinating athletes, Matty darling, let's go and face my mamma.'

'I still don't know what we have to face,' said Martha, rising.

They went out; while Martha acknowledged the homage from various young men, who were putting on the despairing faces required of them by convention, with a careless smile.

'It must be nice to be such a success,' said Donovan spitefully, as the swing doors revolved behind them, for Martha had a self-satisfied look on her face, although she was reminding herself that it was a convention and meant nothing.

They drove in silence to the Andersons' house, where a message had been left by Mrs Quest: 'Sorry have no time to see you again, must go and get Daddy from hospital, such a pleasant morning with Mrs Anderson, will let you know the result of the test.'

With this piece of paper in her hand, Martha followed Donovan into the drawing room, and found Mrs Anderson poised amid clouds of mulberry chiffon on her purple satin chair. She was smiling, but looked annoyed.

'Now, I want to speak to you young people frankly,' she began, and Donovan muttered, 'Oh, hell,' and flung himself down on a settee and took up *Vogue*. 'No, Donny, it's for you too, and you must listen. Now both of you must realize that you are very young and . . .' Here she paused, gave them a doubtful glance and took a cigarette from a tortoiseshell cigarette case. She lit it slowly, and it appeared that the impulse of anger that had carried her thus far was already failing her.

Martha sat on the end of the settee, at Donovan's feet, and tried to smile. 'I don't know what my mother has been saying,' she said, 'but I think you are jumping to conclusions.'

'Yes, yes,' interrupted Mrs Anderson impatiently, though she sounded relieved. 'I expect you think I'm an interfering old lady – ' here she laughed and looked flirtatiously at Donovan, who was looking at her coldly, 'but I feel that your mother has perhaps – I mean – ' She paused and sighed. 'Oh dear,' she said, and she put her hands to her forehead in a helpless way, 'I'm so tired and cross and . . .' Impulsively she rose, came to Martha and kissed her, but Martha accepted the embrace stiffly. 'Well, I daresay I got the wrong idea,' she murmured, and looked in appeal at both of them.

'I think you have, Mamma dear,' said Donovan icily, throwing aside *Vogue* and sitting up. 'Matty and I are ever so platonic, you've no idea, and it's very upsetting to have you two dirty-minded old girls behaving like this.'

'*Donny!*' gasped Mrs Anderson, and she began to cry, pressing a piece of ivory-coloured silk to her eyes in such a way that it would damage neither the silk nor her make-up. Donovan, with elaborate courtesy, handed her a handkerchief, and now she began to cry in earnest, in great shuddering sobs. 'I'm so sorry, darling,' she wept. 'You must forgive me. I don't know why, but I was so upset, and Mrs Quest was – I mean – '

'Well, don't cry, Mamma,' said Donovan gracefully. 'But I really do think you should tell us what this is all about. You can't summon Matty and me for an audience, and then get us all upset, and suddenly say that you're sorry and leave it like that.'

He stood poised on one hip, a brown suede shoe extended easily in front of him, looking sternly down at his mother, who shook herself, laughed as she saw the black streaks on the handkerchief, dabbed her eyes again and said clumsily, 'Mrs Quest was talking as if you were getting married. I told her that you were both too young, and that we hadn't the money for Donny to marry – '

Here Martha flushed with annoyance, and exclaimed, 'It really is the limit!'

'Yes, Matty, I'm sorry – but . . . Oh dear, it is so difficult. You see, we are really very poor and . . .'

Matty suddenly laughed, thinking of the oblique semi-poverty of her home, and of this expensive house, and of the secret luxurious life of Mrs Anderson: also, like a black screen against which this minor anomaly was exposed stood that knowledge she had brought with her from her earliest years: the fact that the poverty of the Quest family represented unimaginable and unreachable wealth to the black serfs who supported them.

'It's not a joke, Matty,' said Mrs Anderson, who was annoyed, although she smiled in the rueful, charming way that Martha herself used when pleading false claims. 'After all Mr Anderson's retired, and we're not rich. I have some money but not much, and living is so expensive these days, isn't it?' So too the millionaire, indicating his several houses, his cars, his yacht: 'But it all costs a lot to keep up,' he says indignantly.

'Well, Mamma,' said Donovan, giving judgment, 'I think you're a naughty old girl, and I'm cross with you.'

Mrs Anderson brightened and reached up to kiss him. He generously extended his cheek. 'I'm afraid I have a dinner engagement,' she said in her normal gracious tone, standing up. 'You two can look after yourselves. Don't forget Mr Anderson's tray – tell the boy scrambled egg, he's sick of boiled eggs, he says.' She smiled humorously. 'Good night, dears, and forgive a silly old woman.' And she swept out, touching her hair delicately with one hand and her smudged and blackened eyes with the other; she was frowning now, at the thought of the time it would take to do her face, for she was very late.

Martha and Donovan, left alone, did not immediately look at each other. They were irritable. They understood that this scene had raised certain problems; and Martha, for her part, was waiting for him to put these problems into words – for a man should surely take the initiative?

And so he did, but not as she expected. 'Well, Matty,' he remarked at last, plucking at the beautiful rose and copper gladioli whose arrangement must have cost Mrs Anderson so much trouble, 'well, it seems that we're supposed to make love,' and he looked at her gloomily, even resentfully.

She gave a snort of astonished and offended laughter. She stopped, then laughed again. She looked at Donovan, who was regarding her with puzzled annoyance, and went off into a peal of laughter that grew hysterical and broke into a fit of coughing. And then silence. She sighed; she was very tired and depressed.

'It's all very well,' said Donovan resentfully, 'it's all very well.' Again that critical, almost angry look; and now there was anger in the look she directed at him; for a few moments their eyes challenged each other, and then dropped away; and if Mrs Quest or Mrs Anderson had looked in then, she might have been surprised, and even disappointed, to find this couple separated by several feet of carpet and apparently on the verge of a bad quarrel.

'I suppose we had better eat,' said Donovan at last.

With the relieved knowledge that the moment of crisis was postponed, they went to the dining room, where Donovan regained his good humour ordering his father's scrambled eggs. And after that they went as usual to the pictures;

and again as usual, on to McGrath's, where Donovan seemed to find no objection to sharing a large table with about a dozen others.

'Our Donny-boy's in good form tonight,' said Maisie, who happened to be near Martha, under escort of one of the sportsmen.

And Donovan was – gay, malicious and amusing. He seemed determined to eclipse the sportsmen; he made fun of them, told spiteful stories at their expense, and then took the sting from it by telling stories against himself; and at midnight withdrew triumphantly with Martha, saying, 'And now, Matty, you must get your beauty sleep, or you'll lose your looks and then none of us will love you any more.'

The sportsmen gallantly insisted that they would love Matty, and all their girls, forever; but without their usual assurance, and this was not only because of Donovan's triumph but because of the discordant note he always introduced.

On the pavement he said lightly, with the astonishing frankness which was possible only because he could not hear the discordancy, 'You must admit, Matty, that I'm much more entertaining than those oafs, who have all their brains in their thighs?' And when she assented he continued, 'I really think you'd better stick to me, you know. The last girl I took out deserted me for them, and really you should have seen her, she was so bored I could have cried for her.'

'And what happened to her?' asked Martha curiously.

'She got married – a businessman from Nairobi,' he said, as if this served her right, a sentiment which Martha could not help sharing; though she began to dissent from it when he continued, 'All you girls get married, you have no strength of mind at all. I really do feel that all this sex is overrated, don't you?'

'I don't know,' said Martha humorously, 'I haven't tried yet.'

But he would not accept the humour. He pressed her arm urgently, and looked down into her face and insisted, 'Well, don't you think so? All you girls want to be made love to, and really . . .' His face faded in disgust.

Although Martha had every intention of agreeing for the sake of good nature, she began to laugh; and he waited until this rather strained laughter was finished, and muttered bad-temperedly, 'Women are oversexed, that's what I think.'

She began to chatter, in her social manner, about a book on the sexual customs of the Bantu, which she had just read; and thought it ill-tempered of him not to accept what she imagined was a pleasant way out of personal comment: she was saying that among primitive races girls were judged to be sexually mature long before they were in civilized communities.

But he remained silent until he dropped her at her door, and slid his customary good-night kiss on her cheek, saying, 'Well, Matty, I've decided to take you to a dance at the Sports Club next Saturday, and risk all; I can see you are tugging at the leash.'

'Poor Donovan,' said Martha, and she laughed again, she could not help it. Suddenly what she at once described to herself as a mischievous impulse (since she was immediately overwhelmed by embarrassment at herself) made her say, 'Kiss me properly, Don.' She held her face invitingly under his, and half closed her eyes, thankful it was dark, for she could feel a hot flush creeping up her cheeks. She waited, watching his furious eyes through her lashes, until he clasped her and shook her hard.

'Now, stop it, Matty,' he said firmly. 'I will not be teased. You must behave yourself, or I won't take you to a dance.'

On this note they parted. In her room, Martha first was angry, and then since it was her instinct to adapt herself, saw herself through Donovan's eyes and became humiliated. Behind this confusion of feeling was another: she murmured to herself that one felt so safe with Donovan; she was relieved she was going to the Sports Club with him; and for a girl whose first article of faith was that one was entitled to lose one's virginity as romantically and as soon as possible, this was surely an odd thing to think? The fact was, the thought of making love with Donovan was rapidly becoming impossible, even indecent: she had several times called him Jonathan, and never noticed the slip of the tongue.

Part Three

In the lives of most women everything, even the greatest sorrow, resolves itself into a question of 'trying on'.

— PROUST

Chapter One

The Sports Club had come into existence about five years before, and in a way characteristic of the country. For when it was first suggested, at a ladies' bridge party, Mrs Maynard said, 'What a pity there isn't a sports club in this town,' and the others assented, without feeling it necessary to point out that there were several; they belonged to the employees of the railways, the post office, various businesses. From half-past four until sundown, every open space in the city was crowded with young people engaged in violent activity.

Mrs Maynard was large, strong-minded, black-browed and energetic, the wife of a magistrate; and she was a lady. That is, in England, where she married Mr Maynard, she had belonged to the governing class by birth. Mrs Lowe-Island was a lady only because she had married Mr Lowe-Island, whose family had connections with the English aristocracy. She was a vulgar, spiteful woman who did not pride herself on saying just what she thought, because it had never entered her head there were occasions when one should not. She at once said, 'I quite agree with you, dear. We need a place with some class. There should be somewhere for civil servants and people like us.' Mrs Maynard, who, because of her upbringing, understood first of all the arts of suggestion, was naturally pained at having her thought so crudely expressed; but she did not snub Mrs Lowe-Island, because she was unsnubbable, and because in her secret heart she considered her hardly worth the effort. A third lady, Mrs Talbot, was so dissimilar to the other two that her continued friendship with them was a tribute to their mutual passion for bridge. She was a charming, elegant lady, whose chief interest was her delicate and artistic daughter; and she now murmured, with a kind of laughing tolerance which was an appeal to her companions, that it would be nice for the children to have a place where they could play games; and it is a remarkable fact that until they were mentioned the claims of youth had not occurred to the other women. Mrs Knowell, the fourth, at once exclaimed warmly and generously, 'Oh yes, we must do something for the young people, my Douggie loves rugger, though I keep telling him he'll break his neck.'

There was a silence, for it was apparent that here was a conflict in intention. But Mrs Knowell was aflame with excitement, and soon began talking again, and in a few minutes the Sports Club was built and furnished, and in the throes of an inaugural ball. They laughed at her, teased her; particularly Mrs Maynard and Mrs Lowe-Island, for they had imagined the Sports Club as a large shadowy veranda, with native servants standing like willing statues around the walls, plenty of sundowners, and that laughter which is the result of personal comment, while behind this imaginary veranda was a bridge room, filled with elderly ladies.

That evening Mrs Maynard talked to her husband, who expressed agreement by saying it was a paying proposition; Mrs Lowe-Island talked until Mr Lowe-Island said he was no snob, but there were times when . . . Mrs Talbot told her daughter tenderly that it was bad to spend so much time on her water colours, a game of tennis occasionally would help avert the migraine and fainting fits to which, like a Victorian maiden, she was addicted. And Mrs Knowell telephoned her son at the office, which he had forbidden her to do, and irritated him until he said, 'Yes, but for goodness' sake, Mater, tell me another time.'

All these ladies were adept at raising money for good causes, and they found it even easier to raise a large sum for what would be a paying proposition; and very soon there was a large committee of about thirty people, not one of whom was under forty-five. They all had determined ideas about the number of bridge rooms, sundowner lounges and bars the place should possess; and they were on the verge of buying a site which would have room for a club building and perhaps one tennis court, when a new factor entered the situation – which is a mild phrase for what happened when Binkie Maynard picked up the architect's plans (marked 'Sports Club') and went off into loud laughter.

'What's this, a home for retired civil servants?' he demanded.

His mother reproached him; his father regarded him with a certain practised apprehension; and Binkie looked at the plans with a growing interest, until at last he said, 'What-ho, chaps, this has got something – got something, hey? He flapped the plans in the air, let out a whoop, and flew out of the house in search of a fellow spirit.

Binkie had first given signs of what he was destined to become when, at the age of four, plated into tight sky-blue satin, he climbed onto the bride's table at his sister's wedding among the flowers and ribbons, and piped, 'And now it is my turn to give you a toast . . .' He was lifted down, kicking and bawling. At school he was at the bottom of his class, and useless at games, but he organized clubs and societies of all kinds. When he left school, his father put him into the civil service, where at least he could come to no harm, and there he soon arranged clubs-for-having-sandwiches-at-lunchtime and associations-for-saving-money-for-buying-presents-on-retirement. He was the thorn in his father's flesh, his mother's pride, the despair of his chief. He was a large ungainly, red-faced, black-locked youth of twenty when those plans fell like manna from heaven into his hands and gave him the outlet he needed for his genius.

He said to his father next day, 'I say, it isn't fair, you need the young element, I mean to say?' His father could hardly disagree.

At the next committee meeting, Binkie, Douglas Knowell, and half a dozen other young men took the floor. Binkie was chairman, not because he had been elected, but by virtue of his deadly singlemindedness. At the second meeting, there were several girls in shorts and sweaters, who were polite to the elderly ladies and coy with the old men, but treated them as if they hardly had the right to be there at all.

Mrs Lowe-Island got up (for she had not understood, as the rest had, their complete rout) and said that she was no snob, but the club must be restricted; and Binkie climbed to his feet before she had even finished, and with those large, black, indignant eyes fixed on her said he was upset, yes, really upset to hear that anyone, even Mrs Lowe-Island, who deserved three hearty cheers for what she had done, could make remarks that really – he didn't think anyone would disagree with him – were not in the spirit of the country. This wasn't England, he meant to say, this was a new country; he wasn't used to making speeches, but really, he was going to suggest that the club should be free to anyone who could find twenty shillings a year, which was a lot of money to some people, though some people (he meant no offence) might not believe it, and that's all he wanted to say, and that was enough. Here there was a murmur of passionate agreement from all the golden girls and boys; and there was never another suggestion about snobs or restrictions.

From that time, and for several months, the Maynard house swarmed day and night with young men and women. Committee meetings were held, but as a matter of form, and to satisfy and support and confirm arrangements already made by Binkie.

There was one afternoon when Binkie caught sight of his mother playing bridge in a corner of the veranda with three other ladies, all huddled forward to escape the pressure from a throng of shouting and arguing youth; and a pang of contrition must have assailed him, for he said to his father afterwards, 'I say, I hope you don't think we've been shoving our way in. I mean, it is a *sports* club, isn't it?'

Mr Maynard, a suave and cultivated man, raised his eyebrows slightly and smiled; but, finding this gesture insufficient, he murmured, 'My dear Binkie, I cannot tell you what a relief I find it that you are not, as I was beginning to suspect, without a natural bent. You have my blessing –

if it turns out you cannot dispense with it, which I am afraid I find it hard to believe.'

Binkie, after a pause, gave an uncertain smile, and said heartily, 'Oh. Well, that's all right, then, isn't it?'

'So I gather you will have no objection if I resign from the committee and devote myself to reducing my handicap at golf – may I point out that you have made no provision for a golf course in your plans for the Sports Club?'

'That's not fair,' said Binkie, in an aggrieved voice. 'We've got first refusal on the land just behind the building site, and it'll fall vacant in six months, so I reckon there'll be a full-size golf course in a year's time.'

'My apologies,'said Mr Maynard. 'I withdraw completely. But, as to my first point, I suggest that I and your mother be allowed to resign. No ill feeling on either side, but now you've agreed that there may be a small side room where the ladies may play bridge, and I'm assured of my golf course, I feel our usefulness is at an end.'

'I say!' said Binkie reproachfully. 'That's not the spirit, Dad.'

'But you've my blessing, as I've already said. After all, we're more of a hindrance than a help.'

'But who's going to raise the money?' asked Binkie. 'We need another ten thousand at least if we're going to have four squash courts and proper changing rooms, and the golf course won't get built for nothing.'

'Let's get this clear,' said Mr Maynard. 'You want myself and your mother to remain on the committee to raise money for you?'

'You can resign if you like,' said Binkie kindly, 'but we must have the finance committee, mother and Mrs Lowe-Island and the rest, to fix the money.'

Mr Maynard's cheeks swelled, buttoned in by a tight and commenting mouth, while his eyebrows rose like black kites; it was an appearance he had evolved for use in the law courts, where he was magistrate, to impress native offenders into an awe-ful frame of mind; but Binkie merely looked impatient. He allowed his brows to fall and his cheeks to deflate. 'Well, well, well,' he murmured. He nodded slowly again. 'Tell me, what makes you think ten thousand'll be enough? Where did you get the figures?'

'Oh, I can show you the figures, if you want. It's ten thousand six hundred and fifty-four pounds ten shillings and fourpence.'

'You worked that out? You worked it out yourself with estimates and a piece of paper and a pencil?'

'I've no head for figures,' said Binkie good-naturedly. 'I got Douggie to do it. He's the tops with figures.'

'Well, well, well, the born organizer. Who'd have thought it? Well, it's worth it. I should have put you into industry,' said Mr Maynard.

'I say,' said Binkie, annoyed, 'you're not going to start changing jobs for me now? I haven't got time. I'm busy with the Club. Besides, they're going to put me up a grade at Christmas. After all, you've got to say that for the Service, they have to put you *up*, it's only fair.'

In 1935 the Sports Club site marked the division between the old residential quarter of shady avenues and rambling veranda'd houses and the naked veld. Its boundary fence ran along North Avenue; and for many years people had used the phrase 'North Avenue' adjectively. 'She's ever so North Avenue,' Donovan might say approvingly. Here lived senior civil servants, the Cabinet ministers, even the Prime Minister. But now they looked across the street, through the tall creamy trunks of a double line of gum trees, over the playing fields to the club house. It was a noble building, in the Cape Colonial style, of smooth dark-red brick, with a green roof all curves and gables, and a deep veranda supported on stately white pillars. The playing fields, several acres of them, were smooth emerald in the rains, but a scurfy brown in the dry season, in spite of the perpetually working hoses, which were dragged all day like thick black coiling serpents into different positions by a team of half a dozen natives.

Inside there was a large, high-ceilinged room with a polished dark-wood floor, comfortable chairs, and a fireplace at each end; and this room was cleared two or three times a week for dances. Off this room, on one side, were a series of bars and sundowner lounges; and on the other, hidden among changing rooms, a small room which could be used for bridge – though any ladies reckless enough to settle themselves in it for a comfortable afternoon were likely to find Binkie's shock head poked through the door at them, with the firm injunction, 'The squash rackets committee will be wanting this in ten minutes, I'm just giving you fair warning.' For at about four in the afternoon, the Club, comparatively deserted until then, suddenly surged with young men in white flannels and striped jerseys, and girls in gym tunics, shorts, or coloured dungarees; and waiters ran to and fro, staggering under trays loaded with the ubiquitous glass mugs of golden beer. The veranda was crowded; dozens of bare, red-brown, hairy legs, male and female, dangled over the edge; all eyes, devoted, expert, and earnest, followed the hockey and rugger, and from time to time the sound of clapping fell thinly across the wide field, or the cry: 'That's *it*, Jolly, old man' or a moan, 'Betty, Betty, you'll *kill* me with that pass'; and an anxious youth might fall backwards, with an exaggerated loosening of his limbs, to lie on the veranda, murmuring, 'That kid Betty'll kill me, she'll kill me, I say!' He lay waiting until someone took the cue and hastened to him with beer, when he slowly sat up, his eyes roving anxiously around his audience to test the effect of his performance, saying apologetically, 'These kids, these girls! I can't stand it, no, they kill me.' And he thoughtfully drank his beer, amid sympathetic laughter, perhaps even applause, with the modest air of a good actor who knows he has been on the top of his form.

And through these groups moved Binkie, the now kingly Binkie, a carelessly generous, untidy, beer-fat young man, his black eyes always on the watch for any sign of dissidence or discord. He would stop beside a young man, murmuring, 'If you've a moment, there's that business of the shower . . .' And the youth would at once move away with him, and the two stood rather at a distance from the others, with a conscious though deprecatory importance, discussing the machinery of living. Or he would saunter down the length of the veranda, nodding here and there, the busy man for once at leisure, while the girls offered, tentatively, 'Hello, Binks?' 'Hullo, kid,' he returned, kindly, and at last might come to a standstill beside one, and put his arm about her, and his face would assume the agonized, frustrated look which was obligatory, while he said, 'You're killing me, baby, you're killing me. Who's your boy friend, let me kill him for you.' She remained passive, with the equally obligatory look of maternal indulgence, while the other girls laughed; they were flattered, for this was a mark of attention to them all; she was their representative. But even as Binkie moaned and offered homage, his eyes were roving in a sharp lookout for the next thing that must claim his attention; and suddenly he straightened, patting the girl lightly, as if to say, 'Well, so much for you,' and on he strolled to tell the next group that they must drink up, they'd had the same round for half an hour, and the Club'd go bankrupt if everyone didn't pull their weight. 'You're not co-operating,' he would say earnestly. And automatically the hands reached out for the mugs. 'Waiter!' shouted Binkie, waving a lordly hand. 'Waiter, fill up here!'

But the Club was flourishing. The subscription might be low, but there were few people under thirty in the city who were not members. For that matter, there were few under sixty, for, while a casual visitor might assume that this was devoted to youth, such was the prestige of the place that people felt impelled to join. 'There's the New Year's Dance,' they said. 'It's worth it, just for that. It's such a nice atmosphere – not noisy, like McGrath's.'

But it was nothing if not noisy; what they meant was that the section of the community which the bridge-playing ladies had at first hoped would exclusively use it did in fact come to the big dances, although in closed groups. The important civil servants, the big businessmen, with their wives and daughters, sat at large tables, smiled with a not too obvious benevolence, and tended to leave unobtrusively at midnight, before 'things began to break up'.

'Here, break it up there,' Binkie yelled, or: 'Come on, let's – tear – it – to – pieces!' And this meant that the groups, the couples, were expected to abandon any remnant of partiality and throw themselves into the dancing, yelling crowd, while Binkie stood, dripping with perspiration, his tie crooked, waving his beer mug and ordering the waiters to fetch free drinks for the band, who played and smiled, smiled and played, until their jaws and arms must have ached; and when, at two o'clock, they smiled and shook their heads and began to pack their instruments, they were at once surrounded by a crowd of remonstrating, reproachful young men, bribing them with drink for just one more, one more, always one more; while the girls stood smiling a little self-consciously, and, if the band were adamant, said soothingly, maternally, 'Now, kids, it's late, you know, we've got to get to work tomorrow.'

In 1935, 'the gang' were certainly all kids, between sixteen and twenty-one or two. And in 1938 they still called themselves kids, though in the daytime, between the hours of eight and four or four-thirty, these children were ambitious young businessmen, rising civil servants, and the girls were their secretaries; and if someone demanded, 'Where's Bobby, why haven't we seen Bobby lately?' the girl who felt herself responsible for him would say with a faraway, devoted look in her eyes, 'He's got an exam,' and everyone nodded understandingly, with a sympathetic sigh.

The girls were, it was assumed, responsible for the men. Even the child of seventeen who had left school the week before, and was at her first dance, taking her first alcohol, would instantly assume an air of madonna-like, all-experienced compassion; she did not giggle when this wolf or that moaned and rolled his eyes and said, 'Beautiful, why haven't I seen you before, I can't take it, I'm dying,' as he clutched his forehead and reeled back from the vision of her unbearable attractions. She smiled a small, wise smile, and might, even before her first visit into the grown-up world was over, find herself exhorting him to 'go on the tack', with a flushed, earnest look of sisterly regard. For they were always going on the tack; a dozen pairs of sympathetic eyes would follow the consciously heroic youth as he wandered down the veranda with a glass of orange juice in his hand; and they asked anxiously, 'How goes it, Frankie?' 'Keeping it up, Jolly?' And he would shake his head, and groan and suffer, with one experienced eye on his public – since he was bound to have done this at least a dozen times before.

The public: it was all so public, anything was permissible, the romances, the flirtations, the quarrels, provided they were shared. These terms, however, were never used, for words are dangerous, and there was a kind of instinctive shrinking, and embarrassment, against words of emotion, or rather, words belonging to that older culture, to which this was an attempt at providing a successor.

If two young men were seen in angry argument, Binkie or one of the older members would hastily go to them, saying sentimentally, 'Break it up, old man, break it up, kids,' and the contestants would be led back to the flock, smiling apologetically, smiling if it killed them. When a couple remained too long together, dated each other too often, half a dozen self-appointed guardians of public safety would watch them, and at last surround them, with 'Hey, hey, what's this?' A young man would say, 'You can't do this to me, Betty,' and for the moment he represented all the young men; and a girl would say, in sour warning (and that sour personal note held a deeper note of danger), 'And who were you with last night?' smiling at the culpable youth with the assurance of a representative so that he accepted the rebuke as a public one, though with unacknowledged resentment because it was also personal.

This system of shared emotions might have been designed to prevent marriage; but if by chance a couple managed to evade Binkie's vigilance and the group jealousy, and presented themselves engaged, they would be received with a groan of protest; it was felt, deeply, as a betrayal; and if they braved it out, shaking their heads smilingly at Binkie's private warnings that 'Man, your work'll suffer,' and 'You don't want to tie yourself down to kids at your age, baby,' then the group, like one of those jellylike spores which live by absorption, swelled out and surrounded the couple, swallowing the marriage whole. They might marry provided they married from the Sports Club, with Binkie or one of the senior wolves as best man, and rejoined the Club at once after the briefest possible honeymoon, prepared to share their joys and sorrows with the rest. But these marriages tended to dissolve rather quickly. There were more than one couple, now returned to the fold as units, who danced with their ex-husbands, ex-wives, in the usual sentimental good-fellowship, even made love to them afterwards, though within the prescribed limits, and in the prescribed place, a parked car; and if these limits proved irresistibly piquant, after the freedom of marriage, so that the couple seemed inclined to link up again, Binkie was likely to take both aside, but separately, saying, 'Now, you've tried it once, it didn't work, now don't fall for it again.' And then, as a desperate second best: 'At any rate, have a bang with someone else. There's Tom' (or Mabel, as the case might be). 'Now, Tom's a good sort, why don't you have a bang with him?'

There were already half a dozen children, club children, who slept in their prams through sundowners and dances, and grew up on the veranda among the hockey sticks, beer mugs and bare legs, like a doom made visible.

A newcomer, hearing the sentimental refrain, 'Look, there's Betty, a nice kid, Betty,' would turn to see a tall young woman in brief shorts and sandals, her face brown and dried by a thousand afternoons of hockey and tennis, her hair tied on the top with a pink or blue ribbon, and imagine that the 'kid' was the small girl she led by the hand, who was likely to be wearing the same coloured shorts above fat and dimpled legs, and a hair ribbon tied in exactly the same way as her mother's.

And so it all went on, through '35, '36, '37, '38; during that Christmas season of 1938, it was as if the Club had existed forever, that it would exist forever; it was like a fairy story, drenched in nostalgic golden light, where everyone is young, nothing changes. The tranquil blue gums at the foot of the playing fields, the banked jacarandas at the back of the golf course, the hedges of hibiscus, splashed with vivid scarlet over the glossy thick green – these enclosed a magic circle, and inside it nothing could happen, nothing threatened, for some tacit law made it impossible to discuss politics here, and Europe was a long way off. In fact, it might be said that this club had come into existence simply as a protest against everything Europe stood for. There were no divisions here, no barriers, or at least none that could be put into words; the most junior clerk from the railways, the youngest typist, were on Christian-name terms with their bosses, and mingled easily with the sons of Cabinet ministers; the harshest adjective in use was 'toffee-nosed', which meant snobbish, or exclusive; and even the black waiters who served them were likely to find themselves clapped across the shoulders by an intoxicated wolf at the end of the dance: 'Good old Tickey,' or 'There's a good chap, Shilling,' and perhaps even their impassive, sardonic faces might relax in an unwilling smile, under pressure from this irresistible flood of universal goodwill.

Chapter Two

On that Saturday morning, Martha was embarrassed because she wanted to leave at twelve instead of at one, and did not like to ask the favour of Mr Cohen. She was in an almost agonized condition, out of all proportion to the cause; partly due to the fact that she had hardly been near the Polytechnic for a week. With one part of her mind she was making resolutions to do nothing 'for at least three months' but study shorthand and speed typing; while with the other she guiltily imagined herself walking into Mr Cohen's office and telling him about the dress she wanted to buy: for she intended to use the charm, the almost stammering diffidence which she knew she should banish from her personality here at work.

At twelve, when she at last rose to her feet, gripping the desk because her knees were shaking, Mr Robinson's door opened, and he called through it, 'Come here a moment, Miss Quest.' He added impatiently, 'If you don't mind,' conforming to the etiquette imposed by Mr Cohen.

Martha went to his office and found she was being given a long and complicated document; on a closer look, she found it was one she had already typed that morning.

'Miss Quest,' said Mr Robinson, with a rather strained smile and embarrassed look, 'you must have been thinking about something else when you typed this.'

Mr Robinson was a young man about twenty-five and he was serving his articles. There was nothing youthful about him. He was lean, of middle height, of the athletic build, though he tended to carry himself in an energetic curve, like a half-tensed bow. He was altogether grey and legal-looking;

his light hair lay stiffly back, brushed with oil to a dun conformity; his mouth was thin, set, impatient; and his fine grey eyes, deep-set and intelligent, had not yet learned to soften into tolerance. He had a good knowledge of the law, but he was not yet a good lawyer, and would find it hard to become one. He tended to get impatient with difficult clients, and more than once he had emerged from his office looking prickly and bitter, after the women had listened for some minutes to his angry voice shouting against another, saying, 'In university they don't tell you the greater part of the law is learning to tolerate fools.' With the women, he was curt, and then softened his orders and reprimands with a stiff smile. It was understood that when Martha was really efficient she would become Mr Robinson's personal secretary; but neither of them looked forward to this arrangement. He liked Mrs Buss, whom he overloaded with work, although she was supposed to work exclusively for Mr Cohen.

Now he was trying his best to be pleasant, but failed: and Martha withdrew with the spoilt document, looking as irritable as he did.

She was relieved. Now she would not be in time to buy the dress before the shop closed. She was saved from spending twenty pounds on a model dress, which she would pay for at the rate of ten shillings a month. The decision had been made for her, her mind was set free, and she typed out the document almost as fast and neatly as Mrs Buss and returned to lay it on Mr Robinson's desk well before one o'clock.

'Wait a minute,' he snapped; then, hastily: 'Please.' He reached for the document, read it through, then looked up at her with his awkward smile. 'If you can do it like this now, why couldn't you before?' he demanded.

Martha hesitated, then watched herself rushing gaily into a story about the dress; she wanted to stop, for she should never have started; the fatal nervous compulsion, similar to that which had made her tease Donovan to kiss her, had her in its grip, and she could neither stop nor speak naturally.

He was uncomfortable, for he could never tolerate the personal, and by the time she had come stammering to an end they were both red and uneasy.

'If you'll take my advice, Miss Quest – though it's nothing to do with me, of course – you'll keep clear of these sharks who try and get you girls in their grip. I get them here as clients, crying their eyes out when it's too late. A dress for twenty pounds – it's ridiculous for a child of your age,' he finished, as if he were an old man himself. Then, with a glance at her sulky face: 'Well, it's your affair. Please send Mrs Buss in. If she's got time, of course.'

Martha went out and found the big office half empty. She took her bag, and quickly left by herself, avoiding the others, and hurried along Main Street to the window where the dress was displayed.

Just before the war, women were supposed to be tall, broad-shouldered, slim-hipped, long-legged. Martha's room may have been littered with books, but it was also plentifully supplied with magazines, where all the women conformed to that shape, and when she saw her reflection, when she imagined herself in this dress or that, she continually strained her mental image of herself upwards, thinning it, posing it; when she saw herself ideally, crossing a room, under fire from admiring eyes, it was in the guise of this other, imposed woman. As for Donovan, he saw her as so much raw material for his own needs. This dress, however, had the power to destroy these false images, and she examined it with love, almost with physical pain, for the shop was closed, and now she would never buy it. She knew that the moment this dress clothed her body she would be revealed to herself, and to others, as something quite new, but deeply herself. That dress was made to clothe the person she knew herself to be. It was of a brilliant dark blue, of fine, transparent silky stuff. Its bodice was close and moulded, lightly sewn with tiny brilliants, and the skirt had knots and ribbons of the same brilliants gleaming from the folds. It was a romantic dress, with its lightly draped shoulders and great flowing skirt; but as she tested the word 'romantic' she could not helping thinking of Donovan, and at once began to feel uncertain, for she knew it was not what he would have chosen for her.

And as she thought, dubiously, of Donovan, she heard a car hooting, and turned to see Donovan himself, trying to keep his place in the stream of Saturday lunchtime traffic. The street was a river of hot and shining metal, the cars were creeping, nose to tail, and she ran along the kerb until she was able to leap in beside him.

'What are you doing day-dreaming beside our wicked Mr Louise's window, Matty dear?' he enquired.

She explained, making herself sound flippant, and disguising all she really felt about that dress; and he said, 'But, Matty, you know you must have my personal supervision. I saw that dress this morning, and really, Matty, you should have learned better by now. It's very pretty and womanly and all that, but it's not smart. Now, don't worry. I'll come with you, and you'll see, I'll make you the belle of the ball.'

She laughed, and after a moment submitted herself to him, and felt grateful; for a moment, however, she had felt the beginnings of something very different, a strong resisting dislike of his pressure on her.

In her bedroom, he took out the two evening dresses she owned, and laid them on the bed, and at once became serious and thoughtful. He sat beside them, fingering the material, and frowning; it was a physical communion between those dresses and himself, from which she was excluded.

There was a knock on the door, and Mrs Gunn came in, and Martha knew it was because she had heard a man's voice.

'Oh, it's you, Mr Anderson,' she said, in doubtful relief.

Donovan, with hardly a glance at her, said that he was busy.

At a movement of Mrs Gunn's head, Martha followed her on to the back veranda. 'You won't take it amiss,' said Mrs Gunn, 'but my daughter made it a rule never to have a man

194

in her room. Not that I'd say a word against Mr Anderson, but . . .'

Mrs Gunn's pale and fleshy face was glistening with sweat, her dry reddish hair was dark in streaks, her dress was soaked from the armpits to the waist: hers was not a type to stand the heat. She went on complainingly, 'I had a letter from your mother, she worries about you, I said I'd look after you, but . . .'

Martha said angrily that she could look after herself.

Mrs Gunn was hurt, and said she didn't want to interfere. Martha replied that in that case she might refrain from doing so.

Their voices had risen, and they heard Donovan calling, 'Matty, come here, I want you.'

The two quarrelling women, who liked each other and knew it, exchanged an apologetic and humorous smile.

Mrs Gunn said plaintively, 'It's the heat, Matty. My temper's awful this weather.'

Martha felt an impulse to kiss her, but it was impossible for her to kiss women; she said rather drily that she did not think there was any need to worry about Mr Anderson.

Mrs Gunn's pale and worried eyes lit with malicious speculation; they met Martha's and suddenly both women began to laugh. 'You're all right,' said Mrs Gunn, laughing hoarsely, with a helpless shaking movement of her big tormented body. She put her arms round Martha and kissed her, and Martha tried not to stiffen against this damp, strong-smelling embrace. 'You're all right,' said Mrs Gunn again, and Martha nodded and laughed, and with a guilty look rejoined Donovan.

'When you disgusting girls have finished,' he said in a light but gruff voice. 'You're as bad as my mother, she's always giggling with *women*. You have no discrimination, Matty. I've told you that before. You always get yourself mixed up with people.'

Martha shrugged impatiently and went to the french window. The lunchtime traffic had thinned to an occasional car that raced past impatiently. The tarmac road glistened oilily, the sun poured down, there was a strong smell of warm tar. The sky was ominous, spaces of intense hot blue between heavy thunderclouds. The trees in the park were motionless, the flowers in the garden hung stricken, with curling leaves. Martha was now both irritable and sad. She did not want to go to the dance, everything disgusted her. Worse, she did not understand these violent fluctuations of mood; it was as if half a dozen entirely different people inhabited her body, and they violently disliked each other, bound together by only one thing, a strong impulse of longing; anonymous, impersonal, formless, like water. She stood there, silent, at the open door, while gusts of hot, tar-smelling air came off the street. Slowly she settled into a mood of rich melancholy, where at least she felt at home, though she distrusted it so persistently; thus had she stood, as a child, watching the slow changes of the veld, where the cloud shadows dissolved like flocks of birds, watching the movements of rain along the hills: at *that* moment she saw herself as a lethargic person, doomed, without energy.

She wished Donovan would go away, for she knew that soon she must rouse herself to meet his wishes; for of course she would go dancing that night, and, long before then, would be vividly, electrically excited. The thought of this other person she would soon become exhausted her anew, and she said crossly to Donovan, 'I do wish you wouldn't fuss so. What does it matter what I look like?'

He did not reply, and she looked over her shoulder to see an expression on his face which meant 'These female vagaries'? – but no, it meant, 'Coquetry'! And he was impatient of it. '*Really*, Matty,' was all he said; and then: 'And now come here, I'm ready to start work.'

She went listlessly to his side, but he said, 'Now take off your dress, Matty – no, don't start these girlish giggles, I really do find them so tiresome.'

She slowly removed her dress, pointing out to herself that this was the first time she had been seen undressed by a man, and wishing that it did not seem so unimportant. Standing in her petticoat, she saw Donovan scrutinizing her shoulders and arms, and he even put out his hand and slowly turned her round, to examine her back.

'That's a good girl,' he said approvingly, screwing up his eyes with a professional look.

He led her to the mirror, lifted her arms, and gently pulled over her head the white cotton dress she had made for the Van Rensbergs' dance. 'This has distinct possibilities, Matty, but anyone can look pretty.' He crouched at her feet and shook out the skirt, and Martha saw a pale, tired-looking girl with untidy hair looking back at her from the mirror. 'Now just look at it,' said Donovan. 'You see?'

She saw that it was similar in shape to that dark-blue dress she coveted; it was, if one may use the term of something which has so many forms, the basic type of an evening dress: small fitting top, full skirt; but the blue dress took its beauty from the fine material, and the delicate tracery of glinting beads, and the suggestion of half-concealed shoulders. Obstinately, despite what he said, she yearned for it; and submitted to being shaped into something very far from the girl who could wear that soft, flowing gown.

Donovan kneeled below her and worked on the white dress. He was quite absorbed, and she turned passively between his hands like a dummy. She felt not a trace of self-consciousness when he reached up to pull the stuff across her breasts, even when he pushed them up with his hands, high into the stiff sharp folds with which he intended to emphasize them.

Mrs Gunn knocked again, and entered with a big parcel. She was panting, her hair was falling damply across her face, and though she summoned energy enough to look drily at the absorbed young man on his knees in front of the girl, her remark, 'My God, isn't it awful?' referred to the heat. 'It's going to rain, shouldn't be surprised,' she said, going out. Thunder was rolling gently among the banked clouds overhead.

Martha looked down at Donovan's dark head, usually so sleek and close. A strand of the rather coarse hair had fallen loose, and hung stiffly over his forehead, and for some reason Martha found that stiff lock repulsive; also the plane of forehead, which showed reddish, coarse-grained, and wet with sweat. There were flakes of sodden dandruff on the line of the parting, which showed dead white, like the belly of a fish. She began to move irritably under his working hands, and restrained herself with difficulty when he said, 'Now, then, Matty, we must suffer in the cause of beauty, be a good girl.'

She told herself that she was bored, looked away, and saw the parcel lying on her bed. Books. Cautiously, she leaned the top half of her body sideways, and extended an arm to pull the parcel closer, and Donovan said, 'Matty, there's a time and place for everything.'

She remained exasperatedly patient.

'What books have you ordered?' he asked.

'I don't know what's come,' she replied evasively, with the feeling that this, at least, should be her own.

'Why don't you arrange your books in a nice case so that people may see them when they come? It's no good having books under the bed. And you're really a clever girl, Matty, but you talk just like everybody else. You'd impress people if you tried.'

Martha put on a sarcastic expression for his benefit, but he was not looking at her.

'Now, take Ruth Manners. She went home to England with her mamma, and she's come back ever so intelligent, she went to the theatres and the galleries, and you've no idea, she's so North Avenue these days – Turn around a little, Matty, lift your hip – that's right. You do slouch, you know, but not in the right way, it's very sexy to slouch, if you know how. Well, it's done everything for Ruth. You haven't got a rich mamma to buy you clothes, but at least you've read everything; but you don't know how to make the best of yourself – Let your shoulders forward a little – you should learn to stand with your bottom tucked *in*, and your hips forward, and your shoulders slightly curved, but held so that your breasts stand out. Like *that*, Matty.'

He rose to his feet in front of her, and with one hand pressed in her buttocks, and with the other pressed down her shoulders so that her breasts came forward, almost against his. His frowning eyes met her antagonistic ones, and he dropped his hands, and his handsome face, now showing coarse-featured, fleshy, shiny with heat and effort, slowly went a sullen red. 'I know what you're thinking,' he said, with an attempt at grace. 'Well, I promise I'll make love to you, Matty, I will, really, but not now.' He looked at his watch, and became himself. 'Now you will lie down and sleep, because you really look awful, you know. I will come and dress you at six. You must have a bath at five, but don't touch your hair, I'll do it.' Waving a cheerful goodbye, he hastened away, and Martha lay obediently, shuddering with dislike of him, and also with gusts of hysterical laughter.

She did not sleep. Soon she rose and filled the bath, and lay in it while the water cooled, listening to the iron roof creeping and tensing with the heat. Through the open fanlight she could hear Mrs Gunn's sighs and complaints, where she sat on the veranda. The thunder muttered and growled like an animal. Soon she fell to inspecting her own body according to that other standard, 'long, lean, narrow,' but it was difficult to respect that standard when she saw herself naked, and soon, with frank adoration, she fell into a rite of self-love. Her limbs lay smooth and light in the water, her thighs seemed to her like two plump and gleaming fishes, she scattered water over her white belly, and watched the drops fall like rough jewels and slide to a perfect quivering silver globule in her navel. Meantime, her body lay unmoved and distant, congealing into perfection under the eyes of this lover; while Martha thought of Mrs Gunn's groaning sweating body, and was fiercely grateful for her own; she thought of the ugly scar across her mother's stomach, and swore protectively to her own that it would never, never be so marred; she thought of Mrs Van Rensberg's legs, and with tender reassurance passed her hands over her own smooth brown legs, murmuring that it was all right, all right, nothing would harm them.

A few heavy drops fell like stones on the iron roof; there was a swish and a swirl of rain and wind and dust; the thunder cracked overhead and the rain plunged like a steel barrage. Her spirits rose like a kite, till she was singing inside the din at the top of her voice; and faintly, through the thunder, the crashing rain, the gurgling bath water, Mrs Gunn could be heard chanting relief like a prayer of thankfulness to the rain god. Martha left the bathroom, her depression flooded away with the bath water, and found that around the table on the back veranda Mrs Gunn and her daughter were drinking tea, their faces bright and soft and smiling. Martha stood by the table in her red dressing-gown and drank tea with them, and they talked and watched the rain drive in gleaming spears beyond the faded green mosquito gauze, and the irritable tension of the early afternoon was so far away there was no need to apologize for it. Mrs Gunn put her arm around Martha's hips and said she was her girl, she was her daughter, now that her own had left her; and the young woman at the other end of the table laughed, and they all laughed, and the rain fell endlessly, everything rushed and gurgled and swam, and they laughed again when the thunder came crashing dangerously over the roof like armies, so loud that they could hear no sound of voices, though they were shrieking at each other like grinning maniacs. With a pantomime of laughing regret, Martha indicated she must go and dress; and was sorry to leave them. She could not understand how she had so disliked Mrs Gunn earlier; and Mrs Gunn's daughter, who had a new baby, and was therefore usually an object of repulsion to Martha, seemed delightfully simple and womanly as she sat there beside her mother, nursing the dribbling, mouthing infant.

She wanted to go to that dance more than she had ever wanted anything; her whole being was poised and dedicated; and when Donovan came in, shrieking with laughter over his damp evening clothes, he found Martha bright-eyed and chattering and amenable, ready to be sewn into her dress.

But it took such a long time. Donovan wiped off her make-up, and made her shut her eyes while he painted her face again. He arranged and rearranged her hair. She was compliant, but impatient. At the end, he led her triumphantly to the long mirror, and said, 'Now, then, Matty . . .'

Martha looked, and, in spite of her pleasure, was uneasy. It was not herself, she felt. The simplicity of that white dress had been given a touch of the bizarre – no, *that* was not it; as she regarded herself, she was instinctively forming herself to match that young woman in the mirror, who was cold, unapproachable, and challenging. But from the cool, remote face peered a pair of troubled and uneasy eyes.

As she saw that glance – her own, it seemed – Donovan came forward quickly, and said, 'Now, listen, Matty, you really must see that you must change yourself for a dress like this. Don't you see?' He bent towards her, his hand hovering, ready to seize on what was wrong. 'Look,' he said finally, 'your eyes too. Lift your head.' As she remained motionless, his palm raised her head. 'With those cheekbones,' he said, 'look, your eyes should be like this.' With something like horror, Martha saw him slide his own eyes slantingly sideways, into a languid, distant gleam. 'You *see*?' he demanded triumphantly. He did it again. For a flash of a second, he was terrifyingly herself; and she stared at him in fascinated disgust. This time her laugh was nervous, and he dropped his hand, and looked at her and flushed.

'You really are – extraordinary,' she said at last, slowly; and the dislike she felt was strong in her voice. The silence was a long one; it was a moment of decision between them. Martha, looking helplessly at him, saw, but remotely, that if she was confused and unhappy, so was he; he had a sullen and little-boy look about him that should have claimed her pity, but merely irritated her; and across this barrier flowed a faint guilt that she could not, for the life of her, say something comforting; it was terrifying, in a different way, to see that assured young man so distressed and lost.

At last he sat himself down, flinging one leg moodily over the other, and he remarked, 'I should have been a dress designer. I would have been a very good one, Matty dear.' That light, 'Matty dear,' fed back his self-belief; he was already recovering. 'But if one is raised in the colonies, then what can one do but go into statistics and wait for one's chief to retire!' Here he laughed with genuine bitterness; and Martha understood that if anything bound them it was their mutual conviction that *if* they had been born into other circumstances, *if only* . . .

'Well,' she said awkwardly, 'don't let's quarrel. You'd better give me up as a bad job, you know. I don't think I'm cut out for a mannequin!' She was laughing at him, but she longed for – what? Some gesture that might express that thing they shared? She felt he should have put his arms around her in a light and brotherly way, and thus the whole incident would have been put behind them.

Instead, he laughed again, angrily, and said, 'Oh, well, to hell with everything, Matty. Let's go to the party, and astonish them all.'

At the door, she saw that the rain had stopped. A dusky sunset was reflected in the lake which lay between them and the gate.

'I suppose you expect me to carry you, like a he-man on the films,' he said. 'But I shan't. Now, don't let the mud get on your skirts.'

He shrieked in gay alarm as she began balancing her way cautiously from the step to a rocking stone, and from there to a small point of brick that stood blackly amid the rosy waters. And here she stood, precariously, laughing at herself, and at him, for he was agitatedly dancing on the steps, saying, 'Matty, Matty, do be careful.' There was something about that shrill and helpless exhortation which turned her mood into defiance. She looked calmly about her: there were six feet of muddy water between her and the gate. 'To hell with it,' she remarked; and fell all at once into her element. She lifted her crisp white skirts in a bunch around her waist, and composedly walked in her gold shoes, the water lapping cool around her ankles, to the sidewalk, saying, 'Oooh, it's lovely, it's lovely, Don,' like a child paddling.

In a series of leaps, he came splashing across to join her. 'Matty,' he said, in distressed and incredulous astonishment, 'Matty, you're mad. I suppose you haven't even paid for those shoes yet.'

'Of course not,' she said recklessly, letting her skirts fall, and laughing at him, despising him, most sincerely, from the bottom of her heart.

'But your feet are wet,' he complained.

'My feet are so wet,' she mimicked him cruelly. 'Oh, dear, I might get a *cold*.' She stopped, already feeling herself uncertain. After all, the shoes were expensive; after all it was rather childish. 'Oh, don't be such an old woman,' she said crossly, and got into the car. 'They won't notice my feet,' she said coaxingly at last. 'They'll be looking at your beautiful dress.' She lifted her feet and examined them. The gold leather had dulled, and was crinkling; there was a faint brown tidemark around her ankles. She could not help looking at them with satisfaction; the elegant, cool white dress seemed quite remote from her, a mere surface to her body, which continued strongly upwards from those reckless strong ankles.

She shook her head to loosen her hair, and laughed heartlessly when he said, 'You look like a nice open-air girl, if that's what you want. But for heaven's sake, Matty, do move carefully, I've just tacked you into that dress so as not to spoil the line, and if you bounce about it'll fall off. I suppose you'd like that.'

'Of course,' she said lightly; but she imagined herself thus suddenly exposed, and laughed on a thrill of excitement. 'Of course,' she said again, and saw his face darken with irritated annoyance.

They arrived at the Club. The veranda was illuminated by strings of coloured lights, and a large electric sign said: 'Three weeks to Christmas – Let it Rip, Boys and Girls.'

The large room was cleared for the dance, and was empty. On the main veranda young men and women were drinking, some in evening dress, some not yet changed from their sports clothes. Martha knew most of them by sight, and was greeted by intimate sisterly smiles from the girls, the usual howls and whistles from the men. Her resentment at this had been not so much dulled as pushed away into that part of herself she acknowledged to be the true one. As for Donovan, she saw he was being received with queries: 'Well, stranger, you back?' – a statement, in fact, which meant that in spite of what he said he was no stranger to the Club. She expected they would sit by themselves, if she expected anything at all – for this way of hers, submitting herself to a person or a place, with a demure, childish compliance, as if she were under a spell, meant that she did not consciously expect or demand; she might dream about things being different, but that, after all, commits one to nothing.

Far from leading Martha away from the others, Donovan held a court for a few minutes, while he debated aloud, gaily, with a frank rudeness, whether Binkie's table or another's would suit him best. At last he took Martha's hand and seated her at a table where Binkie and his lieutenants and their girls were drinking and eating peanuts, saying, 'And now here you are, Matty, all among the huskies.'

He then sat himself between two girls, and ignored Martha completely, which at first annoyed her, and then relieved her, for now she was free to behave as she pleased.

It was about seven in the evening. Beyond the dark spines of the blue gums, the sunset faded in a hushed and tender glow; the playing fields were shimmering green under the water; the clubhouse itself was surrounded by a churned mass of red mud. It was the cloistral hour, the hour of silence, as if the very fact that in the trees, and in the veld that was no more than half a mile's walk distant, the little creatures and birds were sinking into sleep aroused, in these people, though briefly, the memory of that other cycle submerged in their blood. The lights were not switched on; they sat in a flushed half-dark, and unconsciously their voices lowered, though they were teasing each other about the mud on their clothes and because some were reluctant to cross the mud to the cars so that they might go and dress. Martha showed her shoes and made a funny story out of wading through the water; halfway through it she became nervous, because she realized it put Donovan in a bad light, but continued, avoiding his eyes; and the young man next to her said that if he had been there he'd have carried Matty in his arms through the flood. He was a big, blond-fleshed youth, his fair hair crinkled tight over his head, with a reddish glint in it; and in a square, burnt, determined face were blue and direct eyes. Martha thought it remarkable that this young man, whom she knew to be manager of a big insurance company, should be content to appear like a buffooning schoolboy. She began talking to him rather awkwardly, about a book she had just read. He answered reluctantly. When she persisted, he gave a public sigh, which drew all the expectant eyes towards him, and said mournfully, 'Baby, baby, you'll be the death of me.' Then he indicated Martha with an outstretched thumb, and said, 'She's intelligent. This baby's got brains.' And he laughed and rolled up his eyes and shook his head with a kind of subsiding shudder into himself. Martha flushed, and, as soon as the conversation had got under way around them, began talking 'amusingly', as she was expected to do. The uneasy blue eyes fixed on her in relief; his face cleared, and she understood that all was well. Soon he got up, saying that he must go and change; but Matty must remember he would die for her, she killed him, and he insisted on the first dance.

Soon the veranda was half empty, and there remained a few couples in evening dress. Martha was feeling a little sick, for she had hardly eaten all day; but Donovan was talking to the two girls, who were leaning towards him and laughing with a flattering attention; and so she gave up all idea of dinner, pulled a plate of potato chips towards her, and began eating them with the ruminant concentration which means a person is eating not for pleasure but from necessity.

She heard laughter, glanced up, and saw that the people around her were amused. 'I'm starved,' she said firmly, and went on eating.

Binkie got up from his chair, came to hers, and crouched

beside her, his arm lightly about her waist. 'Beautiful,' he said, 'we can't have this, we'll give you some dinner.'

She looked hesitatingly towards Donovan. She had never said to herself that he was mean; and it was with another shock that she saw that here he was known to be, for the glances people directed towards him were spitefully amused. She was hurt for his sake, and said gaily that no, she didn't want dinner, Donovan was quite right, she was slimming and –

Donovan waved a careless hand towards her, and said, 'Matty, dear, do go, if you want to.' Hurt again, this time on her own account, she got to her feet, and thanked Binkie, and said she would like to have dinner with him. And so it was that, at the very beginning of the evening, she was separated from Donovan; it was rather as if he had pushed her away, for she left, smiling an apologetic farewell, and he did not so much as look at her.

Martha walked beside Binkie with the same gentle, submissive gesture that had until five minutes before been Donovan's due; the mere fact that he had asked her to dine with him was as if her emotions had been gathered up, twisted together, by him. And he certainly put his arm around her as they went down the veranda, crooning, 'My baby's having dinner with me'; but the circular look he directed around the veranda over her head was keen and critical and he was summoning his subjects by a nod or a wave of his free hand; for having dinner with Binkie was a communal affair.

A dozen wolves, therefore, with their girls, crowded into cars, and drove down to McGrath's dining room, which they entered royally, welcomed by hosts of waiters. For Binkie's 'gang' might go berserk, had been known to wreck the dining room, but they paid liberally, tipped fabulously. On the other hand, McGrath's was the senior hotel in the colony, and here came important visitors from England and the Continent; McGrath's must maintain its reputation, and, therefore, the waiters' welcome was apprehensive.

They were given a centre table in the big room, which was

chocolate brown and gilt, like the lounge. It was already decorated for Christmas. The headwaiter and the wine waiter, both white men, greeted each wolf by name, were offered Christian names in return, and were slapped across the shoulders. They took orders in voices that were pointedly lowered; while the deferential eyes implored, Please, Mr Maynard do please behave yourself, and persuade your gang to do likewise! The headwaiter, Johnny Constoupolis, even pointed out to Binkie that Mr Player, who was the head of the big company which in fact controlled the colony, was sitting with his wife in a corner under the palms by the band. But at this information Binkie leaped to his feet, and roared out a greeting to Mr Player, so loudly that everyone in the room looked round.

Johnny was distressed, not merely because of the danger that other respectable clients might be annoyed, but because his feeling for the important Mr Player was prayerful; the dark, suave, tired little Greek served the great man with the exquisite tact that had gained him this position; and from Mr Player's table he crossed continually to Binkie's, whose father, he knew, was also an important man, an educated man; and in his heart he shuddered with amazement and awed fear, as at madness. These young people were all mad. They spent money like dirt; Binkie might throw away twenty pounds on one of these dinners; he owed money everywhere, even to Mr Player himself; they all behaved like licensed lunatics, as if there was no future, as if they had no plans to become important men themselves, with wives and children. And their idea of themselves seemed to be accepted by everyone else. Johnny knew that if this was going to be one of the evenings when the wolves decided life owed them a holocaust, and began singing and tearing down the decorations, and dancing on the tables, then the other people, including Mr Player, would regard them with the pained tolerance due to a pack of momentarily overexcited children. Strange and even terrible to the little Greek, who had left his beloved country with his family twenty years before, to rescue them all from poverty so profound that it haunted him even now. Never would Johnny the Greek lose his fear of poverty; never would he lose the knowledge that from one minute to the next a man might lose his precious foothold among the fed and honoured living, and slip down among the almost nameless ghosts; Johnny remembered hunger, that common denominator; his mother had died of tuberculosis; his sister had died of starvation in the Great War, a weightless bundle of rags. At Johnny's shoulder was always this shadow, this fear; and now he stood behind Binkie Maynard's chair, in McGrath's dining room, very slightly bowed forward, and took their orders for the meal, while he kept his dark and sorrowful eyes carefully veiled, lest what he felt might show.

He knew that he must spend time taking orders, while the wolves yearned over the girls, insisting that their slightest wish should be fulfilled; but once this ritual was over, it did not matter what food was actually brought, for they would not notice. They did not care about food, or even about wine. If they ordered wine, they might spend five minutes debating about a title on the wine list, and forget what they had ordered when the bottle arrived. They did not understand, they understood nothing, they were barbarians; but they must be given reverence, for one day (though the gods alone knew how this metamorphosis was to be effected) they would be the grave and responsible fathers of the city, and these girls their wives.

Martha ate the hotel dinner with appetite, if not with enjoyment. The menu was long and in French, and this was the most expensive meal the colony could offer.

They ate a thick white soup, which tasted of flour and pepper; round cheese puffs, the size of cricket balls and tasting of nothing in particular; boiled fish with gluey white sauce; roast chicken, hard white shreds of meat, with boiled stringbeans and boiled potatoes; stewed plums and fresh cream; and sardines on toast. They were all drinking brandy mixed with ginger beer. Halfway through, Binkie began urging them all to 'put some speed into it, kids'; for he was already anxious because the dance might begin without him.

At the end, he flung down silver, handfuls of it, while the waiters smiled and bowed towards him, though their intent eyes were already calculating how much silver, and how it would divide between them. The girls were protesting, as usual, with maternal pride, that Binkie was a crazy kid. They returned in a body to the Sports Club. Martha was thinking, with guilty affection, of Donovan, but could not immediately find him. She was already claimed by Perry, the large blond athlete.

The Club was now filled with people in evening dress, and the band was playing. She found Donovan sitting with a girl whom Martha knew to be Ruth Manners. He waved his hand towards her, like an acquaintance, while he cast a disparaging look at Perry. Martha looked for help to Binkie, who said with that disconcerting frankness, 'Better off with us, baby, he doesn't even feed you properly.' But her eyes were still appealing; and they groaned and sighed and shrugged, and fetched chairs and placed tables together, until Donovan was at the head of a large circle of people, and Martha was facing him.

Ruth Manners was a thin, delicate girl with a narrow white face, short dark springy hair, long nervous hands. Her features were irregular: the thin scarlet mouth twisted to one side when she smiled, her thin nose was a little crooked, her eyebrows were like circumflex accents, sharp and black over pale and watchful eyes. She spoke carefully, with controlled vowels, she moved with care; at every moment, she was conscious of how she must appear. And this consciousness, together with the delicate look – her eyelids were slightly reddened and heavy, the white cheeks had an irregular fading flush – gave her an intellectual look. Yet she was very elegant, with an elegance that none of the other women present could approach. She wore a jade-green dress of heavy thick crepe, which was pleated loosely from the waist, and held around the narrow figure with a flame-coloured sash. The top was cut low, front and back, the material lying lightly over small flat breasts that were like a child's. Her shoulders and neck were thin and bony, of a frail whiteness that looked as if it might so easily flush, like her cheeks, into unbecoming red. And yet, though she was not pretty, and her body – so Martha jealously said to herself – would be better covered up, she undeniably possessed the quality that Donovan admired so much. Her assurance seemed to say, One doesn't have to be attractive, one may have an undesirable body, but what of it? I have this other thing. And Martha, because of that assurance, lost hers. She felt herself to be dowdy and altogether lacking, in spite of the homage of the wolves.

Ruth and Donovan made a pair, and knew it. They talked easily to each other, where they sat side by side at the head of the table, in a light, flirtatious, bantering way that was so much *not* the way of the Club that the rest were a little subdued, listening with uncomfortable attention.

Seeing that he had an audience. Donovan leaned back in his graceful way, and took Ruth's hand and said, 'Well, girls and boys, we should all go to England. You see what it does for us? Now, look at Ruth's dress, Matty dear – you see? It's got what we poor colonials can't achieve.'

Ruth laughed and said, 'Poor Don, but you were in England yourself last year.'

Now, Martha had never been told that Donovan had been to England, and she found this extraordinary. She saw that he was annoyed; for he frowned, and hesitated, before making the best of it and saying, 'Yes, Ruthie, but I had no opportunities to improve myself, for I went under escort with my mamma, and she was much too busy buying clothes in Harrods and Derry and Toms, and I had to go with her, because she can't buy anything without me, as you know.'

These two shops, which had been presented to Martha all her childhood as synonyms for 'niceness', now lost their dull sound, for they could also provide Mrs Anderson's conventional smartness. But Ruth looked amused and tolerant at the names; and there was an allowance of spite in her careful drawl, which said plainly that she found Donovan a little ridiculous. 'But surely you couldn't have spent three months doing nothing but buying clothes – even at Harrods?'

Donovan was annoyed, but he maintained the light note. 'My dear Ruthie, you have the advantage of a mamma who wants to do her best for you. You should have pity for us less fortunate breeds.'

'Poor Donny-boy,' said Ruth, with her short laugh.

'Yes,' said Donovan, now launching himself on the effort to be amusing even at his own cost. 'Yes, it was a great disillusion to me, going to England. You know the way we all think of it – but after all, when one gets there, there are certain limitations one overlooks beforehand. I sat in the Cumberland – because we colonials always go to the Cumberland, and nothing will make my mamma see that there is no need to emphasize an already too obvious fact – and I ate ravishing cream cakes all day, with my father, who grumbled all the time because he said England was over-civilized, though I don't think for a moment he knew what he meant by that. We sat and waited for Mamma to return, laden with yet fresh parcels, from various little expeditions of her own – because my mamma can always be trusted to amuse herself, wherever she is. It was the only time I can ever remember that my papa and myself had anything in common. I said, 'Papa dear, you may like the wide open spaces, and you're welcome to them, but as for me, I'm simply made for decadence. Why don't you give me some money, and I shall apprentice myself to some dress designer, and thus find my niche.'

'Poor Donny-boy,' said Ruth again, this time sincerely.

'So my papa said nothing would give him greater pleasure, he disliked anomalies like myself, but unfortunately, since Mamma had spent the money destined to last three months in the first three weeks, and he had had to cable for more, there was none left over for either of us.' Donovan ended on a squeal of laughter, which sounded so resentful that only Ruth was able to join him. The others sat silently watching; and Martha heard Perry mutter, 'For crying out loud, for crying out loud, come and dance, I can't take it.' He roughly pulled Martha up, and they went inside to dance; and again he complained, 'For crying out loud,' with a reminiscent disgust, as they took the floor.

Perry, because of the character imposed on him, was obliged to stop every few moments, shoot up his arms, and yell like a tormented soul, while people turned to laugh; or he broke suddenly into writhing jive, his head crushed back on his neck, his eyes closed, while he crooned, in a thick, blind, whining voice, in imitation of a Negro singing. In between, he pushed Martha conventionally around the room, in a rectangular progress, and the straight blue eyes assessed her, while his face held its sentimental look.

Martha watched his eyes; she was becoming obsessed by the need to look at the eyes of these people and not their bodies; for they were serious, anxious, even pleading; while all the time their bodies, their faces, contorted into the poses required of them. It was as if their surfaces, their limbs, their voices, were possessed, it was an exterior possession that did not touch them, left them free to judge and comment. Martha continually felt a shock; looking from Perry's eyes to his jerking, shuddering impersonations of Negro singing, she felt uneasy. In the meantime, she danced, smiling brightly, replying to him in the jargon. Towards the end of the dance, encouraged by the intelligent seriousness of the blue eyes, she rebelled, and talked in her normal voice about Donovan, about Ruth, while she felt his arms tightening, his eyes clouding. But she went on; she was resentful because he would not accept her as *herself* – whatever that might mean; for was she not continually at sea, because of the different selves which insisted on claiming possession of her? She meant, she wanted to establish contact with him, simply and warmly; she wanted him to recognize her as a reasonable being. When he rolled up his eyes, and pretended to shudder, and said, 'Oh, baby, but the way you talk,' she kept a determined smile, and waited until he finished, and continued with what she was saying. And, slowly, she succeeded. He was beginning to talk normally, if in a gruff and unwilling voice, when the music stopped, and they had to return to the veranda. There Ruth and Donovan still sat by themselves; and now their voices were lowered, and they looked unwelcomingly around at the invasion of returning dancers. They went on talking. But if their earlier sophisticated talk had upset Binkie because it disturbed the atmosphere, this exclusiveness was much worse. When the music struck up again, Binkie went to dance with Ruth. He hated dancing, but it was his duty; he never danced unless there was a couple too much occupied with each other.

It was quite early; people were still arriving, and remained, as they settled themselves, in their parties or couples, though these couples might join others, or a girl from one group pass naturally to another. It was all so easy and friendly and informal. The waiters came with tray after tray of beer and brandy. Martha, drinking brandy and ginger beer as usual, was instinctively regulating the flame of her intoxication: the men might get staggeringly drunk, the girls should be softened by alcohol, not dissolved in it. Binkie, having returned Ruth to Donovan, switched the lights out in the big dance room, and swirled coloured lights steadily across it, in a slow persistent rhythm, which dulled the mind and heightened the senses.

Martha danced in turn with Binkie, who seemed to think that more than one dance with Perry was dangerous, with Perry, with Donovan. But it did not matter with whom one danced; it was all impersonal: one moved trancelike from one man to the next, one danced cheek to cheek, intimately, body to body, and then the music stopped, one drank again, chattered a little, and plunged back into the hot, coloured darkness of the dance room, while the music throbbed. Three times Martha found herself drawn onto the veranda by one or other of the wolves (afterwards she had to remind herself who they had been) and kissed; and always in the same way. Abruptly, without any sort of preface, she was held rigid against a hard body, whose lower half pushed against hers in an aggressive but at the same time humble way; and her head was bent back under a thrusting, teeth-bared kiss. Afterwards, he breathed heavily, like a runner, and sighed, and said, 'I'm terrible, hey? Forgive me baby, you'll forgive me.' And to this the spirit of the place made Martha reply graciously, 'It's all right, Perry,' or Douggie or Binkie; 'it's all right, don't worry.' She should have said, 'Don't worry, kid'; but that word would not come off her tongue. She wanted to laugh; at the same time she found it revolting that they should become so humble and apologetic, while in those humble eyes was such an aggressive gleam. Each kiss was a small ceremony of hatred; and at the fourth occasion, when some anonymous youth began compulsively tugging her towards the veranda, she resisted, and saw his baleful glance,

'Toffee-nosed, hey?' he demanded. And afterwards, at the table, he indicated Martha to the others, and said, 'This baby's toffee-nosed, she's . . .' And he made a show of shivering and holding a coat around him and chattering his teeth.

Donovan suddenly called, 'Well, Matty dear, and how *are* you?' and it was only after she had seen a couple of the young men exchange grimaces in the direction of Donovan that she understood Donovan had been watching her all evening, that for some reason these young men's attentions to her were a challenge to Donovan. She saw, too, that he was pleased because she had been found lacking. She sat quietly at the end of the table, feeling hurt, and confused; her own idea of herself was destroyed. That other veiled personage that waits, imprisoned, in every woman, to be released by love, that person she feels to be (obstinately and against the evidence of all experience) what is real and enduring in her, was tremblingly insecure. She hated Donovan, with a pure, cool contempt; she looked at the young men, and despised them passionately.

When Perry, for the second time, danced her out of the big room, through the dancing couples on the veranda, and to the steps, she went with him easily. 'But it's muddy,' she said, laughing nervously, looking out at the playing fields, which were saturated with water and moonlight.

'Never mind,' said Perry. 'Never mind, baby.' He tugged at

her arm, and when she did not follow him, picked her up, and lifted her down. She could hear his feet squelching through the heavy mud. He carried her around the corner of the building, and without putting her down kissed her.

This was something different, being suspended strongly, in space. Perry, the individual, was merging easily into that ideal figure, a young strong man, who wooed that other ideal person within her (veiled, but certainly lovely), when she suddenly cried out, 'Perry, my *dress*!'

'What's the matter, kid?' asked Perry, annoyed but devoted. 'What have I done?'

She felt a coldness strike down her thigh, and, peering with difficulty over the thick curve of his arm, said, 'My dress is torn.' And it was.

'Baby, I'm sorry, I'm a clumsy brute,' said Perry sentimentally; and he carried her back to the veranda, squelch, squelch, through the moon-gilded puddles. There she stood, on the steps, examining the damage.

She understood there was a silence, people were watching. Her spirits rose in a defiant wave of elation, and she cried gaily, 'Don, you were quite right, my dress is torn.' She walked calmly to the table, holding the gaping cloth together over her naked thigh, and stood beside Donovan, while Perry followed, muttering, 'Kid, I'm sorry. You kill me. You'll be the death of me.'

Donovan was silent for a critical moment, then he shrieked with laughter. Everyone joined in. It was a relieved laughter, a little hysterical. Donovan said, 'Well, I can't do anything without a needle and thread.'

Binkie told a waiter to go and get these things. The waiter protested, sulkily, that he did not know where to find them, and was dismissed peremptorily with 'Go on, Jim. Don't argue. If I say needle and thread, then get them.' He waved his hand dismissingly, and the waiter went away; and returned after a few minutes with the things.

Donovan, again master of the situation, laughed, and stitched up Martha's dress, while Ruth blinked her short-sighted eyes and watched in her quiet interested way, and

215

Donovan said that Martha was a disgusting girl, she had mud on her dress. For some reason, this incident had released them all into gay amity. Martha sat beside Donovan, who held her hand; Ruth held Donovan's on the other side; Perry lounged beside Martha, watching her curiously. Outside, between the veranda pillars, the moon flooded wild and fitful light over the ruffling dark water. The gum trees moved their black hulking shapes over the stars. The music came pulsing steadily from inside. It was midnight. Some of the older people were going home, smiling in a way which suggested that while youth must have its due, it should not, nevertheless, demand too much. Binkie was muttering, like a storm warning, 'Let's break it up, kids, come on, let's break it up.'

Inside, during the next dance, they broke it up. Whooping and yelling, stamping and surging, they flung themselves indiscriminately around the room, while the band played and played and played, pulling rhythm from their instruments with steady fingers, smiling with conscious power, as if it were they, the human beings, who directed the movements of jerking, lolling marionettes below. Martha caught a glimpse, over Perry's arm, of Donovan, dancing looselimbed, like a jointed doll, flinging out his arms and legs around him, his black hair falling in thick locks over his face, and smiling in a way which plainly said, 'This is quite idiotic, I'm doing it because it's the thing.' Ruth, now no longer cool and possessed, jerked unregarded in the pumping arms of Binkie, with a look of patient suffering on her face. And Martha realized that the ridiculous suffering look was the same as that on her own face; she did not like this, she could not let herself go into it. At the moment she became aware of that critical and untouched person within herself, she looked at Perry, and thought in a flash, Despite what he wants us to think, it's the same with him. Perry, apparently, was in a trance of violence. He was letting his shoulders rise and fall convulsively; his eyes rolled to the ceiling, darted sideways with a flash of white eyeball, and settled glazedly in a stare at the floor. His whole body shuddered and rocked and shook; and all the time he was quite unaffected, for when, by chance, Martha encountered for a moment those blue eyes as they rolled past her, she saw them possessed only on the surface, for underneath they were cool and observant, absorbed in appreciative direction of his frenzy. 'Look how madly we are behaving,' that deep gleam seemed to say. At the same time, it disliked being noticed: during that second when Martha's eyes and Perry's met, it was exactly as if two people supposed to be wholly absorbed in a religious ceremony, turn to spy on each other, and are annoyed and embarrassed to see the other's treachery. She wanted to giggle; she did laugh, nervously; and he pressed her close, as if to say, 'Do be quiet,' and said, 'Baby, you're killing me.' He let out an agonized groan, which made her laugh again.

No, like Ruth, she could not enjoy it. At the end of the first dance – that is, the first dance of abandon – she went back to the table on the veranda, leaving Perry to find someone else, and saw Donovan, already calm and composed, his black hair sleek as ever, sitting with Ruth.

'Really, Matty dear,' said Donovan peevishly, 'these orgies don't do anything for you. You'd better comb your hair – no, let me do it.'

But she did it herself, rather perfunctorily, while the stampede continued inside, and she listened, half scornfully, half regretfully, because of this self-exclusion, which left her cool and mistress of herself, listening while Donovan talked to Ruth.

Soon she heard Donovan let out a grateful yell, and saw two people, thus arrested, pause, laugh, and come towards them. One was a small, striking-looking dark-eyed Jewish girl, dressed in tight striped satin, and the other, in striking contrast to her smooth, smart woman-of-the-world look, a rather large and clumsy man, with a craggy-featured Scots face and blue shrewd Scots eyes.

This couple, it seemed, not merely 'knew' Donovan, but were great friends of his; they sat down, ordering drinks while they protested they must go at once. Her name was

Stella, his Andrew; they were married, and very pleased about it — these facts Martha gathered before the music stopped again and she found Perry beside her. He groaned perfunctorily that she had deserted him, she was killing him; but she could no longer keep it up. She laughed at him, and, keeping her eyes fixed on his, began talking naturally — about what? It did not matter, it was her tone that mattered; she could no longer maintain that maternal indulgence. She watched him grow uneasy, even half rise, with a trapped look, before he sank down again; she had won. She felt a reckless triumph that she had coaxed one of the wolves, Binkie's senior lieutenant, into treating her seriously! And it appeared that he was astonished himself; for when Donovan and Ruth, Stella and Andrew Mathews rose and announced they were going to the Mathews's flat, Perry followed Martha across the big dance room, contracting his face comically as he shouted out to the distressed Binkie, 'This baby's got me, I'm lassoed, I'm done for!' And they drove off, Martha with Perry in the back of Donovan's car, while Ruth sat with him in front, thus acknowledging the change of partners.

Donovan and Ruth flirted pleasantly; as for Perry, he did not even attempt to hold Martha's hand. He allowed that great blond athletic body of his to shake gently with the car's movement, as if all the virtue had gone out of him; and while his head shook where it rested on the back of the seat, he looked at Martha, and said protestingly, 'Hey, baby, what are you doing to me?' while she laughed at him. And when they reached the big block of flats, whose fame was due to their being six storeys high, higher than any other building in the town, he followed her meekly from the car, a tamed and uneasy wolf; and so they all went up, in their couples, to the Mathews's flat.

The flat was bright, modern, compact. The small living room had striped curtains, pale rugs, light modern furniture. Coming into it was a relief; one enters a strange place feeling, To what must I adapt myself? But there was nothing individual here to claim one's mood, there was no need to submit oneself. In this country, or in England, or in any other country, one enters this flat, is at home at once, with a feeling of peace. Thank God! There are enough claims on us as it is, tugging us this way and that, without considering fittings and furniture. Who used them before? What kind of people were they? What do they demand of us? Ah, the blessed anonymity of the modern flat, that home for nomads who, with no idea of where they are travelling, must travel light, ready for anything.

The windows were open; the lights of the city spread glittering below; it seemed very high – like a platform lifted precariously in the great darkness, with nothing but a thin shell of concrete between the lit space and the black and sweeping winds. For the wind was strong again. The sky, cleaned by rain that same afternoon, was already tumultuous with moon-sculptured cloud. The clouds went rolling steadily but swiftly overhead, to bank themselves high under a slanting Southern Cross, in mountainous heaps of black. It was warm; although Martha was naked save for her slip of a dance dress, the tendrils of wind that clung to her shoulders were as soft as fingers. Thunder muttered softly, like something half asleep; a heavy cloud bucketed and rolled like a ship in the hands of a driving wind, its undersurface profound and dim, its upper reaches white and illuminated. The moon went out, and there was a smell of fresh rain pouring across the dark.

Martha turned from the windows, and found Andrew serving drinks. It seemed that, every place one entered, no sooner had one arrived, than out came the alcohol. What would happen, she wondered, if for some terrible and unforeseen reason it did not? But the critical thought lasted just so long as the influence of the night outside; soon she was wholly confined to that small lit space, the Mathews's living room, and she reached out her hand for a brandy, and listened to what was going on.

Here it was not Donovan, or Ruth, or herself, who played lead. It was Stella. She sat on the arm of the chair, talking vivaciously, while her dark eyes glowed, resting on the faces of her audience, seeming to pull them into the circle of her magnetism. She was telling how Andrew's father had forbidden him to marry a Jewess, how they had married secretly, and thus seemed to be living together without grace of state or church, until the old man had come imploring them to marry, because this disgrace was more than his respectable Scots soul could bear. Then they had told him they had been married all the time, given him a whisky, and asked him to stay to dinner. It wasn't the story itself that they listened to, laughed at; for Stella was displaying herself, as it were, with her husband for foil. She poised herself on the chair arm, in her tight bright satin, and her sleek, smooth, golden-fleshed body seemed to speak to every person there in a language of its own. She was alive from her naked silk-covered toes – she had flung off her shoes – to her smooth dark hair, which seemed so sophisticated, though it was arranged as her grandmother's might have been, parted in the middle and coiled behind in a simple bun. Her face glistened with animation, her plump tawny arms flung out and gestured until at the end, where she described her father-in-law's collapse, she let them fall, and dropped her voice to a meek, womanly demureness. 'And now everything's all right. The hell is over. It's not right for a son to quarrel with his father.'

There was a short, astonished silence, while everyone looked at the smooth, down-drooping face in its madonna pose; and Andrew said crudely, 'Fat lot you care,' and gave a sardonic laugh.

But Stella was conscious that this apparent lack of sympathy was only on the surface a discord. She laughed, gave another conquering glance around, and then waited, as if to say, 'Well, I've done my turn, the young married turn, and now are you ready to do your part?' She sat drinking, in silence, waiting for someone to take up the torch of conversation. But no one did. So she continued: Now that she was openly married, she had had to give up her job – her firm did not employ married women; they were very, very poor. (She said this with an appropriate sigh.) Even the furniture would have been hire-purchase but for the grace of Andrew's father, who had come round with it as a belated wedding present. Really, things had been so bad (here she gave a long dark, liquid look sideways at her craggy and forthright husband) that positively it had almost come to sleeping on the floor; she had been prepared to sleep on the floor, to be with her chosen. But here Andrew gave another sardonic snort, which checked her for a moment, and she smilingly took a sip of her drink, and looked with satisfaction down at her extended naked toes – she had beautiful, small feet. Then she complained gently that this was a terrible place to live in, because the neighbours kept protesting because of their parties – but really, one couldn't end a party before dawn, how could you? Everyone went to bed so early in this country, and – here she hesitated the briefest moment before smoothly switching the talk into a more reckless channel – really, what with one thing and another, she and Andy were reduced to making love only in the afternoons, and on Saturdays at that, because the neighbours . . .

And now everyone laughed, with relief, for this note united what she actually said with that other conversation her body held on its own, with everybody, man or woman; and Andrew said gruffly that she was a disgusting wench, and a damned liar, because he couldn't imagine her starving on love once a week; and here she a gave yell of laughter, and said he was a hypocrite.

Martha, even while she was slowly involved in this, the new atmosphere, with its taboos and licence, based on the young couple, understood (though with difficulty, since she had not encountered it before) that the grudging practical look of Andrew, his gruff, protesting voice, was only assumed; or if not he was letting that part of himself out on leash; he was not only prepared to see his wife display herself thus to others, but he was an accomplice. Such a reversal was it to Martha's instinctively held ideas, that she was continually, surreptitiously looking to Stella for signs that she resented being shown off. For she was remembering her own continuous half-suppressed resentment of the way Donovan showed her off.

And in the meantime Donovan was curiously silent, for him; he lounged and watched, and laughed admiringly at Stella; Ruth smiled carefully, blinking her red-rimmed, watchful eyes; Perry sat stiffly in a shallow chair which looked as if it would splay out under the weight of his big body, and listened unsmilingly, while from time to time – at those moments when laughter was jerked out of him by Stella – he threw back his head with a sudden dismayed movement, and flung half a glass of liquor down his throat.

Soon, when the subject of love-making lost its piquancy, Stella put on a womanly, serious look, and began talking to Donovan. They were the greatest friends in the world, it seemed, they knew everything about each other, and yet they had not seen each other for six months, and that was at another party. Similarly, Martha found herself being treated with the same simple, affectionate intimacy by Andrew; she soon felt as close to him as to an old friend. And Perry too: when it was his turn to be charmed by Stella into the circle of amity, he turned his great body over sideways in the fragile little chair, and allowed himself to be coaxed by Stella's merry, warm glance into what was almost loquacity. He was uneasy, he did not like it, but he allowed Stella to hold his hand, and at the same time (as if her naked, gleaming shoulders, that small white hand, could have no connection at all with the words they were using) talked to her slowly, seriously, about the finances of the Sports Club, and listened solemnly to her tales of Hong Kong, where she had been brought up.

It was getting late, and cold too; for outside it was raining from the now slow-moving masses of ragged, fitfully moonlit cloud. But when Stella caught herself in a yawn, she cried out that it was impossible to go to bed and she was starving. They therefore descended through the bowels of the building again, in the big lift, and ran through the rain to the cars, and so off down to the hot-dog stands. The town was dead and asleep, under the slow cold rain; but the hot-dog stands were like a small gypsy camp that had sprung up in a side street. All along the pavements, night after night, until dawn, these small high rooms, lit with swinging hurricane lamps, perched on their wheels, and supplied food to the taste of all comers: big mixed grills, rolls filled with eggs, ham, sausages, cups of hot weak coffee or very strong tea, and there were shelves piled with tinned food, which would be opened to order. Martha had often come here to eat, with Donovan, after the pictures.

Stella did not want to leave the car to join the crowds at the stalls. She was in a sentimental mood. She leaned her graceful head against her husband's shoulder, and, it appeared, was no longer hungry, for she did not eat. No one was particularly hungry. But an inertia had settled on them, they could not bear to go to bed, and all around the stalls were ranks of cars filled with people, similarly afflicted. It was four in the morning, neither day nor night; the lights of the stalls glimmering weakly; the black waiters stood yawning over their trays, or beside the stoves; and half the youth of the town ate and drank, watching the sky for that first spear of red light which would release them, so that they might go to bed, saying they had been up all night. But the sky was obscured. The moon appeared briefly, small and hard and bright in the welter of wet dark cloud, and vanished, this time finally. It rained steadily, making an illuminated yellow mist around the lamps. Martha yawned, and was chided for letting the side down; and they ordered more rolls, more coffee; and at last a grey damp light grew along the streets, the houses seemed to darken, harden into shapes, and a weak pallid glow in the sky announced the dawn, which must be plunging in violent rose and gold above the clouds, but here was no more than a reflection of imagined splendour. And now they could go home.

Martha was dropped at the kerb from Donovan's car, but it was Perry who came to the door and kissed her; from which she understood she was now Perry's girl and not Donovan's. She was alone, it was five in the morning, and there was no point in going to bed if one must be up again in a couple of hours.

She opened her parcel of books and yawned till her jaws

ached, and drank tea, sitting on the floor; and reflected that Stella and Andrew – an already sufficiently interesting combination – and Donovan and Ruth, and she and Perry, six people so ill-assorted it might seem they would have nothing to say to each other, not only had spent a pleasant evening together, but were planning to be together the following evening. For it had been taken for granted, under the spell of that intimacy, that of course they must be together; they could not bear to be separated. They would go dancing, having first taken sundowners in the Mathews's flat; they would then . . .

And here Martha, feeling chilled, moved from where she leaned against the bed, and sat in the elongated square of weak, wet sunlight that already lay across the matting, and slowly succumbed to disgust that deepened coldly within her as her flesh warmed to the warming sunlight. She was thinking that she had not been in town more than a few weeks and already she was bored and longing for something different; also she was consumed by such a passion of restlessness that the conflict made her feel weak and sick. She was thinking that at any moment during the last evening, had she been asked, she would have replied that she was bored; yet, as she looked back on it, her nerves responded with a twinge of excitement. She knew that the coming evening would be as barren, and yet she could not think of it without pleasure.

Even more painful than this cold-minded analysis was the knowledge that it was all so banal; just as the stare from that dispassionate cool eye, which judged herself as adolescent, and therefore inevitably contradictory and dissatisfied, was harder to bear than the condition of adolescence itself. She was, in fact, suffering from the form of moral exhaustion which is caused by seeing a great many facts without knowing the cause for them; by seeing oneself as an isolated person, without origin or destination. But since the very condition of her revolt, her very existence had been that driving individualism, what could she do now?

Slowly, and after a long interval, she began to think of

Joss, who was never in any doubt about what was the right thing to do. Joss would say it all served her right, this was what she could expect; she should have telephoned Jasmine and joined the Left Book Club – and at this point she began to laugh with the nervous helplessness that is the result of an anticlimax. For that was how she felt it: that all the terrific, restless force embodied in her was too powerful to be confined in the Left Book Club, and she began to feel critical and hurt at Joss, as if he had been unsympathetic, unfeeling, as if he had misunderstood her. She was mentally criticizing him, exactly as if he were responsible for her, and her failures and triumphs should belong to him. Since this criticism received no reply, her mental image of him remained stubbornly sorrowfully silent; her mind slipped into a heightened mazy condition, and in a fevered daydream she imagined that some rich and unknown relation would come forward with a hundred pounds, and say, 'Here, Martha Quest, you deserve this, this is to set you free.'

For there was no doubt that the root of all this dissatisfaction was that she deserved something life had not offered her. The daydream locked not only her mind, but her limbs; soon she was cramped and stiff, and she had to get up and move about the room, till the blood flowed back, and she went to the door to receive the flood of now soft and hotly welcoming sunlight. It was as if the night had never been; for the light was heavy and rich and yellow, the sky was as thick with rain clouds as it had been yesterday, there was still the oppressive atmosphere of coming storm. There was the ringing of hard boots on tarmac, and the soft padding of bare feet. She stood quite still while past her moved a file of men. First, two policemen in the boots, their crisp khaki tunics belted tight, their buttons shining, their little hats cocked at an angle. Then perhaps twenty black men and women, in various clothing, barefooted and shabby. Then, following these, two more policemen. The prisoners were handcuffed together, and it was these hands that caught Martha's attention: the working hands, clasped together by broad and gleaming steel, held carefully at waist level, steady against the natural movement of swinging arms – the tender dark flesh cautious against the bite of the metal. These people were being taken to the magistrate for being caught at night after curfew, or forgetting to carry one of the passes which were obligatory, or – but there were a dozen reasons, each as flimsy. Now, Martha had seen this sight so often that she was not dulled to it so much as patiently angry. She marched, in imagination, down the street, one of the file, feeling the oppression of a police state as if it were heavy on her; and at the same time was conscious of the same moral exhaustion which had settled on her earlier.

She was thinking, It's all so dreadful, not because it exists, merely, but because it exists *now*. She was thinking – for, since she had been formed by literature, she could think in no other way – that all this had been described in Dickens, Tolstoy, Hugo, Dostoevsky, and a dozen others. All that noble and terrific indignation had done nothing, achieved nothing, the shout of anger from the nineteenth century might as well have been silent – for here came the file of prisoners, handcuffed two by two, and on their faces was that same immemorial look of patient, sardonic understanding. The faces of the policemen, however, were the faces of those doing what they were paid to do.

And what now? demanded that sarcastic voice inside Martha; and it answered itself, Go out and join the Prisoners' Aid Society. Here she sank into self-derisory impotence, and, leaving the door, returned to her room. A clock was chiming hurriedly from the back veranda. Seven o'clock, time to dress for the office. But first she lifted the books from the floor, and looked through them as if she were looking for a kind of deliverance. An advertisement in the *New Statesman and Nation* had brought her certain poets; and she hastily opened some volumes and glanced through them.

> Now the leaves are falling fast,
> Nurse's flowers will not last,
> Nurses to the graves are gone,
> And the prams go rolling on . . .

She read it with deepening anger, for mentally she was still marching with that file of prisoners.

Did it once issue from the carver's hand healthy? demanded the black print silently; and Martha passionately averred that it had, it had – and turned the page quickly.

> There is no consolation, no none
> In the curving beauty of that line
> Traced in our graphs through history where the oppressor
> Starves and deprives the poor.

This poem she read through several times; and she watched herself sliding into the gulf of rich and pleasurable melancholy where she was so dangerously at home, while a sarcastic and self-destructive voice inside her remarked, Well, well, and did you see *that*?

The clock struck one, a clear dissolving note, and she thought, I must be quick, and snatched up another volume. Not the twilight of the gods, she read, but a precise dawn of sallow and grey brick, and the newsboys crying war . . .

The word 'war' separated itself, and she thought of her father, and with irritation. He would like a war, too, she thought angrily; and she took her things and went to the bathroom. They say there's going to be a war because they want one, she thought confusedly; for since it was necessary to resist her parents, it was necessary to resist this voice too.

She lay yawning in the bath, and then heard herself thinking, What if there is a war? What would happen here? She was thinking that she would take lessons in nursing, and volunteer for service overseas – her blood quickened at the idea of it – and she was picturing herself a heroine in the trenches; she was leaning over a wounded man in the slime and debris of no man's land – the phrase gave her a pang of poetic delight; she would . . . But she suddenly leaped out of the bath in disgust at herself, saying, 'I'm doing it too.' She was not only furious, she was puzzled. These highly coloured fantasies of heroism and fated death were so powerful she could only with a great effort close her mind to them. But shut them out she did; and came staggering, out of the bathroom, telling herself she had a right to be tired, she had not slept that night.

She found Mrs Gunn on the veranda wearing a faded pink nightgown that dragged over her huge sagging breasts. Her dull red hair was uncombed and her eyes bloodshot. 'Well, dear,' she asked, interest beginning to rouse her, 'did you have a nice time?'

For a moment Martha wondered what she meant; then she said brightly, 'Yes, lovely, thank you.'

Mrs Gunn nodded enviously. 'That's right dear, you must enjoy yourself when you're young.'

Martha laughed, at once animated in response to this demand that she should be. 'I'm going out again tonight,' she said, and spoke as if she could hardly wait for that night to begin.

Chapter Three

In this town due honour was paid to holidays. Every year, from the beginning of December, work in the offices began perceptibly to slacken. Young Mr Robinson, for instance, would return hurriedly at four in the afternoon, just to sign his letters, after an early festival lunch. Mr Cohen announced that every girl might take three mornings off (in rotation, of course) to do Christmas shopping. Charlie was kept running to and from the post office, with sacks full of Christmas cards. And that Christmas of 1938 had a feverishness, almost a desperation, about it that seemed to involve the whole town. There were dances every night, often three or four of them, at McGrath's, in the Sports Club; while the Knave of Clubs, the city's only night club, was open every evening instead of twice a week.

There was a new, dangerous spirit in the Sports Club itself. An incident occurred that would have seemed incredible only a few weeks before. Two of the wolves were found fighting, publicly, over a new girl just arrived in town, Marnie Van Rensberg; a shocked and fearful Binkie appealed to them, exhorted – and, for once, failed. The young people of the Club saw something quite new: two wolves not merely not on speaking terms, but with packs of followers who tended to wrangle over the rights and wrongs of the case at the bar, even at meetings which were ostensibly about tennis courts or hockey fields. And they saw it passively – that was the extraordinary thing; this new wind blowing, this disruptive force, was so strong that it even seemed proper and normal that three couples should suddenly get married, that the young men should fight, and with real passion: Binkie had a bruise on his cheek, from trying to separate them.

Meantime, all over the Club were large notices: 'Christmas 1938, Enjoy Yourselves' and 'Give the New Year a Bang of a Start!' and 'Let's Give it Stick!'

That dance Martha attended was the last at which Binkie was to give the signal to 'break it up'; there was already too much of a breaking-up spirit. The Club was full of invisible tensions. That cold orgiastic spirit which he deliberately invoked of a Saturday evening, had been invoking for years, was a pale wraith beside the brooding excitement that was on every face. And although the unwritten law still held – but it would not for long – that there should be no politics in the sacred circle, there was one evening when a girl remarked aloud, in a silence, in a sudden dreamy voice, as if she had not known she was going to speak at all, 'Well, this may be the last Christmas . . . I mean to say – ' Then she blushed, and looked guiltily about her. Binkie exhorted her hastily to play the game, that wasn't the spirit; but no one else spoke, and eyes met thoughtfully, in swift glances, and turned away, frowning in deeper speculation. And these faces wore, though unconsciously, a new look: there were moments when they were stern and dedicated as if they were listening to a distant bugle. It was a look which had the power to pierce like a warning. Binkie, seeing it, would yell to the band, who were perhaps already packing away their instruments, to give them a break, man, give them another tune. The band would most likely oblige. Although, once, two o'clock had been the limit, at two o'clock the musicians had firmly but gently shaken their heads and gone home, now they might play until half-past two, even three, in the morning. Afterwards, everyone went down to the Knave of Clubs. No one slept, it seemed. Night after night they were up till the sun rose, they went to work as usual, and they met again by five in the evening. For into this timeless place, where everything continued dreamlike year after year, had come, like a frightening wind, a feeling of necessity, an outside pressure.

And during those heightened, tense days, Stella and Andrew, Donovan and Ruth, Martha and Perry went about together everywhere, for no better reason than that chance had brought them together, and a kind of inertia made it impossible for them to part. They were friends, they loved each other, a gentle, tender nostalgia made every meeting as vivid as a parting. They met in the Mathews's flat immediately after work, and drank and danced or talked until morning, when exhaustion at last caught up with them, and they would fall like logs around the flat, and sleep on the floor, in chairs, or even tumbled across the big double bed, three or four of them together, in a sexless affection – or perhaps it would be more true to say that during that time the forces of sex hung balanced so precariously that no member of the group of six dared to make a movement one way or the other. During that three weeks, Martha might drive to a dance inside the circle of Donovan's arms, and return from it enclosed within the same gentle protective pressure – this time, from Perry. She might dance half the evening with Andrew, locked in tender nostalgia, and watch Stella across the room, cheek to cheek with Donovan; she might fling herself down on the divan for an hour to catch some sleep, on coming to the flat straight from the office, and wake up to find beside her any one of the three men, who roused himself good-naturedly at her stirring, and then hastened to fetch her, and himself, a brandy. And so it went on. Such dreamlike, compelled amity, such good nature, such tender appreciation, had surely never existed? They felt as if something miraculous had descended upon them; and yet it all vanished, and from one moment to the next.

It was at the Christmas-tide dance at the Sports Club. The band played until three; and at the moment the music finally stopped, Stella was with Donovan under the musicians' platform. The pair sang 'God Save the King' hand in hand; and then, in terror lest the evening might end, Stella leaned over to one of the musicians and said, 'Come and join us, Dolly – and bring your girl, if you've got one.' He nodded with a grateful smile, and indicated that he would come when his violin was safely stowed away. Martha, who was with Andrew, linked arms with Stella, and, as Ruth and Penny came alongside Andrew, and the six of them, pressed side to side, danced slowly across the floor to the table, Martha heard Donovan say in a low grumbling voice he had not used for so long she was startled, 'Why did you ask that damned – I mean, why did you make him come?'

And if Donovan's voice was bad-tempered, Stella's was tart. 'You were going to say "damned little Jew," I think?'

'Jew or not, who cares,' said Donovan, so unwillingly that Stella's eyes hardened, and she took her arm away from his. 'He's loathsome. Adolph *King* – trying to pretend he's not a Jew.'

'Here, you two,' said Andrew pleasantly, but warningly. 'What's going on?' He dropped Martha's arm, and went between his wife and Donovan, and began to laugh them out of their anger. And so they reached their table; and it was so long since this mood of tenderness had been disturbed by even a word or a jarring silence, that all six were troubled, and waited apprehensively for the arrival of Adolph King, who apparently had the power to stir up trouble.

Soon he came, a small, compact man, with a pale face that now glistened with the hours of music-making, smallish eyes of that red-brown, hot colour that goes with a smouldering temperament, and small, pale, rather beautiful hands; while his smile was eager and grateful, but indicated he was ready to take offence at a word.

He stood smiling uncertainly by an empty chair, which Stella pushed out towards him with a warning look at the others from her expressive eyes. Too expressive: he saw that look, and the smile was like the baring of a dog's teeth. But only for a moment; the gratitude settled back as he took his chair. Now, this gratitude had nothing to do with his position as music-maker; for all the members of the band also belonged to the Club, and, on evenings when they were not playing themselves, might stand with the crowd, urging their colleagues to play one more, just one more, exactly as if they too, and perhaps the next evening, would not be shaking their heads with that same smiling obduracy. So the uneasy gratitude was altogether troubling, and Martha felt it as she watched him talk with Stella. They were all watching, Donovan's face dark and hostile, Andrew quiet, supporting his wife by an occasional remark which caused Adolph to turn that quick smile in his direction, while Perry, lying back loosely in his chair, glanced alternately at Adolph and Donovan. He seemed to be remembering how much he disliked Donovan.

Donovan made a remark to Ruth in a low voice, and then let out his squeal of laughter; she answered shortly, seeming not to agree. Then Donovan turned to Martha and said, 'Well, Matty, what do you think of Jew-boys who change their names?'

She replied coldly that she did not see why they should not; though in fact she was struggling with a feeling that it was cowardly – she was remembering what Solly had said about Jews who changed their names. She turned to Perry and asked him, 'Do you know him? Is he nice?'

Perry remarked indifferently that Dolly was a nice kid, he was good-natured too, he often played on by himself when the rest of the band had packed up and gone home. 'He's a good violinist,' he added appreciatively, as if unaware of what all this feeling was about.

Donovan was furious. After a few moments' silence, he said loudly to Ruth, 'Shall we go?' Ruth looked round slowly, blinking her tired, heavy-lidded eyes, and nodded. She and Donovan rose, and once again Stella's eyes sparkled indignation and reproach. But Donovan lounged over to her, kissed her cheeks, and said, 'We'll drop in tomorrow, Stella dear.' He turned away, ignoring Adolph.

Ruth said goodbye to every person individually, smiling especially at Adolph, which caused him to flush and make an instinctive movement as if he were going to rise from his chair. Ruth ignored this movement, and, smiling her steady social smile, followed Donovan.

Martha and Perry, at the other end of the long table, were now by themselves.

'A precious plant, our Donny-boy,' said Perry at last, giving considered judgment, and for himself, not out of that compelled group amity in which he had been stuck with the rest of them, like flies in treacle, for the three weeks which seemed like so many months.

Martha said hurriedly, 'You should remember his – he has a bad time at home,' though until she spoke she had not known she thought he had a bad time.

Perry's blue eyes rested on her thoughtfully, while he crooned, 'You've a good heart, baby, you stick up for your friends.'

Involuntarily, she frowned, and looked away; things hung on balance. For the first time in weeks she was thinking, What am I doing here?

Then Perry said in a low voice, 'Come home with me now, baby?' She hesitated, looking up the table to where the group of three were now laughing together, a little too loudly. 'Come on, they're all right,' Perry said urgently, and hauled that long body of his to its feet; he always looked as if he were troubled by his own size, as if he must keep firmly in his head, which was such a long way from his feet, that those feet were too big and might get him into trouble.

Martha also stood up, saying, 'I think I'll be getting home to bed.'

Stella and Andrew at once exclaimed in dismay that it was too early, she must see Boxing Day in, they must all come and have breakfast at the flat. Martha shook her head, smiling, feeling her arm gripped tight by Perry's big paw.

'I'll drop in tomorrow,' she said, as Donovan had done, and then, afraid that her going might be interpreted in the same way as his, walked up the length of the table to the man they called Dolly, held out her hand, shook his, and said that she hoped she would see him again. She saw Stella's approving nod, and Andrew smiling at her. As for Dolly himself, she was embarrassed by that effusively grateful smile.

She went out with Perry, feeling nervous and excited, for she felt the pressure of his eyes on her. She was wearing a dress of flowered crepe, which she had bought on an impulse, and which was neither what she liked or what Donovan liked, for all he had said when he saw it was, 'Well, Matty, *dear*!' It was going to cost her ten shillings a month for the next year, and she regretted buying it. But the pressure of Perry's arm around her waist seemed to absolve her of bad taste.

The drove in silence back to her room, and he got out of the car without speaking and followed her to the door. She was looking for her key, hoping that no one they knew might choose that moment to drive down the street. A couple of cars from the Club swept by, hooting a greeting, and she muttered a bad-tempered 'Damn!' as she fitted the key, and hastily went in. Again she hesitated, and found the problem solved by Perry, who simply lifted her up and carried her to the bed.

'Shhhh!' she could not help warning him; for Mrs Gunn slept the other side of the thin wall.

'Never mind, kid,' Perry crooned, and leaned over her admiringly. He looked for so long that she began to see herself through his eyes, approving the flushed face, heavy eyes, loosened hair. He bent to kiss her, and she let this image of herself dissolve, and shut her eyes, preparing to be lost. But the kiss persisted, and its hardness seemed to demand resistance, his mouth was boring down into hers so that it hurt, and as her mind remarked; He's calculating, he's testing me, she flashed awake and became conscious again of every part of herself as he might see it. She was locked in watchful resistance. He lay down beside her, and began pressing her to him. Her mind was schooled in poetic descriptions of the love act from literature, and in scientific descriptions from manuals on sex; it was not prepared for the self-absorbed rite which he was following. When he reached for her hand, and pulled it towards the front of his body, it stiffened; he pulled harder, and moaned, 'Give me a break, kid, give me a break'; while at the same time he fumbled with her breasts.

She sat up, and demanded angrily, 'What the hell is it you

want me to do?' An entirely rhetorical remark, which he was taking seriously; for he was adjusting his face to that look of doglike and abashed devotion which exasperated her, and she hurried on, examining with hostility the hostile look in his eyes: 'You're absolutely disgusting!' and then realizing she was misunderstood, she stood up, shook back her hair, and said coldly, 'It's quite all right to mess around, like kids, but to – to make love properly, I suppose you'd be shocked!' She was furious. She saw him slowly gather that great body of his to a sitting position, and thought, How silly he looks. He was so astonished that he had not yet time to be shocked, so she hurried on: 'I wonder how many years you've been – messing with girls in cars. After dances there's nothing you don't do – but the thing itself.' His inarticulateness, which was after all verbal, and nothing to do with the way he thought, was affecting her, for as each precise phrase came to her mind, licensed by her reading, she could not help discarding it, under compulsive pressure from a nervous prohibition; she was slowly growing furious with herself because of her clumsy, childish speech.

By now he had become shocked, and knew it. He was standing up, and his large, strongly featured face was hard, and his eyes had a look of lost illusions. He said warningly, still a little sentimental, 'Kid, you'll get yourself into trouble.'

She gave a snort of scornful but agitated laughter, and demanded, 'What sort of trouble?'

He said, 'I wouldn't have believed it of you, kid, I wouldn't have believed it.' At the same time, the aggressive blue eyes were staring and uneasy. They were staring at her in the most perplexed way – here was a new phenomenon, it seemed; for he said slowly, 'I like you, kid, I like you, let's get hitched.'

And now she stared incredulously at him, and began to laugh. She shook with helpless laughter, while he slowly reddened, and his eyes narrowed, and onto his face came a most unpleasant anger. Then he muttered something, flung himself out of the room and slammed the door.

236

As soon as she heard that slam, she remembered Mrs Gunn, lying on her respectable widowed bed next door, and hoped she had not woken. She heard the stealthy creak of springs, and thought, Oh, damn him! And then, shaken with anger, scorn, and discomfort, she reminded herself (for it seemed it was necessary to do this) that she was in the right, while he was revoltingly in the wrong; while she slowly and neatly undressed, folded her clothes across a chair and got into bed. She said to herself that she would sleep the clock round, she would make up for weeks of sleeplessness.

But she could not sleep at once. She was hot and restless and writhing with shame. She thought of Joss, and was reassured, for she was convinced that her ideas were his also. She said to herself that Perry and all the rest of them were a bunch of kids, messing about for years with every girl in the Club, saying, 'Forgive me, kid,' and 'Please give me a break, kid' – and then he dared to look at her like that – and then asking her to marry him, as if – he was mad, he was crazy.

At last she sat up, to light what must have been the fiftieth cigarette since sundown the evening before. The door opened, and the pale, apprehensive face of Mrs Gunn appeared, followed by her body.

'Come in,' said Martha, in a hard voice.

'I thought I'd bring you in some tea,' said Mrs Gunn, advancing with a brimming cup. She was looking furtively around the room – for *evidence*, thought Martha with angry scorn. 'I heard voices,' said Mrs Gunn delicately. 'Did you have visitors?'

'A young man brought me home,' said Martha, 'and he's only just gone.' Make what you like of that, she thought, staring at Mrs Gunn, who sighed, evaded her eyes, and said it looked like rain again, look at that sky! She added that Martha hadn't been sleeping in her bed much lately, and . . . She glanced at Martha, who returned a calm look of defiance.

Martha finished the tea and handed back the cup, thanking her landlady, and, saying she intended to sleep until tomorrw morning, lay down and turned her back. Mrs Gunn pulled the curtains across, shutting out the first gleams of sunlight, and murmured that she looked as if she could do with some sleep and that was a fact. She shuffled herself around the room in her loose slippers, stared at Martha's clothes lying neatly over the chair and seemed to find comfort in them, for she said dubiously that she expected Martha could look after herself, and withdrew with the empty cup. Martha was already asleep.

She woke to find Stella shaking her, saying gaily that she was a lazy girl, it was six in the evening, time for a drink, and afterwards they were going to the pictures. Martha grumblingly got out of bed and dressed. She did not ask who 'they' were; she was still thinking in terms of the group of six.

'What happened with you and Perry?' asked Stella, jealously, with a gay laugh.

Martha laughed uncomfortably, and said they had quarrelled, to which Stella replied calmly that Perry was a great lump of a thing, anyway, and too dumb for Martha. Thus supported, Martha finally went out to the car, where Andrew and Donovan were silently waiting. Ruth, it seemed, was being kept in bed by her mamma. 'One knows what these mammas are,' Donovan said automatically, and gave his shrill laugh, but it was no good. They were flat and tired; it was all an anti-climax; even the vivacious Stella was daunted, and they separated early, after the pictures, irritable with each other and with themselves.

Martha was thinking that it appeared she had quarrelled finally with Donovan, for he was cold and sarcastic with her, and Perry of course would avoid her in future.

She went to bed determined to devote the first month of the new year to the Polytechnic; she reminded herself that in a month of really hard work she had accomplished more than many girls do in a year. Well then, it needed only determination. Determination, therefore, was what she intended to keep; and she went to the office next morning flat but calm in mind, saying to herself that the New Year's festivities must be ignored. She would work on New Year's Eve, she told herself, and believed she meant it.

That same afternoon she was called to the telephone, to hear a voice she did not know. It was hesitant, and flattened, in the South African singsong manner, it was precise and formal, yet managed to leave the suggestion of something unpleasant, like a snigger. When Martha understood this was Adolph, her first impulse was to say no, she was engaged. Instead, she agreed to go out with him that evening. She put the telephone down thinking that her new regime would begin after the New Year.

When he called for her, he had no plans for their evening, so she suggested they might go to the Mathews's flat. He agreed, but in a way which made her ask doubtfully, 'But you're a friend of theirs, aren't you?' He shrugged, in a large fatalistic manner, and its exaggeration made her stare at him.

'Why did you ring me up?' she asked in that direct way of hers, for he looked anything but pleased with the situation; his reddish-brown eyes flickered continually towards her, while he drove in a way which suggested he was surprised to see her there. She was half offended; perhaps she had become affected, after all, by the adulation of the Sports Club men.

'Why did you come and shake hands with me?' he countered, turning those eyes full strength, very aggressively, onto her.

'Shake hands – where?' she stammered; for she was unaccountably offended that he mentioned the incident at all.

'When I came to that table you were all thinking, Here comes that Jew,' he said unpleasantly, but at the same time gave her a look which pleaded that she might deny it.

She denied it at once, even more hotly because it was half true.

He laughed disbelievingly, and said, 'It was nice of you to shake hands with me like that.'

'You exaggerate everything,' she said uncomfortably.

Then, when he laughed again, she said, 'You talk as if – I mean, there are Jews at the Sports Club, aren't there?' For she had not noticed whether there were or not.

'Oh, they tolerate me, I play for them when the rest of the band has had enough,' he said sarcastically.

'I think you're unfair,' she said, really offended, remembering Perry's attitude.

They were at the block of flats, and Dolly brought the car to a rest, holding it on the brakes, with the engine still running. 'Well, shall we go up?' he demanded.

Again she was puzzled, because he was making a challenge out of it, and asked, 'But you are a friend of theirs, surely?'

He frowned, and then swiftly backed the car out again, saying, 'I'll take you down to the Knave of Clubs, Mrs Spore is a friend of mine.'

'But it's only six,' she protested.

'It's open for me,' he said, and it was a boast. They drove in silence along the five miles of tree-lined tarmac to the night club, a barn of a place – which had in fact been a tobacco warehouse – built against a low kopje. A black sign, 'The Knave of Clubs', was tied by fencing wire to the gate. The space in front of the building was filled with flowering cannas, red and yellow and orange – those fleshy, vulgar unambiguous plants whose masses of clear bright colour, showing against a building, or in a park, are as good as a sign, 'For the Public'. Jacarandas, now in heavy green leaf, surrounded the garden. Inside, the brick walls had been left bare. Fine sacking was slung across the ceiling and held in place by wire, between which it bulged downwards. There was a bare wooden floor, and in one corner a large radiogramophone.

Martha sat on a wooden chair by a bare wooden table, while Adolph went to a door at the back, where he knocked. An elderly female head came out, pale-grey flesh around which hung pale-grey locks; and a pair of large black eyes surveyed Martha. 'We want to dance a little,' he said; and the woman called out, 'Excuse me, duckie, I didn't get the crowd out till six this morning, everyone's mad this year, and I'm sleeping it off.' The head disappeared, and Adolph came back with that uneasy set smile of his.

'Like dancing?' he asked.

Martha hesitated. She did not feel easy about dancing; all she knew was that there were people with whom she could dance, and those who froze her into clumsy stiffness, and this had nothing to do with whether or not they were good dancers. 'I can't dance,' she said hopefully at last; but he said, 'I've watched you at the Club. You've got to learn to relax.'

She laughed nervously, and fell back on the excuse that she'd never been taught.

'I'll teach you,' he promised, smiling, while his eyes watched her closely in a way that made her feel uncomfortable. Never had a man looked at her in that way, though she had not the experience to describe, even to herself, what 'that' way was. She was, however, different from the young girl in earlier generations, in that she knew that everything was allowable. Now she was conscious of her body, and suppressed an impulse to close the opening of her dress, which was impossible in any case, since it was designed to stand open, showing her throat. She forced herself, then, to seem unconscious of his scrutinizing eyes, and felt the warmth of what she hoped was not a bright flush creep up over her face. He was smiling; he had noticed the blush, and was pleased; at once she made an angry movement – so angry she was surprised at herself, for what was there to be angry about? Almost at once, however, his face fell back into the uncertain smile; he unconsciously put out his hand, pleadingly, to check her movement away from him. They looked away from each other uncomfortably.

A waiter came from the back premises, bowed over them, and said that Missus Spore had told him to come and ask what they wanted. His manner said that he resented being sent out before the proper time – no one came here before ten in the evening. He did not wear the white uniform, only a white cotton singlet and rather soiled long white trousers.

But Adolph spoke to him in a friendly, almost intimate way, and asked after his family, so that the man began to smile. He took the liberal tip Adolph slid over to him, and said he could sell them a bottle of brandy, if they wanted. Adolph said yes, but he wasn't going to pay more than in the shops, a joke which the waiter accepted as such, for he merely grinned, and soon the bottle of brandy arrived, with glasses and sandwiches.

Martha sipped her brandy, feeling that her escort would offer her no further entertainment until it had done its work; this, as usual, made her feel resentful, and as usual she repressed it. Soon he put on a rhumba and made her dance. She felt self-conscious, dancing alone in this bare, ugly room, and with someone who was an expert. For he said he had been a professional. She knew at once that this was a man with whom she could not dance; her limbs were awkward and heavy, and the more she tried to loosen, the more she became conscious of every joint and muscle of her body.

A tango was playing, and he was instructing her. 'Look, your knees should be like this. Drop your shoulders like that.'

It reminded her of Donovan, and suddenly she stopped, shook back her hair, laughed and said, 'I'll never make a dancer, you'd better resign yourself to it.' Feeling, for some reason, triumphant and self-confident, she walked away from him back to the table. She was thinking that she did not like this man, and she wanted to go home.

As this thought showed on her face, he said humbly, 'I'm no company for you, am I?'

The way he said it, half pleading and half sullen, struck her again. She was feeling very sorry for him, in an impatient, contemptuous way.

'If the crowd at the Sports Club saw you with me they'd be annoyed,' he offered, hoping she would contradict him.

'What have the Sports Club crowd got to do with it?'

'And your friend Donovan Anderson?'

This seemed to her merely irrelevent; but she unconsciously rose to go, and he followed her, bringing the bottle of brandy.

Again they drove silently. It was dark, the stars flashed out, the hills over which the town sprawled were defined by a deeper, intense black, and over them rose the luminous velvet black of the sky. She was frowning ahead of her; he kept glancing at her furtively.

As he drove slowly past McGrath's, he said, 'You wouldn't be seen dead with me in there, would you?'

She replied coldly that she did not understand him; and it was true that it would not have occurred to her to be ashamed of him unless he had pointed it out; though this attitude was at bottom a sort of *noblesse oblige* – he had abased himself so thoroughly that she was feeling like a princess being kind to a ploughboy. She quite unconscious of it, however; she only knew she was very sorry for him.

'You seem to like being a pariah,' she said, ironically; and now he laughed in appreciation of the irony, but at once slid back, and added aggressively that he was not ashamed of being a Jew. 'No one suggested that you ought to be,' she pointed out, again cold.

Altogether, she was getting more and more angry and uncomfortable; and she walked into McGrath's in a way which was, whether she knew it or not, defiantly calm. She waved to the people she knew, and when she saw Perry she smiled at him as if nothing had happened, receiving in return a curt nod. She found herself wondering whether if perhaps not only Perry but all the others were colder, less welcoming; she saw their eyes following not her but Adolph, who walked behind her; she dissolved in pity, and turned, protectively, so that they might walk through the room side by side, talking. But he did not hear what she said; on his face was a small, self-conscious smile; and she wanted to shake him into pride.

When they were seated, he said, 'I've played in this band.'

She was going to reply, as if accepting information, 'Have you?' Then she understood, and said, with a dry smile that was already, after knowing him not more than three or four hours, like a tolerant, ironic comment, 'Well, and why shouldn't you?'

Again his face was tormented by mingled sarcasm, gratitude and relief. Soon her impatience grew intolerable, and she suggested they should leave. The place was half empty, everyone was dancing up at the Club. Irrationally, she longed to be there. He said quickly, 'You'd like to be dancing with the others, wouldn't you?'

'I could have gone if I'd wanted,' she said, and got up from her chair, adding that she was tired and wanted to go to bed.

She went home, and spent the evening reading. She hoped nervously that he had found her dull, and would not attempt to get in touch with her again. She even brought herself to believe this, so that she succeeded in feeling surprised when the telephone rang next day and he asked her to spend the evening with him. Because of this surprise she felt, she accepted, but in a hasty, confused way, which he complained about the moment he set eyes on her again.

'Why did you sound so cold on the telephone?'

'I didn't – I didn't mean to,' she apologized.

Again they went to the night club when it was still empty; and afterwards to the pictures, reversing the usual procedure; and again she said she wanted to go to bed early. By now she was in a condition of bewildered apathy; her emotions were in a turmoil. By turns she pitied him, hated him, felt protective, despised him, while all the time her imagination was at work, making him into an interesting and persecuted figure. She told herself he was intelligent, meaning simply that her image of him had this dubious, fantastic quality. She had discovered, through persistent questioning, that he was a Polish Jew, that his parents had emigrated to South Africa during the gold rush, that his father had been a jeweller in Johannesburg. All this had a romantic air, she was fascinated, and tried to make him talk of it, but he answered stiffly and reluctantly. Finally, he doused the fires of her imagination, by saying, like any conventional British colonial, that he had come to this country at the earliest opportunity because it was British. He was now naturalized. Martha was thinking of the Cohen boys, she was wondering at the difference between them and this man; but by now her feelings were so deeply involved that she could not afford to think very clearly. She pitied him too much to say he was unpleasant and cowardly; she was ready to fight the world on his behalf – or at least her world.

On the third evening of their acquaintance, she was sitting with him at McGrath's when she understood that someone must be staring at her, because of her strong desire to turn her head. She turned it, and saw Stella and Andrew and Donovan, sitting by themselves in a corner and smiling pointedly at her. She waved and smiled; but Stella made insistent signs that she wanted to speak to her. Martha thought this was an invitation to both of them, and looked at Adolph, who, however, was watching her with a fixed and deadly smile.

'Go on,' he said. 'She wants to speak to you.'

Martha flushed at his tone, and promptly rose and went across to the other table, where she stood waiting by Stella's side.

'You're a naughty girl,' began Donovan. 'You just have to be different, don't you, Matty dear?'

'Different about what?' she said coldly, and turned pointedly away from him, looking at Stella. 'What's the matter?'

'You shouldn't be here with Dolly,' said Stella, in that discreet womanly voice of hers, which was several tones lower than her usual one.

Martha elaborately raised her eyebrows and glanced at Andrew. He, however, looked away; he was obviously embarrassed. 'Why not?' she asked bluntly.

Stella's colour was higher than usual, and her eyes were evasive. At the same time she managed to look both sympathetic and self-righteous. It was this look that Martha could see embarrassed Andrew. 'You should take our word for it,' said Stella softly. 'We're older than you.'

This was a fatal argument to use to Martha; and she looked direct at Stella, meaning to convey by that look that she was shocked by what seemed to be disgraceful dishonesty. Stella maintained the responsible, womanly dignity, while her eyes shone with scandalized delight. Martha therefore said shortly that she was a big girl now and could look after herself. She said goodbye formally, and returned to Adolph, wishing that she did not so vividly feel the glances she received as disapproving. She told herself she was being influenced by Adolph's persecution complex.

She sat down beside him, smiling tenderly for the benefit of observers, but this smile fled as he said, 'Well, they've warned you not to be seen in public with a disgusting Jew.'

'You seem to forget Stella's Jewish herself.'

'Yes, but she's from an old English family, she's not scum from Eastern Europe, like me.'

Martha stared, coloured, then laughed scornfully. 'Really, you are ridiculous,' she said, not realizing that this cold scorn was possible only because she saw these distinctions from the heights of her British complacency. She laughed, but immediately checked herself, for there was a look of such hurt on his face that she could not bear it. 'Don't take any notice,' she said protectively. 'Come on, let's get out of here.'

He rose at once, in his obedient way, and they left the hotel; and this time she did not say she wanted to go to bed early. Instead, she assented when he suggested they might drive for a bit, and found herself pouring scorn on Stella and Donovan (she omitted Andrew, for some reason) for being Philistines, and on the whole Sports Club crowd for being . . . Here she hesitated, before she was off down that slippery slope of compelled confession that was like a moment of madness, but she did not know the words for what she felt; she was thinking of Perry. The men of the Sports Club were disgusting, they were like little boys, they just messed about and . . . her voice lamely faltered into silence. She was blushing painfully, and hoped it was too dark to show. Adolph was watching her intently, and after a moment showed that he had understood her only too well, by saying that it was all very well, but she was rather young. This was unbearable; she protested that she wasn't young; then laughed, remembering that she was, after all, eighteen. But the word 'youth' meant to her only something defiant, a reminder of her right to do as she pleased. Again his quickness took her off guard, for he nodded and said, 'Well, if you know what you are doing.' This checked her; and she did not reply.

He turned the car at a corner, and began driving back to town. She was wondering why she must always rush into these moments of urgent speech; she was feeling lost, self-abandoned and she glanced at Adolph, half hoping that he was taking her back to her room, so that she might evade the choice. Then another emotion, a fearful, clutching need to grasp whatever came her way, made her hope that he was taking her to his; it never entered her head to ask him into her room, the idea would have seemed preposterous.

Soon, outside a big house gleaming with lights which fell across a wide shadowy garden, he stopped, with that characteristic gesture of holding the car on its brakes while he let the engine purr a little louder than usual, as if he would take an opposite course at the drop of her hat. 'Coming in?' he suggested in a soft, suggestive voice. This tone offended her, and she hesitated. At once he said, 'Please come in,' and she saw it as a challenge to her generosity.

'Of course,' she said gaily. She was now on a wave of elation, and walked up the path between flowerbeds, talking rather too loudly, while he followed in silence. There was a side veranda, and he unlocked a door and they went into a large room that had curving windows all around the front, overlooking the garden. This gave a tweak at her memory; and she stood still, frowning, wondering why nostalgia was sickening her nerves, and looked at those curving windows – 'like the prow of a ship,' she thought vaguely. Then she knew he was watching her, and instinctively intensified the dreamy absorption of her face for his admiration.

He said, with his uncertain laugh, 'Don't look so aloof,'

and, stung, she turned swiftly, smiling, to see that his smile had already gone from his face: he could never maintain any sort of criticism for longer than a moment, it vanished instantly, in fear of a snub; and at this thought she again dissolved in pity for him.

He was sitting on the extreme edge of his bed, that small dark man, with his watchful eyes and cautiously poised head, the suggestion of dammed power in the taut limbs. She became nervous; as usual, he was waiting to see what *she* would do. Since she did nothing, he said softly, forcing himself into direct speech, and letting the last words die away into a hesitating mumble, 'I suppose you've changed your mind.'

'About what?' she asked swiftly and quite sincerely, for it is true, though it might seem unlikely, that she had never directly admitted to herself why she was here.

He was now able to be sarcastic, and it was without any hesitation of manner that he said, 'Of course, I knew you wouldn't.'

Recklessly she walked across to him, feeling that again, as usual, she was being pulled down a current which she did not understand, and stood beside him, laughing. He half violently, half doubtfully pulled her to the bed, arranged her on it, looked at her, kissed her in an experimental way, looked at her again, hesitated, then muttered an excuse, and went to the dressing table, from which he returned loosening his tie with one hand while he held in the other a packet that he had taken from a drawer. He sat on the edge of the bed, pulled off his shoes, laying them neatly side by side, and began unbuttoning his clothes. Martha lay as if her limbs had been struck by a nervous paralysis, conquering the impulse to avert her eyes, which might have been interpreted by herself, if not by him, as prudishness. There was something dismaying about these methodical preparations. Like getting ready for an operation, she thought involuntarily.

Then, having made sure that everything was satisfactorily arranged, Adolph swung his legs up so that he lay parallel, and began to make love to her, using the forms of sensitive experience, so that she was partly reassured and partly chilled, while she arranged the facts of what was occurring to fit an imaginative demand already framed in her mind. Nor was she disappointed. For if the act fell short of her demand, that ideal, the-thing-in-itself, that mirage, remained untouched, quivering exquisitely in front of her. Martha, final heir to the long romantic tradition of love, demanded nothing less than that the quintessence of all experience, all love, all beauty, should explode suddenly in a drenching, saturating moment of illumination. And since this was what she demanded, the man himself seemed positively irrelevant – this was at the bottom of her attitude, though she did not know it. For this reason, then, it was easy for her to say she was not disappointed, that everything still awaited her; and afterwards she lay coiled meekly beside him like a woman in love, for her mind had swallowed the moment of disappointment whole, like a python, so that he, the man, and the mirage were able once again to fuse together, in the future.

Almost immediately he remarked that her friends at the Sports Club would be furious if they knew.

'I expect they would,' said Martha indifferently. The Sports Club people, and Stella and Donovan and Andrew, seemed immeasurably distant. The act of love had claimed her from them, and she now belonged to this man. She remained silent, looked at his smooth, dark-skinned body; he was not fat or plump, but the flesh lay close and even over the small bones, like a warm and darkened wax, the dark tendrils of hair on his chest glistened, and she played with them, after an initial reluctance – the thought had flashed through her mind that this man's body was wrong for her, that she was having her first love affair with a man she was not at all in love with. She suppressed it at once, and when they rose and dressed she maintained a simple and demure manner, as if she were altogether at his disposal; and ignored a slow and persistent resentment that was beginning to flood out every other emotion.

They went down to the Knave of Clubs. Martha wondered

why it was that before he had always hastily left when the crowd came in; now he remained, dancing every dance, smiling his uncertain smile, in which there was more than a hint of triumph. It annoyed Martha. Every time she lifted her face and saw that small gleaming smile, she had to smother anger. She was dancing badly; she simply could not dance with him; but she lay smoothly in his arms, her hand meekly lying on his shoulder, in the correct attitude for dancing, as shown on the films or in magazines. But he seemed quite indifferent as to whether she danced well or not; when she stumbled over an attempt to follow his elaborate steps, he quickly righted them both, and his eyes were roaming over her head, around the faces of the other people.

At the end of perhaps the fifth or sixth dance, when it was still early, about midnight, she pulled away from him and said in a bad-tempered voice that she wanted to go home. He hastened to take her, without a word of protest. She went to bed persuading herself that she loved him, that he was intelligent (the two things were necessarily connected), and that he was in every way superior to the Sports Club men. She was annoyed because she wanted to cry; she indignantly swallowed down her tears.

Every evening, they went to the Knave of Clubs; for in this shabby place, into which one sank, in a haze of brandy and churning music, as if half stunned, Adolph seemed as much at ease as he could ever be. Mrs Spore treated him with affectionate indulgence; the waiters, whom he tipped so heavily, hurried to greet him, to bring him what he wanted. For Adolph was very generous. Martha, who had grown used to Donovan's frank stinginess, felt herself royally treated, though it was not long before she began to demur, saying that he should not spend so much money on her. He was some kind of a senior clerk for the municipality, his salary could not be so large; and yet he surrounded her with boxes of chocolates and silk stockings, and grew annoyed when she was embarrassed.

New Year's Day they spent in his room, lying on the bed

and eating chocolates. They were silent, for they had quarrelled the evening before. He had criticized her floral dance dress, but not in a way she would have been pleased for him to use. She knew it was dowdy; if he had laughed at her because of her mistake, she would have felt more easy about it. When he took her home he said that she should make it tighter, and showed what he meant by lifting handfuls of material away from her hips. 'You want me to look like a tart,' she said indignantly, to which he replied by calling her a prude. She asked how he would like her to look, and he suggested Stella Mathews. To this she said, 'There you are, then.' She had not known that she thought Stella in bad taste, but now it became a conviction strong enough to quarrel over. They had parted without sleeping together.

This morning the omission was almost at once made good, he being in a possessive, bullying mood, and she feeling dimly guilty, though she could not have said why. Afterwards, she tried again to make him talk about his childhood in the big city down south, but he answered shortly. There was a long silence.

Suddenly he asked her if she had slept with Donovan. She laughed, and said he had good reason to know she had not. And now he said spitefully that he had thought she was not a virgin. She replied, accusingly, that he had hurt her badly that first time. He said, again brutally, How was he to know? She was now so indignant that she remained silent, her face turned away, and he began to tease her, in his half-brutal, half-deferential way, into good humour. He interrupted himself to ask, as if the question had been wrung out of him, 'Do tell me, I won't mind. *Did* you sleep with Donovan?' In spite of her annoyance, and the conviction of injustice, the idea of sleeping with Donovan seemed so absurd that she laughed wholeheartedly. He grew angry and said that Donovan was her type, while he, Adolph, was not. 'If you say so,' Martha said coldly, and refused to be coaxed out of her bad humour.

At five that evening, when he suggested they should go to dinner, she said she wanted to go home, she needed to sleep early, 'for a change'. Then she added hastily that in any case, now the New Year season was over, she would not be able to see so much of him, because she must study at the Polytechnic.

'That's right,' he said, grinding his teeth slightly as he looked furiously at her, 'I knew you wouldn't last long.'

'It's only till seven at night, I'm free every evening at seven,' she said, frightened into compliance by the spark of anger in his eyes.

Every evening at seven, then, he was waiting for her in his car. She came out gaily, grateful because of the man waiting patiently, only to find that gratitude vanishing in ill-humour as he began to question her about Mr Skye: Was her instructor attractive, did he try to make love to her?

When she had turned sullen and uncommunicative, he asked her what she would like to do that evening. This always confused her; she looked back appreciatively at Donovan, who simply informed her what they were going to do. She would reply to Adolph that she did not mind; there was always a long moment of indecision, which was like a conflict between them, while they both assured the other they did not mind in the least what they did. At last she assented hurriedly to the first challenging proposal he made: Did she want to go to McGrath's and drink? Did she want to go to the night club? This manner of his, putting himself at her disposal, offended her, as if it were an insult. At the pictures, if she lost herself in the film, she would turn with an uneasy feeling that he was watching her; and yes, he would be leaning back sideways in his seat, his shoulder turned to the screen, while he smilingly watched her. 'Why don't you look at the picture, don't you like it?' she asked brightly; and he replied, 'I like looking at you'; which flattered her, but also made her feel lost and confused: she felt as if she were something that must be humoured, that he considered himself quite unimportant.

In fact, they were increasingly uncomfortable together, except during those moments immediately after love-making, when she lay quietly beside him, in a devoted, childlike way. She told him then that she loved him; she found herself saying all sorts of things that it embarrassed her afterwards to remember at all. For, lying close up against that warm, sleek body, which apparently had such a powerful claim on her, waves of emotion came over her which she longed might continue over those other uncomfortable times in between.

Once she murmured, not knowing she was going to say it, 'I should like to have your children.'

'You don't have to say that,' he said sarcastically; and she was hurt, for she had been sincere for that moment.

He laughed unpleasantly, and said he would never have any children.

'Why not?' she asked, now deeply ashamed, because he had shattered the emotion which had made the words true.

He said shortly that the women he liked would never marry a man like him. Because of these pathetic words, she began to comfort him, reassure him; but next day he remarked, 'I wonder what will happen to you. I wonder where we will both be in ten years' time.' This filled her all at once with a terrible feeling of loss and impermanence; for once his tone was pleasant, and tender.

'Why shouldn't we get married?' she asked, her heart sinking at the thought of it.

He laughed at her, and smoothed her hair back, gently, in a paternal way, and said she was crazy. Then, a suggestion of cruelty returning, he held her hair close around her throat, so that it slightly choked her, and said that she would marry a good city father and become very respectable and have five nice, well-brought-up children.

She shook herself free, and said that she would rather die. The suggestion made her furious, he might have been insulting her. Afterwards, looking back on it, she marked that moment as the real end of their affair; at the time, she felt resentment, and under the resentment the old fear of loss, as if she were being cheated out of something.

This occurred about ten days after they first made love.

Two or three days later – it was a Saturday – when he asked her what she would like to do, she said that she didn't always want to make the decisions, that she would like to do something he enjoyed, for a change.

'Very well,' he said, and they spent the afternoon at the races; which revealed to Martha something quite new, a circle of people quite different from the regular Sports Club crowd.

The big oval of the racecourse, fringed and tasselled by rich green grass, banked by trees in full leaf, was a little way out of the town; and outside the clubhouse strolled a crowd of people dressed like those in the magazines from England. Adolph kept pointing out important personages, whose commonplace appearance naturally disappointed Martha, who until then had assumed that the famous must necessarily reflect all one's ideas about them, instead of insisting on mirroring forth their own. The man who caused Adolph the greatest excitement was a Mr Player, whose name was used by the people of the colony in that spitefully humorous, grudgingly admiring way that is the tribute offered to real power. Mr Player, said Adolph, knew more about horses than anyone else here.

Adolph hung about, waiting to catch the great man's eye, and when he did he offered an effusive smile, and received a careless nod in return. Mr Player was fat and red-faced, and Martha thought him repulsive, but Adolph said admiringly that he had an eye for the women, he got all the really attractive women in the town sooner or later; which information caused Martha to look disbelieving, for while she knew, theoretically, that women slept with men for money, she could not imagine herself doing it, which is as good as saying she did not believe it. She therefore decided that Mr Player must be kind and generous and perhaps intellectual, otherwise there was no explaining his reputation.

When Mr Player had moved out of their neighbourhood, Adolph began wandering through the crowd, his eyes busily searching; and when he had found the right kind of face, he would appear to stiffen and wait, that almost servile smile steady on his lips, until he had got what he wanted – a

254

hurried, sometimes annoyed acknowledgment of his presence, which he received gratefully. It annoyed Martha and made her feel uncomfortable. But when the first race began, she saw Adolph transformed. For the first time, she saw him shed his awful burden of self-consciousness. He stood by the rail, forgetting her, forgetting eveything, absorbed in the horses that pranced and curvetted at the starting line, gleaming in the bright sunlight, and when they streamed into movement he leaned forward, his eyes following them, his hands gripping the rail; and when it was all over, he remained motionless for a few seconds, breathing heavily, before he turned to her, with a sigh, and said, 'If I had the money . . .'

He took her to the stables, where he knew all the attendants and the jockeys, knew each horse by name. He stood by a big black powerful horse for nearly half an hour, his hand lying reassuringly on its neck, talking to it in a tone Martha had never heard. It touched her deeply, this passion was something she could respect, she felt a new tenderness for him, even while she wondered at his readiness to give up his regular attendance at the racecourse 'simply to be with me', she said with genuine humility, instinctively seeing that whatever he might feel for her was nothing to this abiding emotion.

But when they returned to the crowd, and he resumed his game of stalking the great for recognition, her irritation came back. At the end of the afternoon, he told her sarcastically that she had been bored; she was insincere when she protested she had enjoyed it. And the racing itself did bore her, she was unable to care which horse came in first. The crowd interested her, the clothes of the women – but most of all, and for the wrong reasons, Adolph's behaviour. He knew this instinctively. She assured him again that she had loved every minute of it; he said roughly that she had no feeling for racing and she was a hypocrite.

When they left the racecourse, with the other cars, he drove past McGrath's. She waited, her nerves on edge, to hear him say that of course she wouldn't be seen dead with him in there, now it was filled with the smart crowd from the racecourse. He said it, and she found herself replying irritably that if he didn't behave like a dog who expected to be kicked, no one would treat him like one. It was the first time she had acknowledged that he was, in fact, disliked; and no sooner were the words out than guilt overwhelmed her.

'Look,' she said gently, 'think of Mr Cohen, for instance. When he comes to the Sports Club, no one dreams of thinking, Look at that Jew!'

He laughed in a hurt, strained way, avoiding her eyes, and said, 'Which Mr Cohen? Those lawyers, maybe, but the Cohen who runs the wholesale business wouldn't dare show his nose in the place.'

'Then it's nothing to do with being Jewish,' she persisted, being reasonable at all costs; and he merely laughed again, and said she was a baby and knew nothing about life, which naturally touched her on her weakest spot, and made her cold and hostile.

She walked in front of him into McGrath's lounge, greeting the people she knew, as usual, but understood that their smiles, their waving, were no longer approving; there was no doubt of it: the Sports Club crowd were watching her in a way which politely did *not* pass comment.

She chose a table, and waited for him to join her, which he did, smiling sheepishly. They were silent, and drank rather more quickly than usual, and when he suggested, as soon as their glasses were empty, that of course she wanted to leave now, she rose at once, and walked out.

He ran up behind her, saying, 'Come home with me now?' It was more than his usual hesitating suggestion, and she replied quickly that she must go home, there were letters to write.

She had never seen him so black and stubborn as he insisted, between set teeth, 'Now – I want you to come home with me now.'

He had never insisted before; it had always been left to

her to make the decision; and now she stiffened into resistance. 'No,' she said coldly, 'I'm going home.'

He grasped her wrist, and said, 'You never come when I want you to, only when you feel like it.'

Now, this struck her as unfair; she thought of herself as soft and compliant, because she saw the whole affair only in the light shed by those tender moments after love. She pulled away her wrist, moved away from the side of his car, where she had been standing, and said she would walk home. He came hurrying after her, already nervous and apologetic.

'You only want me to come now because – well, because you want to prove something to yourself!' she stated, and his face darkened, and all at once it became so urgently necessary for her to escape from the whole situation that she simply turned her back on him and said, 'Leave me alone.' As an afterthought, she flung back over her shoulder, 'I'll see you tomorrow.'

So she walked steadily down the main street, until she heard a car draw up behind her, and hastened her steps, thinking that he had followed her; but Donovan's gay, hard voice called out, 'Matty, where are you off to?'

She stopped, adjusting herself to the idea of Donovan, and he said, 'Yes, Matty dear, I've been looking for you. Come on, jump in.'

She got into the car, asking, 'What do you want me for?'

'*I* don't want you, *dear* Matty. Stella wants to speak to you about something. I said I'd never be able to tear you away from your fascinating new friend, but, as luck had it, we passed you engaged in your lovers' tiff, so I seized the opportunity.'

'But *why* does she want to see me?' Martha sounded like a sulky child, and Donovan did not reply, but drove steadily along.

A car passed them, and she involuntarily glanced to see if it was Adolph. Donovan said, 'If you want to locate your admirer, surely you know where to find him?'

'What do you mean?' she inquired.

They were at an intersection; her room was perhaps two hundred yards down, one way, and the Mathews's flat a couple of blocks further on. 'Your fascinating admirer waits here for you,' said Donovan, indicating a vacant and grass-grown lot at the corner. 'Yes, Matty dear, when you've gone to your virgin bed, he sits here, in his car, watching your room to make sure of your exclusive interest in him – the whole town's laughing its head off about it,' he added cruelly, and glanced swiftly sideways to see how she would take it.

She took it badly. She was stunned. Then she muttered, 'I don't believe it.'

He laughed. 'Look over your shoulder.'

She looked. A couple of blocks behind them crawled Adolph's car. The mere sight of it caused her annoyance, and she involuntarily gave an impatient movement, as if shrugging off a burden. She said coldly, however, 'That doesn't prove anything.'

They had reached the flats. Donovan quickly stopped the car and jumped out. She saw he was waving to Adolph; the car wavered, appeared to be turning into a side street, and then adjusted itself and came straight on. Donovan, looking very manly and decided, strode a few paces to meet it, checked it with an imperiously raised hand, leaned inside the car, and spoke to Adolph; Martha caught a glimpse of Adolph's defenceless smile.

Donovan returned, and she said, 'What's going on?'

'Never mind, Matty dear, you come and talk to Stella, you'll find out.'

They avoided looking at each other as they went up in the lift. Martha hated Donovan, and was thinking of Adolph: she was saying to herself that it would be impossible for him to spy on her, while an inner voice was replying that it was only too likely – it seemed consistent with what she knew of him. Fighting against this new conviction, she entered the flat and found Andrew, looking very embarrassed and concealing it with an assumption of responsibility, and Stella seated waiting on the divan as if the act of waiting was in itself a torment. She leaped up, and came to kiss Martha.

Martha allowed herself to be kissed, and asked, 'What's the matter?'

Stella led her to the divan, her arm around her shoulders with a gentle pressure that said, Be patient; then she went to sit opposite, leaning forward. She was wearing a black cocktail dress with sequins on it, which Martha's eye noted and criticized as too bright even while she was waiting agitatedly for what Stella was going to say. Her hair was newly done, lying smooth and glossy on her small head; her oval face was tinted to an even apricot flush; her eyes glittered with excitement. At the same time, she was trying to subdue this excitement and appear deprecatingly womanly.

She said, in a low, dignified voice, which Martha at once resented as a dishonesty, 'Matty dear, we really feel it our duty to tell you – no, don't speak for a moment.' For Martha's eyebrows had involuntarily risen at the word 'duty'. 'Let me finish, Matty.'

Martha glanced at Donovan, who was watching avidly; at Andrew, whose face suggested that he was bound to agree with his wife, even if what she said continually came as a surprise to him. He refused to meet Martha's eyes, which were an appeal.

'Matty,' continued Stella with that effusive gentleness which was like an irritant, 'you're very young, and you've made a terrible, terrible mistake. You should have listened to us. That man has a bad reputation, he's immoral and – '

Here Martha laughed involuntarily, thinking of the atmosphere of sex that Stella exuded like a perfume.

Stella said hurriedly, 'No, Martha, you mustn't laugh. He's not a nice man. He's been talking about you publicly, boasting everywhere.'

This was another shock. Martha could not immediately speak. That inner voice was saying firmly, No *that's* not true; but she was confused, thinking that if he could spy on her, which she believed, then he might also boast. She sat frowning, looking with dislike at Stella's triumphant face.

They were all gazing at her. In astonished horror of herself, she felt her lips beginning to tremble; the thing wavered this way and that, and then Stella expertly tightened the screw: 'Talking about you all over the *town*, Matty.' And Martha burst into tears. Her chief emotion was anger at herself for crying, for now she was lost. Through her tears, she saw the glint of cruelty in Stella's bright eyes; she saw Donovan smiling, though he at once adjusted his look to sternness. A glance at Andrew showed him to be extremely uncomfortable. He got up, came over to her, and pushed away Stella, putting his arms around Martha.

'Now, don't cry, it's all right,' he said nicely, and looked angrily at his wife, who smiled and stood smoothing her hair reflectively, watching Martha's face.

Almost immediately, much too soon to please Stella, Martha pulled herself together, trying to laugh, and asked brightly for a handkerchief.

'You're not the sort of girl who should cry,' said Donovan, handing her his. 'Stella, now, looks divine when she cries. For goodness' sake powder your nose, Matty dear.'

'That's enough,' said Andrew, annoyed. 'Let's call it a day now, shall we? Let's all have a drink.' He went to pour them.

Stella took over again. 'And now we want you to come with us while we go and talk to him.'

'What for?' protested Martha sullenly. She had imagined it was all over.

'You don't want him ruining you, we must stop him talking, the whole town is gossiping,' cried Stella indignantly.

'I don't see any necessity to go and see him,' said Andrew stiffly.

But Stella and Donovan were already on their feet, waiting, and Andrew rose, too, in spite of himself.

'I don't think we should,' said Martha faintly. 'He won't be in, anyway,' she added hopefully, and this rider was her undoing; for she understood suddenly that Donovan had arranged that he should be in, when he spoke to him in the car. The sense of elaborate preparations, discussions, intrigues which she had not begun to comprehend kept her silent while Stella impatiently pulled her up from the divan and said, 'Oh, come on, Matty, he's expecting us.'

As they drove the few blocks to Adolph's room, Martha, from her worried preoccupation, dimly heard Stella chattering animatedly about how easy it was for a young girl to go astray; it sounded like a magazine story. She looked incredulously at Stella, thinking surely this was an act, but Stella was carried away by the drama, and when Martha glanced towards Andrew, thinking that at least he must be amused, no, he was silent; his wife's self-righteousness seemed to have infected him, for he sentimentally pressed Martha's hand, and said, 'You see, it's all disgusting, isn't it?' Stella promptly said, with a relieved look at him, that yes, it must have been a great shock to Martha. Martha understood that they meant sex; and an uncomfortable but derisive grin appeared on her face, and she turned her face away to hide it, for she felt guilty because she could smile at all; she was by now bitterly regretting being here, and hoped that Adolph would have the sense to avoid this ridiculous scene.

But of course he was waiting. As the four entered the big room with its curved windows – and for the first time it flashed into Martha's mind that the reason she had been so drawn to them was because they reminded her of home – Adolph was standing in the centre of the room, watching them, a small, ugly smile on his face. He looked caged; he stared helplessly at Stella, after a quick resentful glance at Martha, who even found herself signalling with her eyes, Don't take any notice of them.

But he could not take his eyes off Stella, and it was she who conducted the interview, while the two men remained standing in the background, waiting.

Stella began, in that womanly voice, 'You know why we've come.'

'I'm afraid not,' said Adolph, with his scared smile.

Stella drew in her breath, outraged by the hypocrisy. 'I've

come to speak to you, because I feel it to be my duty, I'm a Jew myself and I feel – '

'*Stella!*' protested Andrew and Martha together.

Stella impatiently motioned them to be quiet, and went on, smoothing her black silk skirt with a hand that looked curiously agitated, in contrast with the bland smiling face. 'You know quite well what people say, then why do you add ammunition to it, seducing an innocent English girl.'

'Stella,' said Martha again, but by now neither of them was interested in her.

Adolph moved his lips in his scared, guilty smile, and Martha thought, 'Why don't you stand up to her? Don't look so crestfallen.' She was sick with anger at this scene, and with her part in it.

'You married a Scotsman,' said Adolph at last, weakly.

Stella straightened herself, and said with dignity, 'I married him. I didn't drag down my people to be gossiped about.'

Adolph suddenly let out a nervous giggle; his face was dull purple, his eyes went from one to another of the group in front of him, in angry appeal. And since he said nothing, Stella lost poise; her body was tense with the desire for a good vulgar scene, but it seemed there should be no scene.

She dropped her voice and cooed reasonably, 'You must see you've behaved shockingly.'

There was a silence. Then Andrew said angrily, 'Oh, come on, Stella, that's enough, this is all off the point.'

And at last Adolph flashed into anger, and ground out, 'And may I ask what this has got to do with you?'

'Because I'm a Jewess,' said Stella, with dignity. 'Because I've a right to say it.'

It seemed Adolph had exhausted his anger; and after a pause, Stella rose calmly, remarking, 'I'll leave it to your conscience, then.'

She walked to the door, shepherding her flock before her. Donovan, looking moodily irritable, went out first. Andrew followed, saying uncomfortably to Adolph, 'Goodbye.' There was no reply. Martha looked swiftly over her shoulder at

Adolph in guilty apology and saw his eyes so filled with hatred that she averted hers, and hurried out.

No one spoke. In her mind, Martha was framing words to express what she felt: she wanted to say this was the most dishonest disgraceful scene, she wanted to ask sarcastically why Stella had not said any of the things she had protested she intended to say. A glance at Stella's satisfied face silenced her, and a kind of tiredness came over her.

They went to the car and drove in silence uptown. At the intersection Martha said, 'I should like to get out and go home.'

No, Matty dear,' said Stella maternally, 'Come home and have some nice supper with us.'

'Let her go home,' said Donovan unexpectedly. His voice was sulky, his heavy black brows were knitted together over his eyes; he was scowling.

Andrew stopped the car, and Martha got out. Stella leaned persuasively out of the car, and said, 'Now, go to bed early, Matty, don't worry, you need some sleep, it's all over and no harm done.'

Martha saw that Stella was waiting to be thanked; but the words stuck on her tongue. 'Goodbye,' was all that she could get out; and she sounded cold and reproachful. She was reproaching herself for being a coward.

Stella leaned further out, and said gaily that Martha must look on their flat as a home, she must come and see them next day.

Martha nodded, with a stiff smile, and went home.

And in her room she was so ashamed she could hardly bear her own company. She said to herself wildly that she must rush down to Adolph's room and say she was sorry, that it had had nothing to do with her, she had not known it was going to be like that. But at the back of her mind was a profound thankfulness that it was all over. There was no doubt that it was a relief that she need not see him again. And so, after a while, she soothed her conscience with the thought that she would write to him, she would apologize. Not now – tomorrow, later; she would write when a letter no longer had the power to bring him back.

Part Four

But far within him something cried
For the great tragedy to start,
The pang in lingering mercy fall
And sorrow break upon his heart.

— EDWIN MUIR

Chapter One

Martha was alone in her room. She felt exposed, unable to bear other people. She wished she were ill, and so able to stay away from the office for two or three weeks. Soon she did feel a vague, listless aching, rather like an illness. Her mother had sent her a thermometer to 'help her look after herself'. She took her temperature. It was a little over normal. She assured herself that a temperature might be low in the morning and high in the afternoon, and got Mrs Gunn to telephone the office, saying she was unwell.

In the afternoon, she was standing by the door, with the thermometer in her mouth, when she saw herself from outside, and at the same time remembered her father, medicine bottles stacked in hundreds by his bed – her father, whose image persistently composed itself in her mind as a worried, inward-looking man, standing moodily at a window but seeing nothing out of it, holding one wrist between the fingers of his other hand, to measure his pulse. The thought frightened her; she whipped out the thermometer, and stood hesitating, thinking, I'll throw the thing away. She glanced at the silver thread, for she might as well have a look at it first, and then it slipped from her hand and broke. Before it fell, she had seen that it stood at a hundred. Well, she had a temperature, she was justified. Soberly, she swept up the glass, and said consolingly that she would never buy another thermometer, she would not fuss over her health. But it was a relief, nevertheless, to be slightly ill, to be able to go to bed.

To bed she did not go. She put on a dressing-gown,

arranged books, and prepared for a few days' retreat from the world.

A few days: looking back on that period of her life afterwards, what she felt was wistful envy of the self she had been; she envied her lost capacity for making the most of time – that was how she put it, as if time were a kind of glass measure which one could fill or not.

She had left the farm a few weeks before; but put like that it was nonsense. Those few weeks seemed endless, one could not think of time – which is an affair of seconds, hours, days – in connection with it. It seemed she had been in town for years – no, that was another term for the divisions of the clock. What she had experienced since she got that momentous letter from Joss, which had released her from her imprisonment like the kiss of the prince in the fairy tales, was something quite different from the slow, measured years she had spent on the farm.

She thought of farm time, that strict measuring rod, where life was kept properly defined – for there could be no nonsense when the seasons were used as boundaries. On the farm, it was January, she told herself, it was in the middle of the rainy season. After the rainy season came the dry season; and after that, again, the rains. But when she came to think of it, it was not so simple. What of the season of veld fires, which had a climate of its own: lowering, smoky horizons, the yellow thickness of the middle air, the black wastes of veld? It was an extra season inserted into the natural year. What of October, that ambiguous month, the month of tension, the unendurable month? Again, it was neither dry season nor wet for how can a month be called dry that is spent, minute by dragging minute, thinking of the approaching inevitable rain, watching a sky banked with clouds which must break, break soon? October was another season that was given, offered free, as it were, to vary a climate which is thought of as 'dry season, wet season'. And so the rains break at last, if not in October, then in November, or even, when it comes to the worst, in December; the word 'October' does as well as any other to fix the terrible beckoning period of tension which comes in every year, comes inevitably; one cannot have the breaking of the rains without the time of preparation and agonizing waiting to which one gives the name 'October'. And the word 'October' gave off to Martha (her birthday was in that month) a faint marshlight from another world, that seemingly real but illusionary gleam from literature: overseas, October was the closing of the year, in a final blaze of cold-scorched foliage followed by the ritual lighting of the fire on the hearth. No, it was not easy at all, to moor oneself safely, with the words that meant one thing only, to use names like lighthouses; these rocks shifted, as if they too floated treacherously on water.

But now it was January. Christmas was over. Martha stood at her doorway behind a rather soiled lace curtain, and looked at the street. It was hot and wet. The puddles in the garden never had time to dry – to sink into the earth or lose themselves in the air. The sky sweltered with water; several times a day the clouds drove incontinently over the town, everything grew dark for a few minutes in a sudden grey drench of rain, and then the sun was exposed again, and the tarmac rocked off its waves of wet heat, the trees in the park quivered through waves of rising moisture. January, January in the town.

On the farm, everything was vivid, a violent green, while the earth was a blaring red. The sky from Jacob's Burg to the Oxford Range, from the Dumfries Hills away back, over the unbounded north, was a deep, soft hall of blue; and the clouds wheeled and deployed and marched day and night, flinging down hail, storming down rain, rolling and rocking to an orchestra of thunder, while the lightning danced about the thunderheads and quivered over the mountains. On the farm, the bush on the hill where the house stood was so soaked and lush that walking through it meant red mud to the ankles, and saturated branches springing loads of sparkling water at every step. On the farm, the cattle were grazing with nervous haste on the short, thick grass, which they knew would be tough and wiry in so short a time. For this was the season when it was impossible to remember the burning drought of the long dry season. The veld was like those blackened brittle sticks one picks off a rock on a kopje, apparently dead and ready to rot, which one places into water, only to find an hour later, that this lifeless twig has burst into crisp, vivid little leaves. In January, the drought-ridden, fire tortured veld was as teeming and steamy and febrile as a jungle. In the rotting trunks of trees the infant mosquitoes wriggled like miniature dragons; one might find the energetic creatures in the hollow of a big leaf, or in the imprint of a cow's foot or the tangled wetness of a low-growing clump of grass.

Last January, Martha's eyes (fixed as usual on some image of herself in an urban setting – a college girl in Cape Town, perhaps?) were caught by a slow squirm on a branch which she was just about to allow to splash, like a sponge, across her already drenched head, and she saw, as if the deep-green substance of the leafage had taken on another form, two enormous green caterpillars, about seven inches long, the thickness of a wrist; pale green they were, a sickly intense green, smooth as skin, and their silky-paper surfaces were stretched to bursting as if the violence of this pulsating month was growing in them so fast (Martha could see the almost liquid substance swimming inside the frail tight skin) that they might burst asunder with the pressure of their growth before they could turn themselves, as was right and proper, into dry cases, like bits of stick, and so into butter-flies or moths. They were loathsome, disgusting; Martha felt sick as she looked at these fat and seething creatures rolling clumsily on their light fronds of leaves, blind, silent, their heads indicated only by two small horns, mere bumpish projections of the greenish skin, like pimples – they were repulsive, but she was exhilarated. She went home singing.

One might imagine I was homesick! she said to herself dryly; for she could not return to the farm again, not if it were the last thing she did. And yet, for the moment, it seemed she could not face the town either, for here she was, shut in her room with a dubious illness that could be described by courtesy as malaria. Why not? She had had malaria as a child, and everyone knew that 'once it was in your blood . . .' She had a 'touch' of malaria, then – as one might speak of a 'touch' of the sun – and she was not homesick. Everything was satisfactory, for she was telling herself that her experience with Adolph could be justified as such; one is not an honorary member of the youth of the 1920s without knowing that one is entitled to experience, if to nothing else. And it was true she was not ashamed of the affair with Adolph; she was ashamed – to that point where one bursts into inarticulate exclamations of disgust, alone in one's room, one's face burning – because of that scene with Stella. She told herself that never, not on any account, would she go near the Mathews's flat again.

On the third day of her retirement, she received a large and expensive bunch of flowers from Stella and Andrew, with a gay note saying that they had telephoned the office and heard she was ill. Martha was warmed by this kindness, but no sooner had she become conscious of the flush of gratitude through her veins than she remarked to herself irritably, in the old way, Nonsense, what is kindness then? She just does as comes easiest, and then . . .

She wrote a little note to Mr Jasper Cohen, in the humorous vein she knew she should not use, because it pleaded special privilege; for she needed a doctor's certificate to stay at home any longer.

Then she returned to resume that other journey of discovery which alternated with the discoveries of a young woman loose in town: she returned to her books. She was reading her way slowly and vaguely from book to book, on no better system than that one author might mention another, or that a name appeared in a publisher's spring list. She was like a bird flitting from branch to darkening branch of an immense tree; but the tree rose as if it had no trunk, from a mist. She read as if this were a process discovered by herself; as if there had never been a guide to it. She read like a bird collecting twigs for a nest. She picked up each new book, using the author's name as a sanction, as if the book were something separate and self-contained, a world in itself. And as she read she asked herself, What has this got to do with me? Mostly, she rejected; what she accepted she took instinctively, for it rang true with some tuning fork or guide within her; and the measure was that experience (she thought of it as one, though it was the fusion of many, varying in intensity) which was the gift of her solitary childhood on the veld: that knowledge of something painful and ecstatic, something central and fixed, but flowing. It was a sense of movement, of separate things interacting and finally becoming one, but greater – it was this which was her lodestone, even her conscience; and so, when she put down this book, that author, it was with the simplicity of perfect certainty, like the certainties of ignorance: It isn't true. And so these authors, these philosophers who had fed and maintained (or so she understood) so many earlier generations, were discarded with the ease with which she had shed religion: they wouldn't do, or not for her.

In the meantime, she continued with the process of taking a fragment here and a sentence there, and built them into her mind, which was now the most extraordinary structure of disconnected bits of poetry, prose, fact and fancy; so that when she claimed casually that she had read Schopenhauer, or Nietzsche, what she meant was that she had deepened her conviction of creative fatality. She had in fact not read either of them, or any other author, if reading means to take from an author what he intends to convey.

Those 'few days' were one of those periods which recurred in her life when she read like a famished person, cramming into the shortest possible time a truly remarkable quantity of vicarious experience. She emerged from it on Sunday evening, restless with energy, knowing she must go back to work the following day. It was almost February; already a month had gone from the new year. She must go back and work at the Polytechnic, she must fulfil all her good resolutions, so that by the end of the year she would be embarked properly on a career and know where she was going.

The two authors she brought with her from that period of reading were Whitman and Thoreau — but then, she had been reading them for years, as some people read the Bible. She clung to these poets of sleep, and death and the heart — or so she saw them; and it did not occur to her to ask, not until long afterwards, how it was that she, not more than a few weeks in time from the farm, hardly separated from it in space (since this little town was so lightly scratched on the surface of the soil that one could see the veld by lifting one's eyes and looking down to the end of the street, while the veld grasses sprung vigorously along the pavements) — why it was that she read these poets as if they were a confirmation of some kind of exile?

When she returned to the office, she found that Mr Jasper Cohen had gone abruptly on holiday. His son had been killed in Spain — he had been shot, near Madrid, rather more than a year before; a friend of his had written, on returning safe to England, to tell his father so.

The office was concerned not so much over the death of a hero as over the new regime; for Mr Max Cohen, now in charge, had dismissed three girls, one of whom was Maisie. Mr Max Cohen and young Mr Robinson allowed it to be seen how much they did not approve of Mr Jasper's methods. Martha was interviewed and asked perfunctorily after her health (and she looked extremely well) and told that 'we' were so pleased that she was persevering at the Polytechnic, because the office could no longer afford unqualified girls.

Maisie, placidly under sentence of dismissal, had already found herself another job, at an insurance office; she told Martha that she had taken four days off herself, for the Christmas season had nearly killed her — she had slept for three days without stopping. She manicured her nails, dreamily attended to the filing, and smiled with the pleasantest good nature at Mr Robinson and Mr Max, who were even more annoyed because she seemed not to regard being dismissed as a disgrace. The other two girls had left already, in a fit of outraged *amour propre*, and were employed elsewhere.

'Wait till *our* Mr Cohen comes back,' said Maisie calmly. 'They'll catch it. Nothing but slave drivers.' But it was unlikely that Mr Jasper would be back for some months. It was not only the shock of his son's death; his wife – or so said rumour – was going to divorce him, for she felt that it was all her husband's fault that Abraham had been killed, and the office appeared to agree with her.

Mrs Buss said with mournful satisfaction that if you were going to mix yourself up with the Reds, then you got what you asked for; she couldn't understand Mr Cohen allowing Abraham to get mixed up with that bunch. Martha had her first political argument in the office; she pointed out hotly that it was not the republicans who were the rebels, but Franco. She was well armed with facts from the *New Statesman*. She was even better armed by the conviction of being in the right, but what is the use of being right if one is faced by the blank, unaltered stare of satisfied ignorance? Martha was so new to the game that she was surprised by Mrs Buss's calm remark, 'Oh, well, everyone's entitled to their ideas.' She said it was not a question of ideas, but one of fact. Mrs Buss said tartly that in any case everyone knew what Communists were. Martha said the Government in Spain was not Communist, but Liberal. Mrs Buss looked blank for a moment, and then said that was what she had said all the time, the Government was Liberal, so why did Abraham have to go and fight it? Martha was confused; then she understood, and said that Mrs Buss was making a mistake, Franco had never been elected, but ... Mrs Buss listened, frowning doubtfully, while her hands rested on her keys, her bright little face looking stubborn. She repeated, with a toss of her head, that she was entitled to her opinions, and added that politics bored her, anyway, and at once rattled on with her work, to stop Martha arguing. Martha was furious, chiefly because Mrs Buss not only was inconsistent but didn't mind being inconsistent.

After work, she walked down to the Polytechnic, still angry, and very grieved for Mr Cohen, that kind gentleman whose only son was dead, and his wife on the point of leaving him. She decided that she would borrow some money from somewhere and go to Cape Town: if only she could speak to Joss, he would know at once what it was she ought to do! Finally she steeled herself to take shorthand, and tried to concentrate while Mr Skye dictated a long piece about the prices of cotton waste. She gave up the attempt rather early, and left the Polytechnic, to find Donovan waiting for her in his little car. He said graciously that he would take her to the Sports Club, where there was a dance. Martha said that she did not feel like dancing, half hoping that he would take this as a snub. But no, he seemed relieved, and said that in that case they would go and watch the others dancing, he much preferred watching, for dancing was an overrated amusement. Martha understood that she was provisionally forgiven. She was, however, in no mood to feel penitent.

On the way through the darkening streets, he asked in a falsely casual voice, 'And so now you know all about the facts of life, you naughty girl, and I suppose you are pleased with yourself.'

Martha felt that he wanted to talk about the details of the affair; she felt repelled, and said sulkily that Stella had behaved disgracefully, and that he, Donovan, was a hypocrite. He was almost angry, but decided against it: after a quick look, he laughed, and said that she did not deserve a good friend like Stella. To this Martha maintained a strong dissenting silence, and looked out of the window. She felt she should not have agreed to go to the Sports Club. On the other hand, there would have been something childish in refusing.

They reached the Club without having exchanged another word. The big room was cleared for the dance, but everyone was either down at McGrath's, having dinner, or in the bar. Donovan said they might as well fill themselves on sundowner snacks, there would be sandwiches later on, if they got hungry. Martha indifferently agreed. They sat in moody silence on the veranda, drinking brandy.

Soon a group of men came from the bar and joined them,

greeting Martha with stereotyped emotion. She realized that she had fallen from grace, but not disgraced, no, from this circle one could hardly be cast out; it depended on her to redeem herself, for her mere presence here was as good as a sign of penitence. She listened to their talk, and was astonished to find them discussing war. Not the Spanish war, nor the Chinese war, nor Mussolini's adventure in Abyssinia – these wars had had no existence, in this place. They were saying, devoutly, that things looked like trouble; they did not define this, for it meant what it would have meant to Mr Quest – they would shortly be expected to defend the honour of Britain in some way or another. It would have been difficult for them to define it in any case; they never read anything but the newspapers, and the newspapers were still placating Hitler, while the word 'Russia' was not so much the name of an enemy to be fought immediately (though of course it would be, one day) as it was a synonym for evil.

Soon, however, one of them said that if there was going to be a war, then there would be trouble with the niggers. His voice had that intense, obsessive note which means that the speaker desires a thing although he may be claiming the opposite. Martha found herself remarking belligerently that she did not see why there should be 'trouble' with the natives; and the young men turned, rather startled, for they had forgotten there was a girl present. Their voices lowered to a sentimental level, and they assured her as one man that if there was, by God, the kaffirs would be taught a lesson, and there was nothing for *her* to worry about, and that was the truth.

Martha said coldly that there was certainly nothing for her to worry about, but there might be something for them to worry about unless – but at this point Donovan rose, looked at his watch, and said to Martha that if they wanted a nice table they'd better look for one now, before they were all filled.

She followed him, they settled themselves, and then he remarked, 'You're in a most unpleasant mood, Matty dear.'

She said that she was, and found herself telling him about the death of Abraham Cohen. Why? Did she expect him to sympathize? Of course he replied grumpily that if people wanted to get mixed up with the Reds . . . Martha, who had apparently exhausted the possibilities of indignation with Mrs Buss, shrugged and said sweetly that he was so well informed he left nothing to say.

Donovan did not react to this, because he did not notice sarcasm. He replied, 'I told you before, Matty, that you can't possibly do better than me. Now, if you don't let yourself get carried away by another fascinating Jew-boy, then we might do quite well.'

This astonished Martha into silence; she had not understood that he was proposing that they should carry on as before; she was flattered, and at the same time she despised him. So she did not reply. They were in the half-dark of the veranda, where they could see into the dance room through the open door. She was being greeted by the people she knew, but in a muted, watchful way which reminded her again that she was on trial. Several wolves came up, yearned over her, departed again; but it was not the same; this was the routine homage; she was no longer something special, she was being treated like the other girls, who had been currency in the Club for years. She realized this fully when Marnie Van Rensberg came onto the veranda wearing a bright floral evening dress, into which the projecting shelf of her breasts and her jutting hips fitted like the slack bulging shapes of loosely filled grain sacks. Marnie smiled her good-natured, half-abashed smile, to a chorus of moans and whistles. She was the new girl, she was the fresh arrival, she had taken Martha's place, and this had nothing to do with her looks or her personality. Martha saw this, with a mixture of shame that she had ever been affected by the adulation, even slightly, and resentment that she could be deposed by Marnie Van Rensberg.

This last feeling vanished in guilt as Marnie, giggling helplessly, which showed she was as little fitted to adjust herself to the atmosphere of the Club as Martha, came over to her, and said hurriedly, 'Matty, man so you're here, hey? They said you came in here sometimes, and I didn't see you till just now.'

Martha said she was glad Marnie was in town, and hoped that she was enjoying herself. Mrs Quest had said in a letter that the Van Rensbergs were furious with their daughter for taking a job suddenly in town, without consulting them, it was all as a result of Martha's bad example. So Martha was prepared to join cause with her against the older generation.

But Marnie said indifferently she was having a fine time, and added, 'Heard the news? I'm engaged!'

'Oh, that's nice,' Martha said, and quickly added, 'I'm very glad,' when she saw Marnie disappointed at her lack of warmth. 'Who to?' She was unconsciously looking around the Club, trying to pick the man likely to be attracted to Marnie.

'No, Matty, I'm marrying a boy from home. I'm getting married in church next week.'

Martha introduced her to Donovan, who was polite but cool. So she turned her back on Donovan, pressed Marnie down into a chair, and began talking about the district. The two girls said, 'Do you remember . . . ?' for a few minutes, as if the district were years behind instead of weeks. But what they were really saying was a continuation of that childhood dialogue; Marnie was saying proudly that she had got herself a man, only to find this achievement losing glory under Martha's polite indifference. But they liked each other; while they made small talk, their eyes expressed regret – for what? That they could not be friends? Marnie said at last, with a giggle, that Billy sent his love, and then, hastily, that she must get back to her table. They clasped hands impulsively, then loosed them again as if there might be something wrong with this contact, and Marnie went back across the dance floor, blushing scarlet embarrassment in reply to the wolves' attentions.

'Did you hear, Matty dear? Andy and Patrick were rolling on the floor and biting each other, all for the love of Marnie, only two weeks ago,' said Donovan spitefully.

'What?' exclaimed Martha involuntarily, thinking of Marnie's graceless body.

'Yes, it's quite true. There was such a scandal! Just look at the sensation you girls make when you first come into town. And now you're a back number, Matty, and must make way for youth.'

Martha could not help laughing, and for a little while they liked each other. But not for long.

At twelve o'clock the band stopped, for it was not a special dance: Adolph took up his violin, and played for about half an hour, his small gleaming smile fixed like hatred on his lips, while his eyes searched through the dancers: when they came in Martha's direction, she pretended not to see him. She felt guilty, and decided that she would write him that letter of apology next day. But when he had shaken his head for the last time, and climbed off the platform, there was no more music. Then Martha and Donovan, who had been thinking of going down to the Knave of Clubs with the crowd, saw groups forming themselves in a big circle around the dance floor. There was laughter.

'Come along, Matty,' said Donovan hurriedly. 'We're missing something.'

They squeezed their way into the big circle. Everyone was laughing and watching Perry, who was doing his usual act – imitating an American Negro singing. He strummed an imaginary banjo, while he rolled his eyes and jerked and splayed out his knees. It was funny, but he had done it often before, and it was not enough. So after a few minutes Perry let out a high quivering yell, which was immediately understood: he was no longer an American Negro, he was an African. But for this he could not be alone, he must be in a group, while the banjos and the melancholy sad wail from over the Atlantic were out of place. And soon a group of the wolves, headed by Perry, were stamping with bent knees, arms flexed and slightly held out, in a parody of a native war dance. 'Hold him *down*, the Zulu warrior, Hold him *down*, the Zulu chief . . .' they grunted and sang, while the wide circle of people clapped accompaniment to the thudding feet.

Outside this circle of white-skinned people, the black waiters leaned at the doors or against the walls, looking on, and their faces were quite expressionless. And soon this new amusement worked itself out to boredom, and again the singing and stamping died away. Perry, the indefatigable, stood marking time, as it were, frowning thoughtfully, slightly jerking out his elbows, lifting his heels back alternately, humming under his breath, 'Hold him *down* ... boomalaka, boomalaka ...' He stopped and shouted to one of the waiters, 'Hi, Shilling!'

The waiter thus indicated straightened a little, frowned, with a quick glance over his shoulder as if he wanted to escape, and then came towards Perry rather slowly.

'Come on, dance,' said Perry. 'Come on, man.'

The man hesitated: he was smiling in an annoyed way; and then he shook his head and said good-naturedly, 'No, baas, must work for the bar.'

'Come on, come on,' urged everyone, pressing around. It was all good-humoured and persuasive; they had narrowed to a small space, in which Perry and the black man stood. They were packed six deep, peering over each other's shoulders.

'War dance, war dance, come on,' grunted Perry, hunching himself around on his heels, and levering out his elbows — all in an encouraging and paternal way. Then he stopped, took the waiter by one arm, urged him into the middle of the clear space, and stood back, clapping.

'No, baas,' said the waiter again. Now he was annoyed, and intended to show it.

'Come on, man, I'm telling you,' said Perry. 'I'll lose my temper, I'm warning you.'

So then the waiter, in a perfunctory and hurried way, began jerking his arms and listlessly pounding his feet, while he let out a few grunts. And now Perry was annoyed. He shouted, 'Come on, damn it, don't play the fool.' He rolled his big body loosely into position, and demonstrated

280

again, with his intense emotional, self-absorbed parody of dancing, while the waiter remained silent, watching; and then, when Perry straightened himself out and waited, he made the same actions himself. It was not a parody of Perry, a mockery; he was simply trying to get the thing over as quickly as he could, and his eyes flickered worriedly over the heads of the white people to where his fellows stood, watching. Perry tried again; this time the waiter performed a mere sketch of the dance, hardly moving his feet. A girl laughed, on a high, foolish note.

'Come on, damn it,' said Perry frowning. He stood staring at the waiter as if he simply did not understand, while the man avoided his eyes. Then the blood rushed to Perry's face, and he muttered 'You damned black . . .' He had lost his temper completely.

The waiter shrugged, a controlled disdain, and walked towards the white wall of people, which divided instinctively to make way for him. He strolled through, and when he was near a door he suddenly broke into a run and vanished; he had been afraid.

'Gently, kid,' said one of the girls maternally, clutching Perry's arm. 'Don't lose your temper, it's not worth it, kid.'

Perry stood breathing heavily, and even looked rather puzzled. 'All I wanted was him to dance, that's all, for crying out loud,' he said noisily, looking around him for appreciation and support. There were consoling murmurs from the girls. 'That's all I asked, that's the bloody kaffirs all over, I ask him to dance and he gets cheeky.' He looked towards the doors, but there was not a waiter in sight, they had all vanished.

And the white people were left unaccountably bad-tempered, and rather sorry for themselves. They drifted off in groups, Martha walked away with Donovan, who had not said a word. And it was not until they reached his car that he said coldly, in that well-bred indifferent voice, 'I suppose you're feeling sorry for the kaffir.'

For a moment Martha was silent; what struck her was the deliberate way he said it, as if intending to provoke her. And the scene had made her very angry; also, which was worse, had made her afraid. What was terrible, she felt dimly, was the sentimental grievance of Perry and his friends: they really felt ill-used and misunderstood. It was like a madness.

'Not at all,' she said, intending not to quarrel; but then she could not help adding, 'I'm sorry for us, I think it's disgusting.'

'I thought you would,' said Donovan coldly.

They did not speak again for a few moments; they were both thinking of things to say.

'I suppose you thought it was a charming idea to ask him to sing. "Hold him *down*, the Zulu warrior,"' said Martha angrily, giving in to the silence; and she rather clumsily mimicked the pseudo-manly tone of the 'hold him *down*'.

At once he said, 'If you're not careful, Matty dear, you'll become a proper little nigger-lover.'

At this she laughed in astonishment: it was his inevitable fatal false note. Now she had the advantage, and she went on: 'Dear, dear *me*, how *awful*, isn't it, I should be such a naughty, *naughty* girl to have such wicked, unpopular opinions, and just *think* what people might *say*!'

And now he was furious, for she had minced out the sentence with a really unpleasant parody of his mannerisms. She had wounded him in his vanity, and so it was no longer a question of her opinion or his. They drove for a block or so in silence, while she waited for the thunderbolt to fall. She glanced at him nervously, wondering why he was so silent, but frowned blackly, his face averted.

Then he said, 'Well, Matty, we don't seem to go together at all, do we. I'm simply not broadminded enough for your Jews and your niggers.'

And now she was very angry. She said, 'You needn't flatter yourself you have a mind at all.' It sounded so childish, she would have recalled it, if she could, in favour of something calm and dignified. But it was too late.

The moment the car stopped, she jumped out, and went to her room, without even looking at him. She was furious with herself; alas, with what self-command do we conduct these arguments in imagination!

'Well,' she said finally, in a mood of wild elation, 'that's over, I'm finished with *that*.'

And what she meant was she was finished with the Sports Club, and everything it stood for.

Chapter Two

Martha was again solitary, for a few days. She told herself it was only February, to still her extraordinary panic; she was so restless she could hardly bear to sleep; she would start awake after an hour's light doze, feeling that life was escaping her, that there was something urgent she should be doing. She flung herself into work at the office, which all at once seemed easy instead of tedious; she studied at the Polytechnic with all her concentration, and was commended by Mr Skye. Afterwards, avoiding speaking to anyone, she walked home to her room through the park. There was a drought; the sun shone steadily all day, the sky was strong and blue, there was a smell of dust. (On the farm, the scents and wet heat of the jungle had vanished, and the grass was yellowing.) She tried to read, and could not. While the darkness settled over the town, she stood at her door, listening. For, night after night, music came from across the park, from down the street, from the hotel half a dozen blocks away: the whole town was dancing. The dance music flowed from all over the town, like water throbbing from dark sources, to mingle in a sound that was not music but could be felt along the nerves like the convulsive beating of a vast pulse. And there stood Martha at her doorway, carefully keeping out of sight behind the soiled lace curtain, watching the cars pass and hoping that none would stop, for she feared being dragged back to the compulsion of pleasure, saying that she should be studying – but what? – and feeling like a waif locked out of a party; she was missing something vitally sweet.

During those few days she made various inconclusive

attempts to escape. At a sundowner party weeks before, she had met a young woman who dressed windows for one of the big stores. Martha, buoyed as usual by the conviction that there was nothing she could not do, given the opportunity, sought out this young woman, and went to interview a certain Mr Baker, who owned the biggest store in town, offering herself as a potential window dresser. Mr Baker, far from being discouraging, seemed to approve; and it was not until the unpleasant subject of money was approached that Martha realized she was being engaged for the sum of five pounds a month, which, Mr Baker blandly assured her, was the salary all his girls were first employed at. Martha asked naïvely how it was possible to live on it. The gentleman replied that his work girls lived at home, or, if this were not possible, he arranged for them to live in a certain well-known hostel. Now, Martha knew this hostel was run on charity, and that Mr Baker was a town councillor, a very influential person. She was young enough to be surprised and shocked that he should get his labour so cheap by such methods. Mr Baker, who had imagined that he was on the point of getting a young and attractive girl 'of a good type' (this was his particular euphemism for the uncomfortable word 'middle class') for five pounds a month, was astounded to find this same apparently mild and amenable person suddenly half inarticulate with fury, informing him in short and angry jerks that he ought to be ashamed of himself. Mr Baker at once grasped the situation, said to himself that this spirit could be useful if properly handled, and, in the suave and reasonable voice of an experienced handler of labour, began handling her. He said her views did her credit, but that she was mistaken. His salesgirls were contented and happy – why, they stayed with him for years! After all, if one was training to become a servant of the public, one expected to pay for that training: if Martha was going to be a doctor, for instance, she would have to spend thousands on it, whereas he was offering to *pay* her (though admittedly not enough to live on) to learn a skilled job. Surely Miss Quest was reasonable enough to . . . Martha could not stand up to this urbanity. She collapsed, not into agreement, but into a stubborn silence, trying to find reasonable words to express her anger. Why, it was only last week that Mr Baker had made a compassionate speech appealing for public money to support the hostel 'for those unfortunate girls at the mercy of . . .' She could not speak, but she abruptly left, slamming the door, only to collapse immediately afterwards into a most familiar rage at herself for her ineffectiveness.

She paid a second visit to the *Zambesia News*. Mr Spur was delighted to see her. She was cool, like an acquaintance, though one day she would remember with gratitude that it was in his library she had first heard the words, 'Yes, my child, you must read. You must read everything that comes your way. It doesn't matter what you read at first, later you'll learn discrimination. Schools are no good, Matty, you learn nothing at school. If you want to be anything, you must educate yourself.' But that remark had been addressed to a child, whose affectionate admiration she now entirely disowned. She was, however, troubled by a vague feeling of indebtedness.

Mr Spur said that since her shorthand was now passable, and her typing fast, if inaccurate, she could certainly have a job with the woman's page. But – how it happened she did not know – she found herself arguing with half-inarticulate anger about the capitalist press. The *Zambesia News* was a disgrace, she said: why didn't it print the truth about what was happening in Europe? Mr Spur said, half annoyed, that the truth was always a matter of opinion; and then, controlling himself, said with the humorous gentleness of old age that on the woman's page she would be corrupting no one.

'The *woman's* page!' said Martha indignantly.

It was only afterwards that it occurred to her that he might perhaps have inquired, 'Why do you come asking for a job when you despise the paper so thoroughly?' But there was only one paper; if she was going to be a journalist, then she would have to make use of it.

She went back home, and dreamed of herself as a journalist, as a window dresser, applied for a job as chauffeur to a rich old lady, and was thankful when she was turned down, on the grounds of her youth. She decided she would become an inspired shorthand writer, like Mr Skye; and answered an advertisement to help a mother across the sea to England with her three young children. This woman, a rather supercilious middle-class female whom Martha instinctively loathed, asked Martha if she liked children. Martha said frankly that no, she did not, but she wanted to go to England. The woman laughed, and there was a moment of indecision, which was ended when the lady noticed her husband's eyes resting on Martha with rather too much appreciation. Martha was naïve enough to think she had lost this opportunity because of her clumsy answer, and once again made resolutions, in privacy, to control her tongue, to behave sensibly.

But she was still working at Robinson's; she was, in fact, neither a journalist, a chauffeur, a shorthand writer, nor on her way to England.

For a few days then she dreamed of herself as a writer. She would be a freelance. She wrote poems, lying on the floor of her room; an article on the monopoly press; and a short story about a young girl who . . . This story was called 'Revolt'. She dispatched these to the *Zambesia News*, to the *New Statesman* and to the *Observer*, convinced that all three would be accepted.

She remembered that as a child she had had a talent for drawing. She made a sketch there and then of the view of the park from her door; it really wasn't too bad at all. But the difficulty with being a painter is that one must have equipment. Ah, the many thousands of hopeful young writers there are, for no better reason than that a pencil and writing pad take up less room than an easel, paints, and drawing boards, besides being so much less expensive.

Martha, then, would be a writer: it came to her like a revelation. If others, then why not herself? And how was she to know that one may live in London, or New York, a village in Yorkshire, or a dorp in the backveld, one may imagine oneself as altogether unique and extraordinary (so powerfully does that pulse towards adventure beat), but one behaves inevitably, inexorably, exactly like everyone else. How was she to suspect that at least a hundred young people in the same small town stuck in the middle of Africa, kept desks full of poems, articles and stories, were convinced that *if only* . . . then they could be writers, they could escape into glorious freedom and untrammelled individuality – and for no better reason than that they could not face the prospect of a lifetime behind a desk in Robinson, Daniel and Cohen.

Almost immediately, the article on the monopoly press was returned from the *Zambesia News*, and the rejection slip dismayed Martha so much that she let the idea of being a freelance writer slip away.

And all the time that she dreamed with a fierce hunger of escape, and doing something vital and important, the other secret pulse was beating. There she stood, behind the curtain listening to the slow throbbing of the dance music, and wanted only to dance, dance all night; not at the Sports Club, but with some group of young people who were faceless, almost bodiless, imagined as a delicate embodiment of the dance music itself.

About ten days after she had quarrelled with Donovan, she was telephoned at the office by Perry, to ask if she were free the following evening, for there was a visiting team of cricketers from England; would she like to be one of the girls?

Martha refused. She was now finally sickened by her own inconsistency – so she said, as she proudly put down the receiver, suppressing a surge of longing and regret that she was wilfully refusing an evening of delicious pleasure. Nonsense, she told herself, it would not be pleasure, she would be bored. The thought that remained in her mind was that she was now casually rung up to fill in – to be 'one of the girls'.

That evening, however, there was a letter from her mother. She picked it up gingerly. She was accustomed to reading the first paragraph of a letter from home and then flinging it in a crumpled mess of paper, into the wastepaper basket.

My Darling Girl,

I sent Sixpence in to the post this afternoon, expecting a letter from you, and there wasn't. It really is unfair of you. I've not heard for a week, and you know how worried Daddy gets over you, he can't sleep at night worrying about you, and besides, we cannot afford to send boys in like this, and I've only got three now, I sacked Daniel for stealing, I missed my pearl brooch and I know he took it, but of course he denied it, though I sent for the police, and they gave him a good hiding, and they searched his hut, I expect he's hidden it in the thatch, so I have a lot of work to do, my new cook can't even boil an egg, they really are an ignorant lot, and so it's not fair of you to make me send in the boy for nothing.

I had a letter from Mrs Anderson, she told me she hasn't seen you, I wrote to her asking about you, since you never say anything, and if you've quarrelled with Donovan, I do think you might have told me, because it puts me in a false position, with his mother. She seemed to think you might marry, she was pleased, though of course you are too young, but he's such a nice boy, one can see that, and of course there's money there too . . .

Martha threw away the letter; there were twelve pages of it, crossed and re-crossed like the letters one reads of in Victorian novels – the letters of leisure. But as the crumpled ball flew across the room and landed rather short of the wastepaper basket, a postscript written in darker ink caught her eye, and in unwilling curiosity she went to pick it up.

I found my brooch this morning, it fell into a flour sack in the storeroom. But he's a thief in any case, I know he took my silver spoon, though of course he said he didn't. They're all thieves, every one, and the trouble with you Fabians is that you're all theory and no practice. One has to know how to handle kaffirs. The *Zambesia News* said last week the Fabians in England were complaining in Parliament again about how we treat *our* niggers!!! I'd like to get a few of them here, and then they'd see how filthy and dirty and disgusting they all are, and thieves and liars every one, and can't even cook, and then they'd change their tune ! ! ! !

The effect of this letter on Martha was hardly reasonable. After half an hour of violent anger, a feeling of being caged and imprisoned, she went to the telephone, rang the Sports Club, asked for Perry, and told him she would be delighted to help entertain the visiting cricketers tomorrow.

Chapter Three

In the event, the visiting sportsmen seemed disinclined to make much of the girls provided for them.

The dance was held at McGrath's. The big dining room now showed its oblong of bare boards, for the tables were pushed against the wall, their stained brown surfaces showing faded rings from wet glasses. The musicians were on the platform in their bower of ferns and potted shrubs. The tables in this room were mostly occupied by the young married crowd, while the cricketers, with the Sports Club men and the girls, were in the lounge, around a long improvised table that stretched almost from wall to wall of the enormous room. But the cricketers drifted off to the bar and remained there, and the girls, who were after all not forced by any pressure from statistics into being good-natured wallflowers, soon drifted off in the arms of local men, who had come prepared to remain womanless for the evening. Martha danced when she was asked, and quite late in the evening returned to the table to find that half a dozen or so of the cricketers were now seated at the table, for the girls had become absorbed elsewhere. They did not seem to mind, they were drinking and talking and looking at their watches, though one of them rose and asked Martha to dance. She tried to talk, but found it difficult, and, being the prig that she was, was disgusted that people whose names were commonplaces in the news, idols of England, talked of by the Sports Club crowd with reverence, were like schoolboys in conversation. She was surprised, in short, that athletes were not intellectual, for somewhere within her was still a notion that famous people must necessarily be brilliant in every way. Besides, only that morning the *Zambesia News* had devoted three columns to the opinions of the captain of the team: the international situation, he said, was uncertain, but if sportsmen of all countries could play together regularly, unhindered by their governments, peace would be assured; all day businessmen, Rotary members, and civil servants had been quoting this judgment with approval and saying, yes, he must be a fine chap.

Martha danced with this same man later, and was piqued that he was as bored as she – or rather, his attitude was so different from the Colonial men that she at first thought he was bored. She was accustomed to wait for attentive appreciation, while he, it seemed, wanted her to flatter him. When the dance was over, she sat down, shaking her head at an invitation to dance again, and reminded herself that 'millions of women' would envy her, but was unable to find pleasure in the thought. For McGrath's was ugly, the band was bad, and though she was drinking steadily as usual, her brain was critically alert. She wished herself back in bed. At the same time, she observed herself chatting brightly; her face stretched in a smile, just like the few other girls who remained; and when a pert 'amusing' remark ended unexpectedly in a yawn, she shook herself irritably into attention, and rearranged the smile.

Maisie, who happened to be there, remarked in that indolent voice, 'Ohh, our Matty's been having too many late nights.' This was offered to general entertainment, and received with laughter, while Maisie was teased about her own popularity. Through this she smiled sleepily, and then she said in a low voice to Martha, 'For crying out loud, these English boys give me the pip, they're so stuck-up, you'd think they were doing us a favour.' She then got up to dance with one of them, offering herself to him with a meekly submissive movement of her body as she slid into his arms, while her eyes arched upwards in attentive silence. Over his shoulder she winked at Martha, which lit her face into spiteful but resigned mockery. She was danced away, the very image of a willing and admiring maiden.

It was at this point that Martha found herself addressed by the routine 'Hullo, beautiful, why haven't we met before?' She got up to dance, the responsive smile already arranged in her eyes. She saw that this was a young man she had seen occasionally at the Club. His name was Douglas Knowell, which inevitably became Know-all. He was a cheerful, grinning young man, of middle height, rather round than lean, with a round fleshy face, light-blue eyes, a nose that would have been well shaped had it not been flattened by an accident of sport, and palish hair plastered with water into a dull sodden mat. He bounced rather than danced Martha around the room, and from time to time let out a yell of triumph, while Martha automatically soothed and admonished him into civilized behaviour.

'Who are you?' she asked at last flirtatiously, and he said, 'Ah, that's asking, but I know who you are.'

'Then you have the advantage,' she said, wanting him to tell her his name, for she was perhaps a little piqued that he had not made any attempt to get to know her before.

'Adam,' he said, twinkling his blue eyes at her in a consciously merry look; and Martha glanced at him, startled, for this was more literary than one might expect from a wolf, and she knew that he was one of the senior members of the pack: he had helped Binkie start the Club, so she had been told.

'What a pity I can't be Eve, since you know my name,' she said, and instinctively dropped, without knowing it, the maternal note from her voice.

'Oh, but you can be Eve, you are,' he shouted, drawing her closer, in his reckless bouncing dance around the room.

When the band stopped playing, Martha was startled that it was so late; she had enjoyed herself. Douglas told her it was a matter of luck he had come at all, he had not been going out much recently. 'So I'm in luck, because you are rather – rather a fine,' he said, with a beaming pressure from his eyes.

'I'm what?' she asked, startled.

'You're really a fine,' he said again, using the adjective as a noun, which was a trick of his, as was his way of isolating each word as if considering it, so that his slangy speech had a curious effect of pedantry.

She asked him why he had not been going out, why he was so seldom at the Club, and he replied, quite in the code of the pack, that he was studying for an exam, and besides, he was on the tack.

Habit almost made Martha approve, 'That's the ticket, kid, that's the style,' but instead she asked bluntly, 'Why, do you drink too much?'

He replied seriously that now he was too old for rugger, he was not as fit as he had been, he must keep his weight down, and besides, the doctor said he was getting an ulcer. Now, most of the men at the Club had stomach ulcers, and they all spoke of it in this same way, a protective way; they said, 'No, that's not my line, I can't eat that,' or 'My ulcer won't allow me that,' like a mother crooning over a baby. They addressed that part of themselves which was the ulcer as if promising to protect and look after it. They sounded proud of it.

She said flippantly, 'Having ulcers is positively an occupational disease of a wolf.'

'What's that?' he demanded quickly, ready to be offended; then he laughed and repeated, smiling with his eyes, 'Yes, you-you are really-really rather a fine.' And now Martha noted that stammer which was no stammer, not a nervous thing, but a trick of speech.

But she liked him, she was warmed by him; she went home looking forward to having tea with him next day. 'Having tea,' too, was exciting. One did not 'have tea' with a wolf, it was a meal that had no social place in their lives. Douglas was already appearing to her as something new and rare, he was so different from the Sports Club men!

And so they ate strawberries and cream at McGrath's, and she insisted on paying for her own, for he said casually he had sold his car, he could not afford it. If one could not afford a car, that was a confession of poverty indeed; for a reliable secondhand car could be bought at twenty-five pounds, and the most junior clerk owned one as a matter of course. Martha pitied him for this cheerful confession, and wondered at what must be a romantic reason for it, because he was fairly high in his department; at his level in the Service, one was not poor. But all this was confused in her mind, she was always vague about money; all she felt was a pitying admiration; and after tea, when he asked her to walk with him to the office, as he intended to work late, she went willingly.

When they reached the big block of Government offices, it was natural she should go in with him. His office was a large and airy room overlooking the tree-lined avenue. She wandered around it, trying to be interested in calculating machines and other appurtenances of finance; for she always felt an instinctive revulsion when confronted with what she still referred to as arithmetic. In fact, it chilled her so much that she was wondering if she might politely take her leave, when she caught sight of a magazine lying on the desk, and darted forward to pick it up, exclaiming, 'You didn't tell me you took the *New Statesman*!' She might have been saying, 'Why, we are members of the same brotherhood!'

'Yes, I do take it, it's a fine-fine paper,' he said.

She looked at him with wide and delighted eyes; she even unconsciously went across to him and took his hand. 'Well,' she said inarticulately, 'how nice, well then . . .' Suddenly she saw herself behaving thus, and flushed, and dropped his hand, moving away. 'All the same,' she said resentfully, 'it's nice to meet someone who – In the Club, everyone is practically mentally deficient!'

He laughed with pleasure at this sincere flattery, and they began to talk, testing each other's opinions. Or rather, Martha flung down her opinions like gages, and waited for him to pick them up; and when she said aggressively that she thought the natives were shockingly underpaid, and waited for him to say, 'It's no good spoiling kaffirs, they don't understand kindness,' and he said instead: 'Oh, yes, it would be desirable if there were a change of policy,' she gave a large, grateful sigh, and relapsed into the silence of one who has at last come home. But it was an expectant silence. It seemed to her that now their friendship was on an altogether new plane; and when he said, 'I ought to be doing some more work,' she exclaimed, as if he were insulting their friendship, 'Oh, no, you must come home with me to my room, I've just got a new parcel of books from England, I wired for them.'

And so he went with her, not so much surprised as bewildered. For Martha had all at once turned into something quite different. She would have been indignant had anyone told her that weeks of the Sports Club atmosphere had altered her manner. Martha Quest, at McGrath's or at a dance at the Club, was either a bored, sullen, critical young woman with a forced smile or a chattering ninny with a high and affected laugh. Now her acquired manner dropped from her, and she could be natural. She was herself.

'Herself', in her room, making tea, and then sitting on the floor with the new books spread out all around her, was completely childlike. Her hair fell out of the careful loose waves and was pushed hastily back, her eyes were bright and fixed on his with a delighted wonder; she talked quickly, as if the shock of finding a fellow spirit was so exquisite that she could not hurry fast enough to the next confirmation of it. She was altogether confiding and trustful. Not to tell him *everything* would have been a betrayal of their relationship; she felt as if she had known him forever; the world was suddenly beautiful, and the future full of promise.

And it was the future they spoke of; for she found he was as dissatisfied as herself with the present. He wanted to go to England, he said; he had plans, too, to live in the South of France and become a wine farmer. That would be the life; one could live cheaply and be free, and his father had been a farmer: he wanted to get back to the soil.

She urged him to describe these plans in more detail, but since they were still hazy, she made them for him. He must borrow a little money, enough to get over there – fifty pounds would be enough, living was so cheap in France, everyone said, all one had to do was to get there, and then life would begin.

It was midnight when he said he must leave; which he did reluctantly. A serious, responsible young man, he seemed to Martha, with his warm and approving blue eyes, and that touch of hesitation in his speech, which made everything he said so deliberate, so considered.

Martha told herself fiercely that he was a man, at least, and not a silly little boy. And so intelligent too! She slept that night deeply and dreamlessly, for the first time in weeks; she did not start up, half a dozen times, with the feeling that there was something she ought to be doing, if she only knew what it was; she woke on a delicious wave of anticipation, the day beckoning to her like a promise. But she did not say she was in love. For of course she was going to have a career. Besides, when she said, 'He's a man, at least,' that 'at least' was by no means rhetorical. She was still capable of being critical. For several days they were together all their leisure time, and she looked surreptitiously at him, with a feeling of disloyalty, and the round, rather low forehead struck her unpleasantly – there was something mean about it, something commonplace; the shallow dry lines across it affected her; as for his hands, they were large and clumsy, rather red, heavily freckled, and covered with hair. Soon she averted her eyes from his hands, she did not see them; she did not see his forehead, with those unaccountably unpleasant lines, like the lines of worry on an elderly face. She saw his eyes, the approving and warm blue eyes. She had never known this easy warm friendliness with anyone before; she could say what she liked; she felt altogether approved, and she expanded in it delightedly, and her manner lost its half-timid aggressiveness.

Also, he was so sensible! When she told him, making a funny story of it, how she had nearly gone to England as a nursemaid, he listened, seriously, and said she should not go to England without being sure of something to go to; and that it was 'ill-advised' to become a chauffeur, because the job had no prospects, while at her remark that she thought of becoming a freelance writer, he produced all kinds of practical objections, the least of which was the question of talent, for it seemed he had once had the same notion himself, had 'gone into the question from every angle,' in fact. He found a folder packed with sketches she had made of the wardrobe, the flowers in the garden, and evolved a most sensible plan. She should take a course in commercial art at the Polytechnic, and then she would be equipped to move from country to country as she liked. And Martha caught at this with enthusiasm, the idea gripped her completely for a couple of evenings. Then she began to condemn herself bitterly, as usual, for indecision; a creeping reluctance came over her at the mere idea of two or three years' serious study. But what she was thinking involuntarily was, What's the use of it? – meaning the war. 'Two years?' she murmured, looking at him evasively. That knowledge of urgency was in her, stronger than ever. Unconsciously, the coming war was there, before her, like a dark chasm in her spirit. And when he said, 'Well, two years isn't long,' she laughed suddenly, and the maternal note was back in her voice, so that they both felt uncomfortable. It was a discord in their relationship. And they continued to talk, like two children at college, about growing grapes in France, or going to America, delightedly planning half a dozen different careers at once.

And this continued for what seemed to be a long time, though it was not much more than a week. And then one evening they had returned from the pictures, and were walking slowly towards his room under the long canopies of heavy leafage, and she was telling him, for some reason, about Perry, and how he had flung out of her room 'in a rage', as she explained laughing. Douglas exclaimed, 'You really are rather-rather a fine . . .' and kissed her. This was no romantic kiss, but more a friendly and companionable one; they clung together, and what she was most conscious of was the warmth of his arm against her back. And then she was flung into dismay because he broke away with a sigh, and muttered, frowning, 'I shouldn't . . .' He walked on a few steps, and the boyish face was troubled, his eyes clouded.

'Why ever not?' she demanded, laughing, running up to overtake him, for now she felt that of course, since he had kissed her, he had in some way claimed her, and they would make love.

He looked embarrassed, so that she gave an uncomfortable laugh. She was offended.

'I – well – I . . .' He looked away, his face clenched in indecision; then he again turned to her, and kissed her, muttering, 'Oh, to hell with it, let them all go to hell.' She hardly heard this; she was now possessed by a fierce determination not to be deprived of what was her right. He had kissed her, that was enough.

They reached his room locked together, their steps lagging, and he did not switch on the light. He took her to the bed, and they lay on it. He began to kiss her, caressing her arms and her breasts with a hard and trembling hand. She was ready to abandon herself, but he continued to kiss her, murmuring how beautiful she was. Then he smoothed her skirt up to her knee, and stroked her legs, saying over and over again, in a voice troubled by something that sounded like grief, that her legs were so lovely, she was so lovely. Her drowning brain steadied, for she was being forced back to consciousness. She saw herself lying there half exposed on the bed; and half resentfully, half wearily partook, as he was demanding of her, in the feast of her own beauty. Yes, her legs were beautiful; yes, she felt with delight (as if her own hands were moulding them), her arms were beautiful. Yes, but this is not what I want, she thought confusedly; she was resenting, most passionately, without knowing that she resented it, his self-absorbed adoration of her, and the way he insisted, Look at yourself, aren't you beautiful? Then he raised himself and pulled back the curtains. Immediately, the trees in the street outside lifted themselves in the moonlight, moonlight and yellow street light fell over the bed in an unreal flood of glamour, and in this weird light her bronze legs, her tumbled skirt, her loosely lying brown arms, lay like a statue's. He pulled aside her dress, and fell in an ecstasy of humble adoration on her breasts, cupping them in his hands and explaining how they were so sweet. During this rite, she remained passive, offering herself to his adoration; she was quite excluded; she was conscious of every line and curve of her own body, as if she were scrutinizing it with his eyes. And for hours, or so it seemed, he kissed and adored, pressing his body humbly against her and withdrawing it, and she waited for him to sate his visual passion and allow her to forget the weight of her limbs, her body, felt as something heavy and white and cold, separate from herself. At last, her spirit cold and hostile, she said she must go home, and sat up brusquely, jumping off the bed. He came to her and helped her button up her dress, still self-absorbed in his fervent rite of adoration.

'How sad-sad to shut them away,' he said, closing the material over her breasts, and she felt as if they were burying a corpse. She thought angrily, *Them* – just as if they had nothing to do with me! Yet as she crossed in front of a mirror, she glanced in, from habit, and straightened herself, so that the lines of her body might approximate to those laid down by the idea of what is desirable. She settled her shoulders, so that her breasts, *they*, should stand out; and, with a rather impatient movement, she walked away from Douglas, who followed her meekly. But when they reached the gate and were ready to walk down the road, some kind of guilt, like a tenderness, made her slide obediently into the curve of his arm.

The moon stood high and cold, above a flood of stars, the trees glittered off a greenish light, the street shone like white sand. Suddenly she heard him say, in a different, half-sniggering voice, which struck her apprehensive with shock, 'I-I can't-can't walk.' He gave her a guilty, aggressive glance, and laughed. 'Never-never mind,' he said, still laughing suggestively. 'But that-that was rather-rather a strain.'

She did not understand him. She looked at him, bewildered. Also, she was disgusted and impatient. Her own body was aching, even her shoulders ached, and her breasts felt arrogant and chilled. But she was bound to love him, that claim had been laid on her. Yet she resented him so terribly, at that moment, she could not look at him. She was remembering Perry. She was wishing that men were not like this. She did not know, clearly, what she wished; all she knew was that she ached, body and spirit, and hated him. She walked silently down the moonlit street, looking ahead of her.

He said unexpectedly, without stammering, 'I ought to tell you that I'm engaged to a girl in England.'

Martha stared at him. She thought scornfully, How conventional. She despised him even more. She shrugged, as if to say, 'What of it?' The girl in England seemed remote, quite irrelevant. At the same time, she felt all at once deprived and lost and unhappy, a flood of unhappiness came into her, so that, watching it from outside, as it were, she said irritably of herself, What's the sense of *that*?

To him she said sarcastically, 'I suppose now you think everything's all right, you can say to her quite truthfully that you've been faithful.'

He laughed uncomfortably, pressed her arm to his side with a quick, nervous squeeze, and said, 'No – no, I didn't think, I was waiting all the time for you . . .'

'Waiting?' she asked, again at sea. Then she shrugged again. She said to herself, Oh, to hell with him. What she meant was, To hell with men.

When they reached her home, she nervously said good night, and turned to go in. But her coldness troubled him; he stopped her, holding her irresolutely for a moment. Then he said inarticulately again, 'Oh, to hell with it,' and came in with her.

She thought, amazed, Surely he's not going to make love to me *now*? For it seemed quite outrageous, even insulting, that he should. The moment had passed. But he did. She acknowledged to herself that this was quite different, not at all the same thing as with Adolph. Then she supressed the disloyal thought. Afterwards he remarked, with a proud, shy laugh, 'You're the first girl I've made love to.'

'*What?*' she exclaimed indignantly. She felt furious. She suppressed that too.

'Well, there was a prostitute in Cape Town, but I was drunk and . . .'

The prostitute seemed neither here nor there. 'How old are you?' she asked bluntly.

'Thirty.'

She digested this information silently. She was shocked. But it was not so easy to be shocked, for that claim on her was so strong. She stroked his head, acknowledging the claim, and thought uneasily that he had been messing about with the Sports Club girls for years. It was so unpleasant, she immediately forgot the fact. Then, like a ribald and mocking spirit housed somewhere disconcertingly within her, the thought arose: Gallantly preserving himself for the *right* girl! How touching! How disgusting! She tried to shut a lid on this disconcerting spirit, and succeeded, but not before it had said derisively, in a pious voice, Keeping himself clean for his wife. She turned towards him, and began caressing his head and hair in a passion of tenderness.

After a while she told him about Adolph. Now, this was no confession, but a statement of fact. And whatever Douglas might naturally have been inclined to do, such as forgive her, for instance, was put on one side, for if one has a relationship with a girl based on an assumption that one is in all things free and unprejudiced, and she remarks, taking it for granted that it has nothing to do with you, that she is not chaste, and it is to her a matter of no importance one way or the other, then a man can hardly do otherwise than conform. Douglas accepted the statement, in the spirit in which it was offered. Soon he was comforting her; Martha was sitting up in bed, her voice wrung with anguish, saying, 'I can't understand how I behaved so terribly, I can't bear to think of it.' He understood she did not mean sleeping with Adolph, she was ashamed because of something else. He comforted her, though it was not clear to him what it was all about. Finally he said, 'Well, I know old Stella, she's a good sort, she's a good kid, she meant well.' Martha did not reply, she withdrew from him into that glacial region where it seemed he was hardly worth criticizing. Soon he kissed her, and went home.

In the morning Mrs Gunn was acidly correct, but Martha no longer cared about Mrs Gunn. She was extremely depressed.

After work that day, Douglas waited for her, and took her to his room at once, saying that it was necessary for them to discuss a certain matter. She had not seen the room by daylight. It was quite large, an ordinary furnished room, with cretonne-covered chairs, a cretonne-covered daybed, coconut matting on the red cement floor. There was a writing table against one wall, however, and this was piled with ledgers and files from the office. She admired this, her respect for him was instantly restored. She was seeing him again as a sober, responsible man to whom she could defer.

He remarked nervously that he was in a hell of a fix. He moved around the room, stopping for a moment at the window, staring out of it, returning to the desk to finger a ledger or pick up a ruler. Martha watched him move, and what she felt was, This won't last long. She meant that her will was set hard on his saying he would give up the girl in England. It was remarkable that it had never entered her head to feel guilty about the girl in England; no, Martha was in the right, the other girl was the interloper. If someone had asked her, just then, if she wanted to marry Douglas, she would have exclaimed in horror that she would rather die. But she sat there quietly, her face troubled and her eyes thoughtful, and at the same time every line of her body expressed quiet, set determination.

As for Douglas, he looked altogether like a rather worried boy. He wore an old pair of flannel trousers, a white shirt rolled up at the sleeves and open at the neck. There was a fresh cleanliness about him. Martha was already feeling maternal. She sat and waited.

He began to talk, in an absorbed troubled way. He was talking to himself, trying to present the problem to himself, as it were, with Martha as passive audience. He said he had met the girl in Cape Town. She had been on holiday there with her aunt. 'Come out to get herself a husband in the colonies,' Martha thought scornfully. He had taken her out several times. Then his leave was finished, and she returned to England, and he to his home town. Then, afterwards, he had written to England, asking her to marry him.

'You mean you *wrote* – you got engaged by *post*?' asked Martha in a scandalized voice.

'Yes. Yes. She was ever such a fine. She was such a sweet.' He half stammered looking as bewildered as she. 'I told her,' he added, suddenly quite firm, and speaking without a suggestion of hesitation, 'that we could not marry yet, I can't afford it, we must wait two or three years.'

She was silent. Again she was wondering why he was so poor. She asked hesitantly, not wanting to 'interfere', 'Why are you – I mean, why couldn't you marry?'

'Well, the Sports Club racket is a helluva expense. You can't save money if you're in the Club much.'

'Do you owe money?'

'No, I don't owe-owe money. But I thought, if I was going to marry, I ought to offer her a proper home.' This last was said as if quoted.

She shrugged, dismissing the question of money. She felt there was some kind of discrepancy, but could not be bothered to think it over. What does money matter? she thought dimly.

He came to her helplessly, saying appealingly, 'I don't-don't know, Matty.'

She comforted him. Soon they made love. Physically it was a fiasco, which only made her more tender. By the end of the evening, it was decided they would marry. When she went home, she walked with calm angry contempt into the back veranda, informed a silent and critical Mrs Gunn that she was going to get married, and turned on her heel and went out before there could be any reply. She then sat down and wrote to her parents that she was marrying 'a man in the civil service', that they would be married in ten days, and she would bring him out to the farm 'for inspection' the following weekend. 'It went without saying' that they would marry at a register office.

On the following morning she woke in a panic. She told herself she was mad, or rather, had been, for now she was quite sane. She did not want to marry Douglas, she did not want to marry at all. With a cold, disparaging eye, she looked at the image of Douglas and shuddered. She told herself that she would ring him from the office and tell him they had both made a terrible mistake. Calm descended on her, and she went to the office, spiritually free once again. In this mood she walked into the office, and was greeted by congratulations.

'But how do you know?' she asked, annoyed; although warmth was already rising in her, in answer to the spontaneous pleasure on every face.

It appeared Maisie had telephoned Mrs Buss from the office where she now worked.

'But how did Maisie know?' inquired a completely bewildered Martha.

'She said your – your *fiancé* was up at the Club last night, he was giving it a real bang, he's off the tack again.'

Martha nodded, and began taking the cover off her typewriter, to give herself time. Douglas had taken her home at midnight. He had then gone up to the Club? She could imagine the scene only too vividly; and disgust and anger, heightened by a sickly, unwelcome excitement, began plucking at her nerves.

The telephone rang for Martha. It was Maisie, being calmly, amusedly informative. Having congratulated Martha on 'hooking Douggie – no one ever thought Douggie'd get hooked,' she went on to say that the wolves had practically wrecked the town, they'd torn up the whole place. There was a chamber-pot on the statue of Cecil Rhodes that morning, and all the lamp-posts were slashed with red paint. Perry, Binkie and Douglas had spent the hours between four and seven not in a prison cell, which was hardly fitting for people of their standing, but drinking brandy with the policeman on duty at the charge office. They had been fined ten shillings each and presumably were now back administering the affairs of the nation.

'Douglas was *with* them?' said Martha, dumbfounded.

'You're telling me he was with them, you haven't seen our Douggie when he gets going.'

Martha put down the telephone, and found Mr Robinson waiting to congratulate her. There followed Mr Max Cohen. Both shook her hand, smiling with an altogether new emphasis, like those welcoming a new member (But of what?). She understood, however, that she had done well for herself. That was implicit in every smile, every gesture, every inflection of their voices. Mr Robinson smiled continually, the same eager, interested, rather wistful smile that Martha was to see on every face for the next few weeks. He said, 'Your young man has just telephoned me. Off with you and enjoy yourself. You only get married once – or so I hope,' he added, with a glance at his girls, and they laughed dutifully.

Martha lingered in the cloakroom, powdering her face, while she tried to examine the idea that she was doing well for herself. It made no sense to her. And in any case, of course it didn't matter. So she went downstairs, and found Douglas on the pavement. He was transformed. Martha felt a disgust at the first glance, which she immediately banished. He was red-eyed, his plump cheeks were darkened with stubble, his clothes were crumpled.

'Come on,' he cried, 'we'll give it a bang.' He gave a whoop, standing there on the pavement, so that people turned around and smiled: it appeared that everyone in the city knew. 'I haven't been in bed yet,' he said triumphantly; and she laughed, even while she felt a stab of irritation at the self-satisfied look on his face.

Martha found herself being led to the Mathews's flat. She hung back, protesting. But it appeared that Stella had known Douggie for years, they were the greatest of friends, Stella had rung Douggie at nine that morning to ask the happy couple to lunch.

In the flat, Stella took Martha into a warm embrace, her eyes shone with tender emotion, and even tears; she murmured, 'I'm so glad, Matty dear. Now everything's all right, isn't it.' The slightly sustained pressure of her embrace was the only reminder, for that moment, of the incident with Adolph, though at any point in the conversation where there might be an opportunity for remembrance Stella smiled in a secret, warm conspiracy over at Martha. Martha did not return these smiles; this was the only way in which she remained loyal to herself.

They drank all morning. Long before lunchtime, Martha was gone on the tide. She was wildly elated. They had a long and alcoholic lunch at McGrath's, where they were interrupted every moment by people coming with congratulations; and no sooner had lunch finished than they went to the Sports Club, where the crowd was arriving, for it was then four o'clock. At the Club, Martha and Douglas were kissed and clasped and slapped by dozens of people; they were half drowned in champagne, to the refrain, 'I never thought anyone'd hook our Douggie.'

Binkie danced with Martha several times, in a puzzled, angry sort of way, repeating that she was a nice kid; then he gave it up, with the remark that there was something in the air, everyone was getting married, he'd have to get hooked himself in self-defence soon, though of course now Matty was out of the question there was no point in it. And he heaved a large sigh, which was genuine; he had lost control of his Club, and he knew it.

The party went down to the Knave of Clubs at four in the morning, and at sunup returned to the flat, where Martha and Douglas collapsed on the divan and slept. They woke to find Stella, attractively sluttish in a rather soiled purple satin dressing-gown, her ropes of dark glistening hair falling like a corrupted schoolgirl's over her shoulder, waiting with cups of tea, and suggestive jokes, because the loving couple had been sleeping back to back, with several inches between them.

Douglas told Stella that she was a dirty-minded girl, which was an echo of Donovan that made Martha cold and thoughtful. Douglas followed Stella into the kitchen, where the pair of them cooked breakfast and flirted until Andrew became annoyed. Miraculously, Stella transformed herself into the image of a quiet, devoted wife ministering to others. She served the breakfast, garbed in a white linen dress as simple as that of a nurse. Her hair was now coiled meekly around her exquisite head. She was so attractive that neither her husband nor Douglas could take his eyes off her. Martha did not notice this, for she was sunk in depression. But soon after that late breakfast they began to drink again, and again Martha was elated.

And so it went on for the whole of that week. In the office Martha was treated like a queen, she was allowed to come late, to stay away for three hours for lunch, even not to come at all. The four of them spent their time together, while Stella's calm assumption that she was in some way fitted to lead the couple along the flowery road to matrimony was accepted by them quite naturally. And Martha was completely swept away by it all. There were occasional cold moments when she thought that she must somehow, even now, check herself on the fatal slope towards marriage, somewhere at the back of her mind was the belief that she would never get married, there would be time to change her mind later. And then the thought of what would happen if she did chilled her. It seemed that half the town was celebrating; she had not begun to realize how well known Douglas was; the Sports Club were magnificently marrying him off, with a goodwill in which there was more than a hint of malice. The wolves fêted him and toasted him; several times in an evening he was rushed at by a group of them, and tossed protesting and laughing into the air, while Martha stood by smiling uneasily, feeling that she must be perverse to dislike what everyone else thought so amusing and natural. But she was uneasy about Douglas himself. The quiet, responsible, serious young man she had imagined she was marrying had vanished, for the time at any rate. He was jocular, he wore a steady smile of triumph that deepened self-consciously when he entered a room with Martha; and towards the end of an evening he was likely to vanish into a pack of stamping, yelling young men who moaned inarticulately in an ecstasy of frustrated energy, 'We'll tear the place up, we'll give it a bang.' Martha thought secretly that there was something very strange about it all, for if the point of this public orgy was sex – which surely it must be, judging from the meaning smiles, the jokes, and the way Douglas was continually taken aside by a young man, and teased until he began directing uneasy, proud, guilty looks at Martha which she tried hard not to hate him for – then sex, the-thing-in-itself, had mysteriously become mislaid in the publicity. For after a dance the couple found themselves back in the Mathews's flat, half-drunk, completely exhausted, and Douglas in this mood of jocular triumph was so repulsive to her that she nervously protested she was tired, and he at once dropped off to sleep as if the thing were of no importance. She was, in fact, already feeling a creeping disgust of him. It would, however, all be all right when they were married. It was odd that Martha, who thought of the wedding ceremony as an unimportant formula that must be gone through for the sake of society, was also thinking of it as a door which would enclose Douglas and herself safely within romantic love; in fact, in a contradictory, twisted way, while she slept limb to limb with Douglas every night, she was thinking of that unimportant wedding ceremony rather as her mother might have done. Naturally this comparison wouldn't have dared to enter her head. She thought of the marriage as a door closing firmly against her life in town, which she was already regarding with puzzled loathing. She was longing for the moment when it would no longer have anything to do with her.

By the Friday of that week, Martha was tired and irritable. She was also persistently depressed, which no one would have guessed from her smiling face. On that evening she was unresponsive when Douglas suggested they should go and see Stella, and said she would rather stay in her room.

'Come on, you only-only get married-married once,' he said coaxingly; so they went to the flat and drank, but when Stella suggested they should go and dance, Martha said she was tired, and wanted to go to bed.

'Ooooh, naughty, naughty Matty,' sang Stella, waving her tinted forefinger at the couple, her eyes bright with complicity and curiosity.

Douglas smiled and said proudly, 'Give-give us a break, Stell.'

They went home. There Douglas produced a book and said, 'We can't go wrong with this, can we?' It was Van der Velde's treatise on marriage. It may be said that few middle-class young couples dare marry without this admirable handbook; and as Douglas had seen it in his young married friends' bookcases, he had bought it.

Now, the sight of the scientific and modern book had a double effect on Martha. (She had of course read it.) It gave her assurance and made her feel a woman experienced in love, while at the same time she felt unaccountably irritable that Douglas should produce it now – like a cooking book, she remarked to herself before that persistently disagreeable voice was silenced by an effort of will. On the one hand, the gleam in Douglas's eyes excited her to try . . . but here that irritating voice remarked, Position C, subsection (d); and once again it was squashed. She was adapting herself compliantly to Douglas's attitude (the book was lying open at the chosen recipe) when suddenly a wave of exasperation swept over, and she said angrily that she was tired, she was exhausted, she was fed up with the whole thing; she sat up with a jerk, and burst into tears.

Douglas was astounded. However, the thought that women are . . . came to his aid; he asked her nicely what was the matter, said 'Don't cry,' and comforted her like a brother. Martha wept unrestrainedly, loved him for his kindness; and in due course they made love, and for the first time, and without the aid of the book, in a way that pleased them both.

He went home early, saying she needed sleep. He promised not to go to the Sports Club, which for some reason seemed important to her, though he could not imagine why. Martha woke with the feeling of a prisoner before execution, and said to herself that she would ring him up and say she could not possibly marry him.

When she got up, there was a letter from her mother, ten pages of every sort of abuse, in which the phrases 'you young people', 'the younger generation', 'freethinkers', Fabian sentimentalists', and words like 'immoral', were repeated in every sentence. Martha read the first page, flew to the telephone, and implored Douglas to come to her at once. He came, within fifteen minutes, to find Martha in a state of locked hysteria. She was dangerously calm, very sarcastic, shooting out epigrams about virtue and conventionality like bullets. She then burst into tears again, and said, half crying and half laughing, 'How dare they? How dare she? It's not as if . . . If only they – well, it's not as if they cared a damn *really* one way or the other, and . . .'

Douglas calmed her, but did not make love to her, thinking this was hardly the moment, poor little thing. Martha was soon calm again, and Douglas was perturbed that now it seemed she was cold with him as well as with the rest of the world. However, he used the ancient formula, She'll be all right once we're married, and reminded her that today was the day they had arranged to go to the farm.

She seemed to feel annoyed that he thought it necessary to remind her. He went to fetch Binkie's car, which he was borrowing, and when they had packed their things they started, Martha rather subdued and silent, he transformed back into the serious and sensible young man whom it was easy to love.

The road drove straight across country, twinkling off sunlight from the marbling lanes of asphalt, up the side of a vlei, down the next, between low walls of yellowing grass whose roots were still cluttered and bedded in the mess of last year's subsiding growth – that is, save where the veld fires had swept and blackened soil (charred and cracked even after the drenching rains), so that new stems rose glistening, as clean as reeds from water. The sky was as deep and blue and fresh as a sweep of sea, and the white clouds rolled steadily in it. The veld, so thickly clothed with grass, broken with small tumbling kopjes which glittered with hot granite boulders, lifted itself unafraid to meet that sky. This naked embrace of earth and sky, the sun hard and strong overhead, pulling up the moisture from foliage, from soil, so that the swimming glisten of heat is like a caress made visible, this openness of air, everything visible for leagues, so that the circling hawk (the sun glancing off its wings) seems equipoised between sun and boulder – this frank embrace between the lifting breast of the land and the deep blue warmth of the sky is what exiles from Africa dream of; it is what they sicken for, no matter how hard they try to shut their minds against the memory of it. And what if one sickens for it when one still lives in Africa, one chooses to remain in town? Living in town, Martha had forgotten this infinite exchange of earth and sky. She met it again as if she had returned from the North, where veils of mist and vapour and pollution hang over the land, where a dim and muted sunset seems to be taking place in another universe, the sky is self-contained, it broods introspectively behind its veils, the sun shines, the rain falls, but absently, dreaming, and the people on the earth accept what comes, with hardly a glance at their cold partner. And Martha came out of the town into the veld like an astonished stranger; she had been shut from it by a matter of a few weeks among the shells and surfaces of brick and concrete. She might have been in another country.

She was hurtled along this straight road, and it seemed as if the framework of the car hardly existed; she was carried along on movement itself, the sun immediately above, naked and powerful, the loins and breast of light, while the earth's heat rose to meet it, in a rank and swelling smell of growth and wetness. The car flung her, so it seemed, through the

311

air; and other cars, flying past, signalled the recognition of travellers in space with the flash of sunlight from hot metal. On and on; the town was a long way behind, the farm was not yet reached; and in between these two lodestones, this free and reckless passage through warmed blue air. How terrible that it must always be the town or the farm; how terrible this decision always one thing or the other, and the exquisite flight between them so short, so fatally limited . . . Long before they had reached the station, the wings of exaltation had sunk and folded. Martha was bracing herself to meet her parents. She was going to fight and win. They tore through the station. She noted briefly that not only the Cohens' store had 'Socrates' written over it; the Welshman had gone – it was Sock's Imperial Garage now. The puddle by the railway lines was brimming. The sky shimmered bluely in it, and through this illusory sea floated some fat white ducks, each leaving a ruffling wake of brown water.

The car turned, with a bounce, into the farm road. In the dry season, it was thick brown dust. In the wet, it was a lane of rich, treacly red mud. Now, in the short drought, the mud had hardened in deep fanged ruts where the wagons had passed. Binkie's town car began to groan and rattle.

'You can't go fast over this road,' said Martha, and it was the first remark she had made for half an hour. She added nervously, 'You know, I think I ought to say . . .' She stopped, feeling disloyal to her parents. It flashed across her mind that Douglas might be shocked by their poverty; but since she was now allied to him, and she would have scorned to be shocked by anyone's poverty, this was a new and confusing sort of disloyalty. She left this problem to fend for itself, and finished what she had intended to say. 'About my father. He wasn't actually wounded or anything, or at least not much, just a flesh wound, but – well, the war seems to have got hold of him. He doesn't think about anything but war and being ill,' she concluded defiantly.

Douglas said pleasantly, being the decent young man he was, 'Well, Matty, I'm marrying you and not your father.'

She reached for his hand. Clinging to it, she allowed

herself to be comforted into security. Suddenly they reached the spot where the road entered the big field. 'I say, this is-is something like,' approved Douglas, slowing the car. The maize was strong and green, a warm green sea glancing off golden light, while the dark red earth showed momentarily along the dissolving lanes as the car crawled past. But Martha was looking apprehensively at the house. Now the trees had filled with leafage, the house was crouched low among them, nothing but a slope of dull thatch. She said to herself, Now, don't let yourself be bullied, don't give in. And with Martha in this defiant mood, they reached the homestead.

Mr and Mrs Quest were standing waiting outside the house. Mr Quest was smiling vaguely. Mrs Quest's smile was nervously welcoming; and at the sight of it, Martha began to feel uneasy. All through her childhood, at school or when she was away staying with friends, those letters had been flung after her, terrible letters, so that reading them Martha had cried, She's mad, she must be mad! She had returned determined to resist the maniac who had written those letters, only to see her mother smiling uncertainly, a tired-looking Englishwoman with unhappy blue eyes. And so it was now: before Martha had even got out of the car, she knew a most familiar feeling of helplessness. Douglas glanced at her, as if to say, You've been exaggerating, and Martha shrugged and looked away from him.

Douglas shook Mr Quest by the hand and called him 'sir'; when he reached for Mrs Quest's hand, she bent forward and kissed his cheek. She was now smiling a timid welcome.

'Well,' she said humorously, 'and so you crazy youngsters have come, I'm so glad.'

Martha, stunned as usual, was kissed by her mother, and received a pleasant 'Well, old son?' from her father. Then he said, 'If you don't mind, it's time for the news, I must just go inside for a minute.'

'Good heavens,' said Mrs Quest, 'so it is, we can't miss that.'

They went inside to the front room, and turned on the wireless. Mr and Mrs Quest leaned forward in their chairs, listening intently while an announcer repeated Hitler's assurances that he intended no further conquests in Europe. When the announcer began to talk about cricket, Mrs Quest turned the wireless down, and said with satisfaction that it wouldn't be long now before war started. Mr Quest said that if Chamberlain didn't listen to Churchill, England would be unprepared again, but it didn't matter, because England always won in the end.

Martha was opening her mouth to join in angry argument, when she noted that Douglas was politely agreeing with both her parents. She therefore deflated, sat back, and listened while Mr Quest explained to Douglas that, according to prophecy, Armageddon was due almost immediately, there would be seven million dead lying around Jerusalem, the Mount of Olives would be split in twain (probably by a bomb) and God would appear, to separate the believers from the faithless. Here his voice changed, and he remarked, with an irritated eye fixed on Martha, that Douglas might not know it, but Martha was not only a socialist, which was not important, since it was only a disease natural to her age, but an atheist as well.

Martha was expecting Douglas to say that he was also an atheist, but he merely said that he thought what Mr Quest said was so interesting, and perhaps he could borrow some pamphlets sometime.

Martha therefore sank into comforting dependence on Douglas, although somewhere within her was a protesting voice remarking that he needn't treat her father as if he were a child. Then she told herself that he *was* a child, and Douglas was quite right. At the thought, she felt sad, and looked unhappily at her father, for he seemed even more distracted than before. He seemed to be thinner, and his hair was greying fast. The handsome dark eyes peered with a remote and angry gleam from under shelves of bristling white hair. Surely, wondered Martha, he has not changed so much in a few weeks? Was it that she had not noticed, living so close to him, that he was becoming an old man? At the thought that her father was old, her heart contracted painfully; and she said to herself, Nonsense, most of his diseases are imaginary, and anyway, people can live for years and years with diabetes. In fact, because *she* could not endure the thought that her father might die, she assured herself he was hardly ill at all. All the same, she longed to comfort him, but this was impossible, for one half of her attention was still standing at the alert, waiting for the scene which surely was due to start at any moment. She was nervously watching her mother, but quite soon Mrs Quest said she must go and give orders about lunch, the new boy was so stupid he couldn't even lay the table, and she had to do everything herself.

Mr Quest, having finished a long explanation of how Russia was the Antichrist, and therefore the war could not start until the sides had become reshuffled in some way, remarked, 'Well, there was something I wanted to say.' He glanced apprehensively over his shoulder towards where his wife had gone, and said, 'I didn't want to say anything in front of your mother, she's not – well she doesn't understand this kind of thing.' He paused, staring at the ground for a few moments, and then went on, as if there had been no interruption: 'I suppose you two are not getting married because you've got to? Matty isn't in any sort of trouble?' He looked uncomfortably at the silent couple, the frail white skin of his face flushing. He does look old, thought Martha miserably, trying to look courageously at this new vision of him; for, in spite of everything, she had always thought of him as a young man.

Douglas said, 'No, sir, there's nothing of the kind.'

Mr Quest stared disbelievingly at him. 'Well, why get married in such a hurry, people will talk, you know.'

'*People*,' said Martha scornfully.

'I daresay,' said her father angrily. 'Well, I don't care, it's your affair, but what people say causes more trouble than you seem to think.' He paused again, and said appealingly, 'Matty, I wouldn't like to think of you getting married when you didn't really want to – of course, this has nothing personal in it, Douglas.' Douglas nodded reassuringly. 'Because if you are in the family way, then we'll do something about it, provided your mother doesn't know,' he said aggressively, with another glance over his shoulder.

The words 'family way' caused Martha acute resentment, and with a glance at her face, her father said, 'Oh, very well, then, if it's all right, I'm glad to hear it.' He then began telling Douglas about his war, while Martha waited, with her nerves on edge, for him to say, 'But that was the Great Unmentionable, and of course you don't want to hear about that, you're all too busy enjoying yourselves.'

Douglas said politely that he was very interested in everything Mr Quest said; and Mr Quest's face brightened, and then he sighed, and said, 'Yes, it's starting again, and I'm out of it, they wouldn't have me. I'm too old.'

Martha could not endure this. She abruptly got up and went out.

Her mother was returning from the kitchen. Martha braced herself for the opposition that must come, but Mrs Quest hurried past, saying, 'I must get him his injection, and there's his new tonic, oh, dear, and where have I put it?' But she checked herself, and came back, saying quickly, with a downward look at Martha's stomach, 'You're not – I mean, you haven't . . . ?' Her eyes were lit with furtive interest.

Martha snapped out coldly, with as much disgust as Mrs Quest might have considered due to the cause of the possible event, 'No, I'm not pregnant.'

Mrs Quest looked abashed and disappointed, and said, 'Oh, well, then, if you are – well, I mean, but your father shouldn't know, it would kill him.' She hurried away.

At lunchtime Mrs Quest inquired whether they wanted to be married at the district church, and Martha said hotly that they were both atheists, and it would be nothing but hypocrisy to be married in church. She was expecting an argument, but Mrs Quest glanced at Douglas, and sighed, and let her face drop, and finally muttered, 'Oh, dear, it really isn't very nice, is it?'

That evening, when Martha went to her bedroom, she sat on the edge of her bed, and pointed out to herself that not only had her parents accepted the marriage, but she could expect her mother to take full control of the thing. In fact, she already felt as if it concerned her mother more than herself. The door opened, Mrs Quest entered, and she said that she was going to come into town with Martha on Monday to buy her trousseau. Martha said firmly that she didn't want a trousseau. They wrangled for a few moments; then Mrs Quest said, 'Well, at least you should have a nightdress.' She blushed furiously, while Martha demanded, 'Whatever do I want a nightdress for?'

'My dear child,' said her mother, 'you must. Besides, you hardly know him.' At this she blushed again, while Martha began to laugh. Suddenly good-natured, she kissed her mother and said she would be delighted to have a night-dress, and it was very nice of her to suggest it.

But Mrs Quest hesitated, and then asked, 'What kind of an engagement ring is he getting you?'

Now, neither Martha nor Douglas had thought of an engagement ring, and Martha said, 'There isn't any need for an engagement ring. Anyway, he can't afford it.'

Mrs Quest took a diamond ring from her finger, and said nervously, sounding guilty, 'Now, do be sensible, think what people will say, wear it for my sake, so people won't think . . . I mean, Marnie had such a lovely ring, and . . .'

The usual anger rose in Martha, succeeded by a kind of apathy. She took the ring, and slipped it on her engagement finger. It was a fine ring, a conventional five-stoned affair, but it had no beauty; it was a ring that said, Here are five expensive diamonds displayed in a row. Martha thought it unpleasant; besides, the cold metal sank into her flesh like a chain. She hastily took it off, and handed it back, laughing weakly and saying, 'Oh, no, I don't want a ring.'

'Now, please, Matty,' said Mrs Quest, almost in tears.

Martha looked at her mother in astonishment. She shrugged, and put the ring back, while Mrs Quest embraced her, and again there was a guilty look on her face.

When her mother had gone, Martha removed the ring and laid it on the dressing table. She was now feeling lost and afraid. She was vividly conscious of the night outside, the vast teeming night, which was so strong, and seemed to be beating down into the room, through the low shelter of the thatch, through the frail mud walls. It was as if the house itself, formed of the stuff and substance of the veld, had turned enemy. Inside the thatch, she knew, were a myriad small creatures, spiders, working ants, beetles; once a snake had been killed – it was coiled between the thatch and the top of the wall. Under the thin and cracked linoleum that clothed the stamped mud floor, the shoots from the trees cut two decades ago were struggling upwards, sickly white, to seek the light. Sometimes they pushed the linoleum aside, and had to be cut level. Martha, hating the room, went to the window. The light of the stars was strong and white, there was a sheet of white hazy light over the mealie fields. She was even more afraid. She looked at the door leading to her parents' room. It was open. It had stood open all night ever since she could remember. She thought now, with a half-derisive grin, how often her father had complained, 'Can't we shut the door now, May? The kids are old enough, they won't choke in their sleep.' But Mrs Quest could never bring herself to treat that door as one that might be shut. The other door, which opened into the end room, had also stood open. In fact, it could not shut, because the lintel had swollen to a bulge. Now, however, this door was closed and fastened with a heavy padlock, of the kind that was used to secure the storeroom against the native servants. Martha went silently to examine this door, and found that the lintel had been planed flat, showing startlingly white, like new wood.

She slipped out of the door that led into the garden, receiving a drench of glittering starlight faintly perfumed with geranium. She looked over the landscape of her childhood, lying dark and mysterious, to the great bulk of Jacob's Burg, and tried to get some spark of recognition from it. It was shut off from her, she could feel nothing. There was a barrier, and that barrier (she felt) was Douglas. And as she thought of him, she turned sharply at a sound, and he came towards her grinning from the end bedroom.

He slipped his arm around her, and said, 'You musn't get so prickly with your parents. After all, we've rather sprung it on them, and they've been very decent.'

She assented, and could not help feeling that even this mild protest was in some way a betrayal to their side.

'You'll see,' said Douglas consolingly, 'it'll be ever-ever such a fine wedding, and you'll like it.'

Again she assented. It had been arranged that they would be married by Mr Maynard, Binkie's father. He would marry them, as a favour, in their own flat – the flat which Douglas had already found for them 'from a pal'. Afterwards they were going off on a honeymoon with Stella and Andrew to the Falls. She had hardly listened to these arrangements, because all these formalities were so unimportant.

He remarked, 'I must say, all this looks as wild as hell, gives me the creeps.' She said yes, rather forlornly, for it did look wild and lonely; and she had never felt lonely in the veld before. The pressure of his arm on her shoulder suggested she should move beside him back to his room, and she went, gladly, with the warmth of his arm as guide.

She said passionately, 'I wish it was all over.' She repeated it desperately, as if she were talking about an unpleasant if not dangerous operation.

But inside the end room, which had been her brother's, she began to laugh at herself. One could almost think of this room as disconnected from the rest of the house. It was small and quiet, with whitewashed walls, and the glistening thatch slanting low over a small window. The low hissing of the oil lamp was soothing, and she sighed comfortably when she heard an owl hooting from the trees.

Douglas was a wall of strength; and from her clinging to him, and his calm reassurance, their love-making flowed out, and died into sleep. The 'act of love' – that fatally revealing phrase – was no act at all tonight, if one gives to the words what is due to them of willed achievement. For both these people were heirs, whether they liked it or not,

319

of the English puritan tradition, where sex is either something to be undergone (heard in the voices of innumerable chilled women, whispering their message of endurance to their daughters) or something to be shut out, or something to be faced and overcome. At least two generations of rebels have gone armed to the combat with books on sex to give them the assurance they did not feel; for both Martha and Douglas, making love when and how they pleased was positively a flag of independence in itself, a red and defiant flag, waving in the faces of the older generation.

In the morning Martha woke first, and found herself curled delightfully against Douglas's inert and heavy body. She was floating free and away from all the strained preoccupation of the day before. She thought with good humour of her mother's absorption in the wedding arrangements, and with amusement of her father, who would probably not notice the wedding ceremony at all if not reminded to do so. She lay gently, feeling the slow rise and fall of the warm flesh, and listened to the servant chopping wood outside, and watched the light from the window deepen on the white wall to a reflected yellow glow from the warming soil. Then the yellow patch began to shake and tremble – the sun had risen to the height of the tree outside; and slowly a pattern of leaves grew dark against a clear, luminous orange, and trembled as if a breeze were flowing through the room itself.

Douglas stirred and greeted her with an affectionate 'Well, Matty.' Then he turned over, and her body began to tense into waiting. 'Let's try like this,' he said with determination, and she caught a glimpse of his face, which was rigid with concentration, before she closed her eyes and lay alertly ready to follow what he intended to do. What she was thinking was, and with a really extraordinary resentment, Why does he have to spoil last night? Her attention was so strained to miss no new movement of his, for she was terrified he might find her lacking, that the end came unexpectedly for her, and left her reassuring him, as usual, that all was well. She was very tender and consoling, and lay stroking his hair, while she thought, Well, it was lovely last night, at any rate. Now, last night she had not been conscious of anything very much; she was in fact arranging the dark, underwater movements of last night into a pattern to measure against this morning's failure. She was also thinking worriedly about her mother. It no longer seemed unimportant or amusing that her parents were as they were. She was apprehensive. Back in her room, she looked at the open door into her parents' room, which had the force now of a deliberate reproach, and waited until Douglas was ready to go with her to the breakfast table, so that she need not face her parents unsupported.

That her mother had been in her room during the night Martha could see from her look of strained curiosity. And yet, this was surely no more than could be expected from a conventional middle-class matron concerned that her daughter might go to the altar, or rather to the table at the register office, a virgin? That square, vigorous, set face, the small blue eyes, always clenched under a brow of worry, were now directed persistently towards Douglas. Mrs Quest could not take her eyes off her daughter's young man. She talked to him like a reproachful but eager girl, there was an arch and rather charming smile on her face, even while the gaze was persistent, tinged with guilt. She looked as if she had been done out of something, Martha remarked unpleasantly to herself; and she knew that immediately after breakfast her mother would come to her, on some pretext or another, but really fulfilling a driving need to talk about what had happened. Martha felt exhausted, a dragging tiredness overcame her at the idea of it, and as soon as they rose from the table she attached herself to her father; and at last Mrs Quest went off with Douglas, since it seemed Martha was deaf to any suggestions that it would be nice to discuss the wedding.

Mr Quest took his deck-chair to the side of the house, and leaned back in it smoking, gazing over the slopes of the veld to Jacob's Burg. The great heave of blue mountain was this morning towering up into the blue sky, and wisps and wraiths of cloud dissolved around it. Martha sank beside him, with the comfortable feeling of repeating something she had done a thousand times. The sunlight slowly soaked into her flesh, she felt her hair grow warm around her face, she sighed with pleasure, and prepared to let the morning slide past, while her thoughts drifted away – not towards the wedding, that annoying incident which must somehow be accepted, but to the time afterwards. They would go to England, or to the South of France; Martha dreamed of the Mediterranean while her father thought of – but what was it likely to be this morning? After a while he began talking, after the preparatory 'Well, old son!' and she listened with half her mind, checking it up, as it were, on the landmarks of his thought. He was thinking of her brother who (lucky devil) would be allowed to fight in this new war. From there he slid back into his tales of the trenches, of the weeks before Passchendaele, from which he had been rescued by that lucky flesh wound: none of his company had come through it, all were killed. From there he passed to the international situation.

Martha lit another cigarette, lifted her skirt so that the sun might deepen the brown of her legs, and asked suddenly, 'Do you like Douglas?' She might have been talking about an acquaintance. When she heard the tone of her voice, she felt guilty, because of this unwelcome, deep understanding with her father that lay beneath 'all this nonsense about the British Israelites and the war' – the understanding that made Douglas seem like a stranger whom they might discuss without disloyalty.

'What?' he asked, annoyed at being interrupted. Then he collected himself, and said indifferently, 'Oh, yes, he's quite all right, it seems.' After a pause he said, 'Well, as I was saying . . .'

Some minutes later Martha inquired, 'Are you pleased I'm getting married?'

'What's that?' He frowned at her, then seeing the sardonic lift of her brows, said guiltily, 'Yes – no. Oh, well, you don't care what I think, anyway.' This had the irritability due to the younger generation, and she giggled. Slowly he began to smile.

'I don't believe you've even understood that I'm getting married in five days,' she said accusingly.

'Well, what am I expected to do about it? There was one thing I wanted to say. What was it, now? Oh, yes. You shouldn't have children – I mean, that's in my view, it's not my affair, but there's plenty of time.'

'Of course not,' said Martha vaguely. That went without saying.

'What do you mean, of course not?' he said crossly. 'You may think you're better men than your parents, but we didn't mean to have you, the doctor said we were neither of us in a fit state, but you happened along nine months to the day. But then we didn't anticipate the wedding ceremony. We were both having severe nervous breakdowns, due to the Great Unmentionable' – he snarled this phrase over at her, but without any real emotion, so that she smiled patiently – 'so we were taking all the necessary precautions, or rather your mother was, she's a nurse, so it's in her line, that sort of thing. So I thought I'd better point out, children have a habit of resulting from getting married.'

Since her earliest years Martha had been offered the information that she was unwanted in the first place, and that she had a double nervous breakdown for godparents, and so the nerve it reached now was quite dulled; and she merely repeated casually that she had no intention of having children for years and years.

Mr Quest remarked with relief that that was all right, then, and – his duty as father done – began talking about what they would do when they left the farm. If Martha had been listening, she might have noted that these plans were much more sensible and concrete than they ever had been; but she was not listening.

Soon the sun grew too warm, and they moved their chairs under the sheltering golden shower, and now faced out-wards to the Dumfries Hills. They were low and clear today; the rocks and trees showed across the seven miles of distance as if the heights of this hill and the height of that range shared a dimension where the ordinary rule of space did not apply. Martha felt she could lean forward over the lower slopes of ground between (where the Afrikaans community lived) and stroke the bluish contours of those brooding sunlit hills.

The servant brought morning tea, with the message that the Little Missus and the Big Baas must take it by themselves, for the Big Missus and the New Baas had gone off to the vegetable garden.

'He's being awfully tactful, isn't he?' remarked Mr Quest half sarcastically. 'He's being so well behaved. Well, I daresay that's the way to get on in this world.' This was the nearest he had got to comment or criticism; and Martha invited him to continue with a glance and a receptive silence. He said: 'Sex is important in marriage. I do hope that is all right. Your mother, of course . . . However . . .' He paused, with a guilty glance at her, and Martha was filled with triumph, though she could not have said why. 'All your generation' (and the usual irritation was applied to the surface of his words) 'take it in your stride, or so I understand.' The look he gave her was an unwilling inquiry. How much she would have liked, then, to talk to him! She had even leaned forward, opened her mouth to begin, though she did not know what it was she was going to say, when he said hastily, 'So that's all right, then, isn't it?' He handed her his cup for some more tea. There was a silence, but it lagged on unbroken. Martha was now restrained by that reiterated 'young people', 'your generation'; she owed it to her contemporaries to treat the whole subject with nonchalance. And soon he began talking about a girl he had been in love with before he met Mrs Quest. 'Lord, I was in love,' he said longingly, trying to sound amused. 'Lord, Lord, but I had a good time – but that was before I married, before the war, so it wouldn't interest you.' He was silent, smiling thoughtfully over at the Dumfries Hills, his whitening eyebrows lifted in perverse and delighted comment, while he occasionally glanced towards Martha, and then withdrew his eyes as if those glances were the results of thoughts he would rather not own.

As for Martha, she was now unhappy and restless, and wished that Douglas would return from the vegetable garden.

Immediately after lunch, it was time for them to go back to town. During the drive, Martha was telling herself that the last hurdle was past, she had 'obtained her parents' permission'. She used the phrase half humorously, half with spite, for she was feeling, contradictorily enough for a girl who refused formalities with such vehemence, that surely there had been something wrong with that weekend at home? Surely (or so she dimly felt) she should have had to fight, face real opposition, only to emerge a victor at the end, crowned by the tearful blessings of her father and mother? Surely there should have been some real moment of crisis, a point of choice? Alas for the romantic disposition, always waiting for these 'moments', these exquisite turning points where everything is clear, the past lying finished, completed, in one's shadow, the future lying clear and sunlit before! For, looking back on the weekend, Martha felt nothing but that she had been cheated; her mother's attitude and her father's seemed equally wrong and perverse.

So, as usual, she gave an impatient shrug, and dismissed the whole thing; soon that door would be closing on her past; all the mistakes and miseries of her time in town would be forever behind her. She had merely to live through five days to the wedding. She asked Douglas what her mother had arranged with him, intending that the undertone of sarcasm should provoke him, but he did not hear it. He replied enthusiastically that everything would be fine, everything would be satisfactory. He continued to talk of various details, and Martha understood, and with amazement, that she would not be getting married under the aegis of the Club; she had had a vague idea that surely they would all be there, wolves and virgins. For Douglas was remarking casually, as if he were not a senior member himself, that they 'must keep it dark, we don't want that crazy bunch spoiling it.' He added with mixed pride and shame that if Binkie knew the exact time and place he'd turn it into a proper-proper scrum. Mr Maynard, it seemed, had promised to keep it all secret, even from his son.

As they entered the town, rather late in the evening – for they had stopped to visit a tobacco-farmer friend of Douglas on the way – Martha happened to glance down towards the Club, and saw a crowd of people massed under the illuminated trees. 'Let's drive past,' she suggested, and they did so. 'What on earth is going on?' There were three packing cases stood on end on the pavement, and on these stood three men. 'An open-air meeting?' she suggested; and Douglas said critically, 'Gang of cranks.' She asked coldly why one shouldn't have an open-air meeting, but he was frowning, and looked disturbed.

He stopped the car at a distance, and they leaned out; the moon was pouring out light, and it was easy to see. The crowd was entirely white, save for half a dozen native stragglers who were on the outskirts of the crowd, ready to move off if challenged. Policemen stood waiting, white policemen, and their expression of scandalized interest was shared by most of the listening people. The speaker on the tub was a short, strongly built man with rough copper-coloured hair; fragments of Irish speech came floating over the heads of the crowd; 'humanity', 'drift to war', 'fascism', Martha heard and looked at Douglas to share her excitement. But his expression was that of an official faced with something new. It was not usual to have open-air meetings, there was something lawless about them, and therefore he disapproved. It was as simple as that. Martha felt her heart sink, looking at the frowning, rather pompous face. Then she turned to look again. It was rather beautiful. The trees were shining with an intense green, like trees seen through water, and they shook in a faint wind. Overhead, moon-illuminated clouds drifted quietly. The light shone on the rough copper hair of the speaker, and his eyes glittered steadily. Martha could hardly hear what he said. He was speaking about the necessity for making a pact with Russia to defeat Hitler; the faces of the audience had the passive, watchful look of public opinion faced with something it allows but does not approve. Then Martha, looking into the shadows behind the three men on the boxes, saw Joss and Solly, and Jasmine Cohen; they were with the people Martha had met at the tea party at the school; there was also a rather slight, tall young woman with fair hair wound around her head in plaits, like a school-teacher's; and Martha found herself vividly jealous of this girl. She longed to leave the car, to go over to the Cohens, and stay with them. The impulse to do so surged up in her, and died as a tired shrug at the thought of undoing all the arrangements that had been made. She turned away quickly, afraid they might have seen her. She was afraid of how they might criticize Douglas; she could see him through their eyes only too clearly.

She saw Douglas looking at her with a cold antagonism. 'Finished?' he inquired, as if he had been listening only to please her. He started the car.

'How conventional you are,' she remarked acidly, as they went down the street.

'Trying to draw attention to themselves,' he said, for some reason red with anger, his eyes protruding. She had never seen him like this.

She said, with quiet dislike, that the essence of a public meeting was to draw attention to oneself.

He was feeding the petrol into the car so fast that it choked, spluttered, stopped. They rolled down the street in silence, while he tried to start the car. When it started, he turned to her, and demanded like a child in a temper, 'If you've changed your mind, Matty, now's the time to say so,' and she inquired, 'About what?' though she knew quite well. His face grew more red, and seemed to puff out; his eyes were inflamed. She was now wondering sincerely why he was so extremely angry. She asked, reasonably, if he thought there was any necessity to lose his temper over a meeting he did not agree with. He was silent, breathing heavily; she was more and more astonished; at the same time, she was revolted; she thought he looked vulgar and ugly, puffed out and red with temper, his neck swelling over his collar. She said to herself that now she could free herself, she need not marry him; at the same time, she knew quite well she would marry him; she could not help it; she was being dragged towards it, whether she liked it or not. She also heard a voice remarking calmly within her that she would not stay married to him; but this voice had no time to make itself heard before he turned to her, and asked again, this time quietly and pleasantly, for his anger had subsided, whether she wanted to change her mind. She replied that she did not.

They went straight to the Mathews's flat, where they were welcomed with food and, above all, drink.

Next day Martha and Douglas moved into their new flat, so that Binkie and his lieutenants could not find them; and lived there like people under siege, while the Mathews brought them supplies. All four spent that time in a state of wild excitement, like a permanent picnic. Also, there were curtains to hang and furniture to arrange, which Stella took it for granted was her prerogative. Martha was rather surprised at the way Douglas recklessly bought whatever took his fancy or hers; the delivery vans were rolling up several times a day with carpets and cupboards and bales of stuff, and when she said nervously, 'Look, darling, if you're broke, there's no need to have all this stuff, surely?' he exclaimed with a whoop that one only got married once. 'But you did say you were short of money,' she suggested, still nervous, for she could not rid herself of the feeling that to make detailed inquiries about his finances would be an unpardonable interference. Besides, he was paying the forty pounds she owed as a result of not being able to live on her salary, and she felt guilty about it. Douglas said that he had saved some money, he had about a hundred pounds, and he was heavily insured and could borrow on it. In fact, what he said now was in contradiction to what he had said before, but Martha as usual shrugged her shoulders. For the Quests' attitude towards money could hardly be described as practical.

This letter arrived from Mr Quest on the day before the wedding.

Dear Douglas,
My wife tells me I should make inquiries as to your financial position, which I forgot to do; she, however, seems to have fairly accurate information, so I take it everything may be considered satisfactory. [At this point, that prickling irritability that always lay in Mr Quest, like a poisoned well, made itself felt through the words of the letter.] At any rate, under instructions, I am making a formal inquiry as to whether you are able to properly keep and maintain my daughter; which you are quite entitled to resent, since I have never been able to maintain her properly myself. I expect my wife will discuss the whole thing with you in due course. I am informed we are providing the linen and the blankets, but since my debt to the Land Bank is due for repayment, I trust you will discourage my wife in any unnecessary generosity.

Yours sincerely,
Alfred Quest

P.S. – I do hope everything goes well with the arrangements. I am persuading my wife not to come in to town until the day itself. I take it this will meet with your approval.

This letter was read by Douglas with an amused grin; while Martha hoped nervously that her father's persuasion might in fact keep her mother out of town, though she doubted it. Then he let out a whoop, and did a war dance around the room among the bottles and ham rolls and eggs, and said, '*We're* all right, aren't we?'

For he was very well pleased with everything. The wedding was working out well, for the arrangements were by no means as casual as might appear.

The people who were to be invited were all 'old friends' of his whom she had not been told of until that moment. Mr Maynard, for instance, that respected magistrate; Douglas's voice had a ring of satisfaction when he mentioned him. There was a Mrs Talbot too; Martha knew her as a very rich and respected lady, who, it seemed, had known Douglas since he was a child. She was giving them a generous cheque. There was to be present, too, a certain member of

Parliament, a Colonel Brodeshaw, who had been a friend of Douglas's father. The head of the department and his wife were to drop in for a glass of champagne afterwards; for there was to be a garden party at Government House that same afternoon, which it was hardly reasonble to expect them to miss, even for a wedding.

It was being impressed on Martha that the wolves, though it seemed Douglas did not consider himself to be one, were also the rising young men of the town, with futures to consider. It made her uneasy, until she comforted herself with the thought, Well, we're leaving the town, anyway, we're going to Europe.

When Douglas asked her whom she wanted to invite, she looked at him in amazement, and replied that she didn't mind. For she persisted in feeling that all this was quite unimportant, her only part in it was to get through with the distasteful business as quickly as possible. And since this feeling remained with her to the end, there is very little to say about the wedding itself. Mrs Quest, certainly, was too upset to describe her emotions when she arrived at ten in the morning to order to 'dress the bride' and found that most of the wedding guests were already seated around the bedroom – where Martha was trying to pack – perched in the bed, on top of the dressing table, even on the floor.

Martha was 'quite wild with happiness'. This is what Stella and Mrs Quest told each other, as they fought, with deadly politeness over who was to arrange the buffet. The two women loathed each other at first sight, and, in consequence of this passion, were inseparable all day. Martha and Douglas were laughing and making jokes against themselves and this unorthodox wedding, trying to finish packing amid clouds of confetti, and drinking champagne in tumblers. At lunchtime about twenty people, already slightly tipsy, were seething about the tiny flat eating sandwiches and drinking, while Mr Quest, looking resigned but slightly irritated, sat in a corner, flirting with Stella when she came near him, which was not often, since she had to keep an eye on Mrs Quest.

330

It could be said, then, that the wedding began at about ten in the morning; there was no *moment* at which poor Mrs Quest might emotionally take leave of Martha. Shortly after lunch, Mr Maynard arrived, looking urbane. He shook Douglas by the hand and called him 'my boy', was pleasant to Martha, and then suggested that as he had to marry four other hopeful couples that afternoon he would be obliged if they might get it over, otherwise he'd never get finished with the business. Mrs Quest hurried her husband into a position where he could give Martha away, for she had not understood that it was unnecessary in this kind of ceremony.

There was a long pause of unwillingly suspended emotion while Martha signed about nine different documents – 'In triplicate, too!' she exclaimed aloud, exasperatedly, while her mother said, 'Hush, dear,' and Douglas said soothingly, 'It's all right, Matty, I thought we might as well get it all done with.' What the documents were she had no idea.

Mr Quest, seeing that his presence was not needed, retired to stand by Stella, who could now give her attention to fascinating him, and succeeded completely. This afternoon she was brilliantly attractive. She wore sleek black, and a hat streaming with bright green feathers, and supplied a cosmopolitan smartness to the dowdy colonial gathering. Martha was atrociously dressed, and knew it, but had decided it was of no importance.

Mrs Quest waited anxiously immediately behind Martha's left shoulder, and at the crucial moment when the ring must be put on she grasped Martha's elbow and pushed forward her arm, so that everyone was able to see how Martha turned around and said in a loud, angry whisper, 'Who's getting married, me or you?'

The group then dissolved in tears, kisses, congratulations, and alcohol. In this manner, therefore, was Martha Quest married on a warm Thursday afternoon in the month of March, 1939, in the capital city of a British colony in the centre of the great African continent. Afterwards she could remember very little of the occasion. She remembered a wild elation, under which dragged, like a chain, a persistent misery. She remembered (when time had sorted out what was important from what was not) that someone had been saying that Hitler had seized Bohemia and Moravia, while everyone exclaimed it was impossible. She had heard the information with the feeling she must hurry, there was a terrible urgency, there was no time to waste.

She remembered too, that as she and Douglas, Stella and Andrew were about to leave on their joint honeymoon (for, as Stella was explaining to everyone, she had never had a proper honeymoon before), Mrs Quest stood shaking Mr Maynard by the hand, her face lit by the timid charming smile which was so strange a contrast with the formidable masculine face, while Mr Maynard smiled his usual tolerant comment on life and people.

'Mr Maynard, you must agree with me, it's *such* a relief when you get your daughter properly married!'

And Mr Maynard replied, 'Unfortunately I have no daughter, but if I had, it would be my first concern.' He involuntarily frowned as he glanced at his watch, and added, 'I must ask you to excuse me, I'm late for my next, I cannot understand what is coming over our gilded youth, I've never known such a year for weddings.' He hastily flung a handful of confetti in the direction of the departing car, and hurried off on foot to the Magistrate's Court, which was just down the road.

Halfway there, he saw the wedding car trying to turn down a side street, away from half a dozen pursuing cars. 'The pack are on the scent,' he murmured, as he caught sight of Binkie leaning out of the front car, his mouth open in a yell, his eyes staring excitement. The car recklessly shot across the corner of the pavement. It skidded. The following car collided with it. There was a general screeching of brakes, a smashing of glass, and yells and shrieks of all kinds. The Mathews's car, hooting derision, sped rocking down the main road south.

Mr Maynard scrupulously averted his eyes from the accident, for he was likely to have to judge it in court – if it came to court, which he hoped they would have the sense to avoid. Really, he thought, it would be the limit if he had Binkie up in front of him on a charge of – what? He glanced over his shoulder. The cars, locked together, were surrounded by a mass of humanity, girls and boys; but they were not arguing with each other, but standing over a black man who had apparently been knocked down. 'Damn the boy,' said Maynard furiously, meaning his son. From behind a building, he peered out cautiously. No, the native was getting to his feet and shaking himself. And now it looked as if silver rain were falling from heaven around the man, for the wolves were flinging handfuls of money at him, slapping him on the shoulder, and assuring him he was all right, no bones broken. They were already climbing back into the undamaged cars, to resume the chase after the Mathews's car.

Mr Maynard walked on, very shaken, very unhappy. No sense of responsibility, competely callous, thought they could do anything if they could buy themselves out of it afterwards ... His thoughts turned to what was happening in Europe. His views were liberal, in the old, decent sense; he hoped there would not be war, he knew there would be. Suddenly he found himself thinking, Poor kids, let them enjoy themselves while they can – He shook himself furiously; this was a first infection from that brutal sentimentality which poisons us all in the time of war. He recognized it, and dismissed it, and walked on, more slowly. Four more weddings to get through. Well, he thought cynically, that would be four divorces for him to deal with, in due time. Five, counting the one he had just finished. Marry in haste, repent in leisure: he believed this firmly, though he had been engaged to his own wife for over a year and knew that he had disliked her for the past fifteen.

He thought, Well, Douggie's got married, that's a step in the right direction; more than I can hope for Binkie. He began thinking, with the wistfulness of a lonely and ageing man, of possible grandchildren; for to a man like Mr Maynard a son like Binkie is as good as having no son at all.